TOMARE!

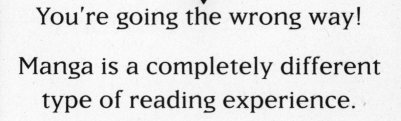

止まれ
[STOP!]

You're going the wrong way!

Manga is a completely different type of reading experience.

To start at the *beginning*, go to the *end!*

That's right! Authentic manga is read the traditional Japanese way—from right to left, exactly the *opposite* of how American books are read. It's easy to follow: Just go to the other end of the book and read each page—and each panel—from right side to left side, starting at the top right. Now you're experiencing manga as it was meant to be!

Fairy Tail volume 28 is a work of fiction. Names, characters, places, and incidents are the products of the author's imagination or are used fictitiously. Any resemblance to actual events, locales, or persons, living or dead, is entirely coincidental.

A Kodansha Comics Trade Paperback Original.

Published in the United States by Kodansha Comics, an imprint of Kodansha USA Publishing, LLC, New York.

Publication rights for this English edition arranged through Kodansha Ltd., Tokyo.

First published in Japan in 2011 by Kodansha Ltd., Tokyo
ISBN 978-1-61262-270-5

Printed in the United States of America.

www.kodanshacomics.com

9 8 7 6 5 4 3 2 1

Translator: William Flanagan
Lettering: AndWorld Design

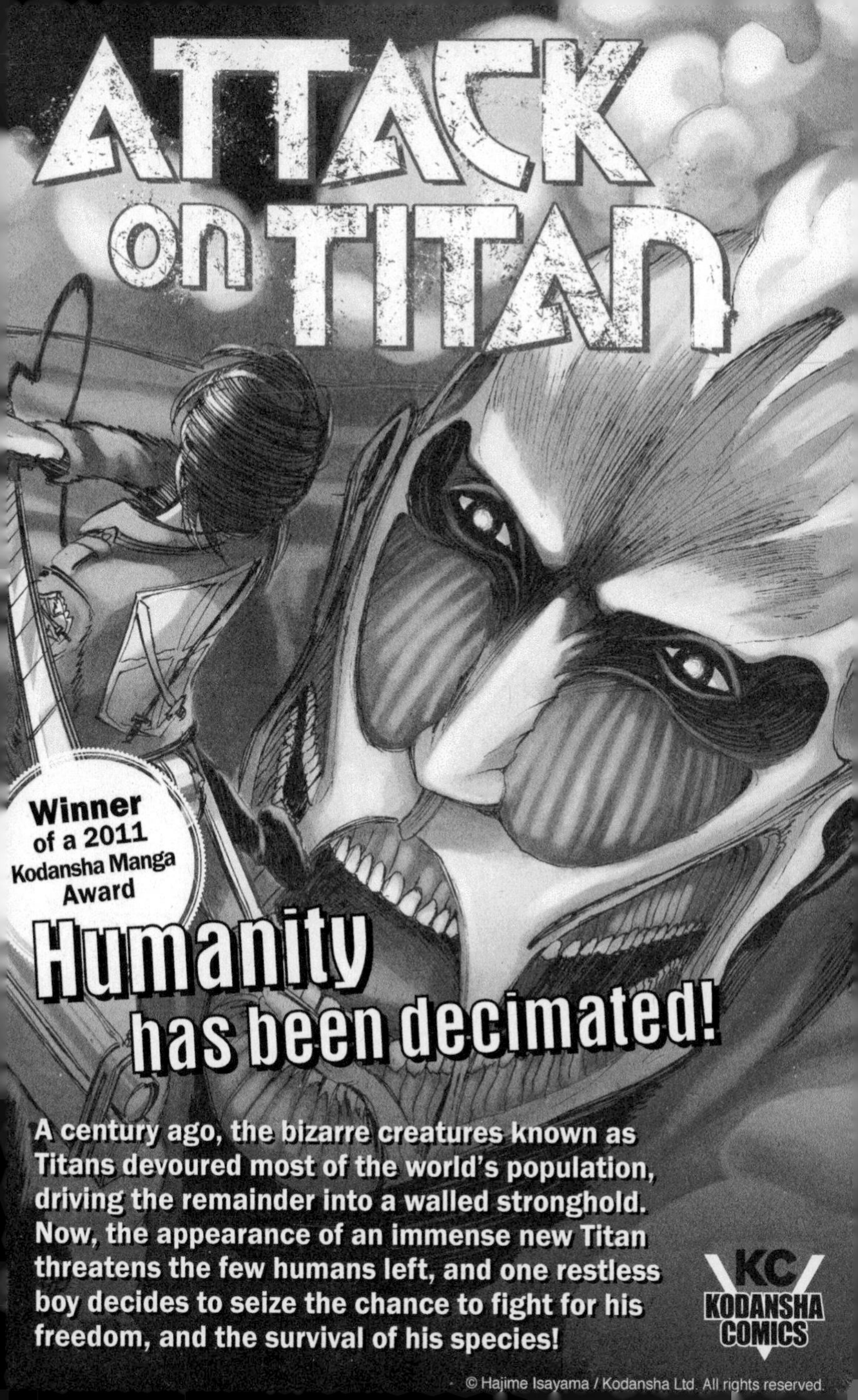
ATTACK on TITAN
Winner of a 2011 Kodansha Manga Award
Humanity has been decimated!
A century ago, the bizarre creatures known as Titans devoured most of the world's population, driving the remainder into a walled stronghold. Now, the appearance of an immense new Titan threatens the few humans left, and one restless boy decides to seize the chance to fight for his freedom, and the survival of his species!
KC KODANSHA COMICS
© Hajime Isayama / Kodansha Ltd. All rights reserved.

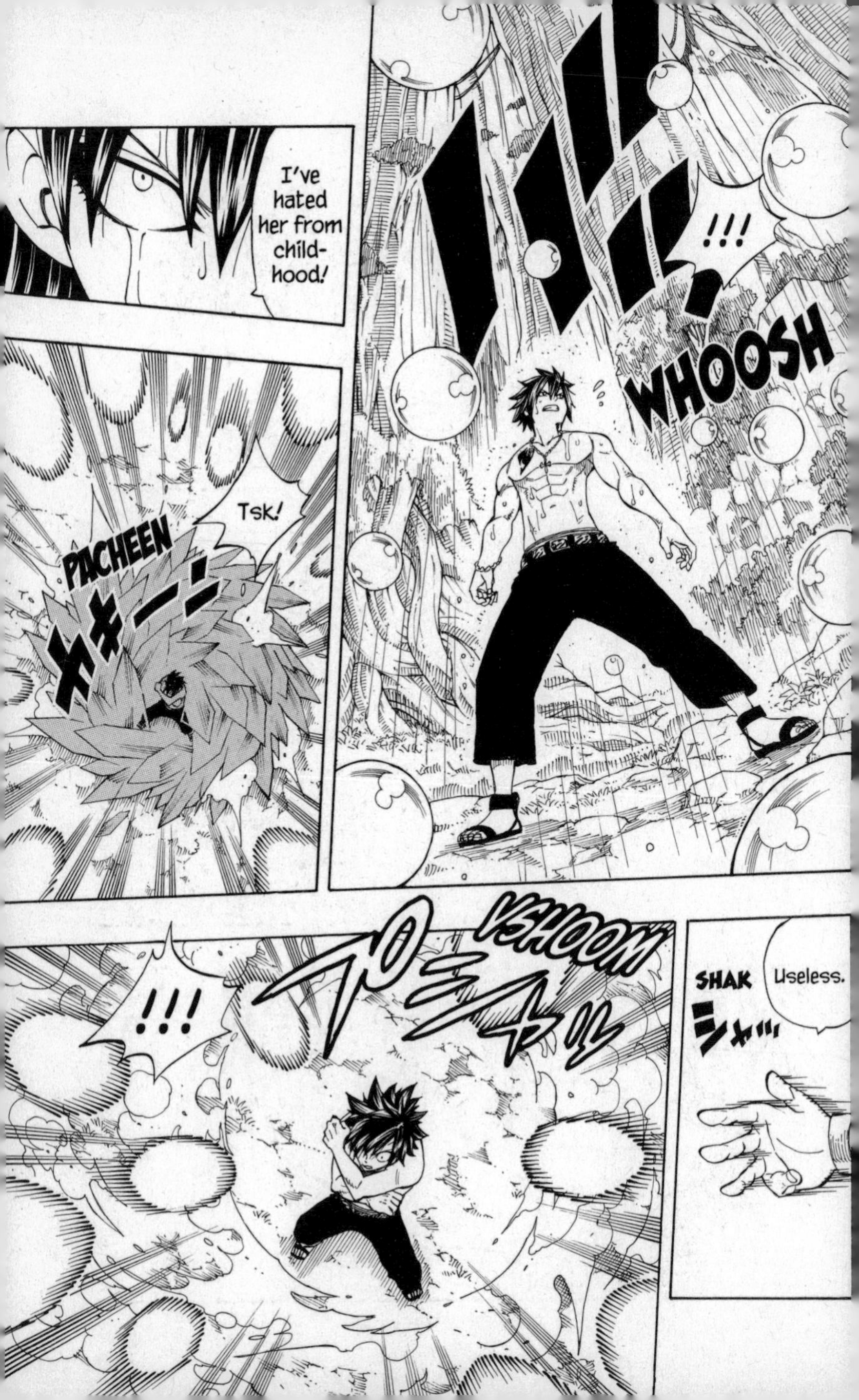

!!!
WHOOSH
I've hated her from child-hood!
Tsk!
PACHEEN
Useless.
SHAK
VSHOOM
!!!

FAIRY TAIL

28

フェアリーテイル

Magnolia
SPIRIT
Boots

HIRO MASHIMA

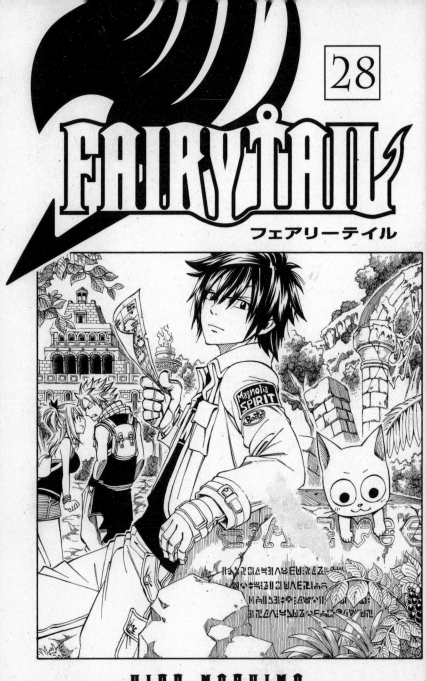

The Contents
for Fairy Tail
Volume 28

CONTENTS

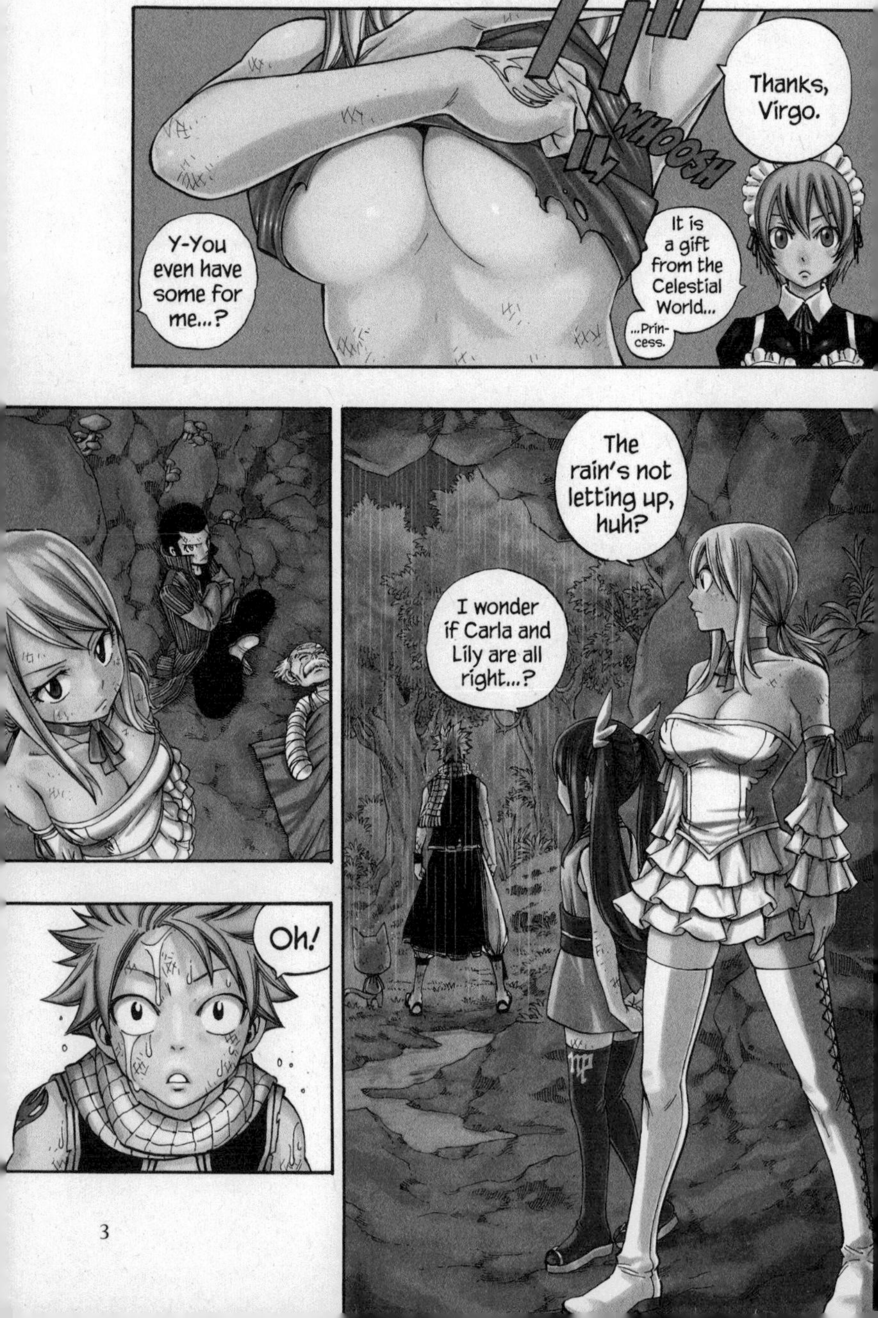
WHOOSH
Thanks, Virgo.
It is a gift from the Celestial World...
...Princess.
Y-You even have some for me...?
The rain's not letting up, huh?
I wonder if Carla and Lily are all right...?
Oh!

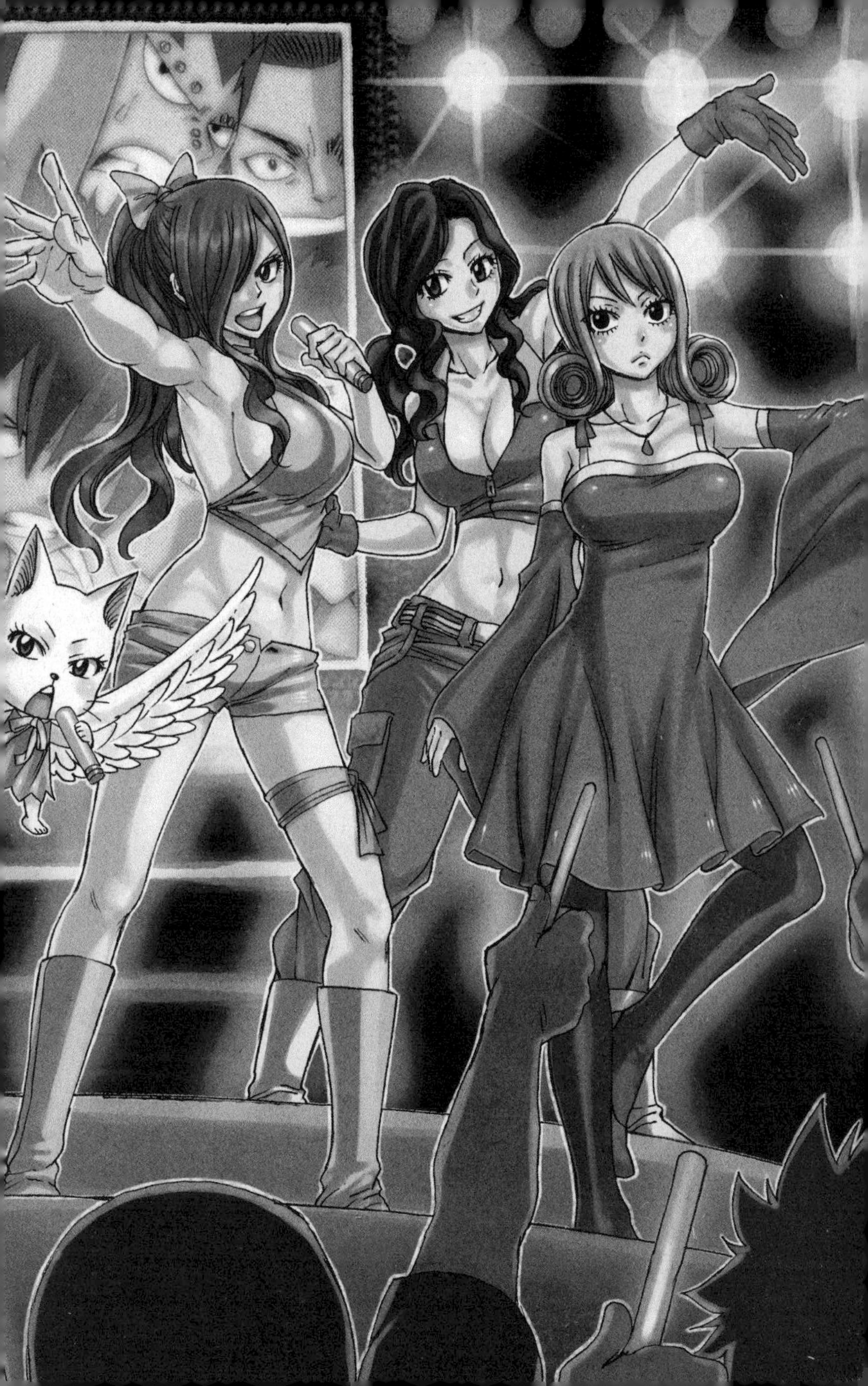

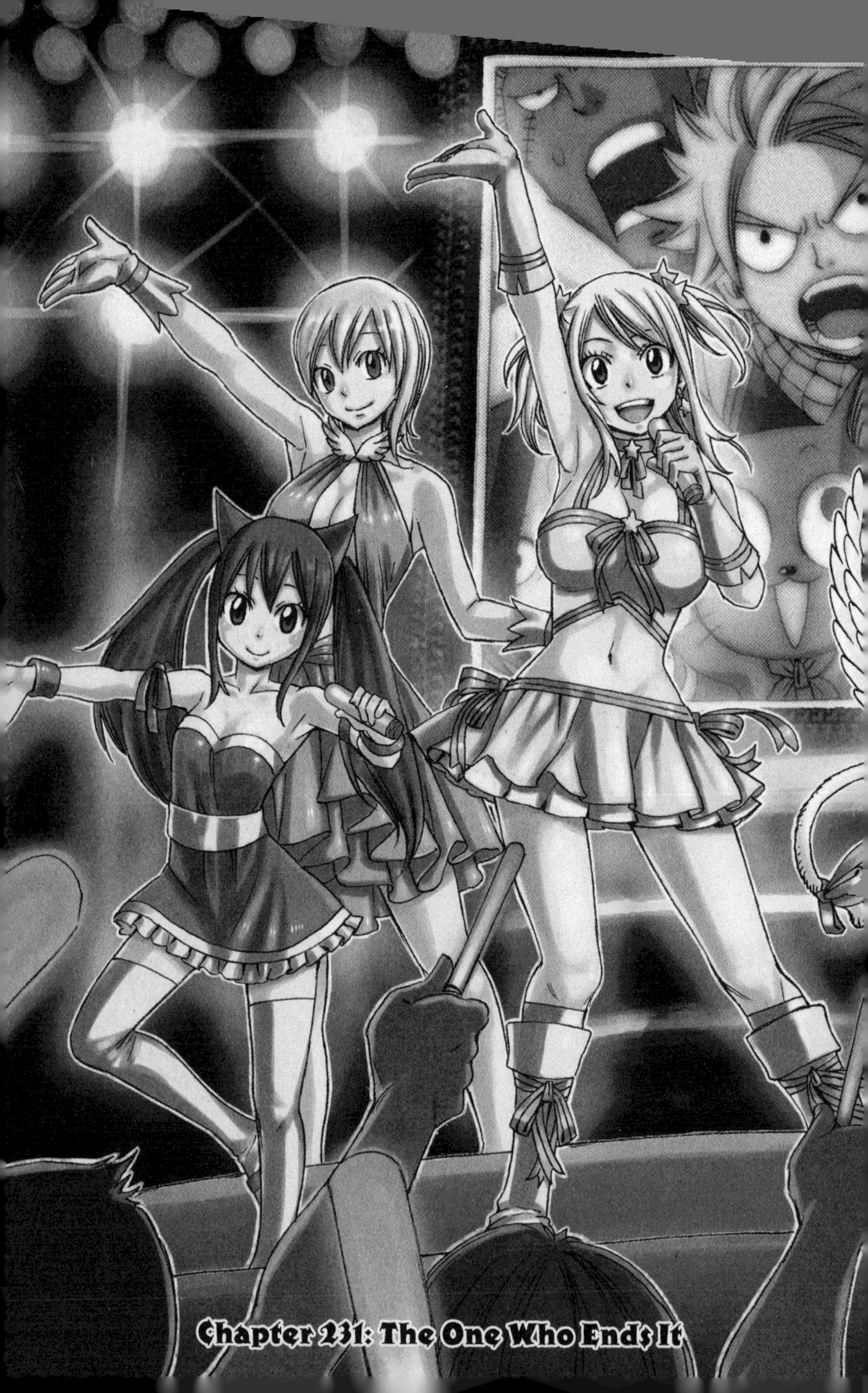
Chapter 231: The One Who Ends It

FAIRY TAIL

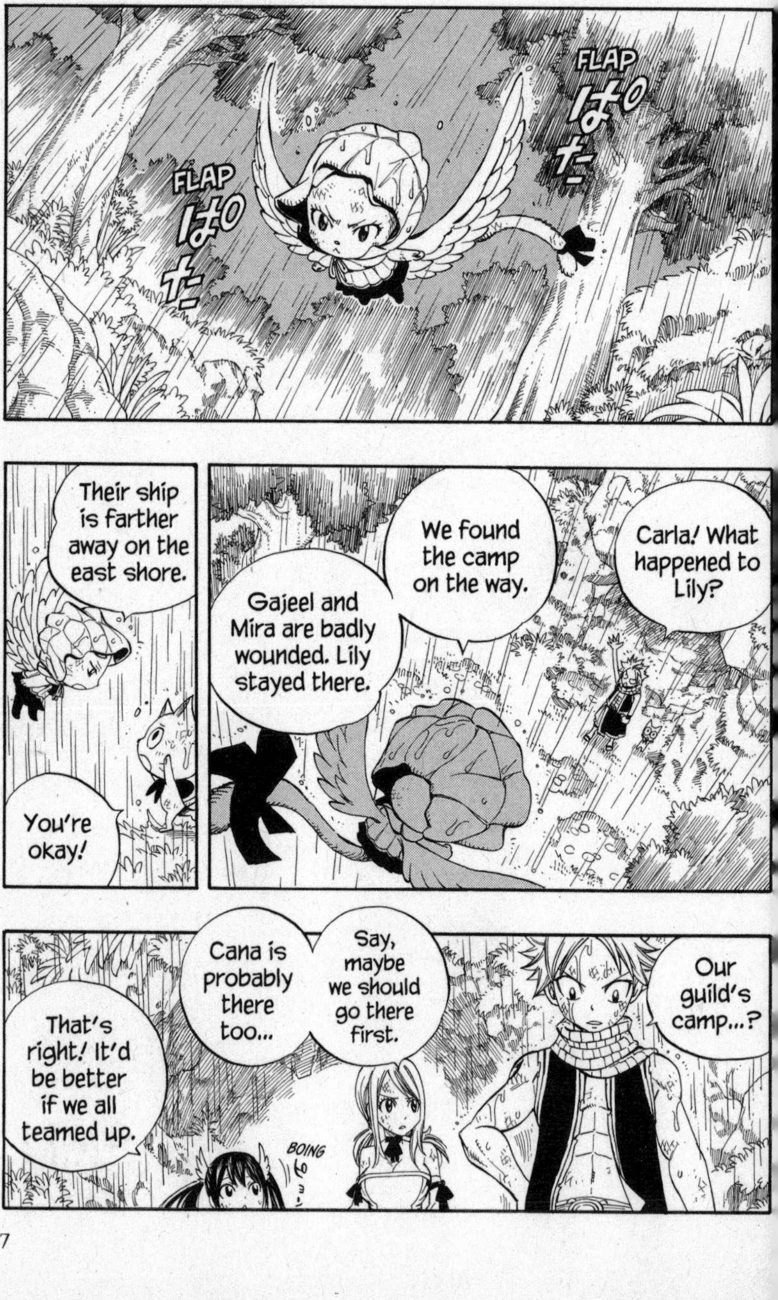
FLAP
FLAP
Carla! What happened to Lily?
We found the camp on the way.
Gajeel and Mira are badly wounded. Lily stayed there.
Their ship is farther away on the east shore.
You're okay!
Our guild's camp...?
Say, maybe we should go there first.
Cana is probably there too...
That's right! It'd be better if we all teamed up.
BOING

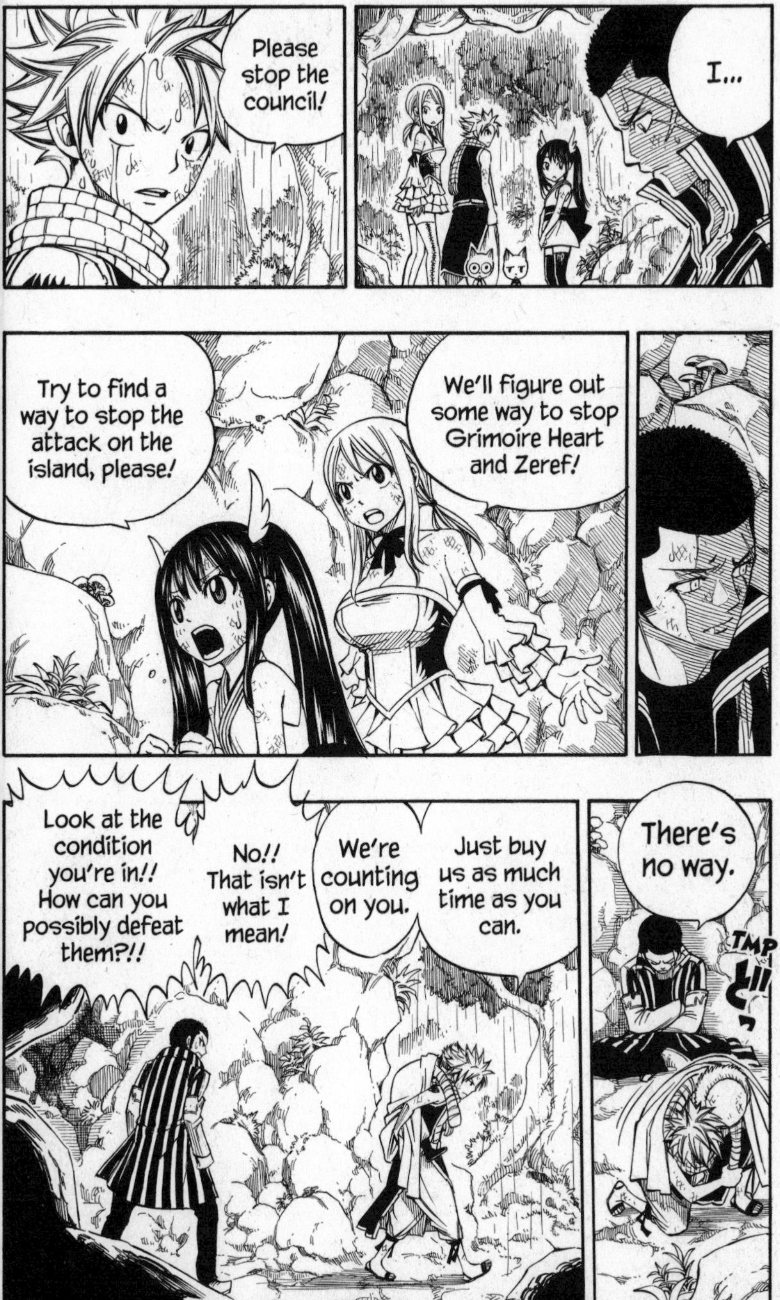
I...
Please stop the council!
We'll figure out some way to stop Grimoire Heart and Zeref!
Try to find a way to stop the attack on the island, please!
There's no way.
TMP
Just buy us as much time as you can.
We're counting on you.
No!! That isn't what I mean!
Look at the condition you're in!! How can you possibly defeat them?!!

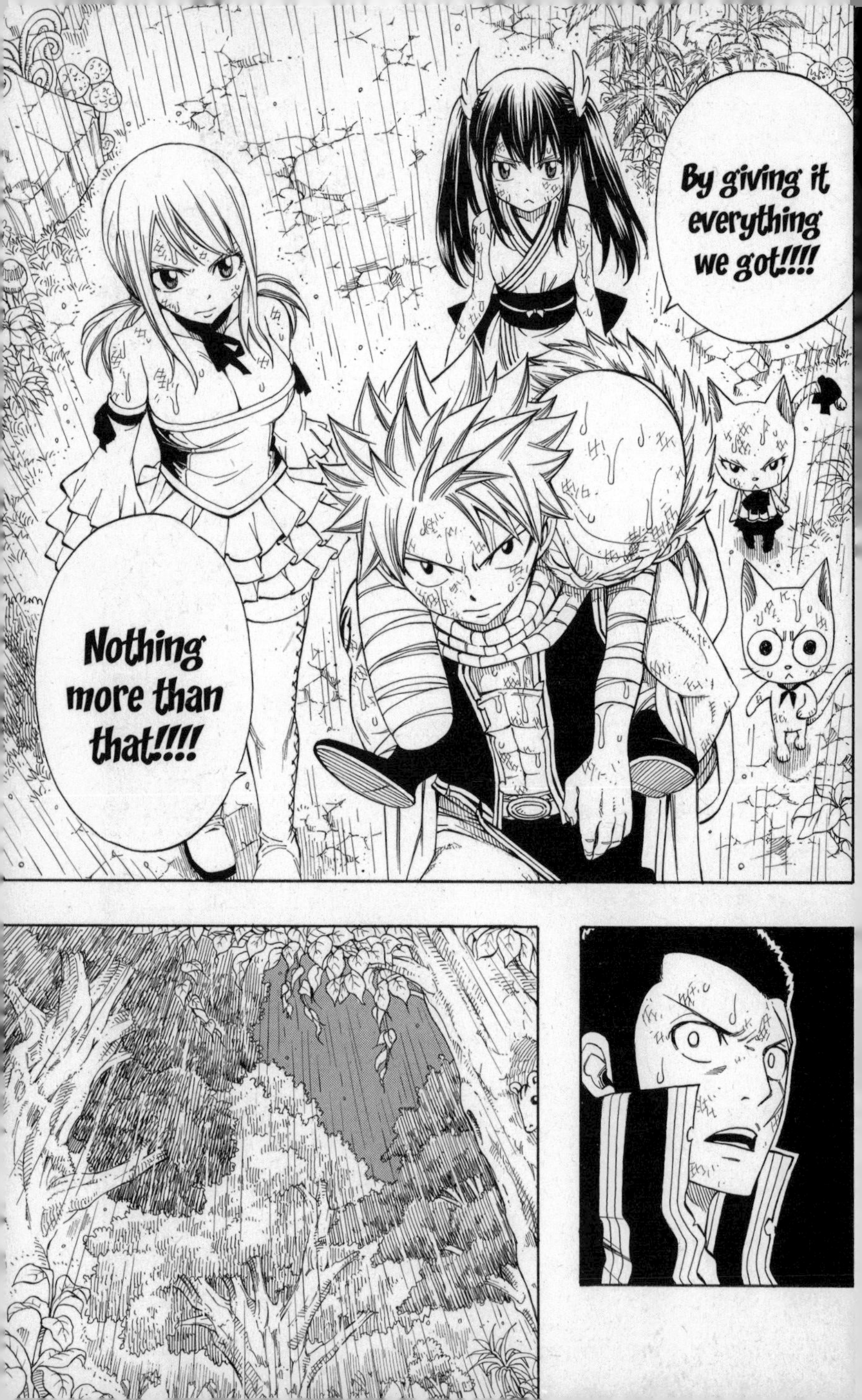
By giving it everything we got!!!!
Nothing more than that!!!!

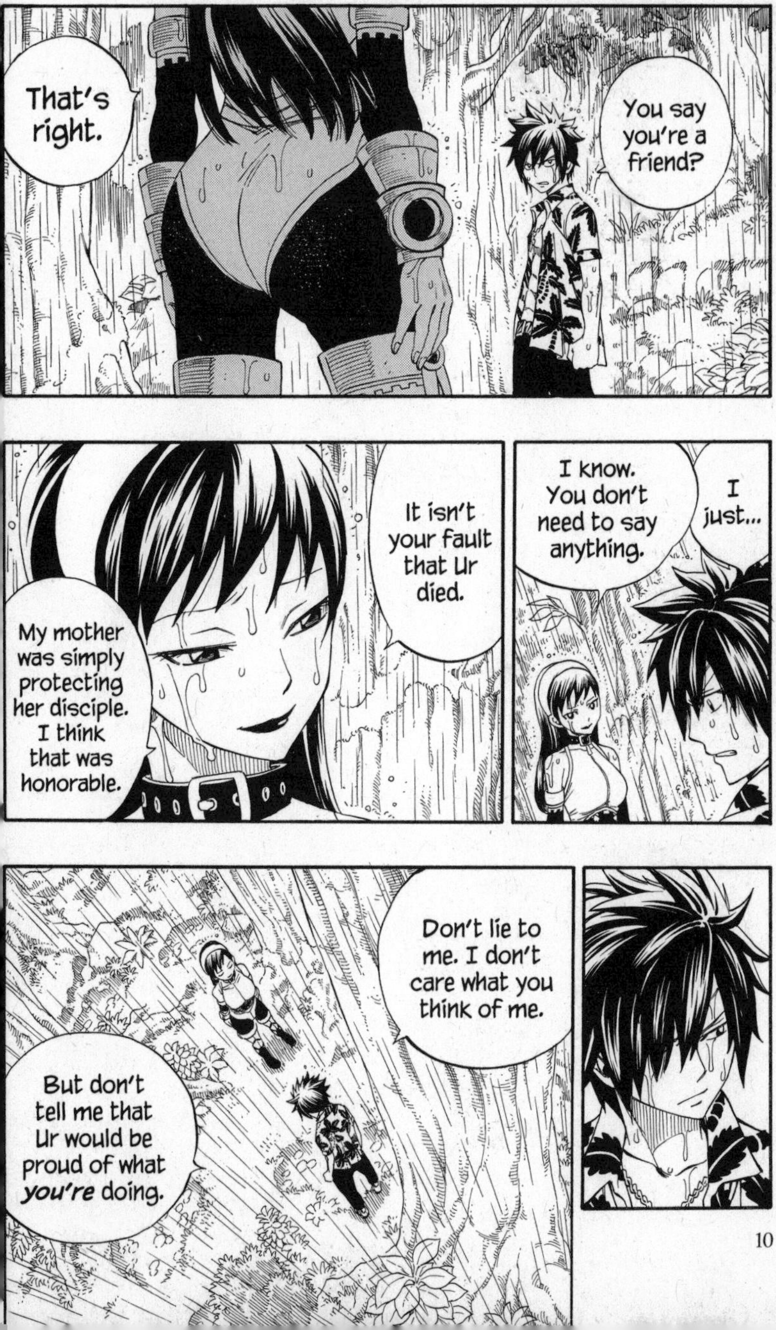
You say you're a friend?
That's right.
I just...
I know. You don't need to say anything.
It isn't your fault that Ur died.
My mother was simply protecting her disciple. I think that was honorable.
Don't lie to me. I don't care what you think of me.
But don't tell me that Ur would be proud of what *you're* doing.

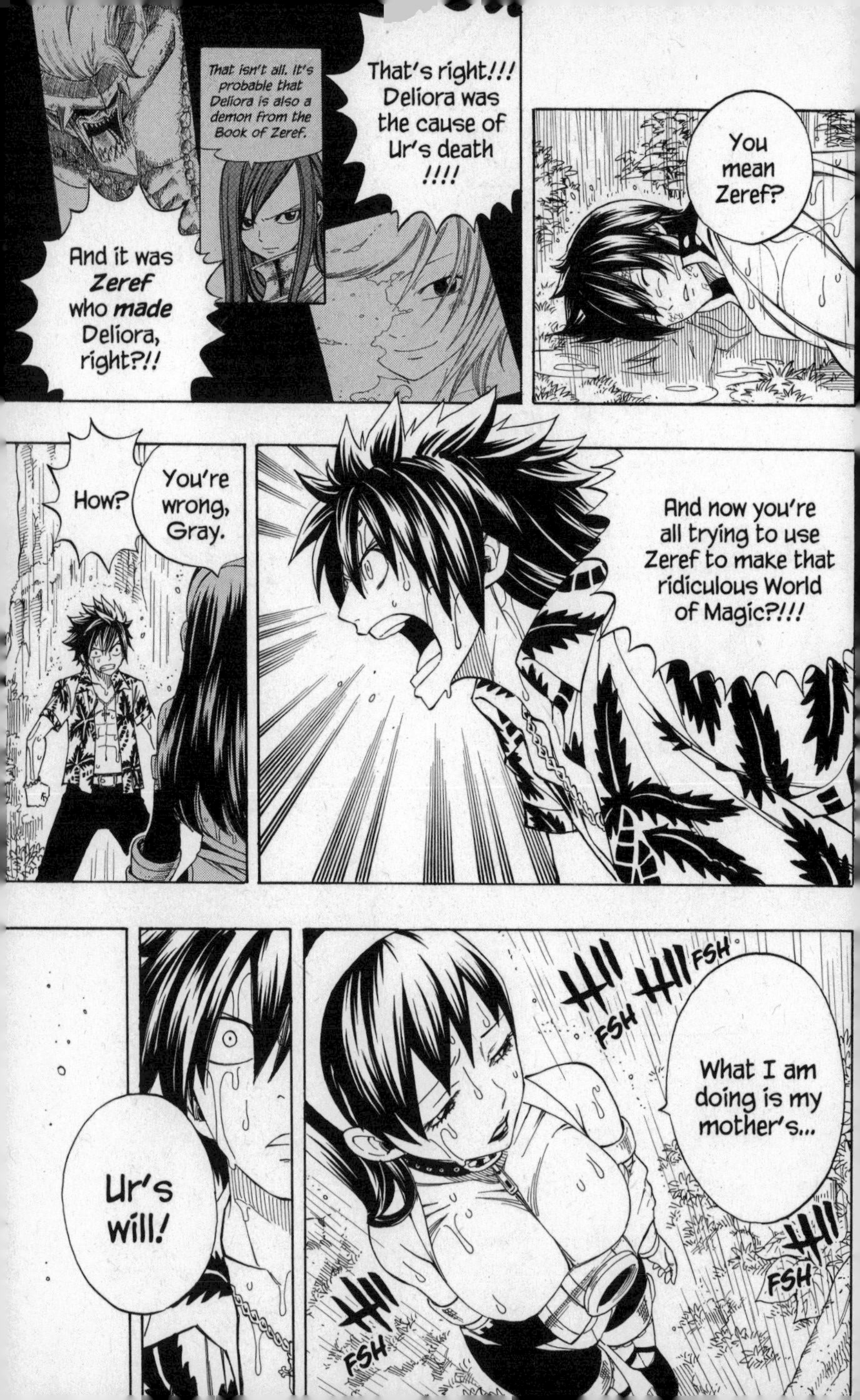
You mean Zeref?
That's right!!! Deliora was the cause of Ur's death !!!!
That isn't all. It's probable that Deliora is also a demon from the Book of Zeref.
And it was *Zeref* who *made* Deliora, right?!!
And now you're all trying to use Zeref to make that ridiculous World of Magic?!!!
You're wrong, Gray.
How?
FSH
FSH
What I am doing is my mother's...
FSH
FSH
Ur's will!

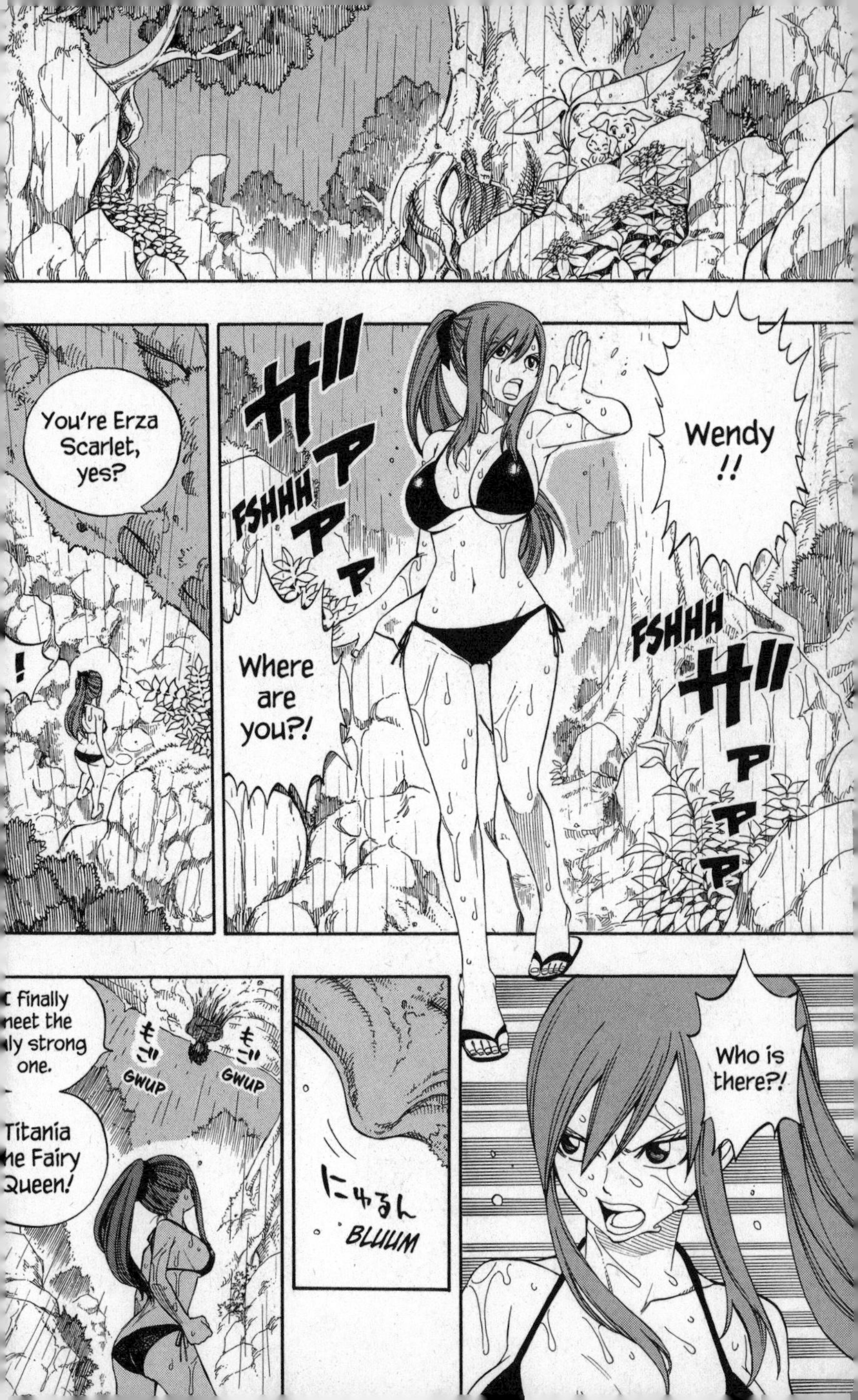
Wendy !!
FSHHH
ザァァァ
Where are you?!
FSHHH
ザァァァ
You're Erza Scarlet, yes?
!
Who is there?!
にゃるん
BLUUM
finally eet the ly strong one.
もご
GWUP
もご
GWUP
Titania he Fairy Queen!

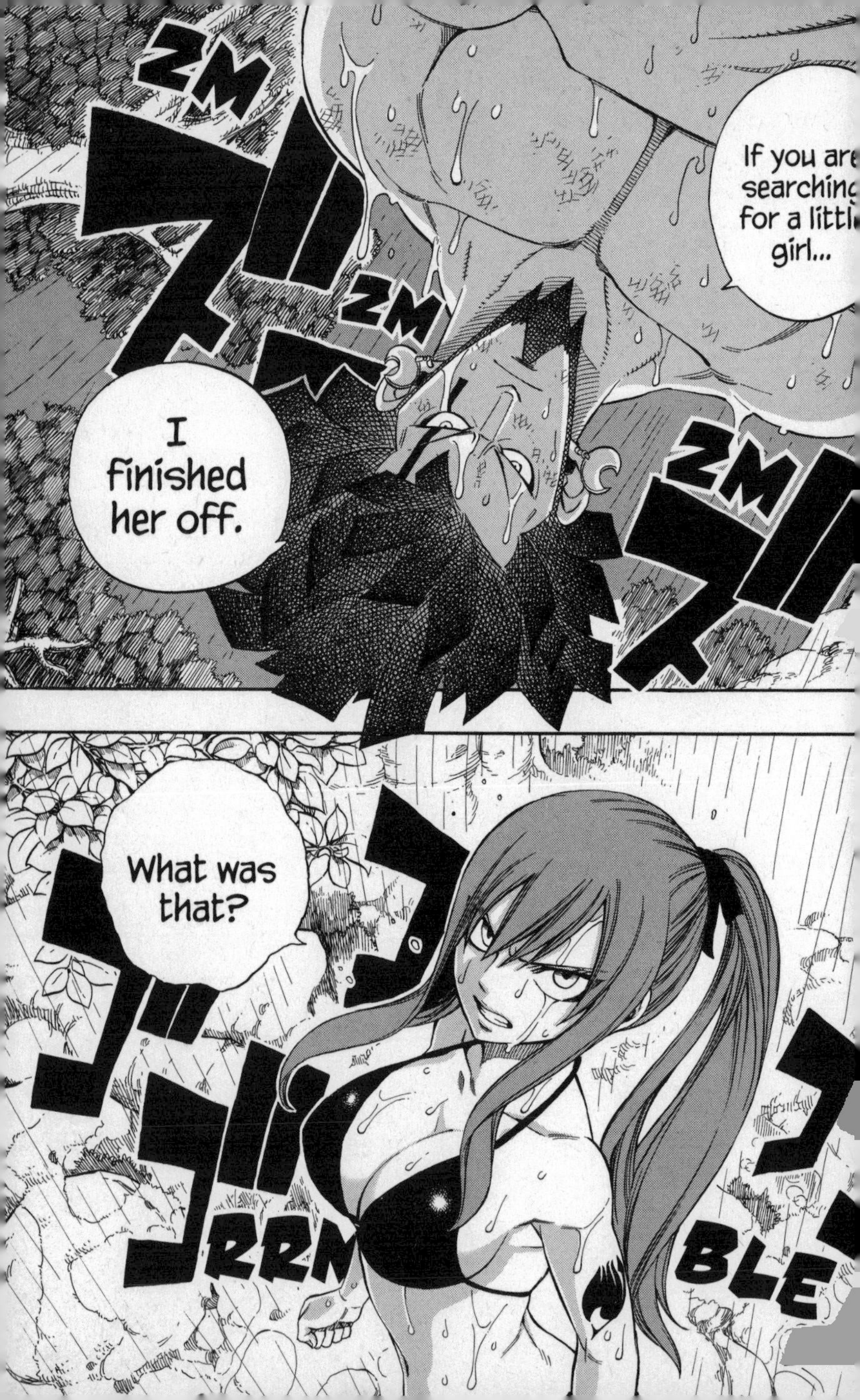
If you are searching for a little girl...
ZM
ZM
ZM
I finished her off.
What was that?
RRM
BLE

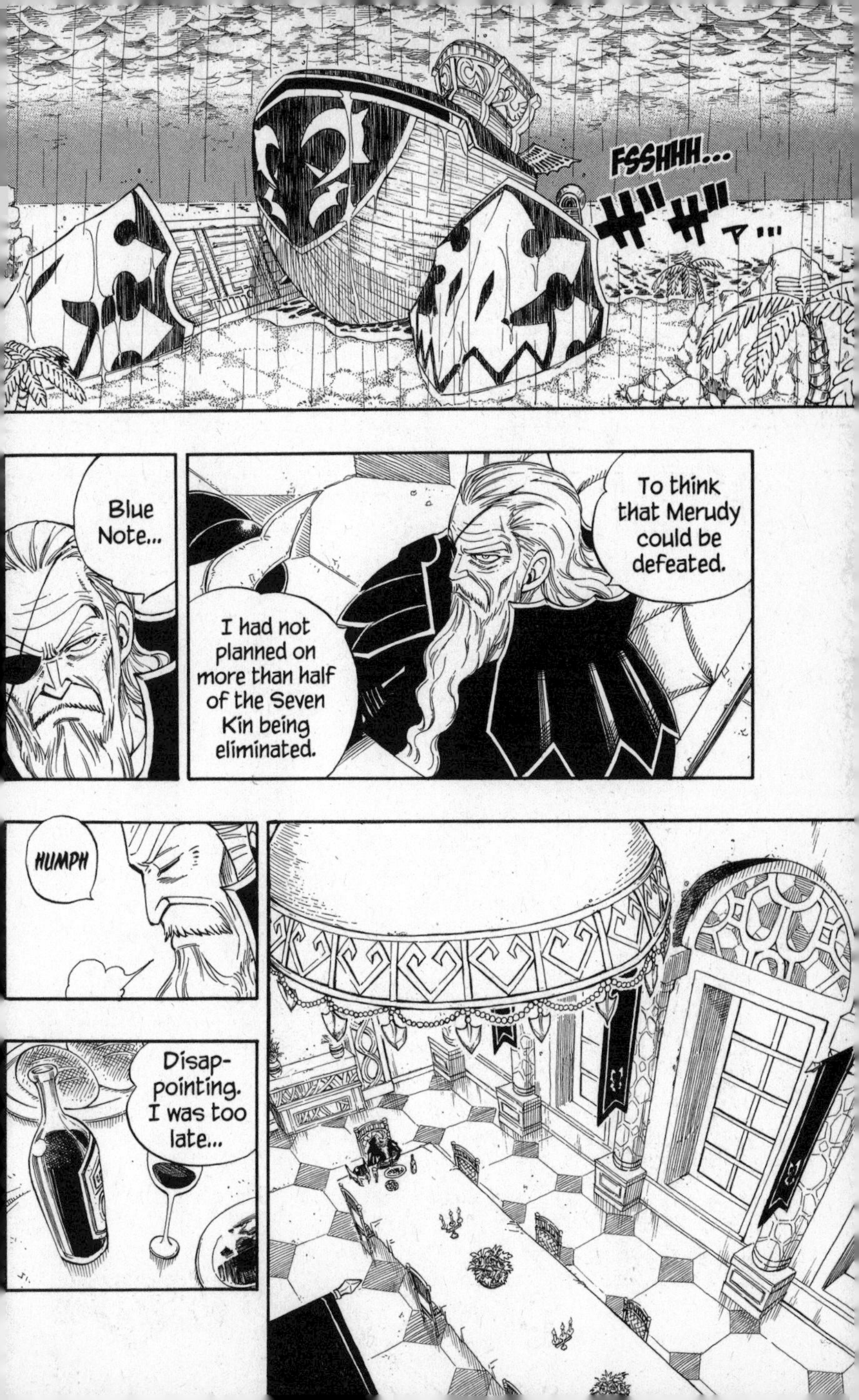
FSSHHH...
ザザァ...
To think that Merudy could be defeated.
I had not planned on more than half of the Seven Kin being eliminated.
Blue Note...
HUMPH
Disap-pointing. I was too late...

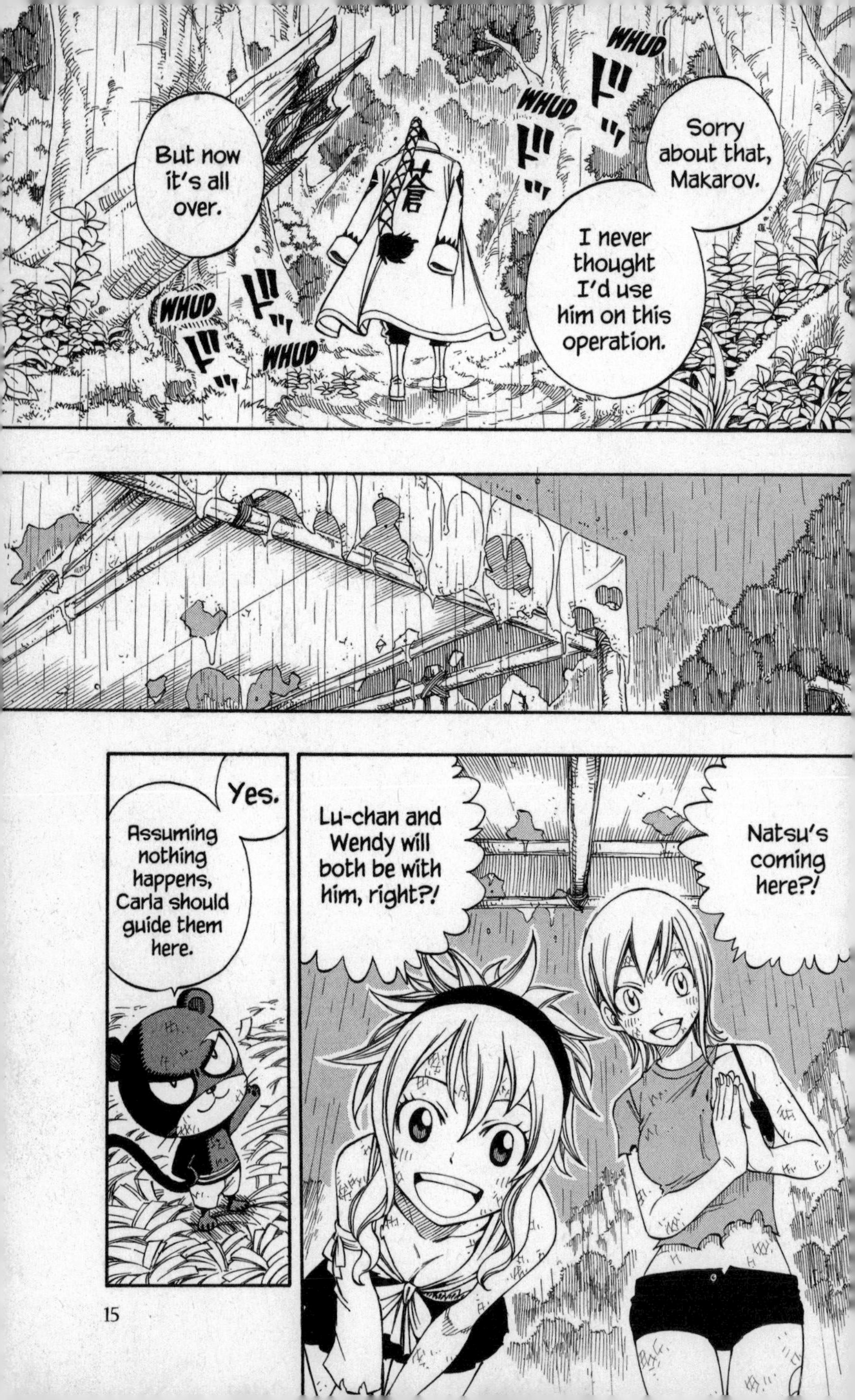
Sorry about that, Makarov.
I never thought I'd use him on this operation.
WHUD
WHUD
But now it's all over.
WHUD
WHUD
Natsu's coming here?!
Lu-chan and Wendy will both be with him, right?!
Yes.
Assuming nothing happens, Carla should guide them here.

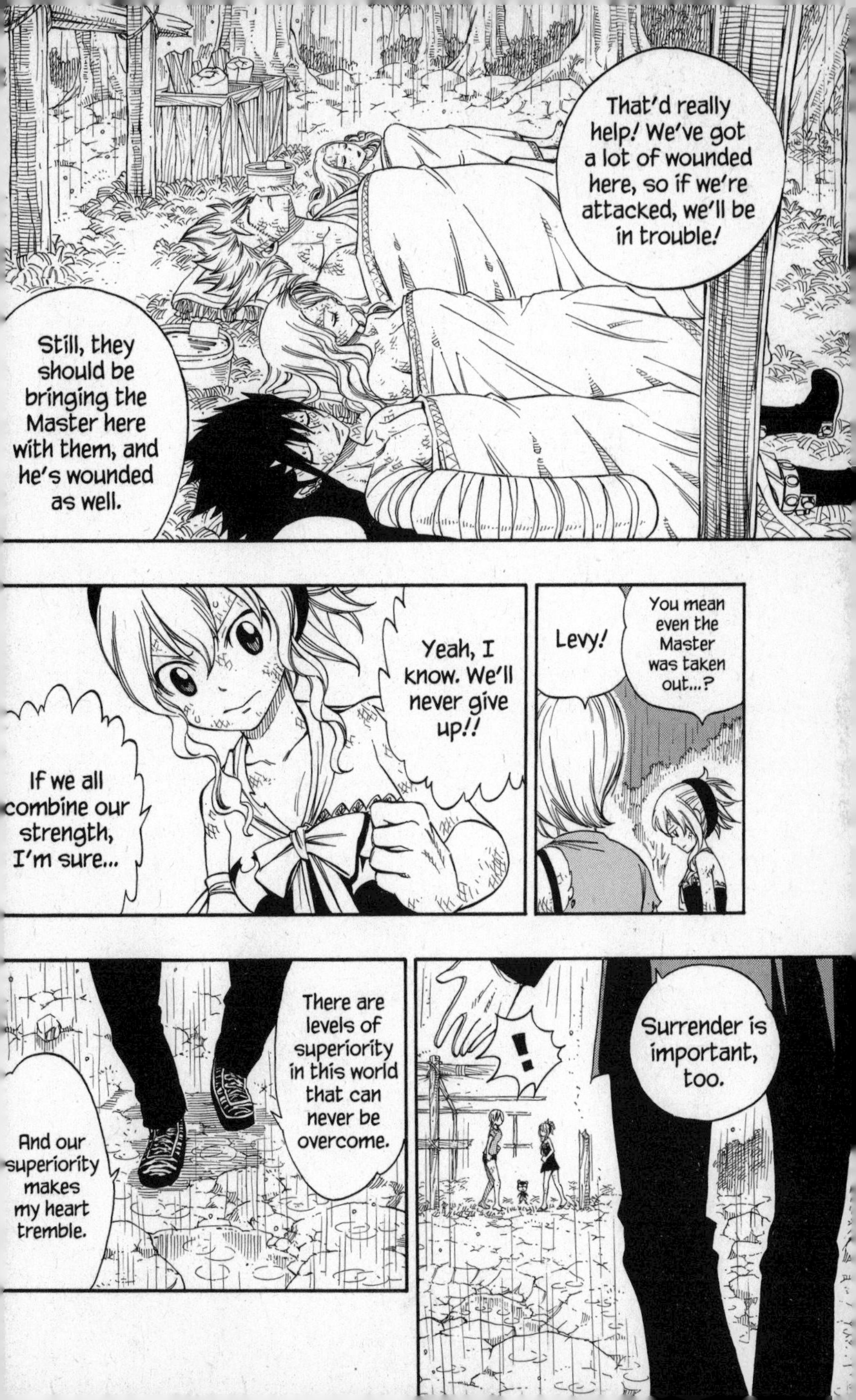
That'd really help! We've got a lot of wounded here, so if we're attacked, we'll be in trouble!
Still, they should be bringing the Master here with them, and he's wounded as well.
You mean even the Master was taken out...?
Levy!
Yeah, I know. We'll never give up!!
If we all combine our strength, I'm sure...
!
Surrender is important, too.
There are levels of superiority in this world that can never be overcome.
And our superiority makes my heart tremble.

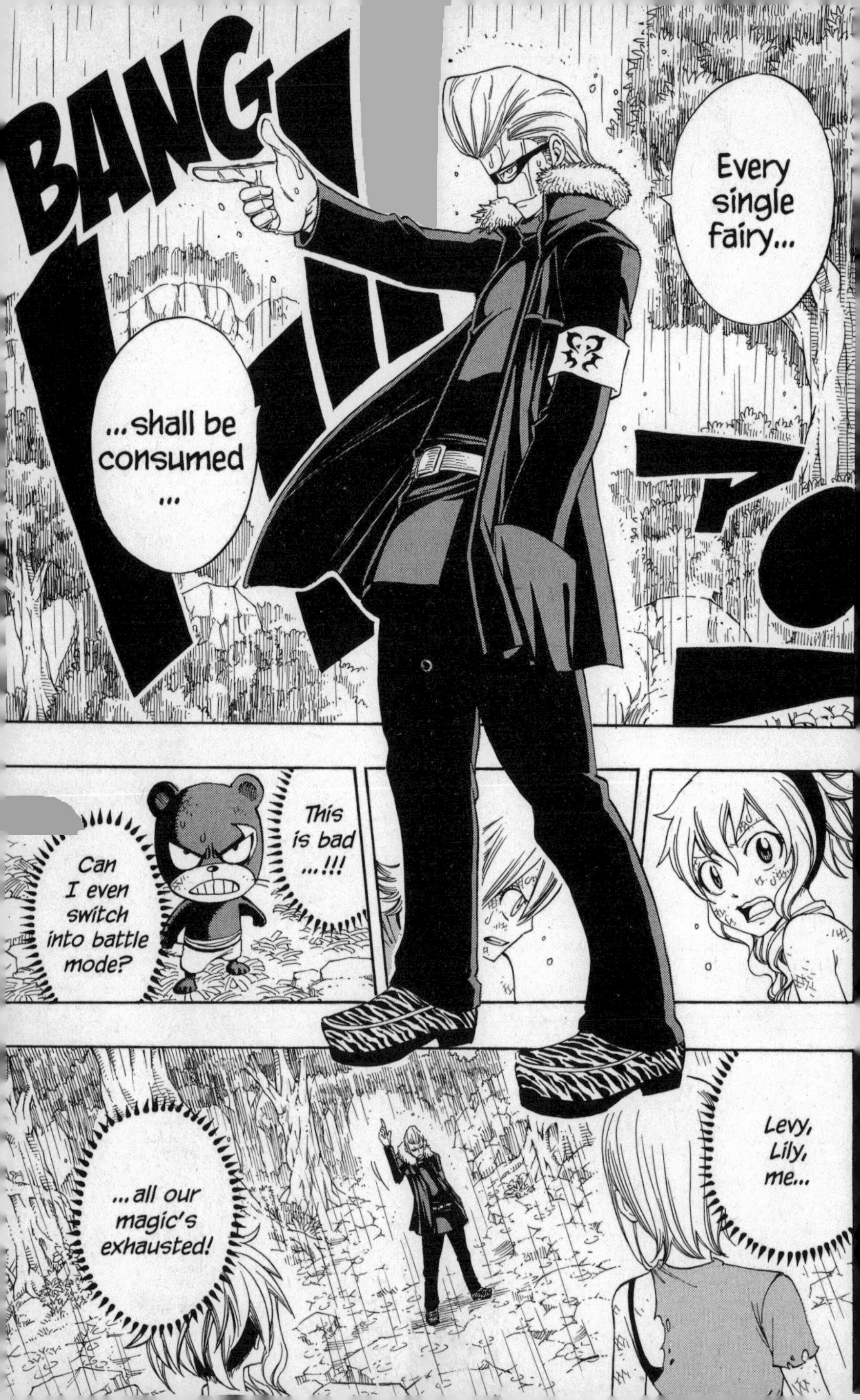

Every single fairy...
BANG
...shall be consumed ...
This is bad ...!!!
Can I even switch into battle mode?
Levy, Lily, me...
...all our magic's exhausted!

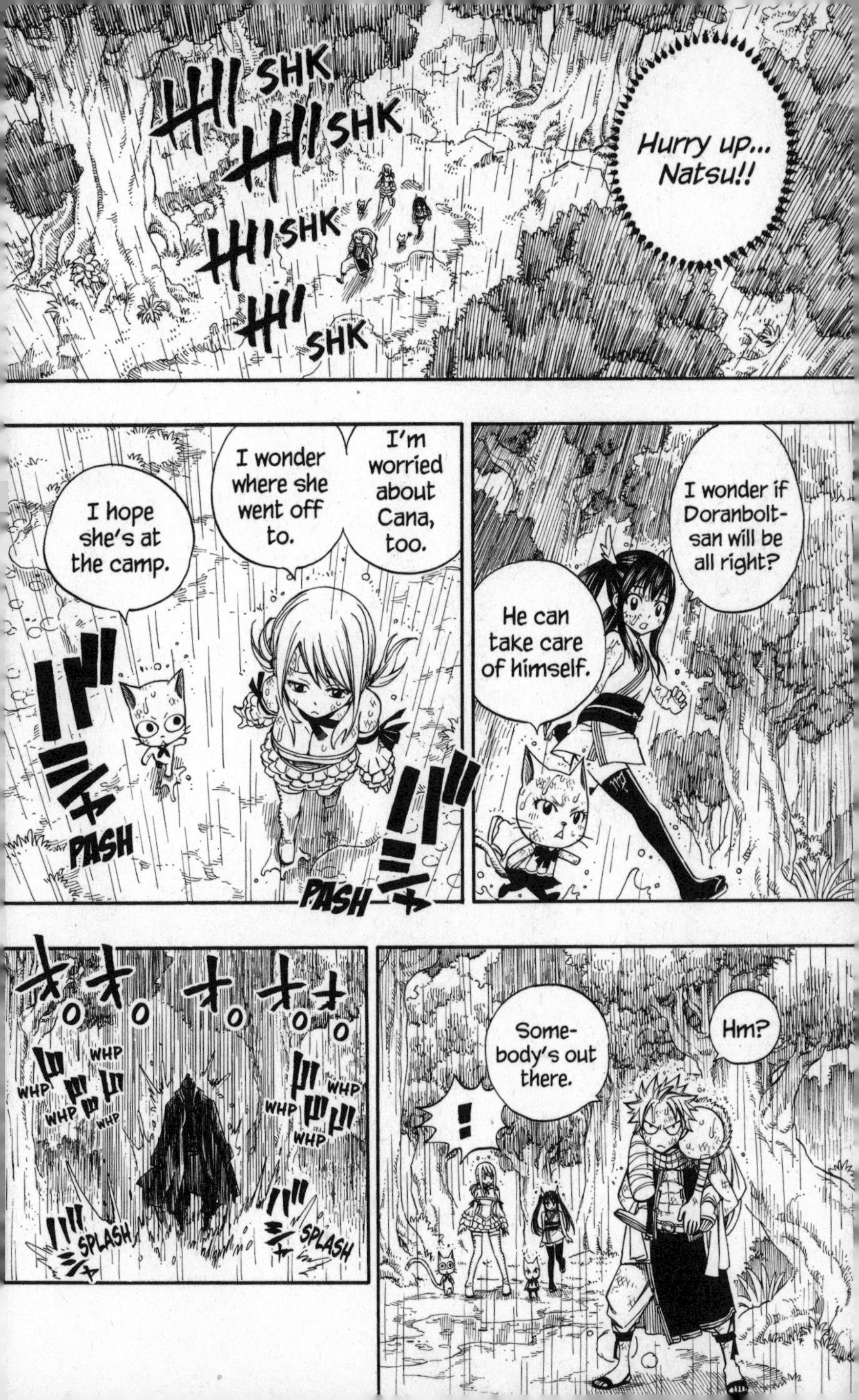
SHK
SHK
SHK
SHK
Hurry up... Natsu!!
I wonder if Doranbolt-san will be all right?
He can take care of himself.
I'm worried about Cana, too.
I wonder where she went off to.
I hope she's at the camp.
PASH
PASH
Hm?
Somebody's out there.
!
WHP
WHP
WHP
WHP
WHP
WHP
SPLASH
SPLASH

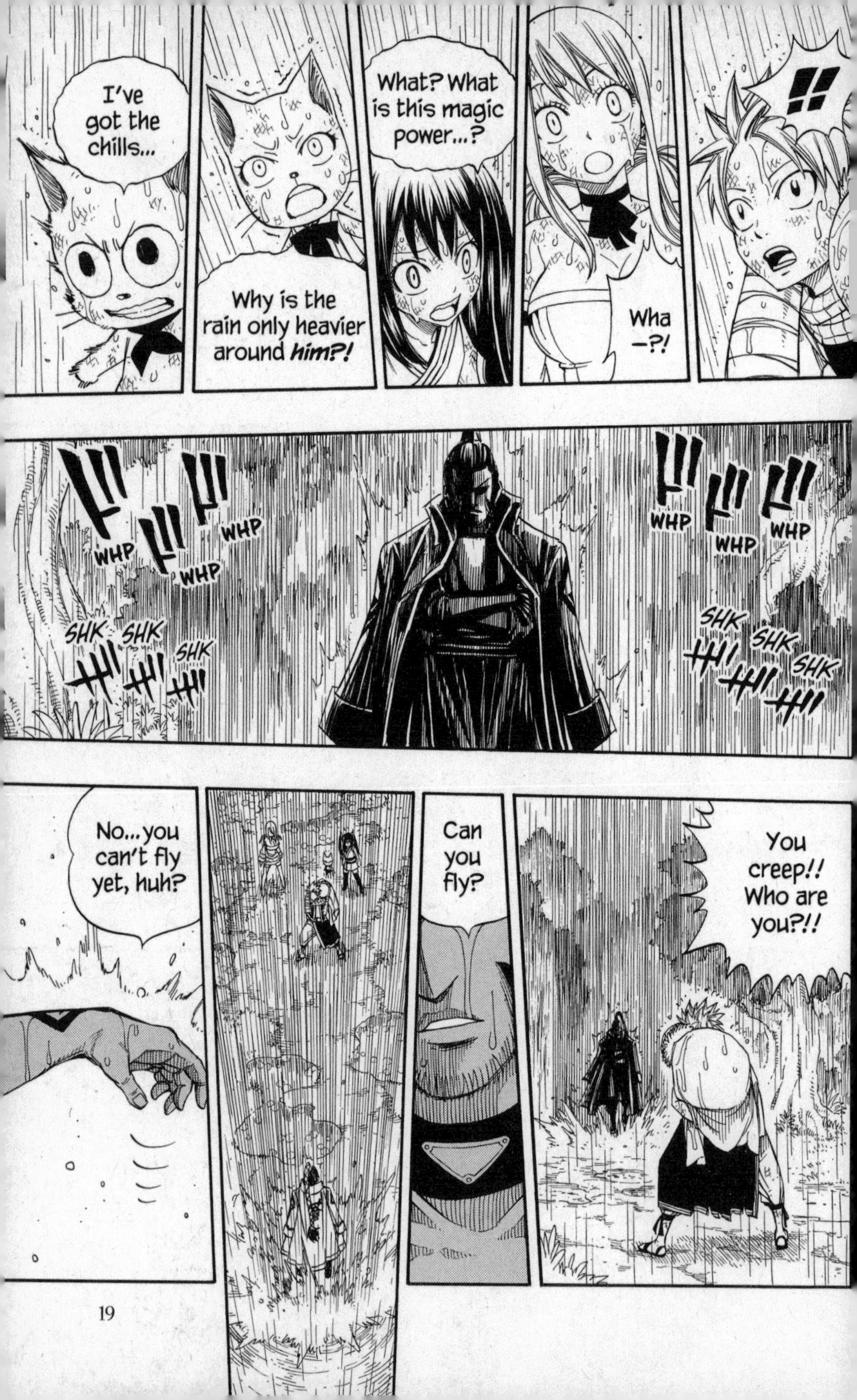
Wha
—?!
What? What is this magic power...?
Why is the rain only heavier around *him*?!
I've got the chills...
WHP WHP WHP
SHK SHK SHK
WHP WHP WHP
SHK SHK SHK
You creep!! Who are you?!!
Can you fly?
No...you can't fly yet, huh?

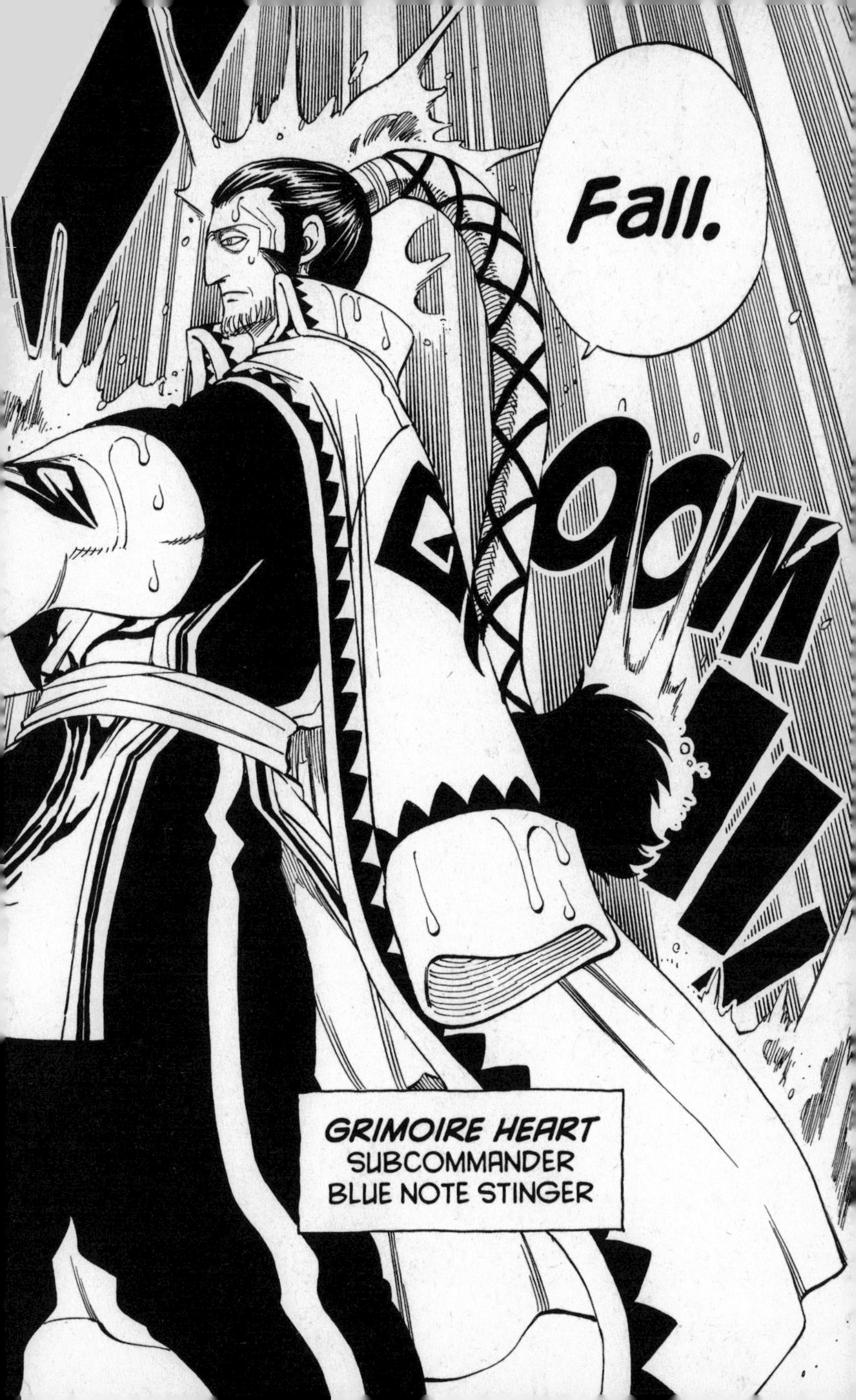
Fall.
DOOM!!
GRIMOIRE HEART
SUBCOMMANDER
BLUE NOTE STINGER

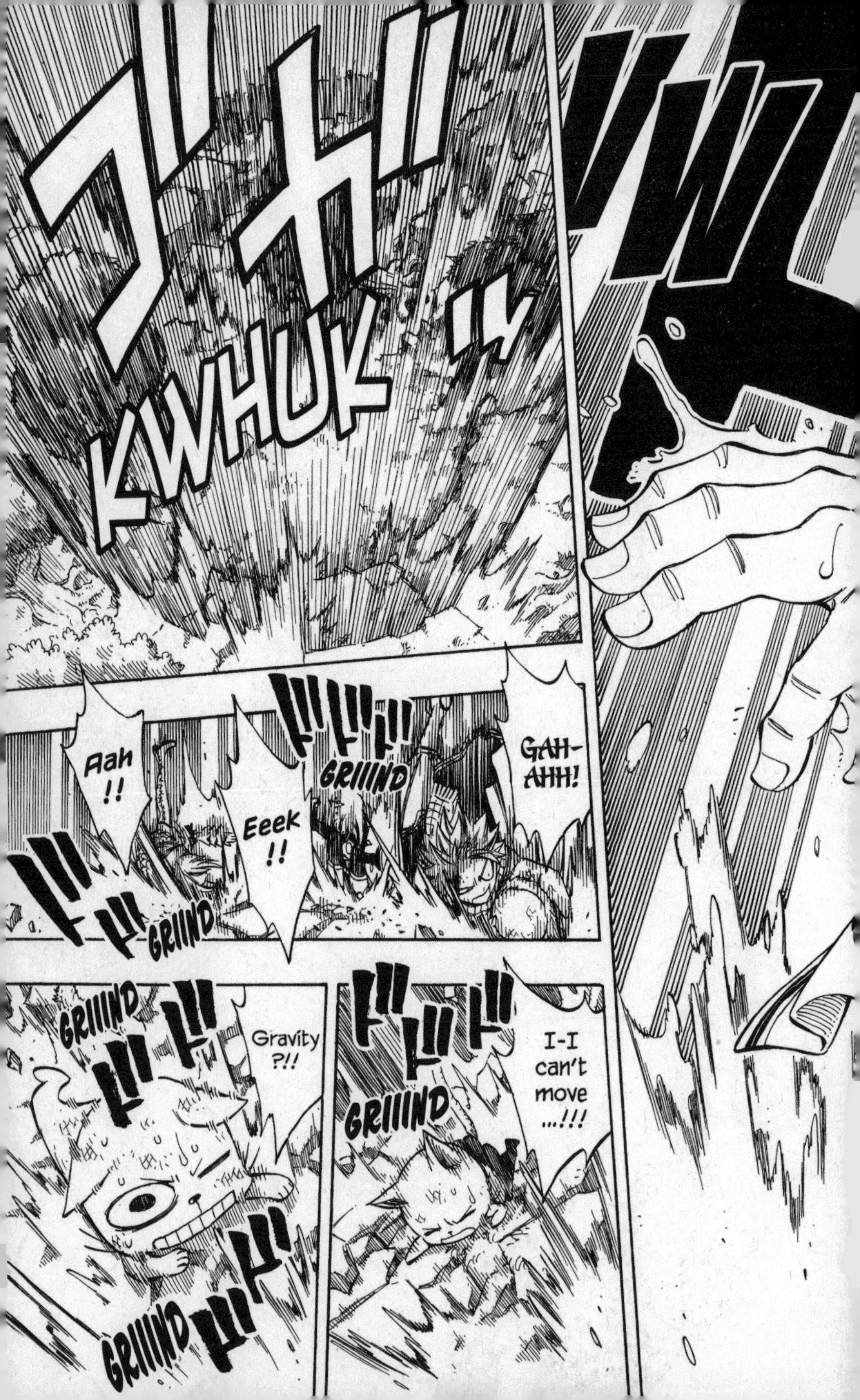
KWHUK
GAH-AHH!
GRIIIND
Eeek !!
Aah !!
GRIIND
I-I can't move ...!!!
GRIIIND
Gravity ?!!
GRIIIND
GRIIIND

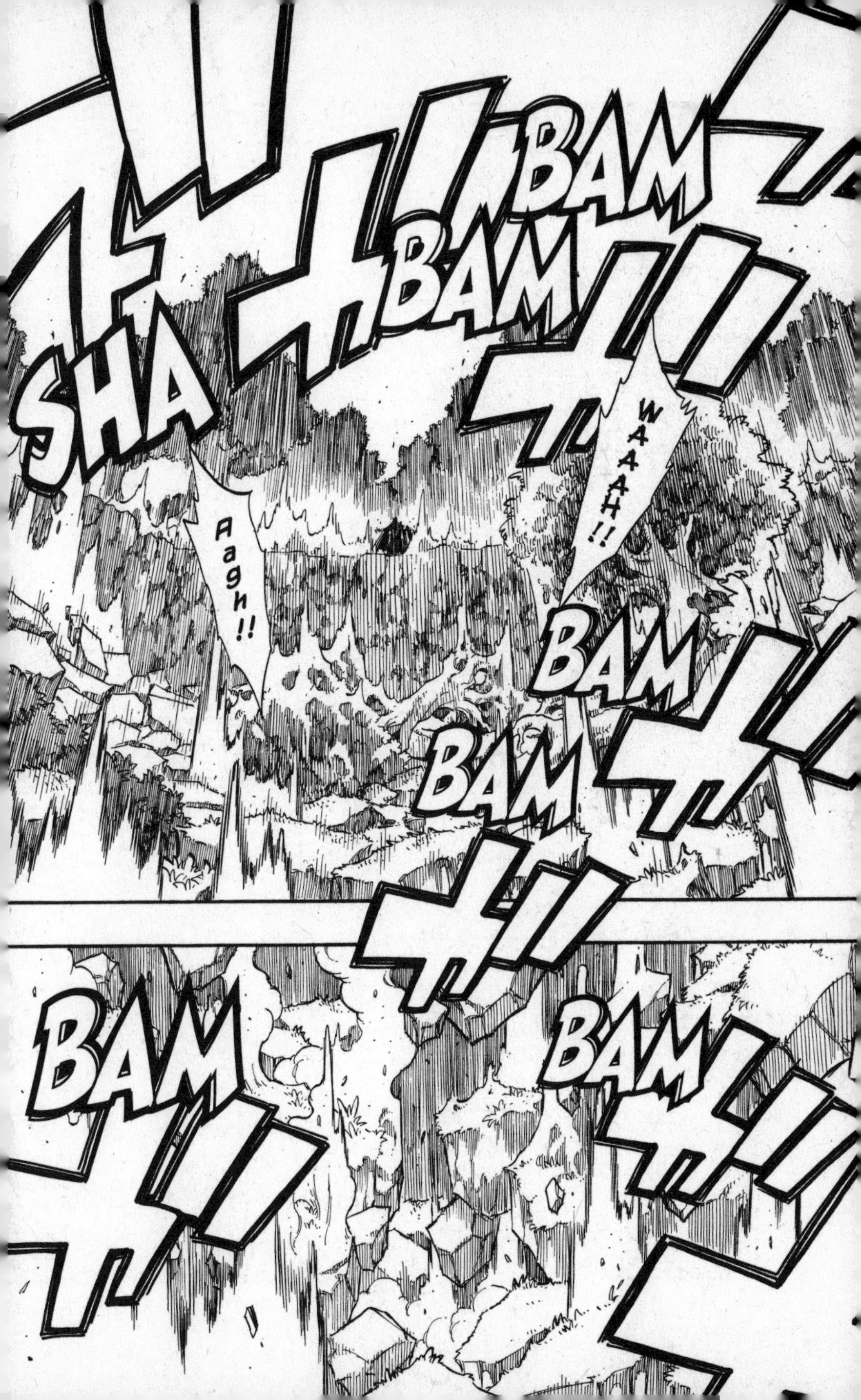
BAM
BAM!!
SHA
WAAAH!!
Aagh!!
BAM
BAM!!
BAM!!
BAM!!

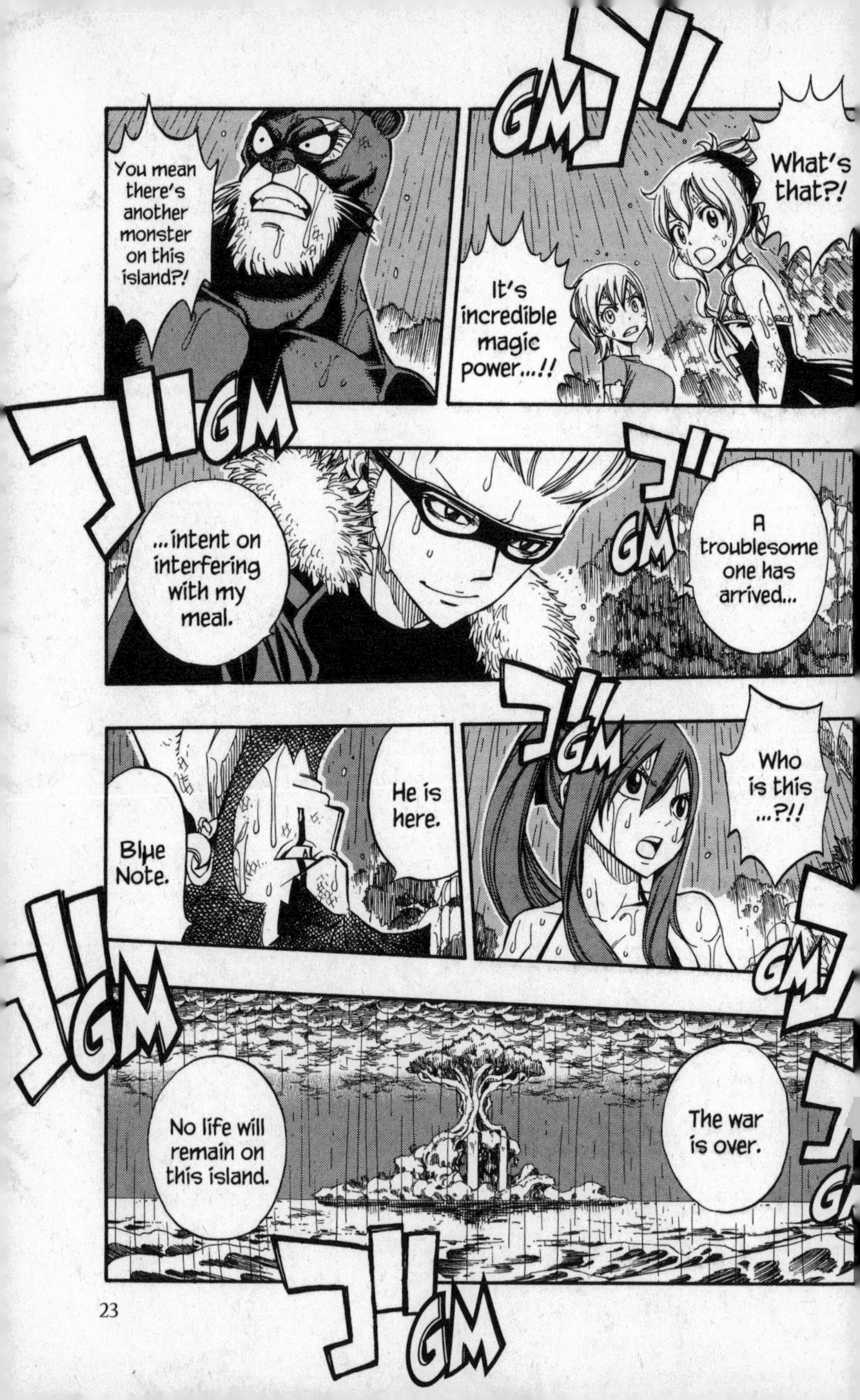

GM
What's that?!
It's incredible magic power...!!
You mean there's another monster on this island?!
GM
GM
A troublesome one has arrived...
...intent on interfering with my meal.
GM
Who is this ...?!!
He is here.
Blue Note.
GM
GM
The war is over.
No life will remain on this island.
GM

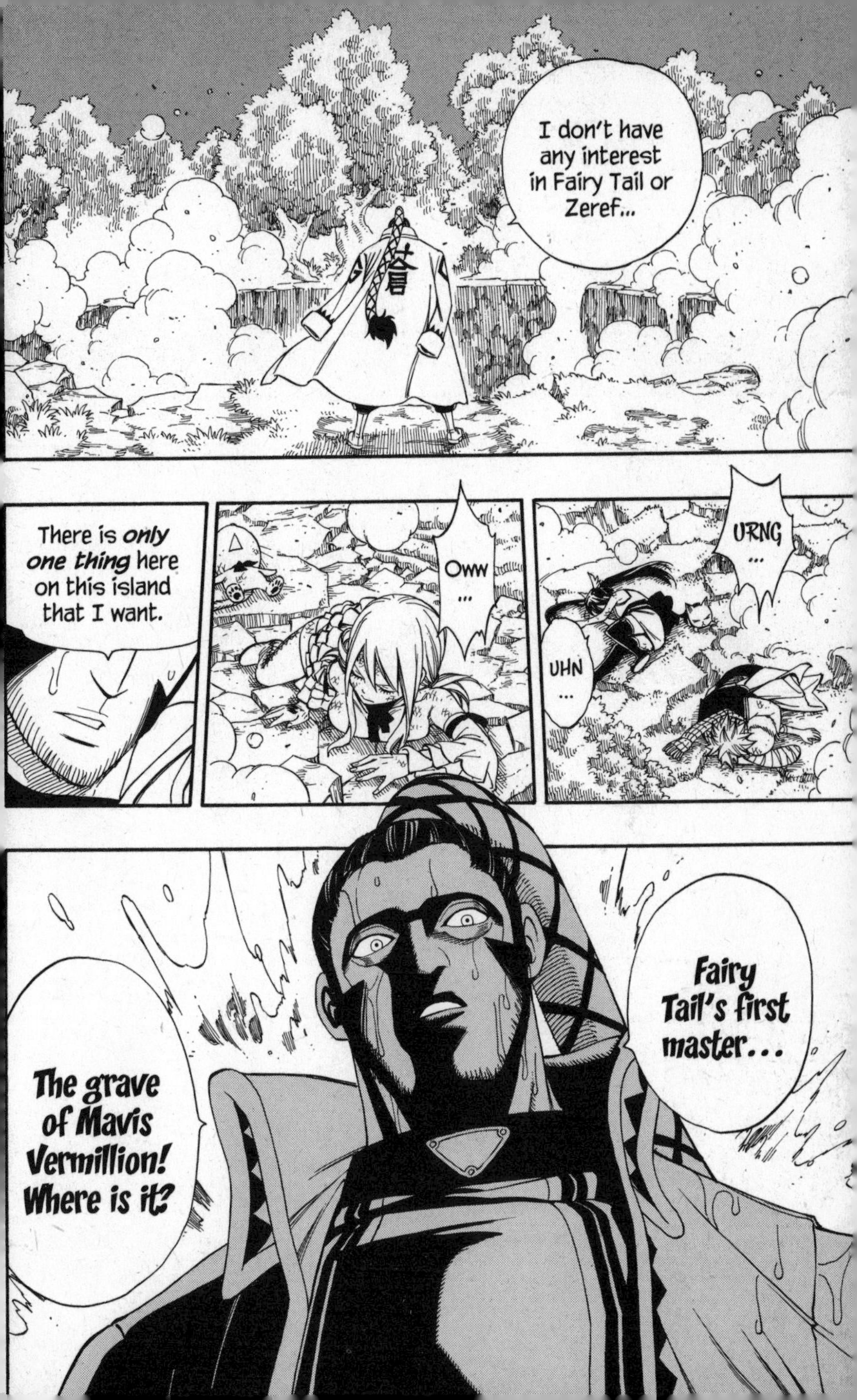
I don't have any interest in Fairy Tail or Zeref...
URNG ...
UHN ...
OWW ...
There is *only one thing* here on this island that I want.
Fairy Tail's first master...
The grave of Mavis Vermillion! Where is it?

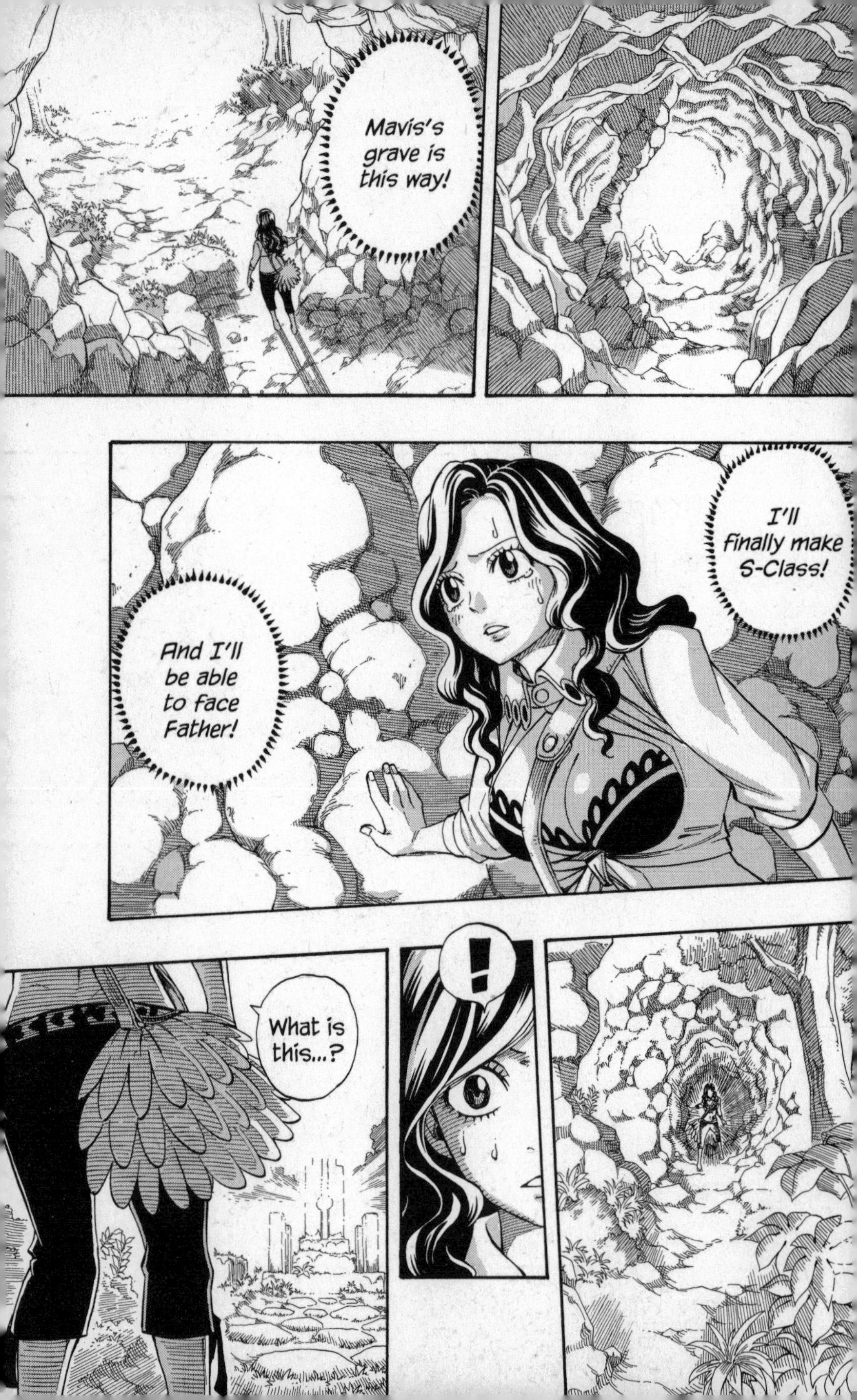
Mavis's grave is this way!
I'll finally make S-Class!
And I'll be able to face Father!
!
What is this...?

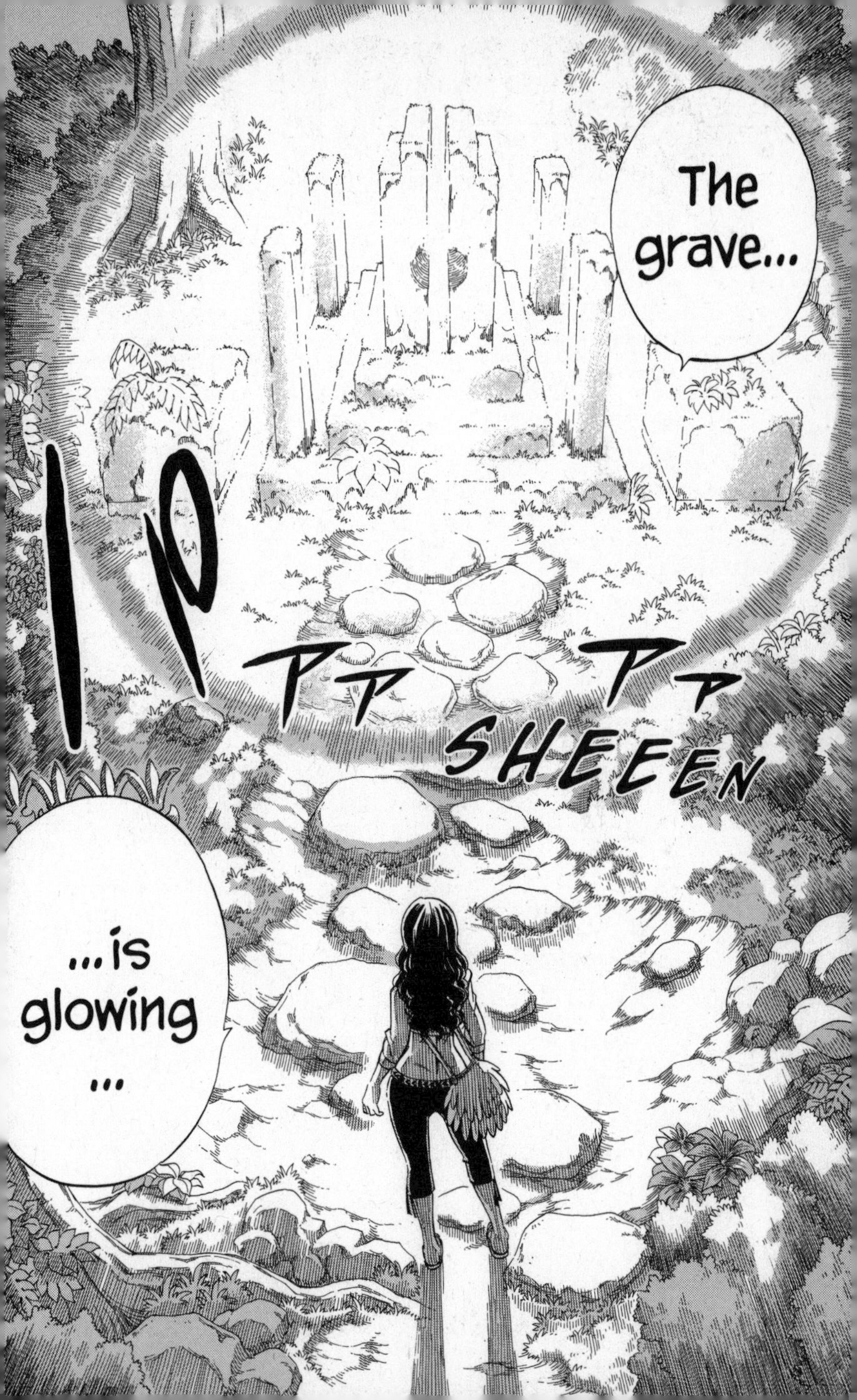
The grave...
SHEEEN
...is glowing...

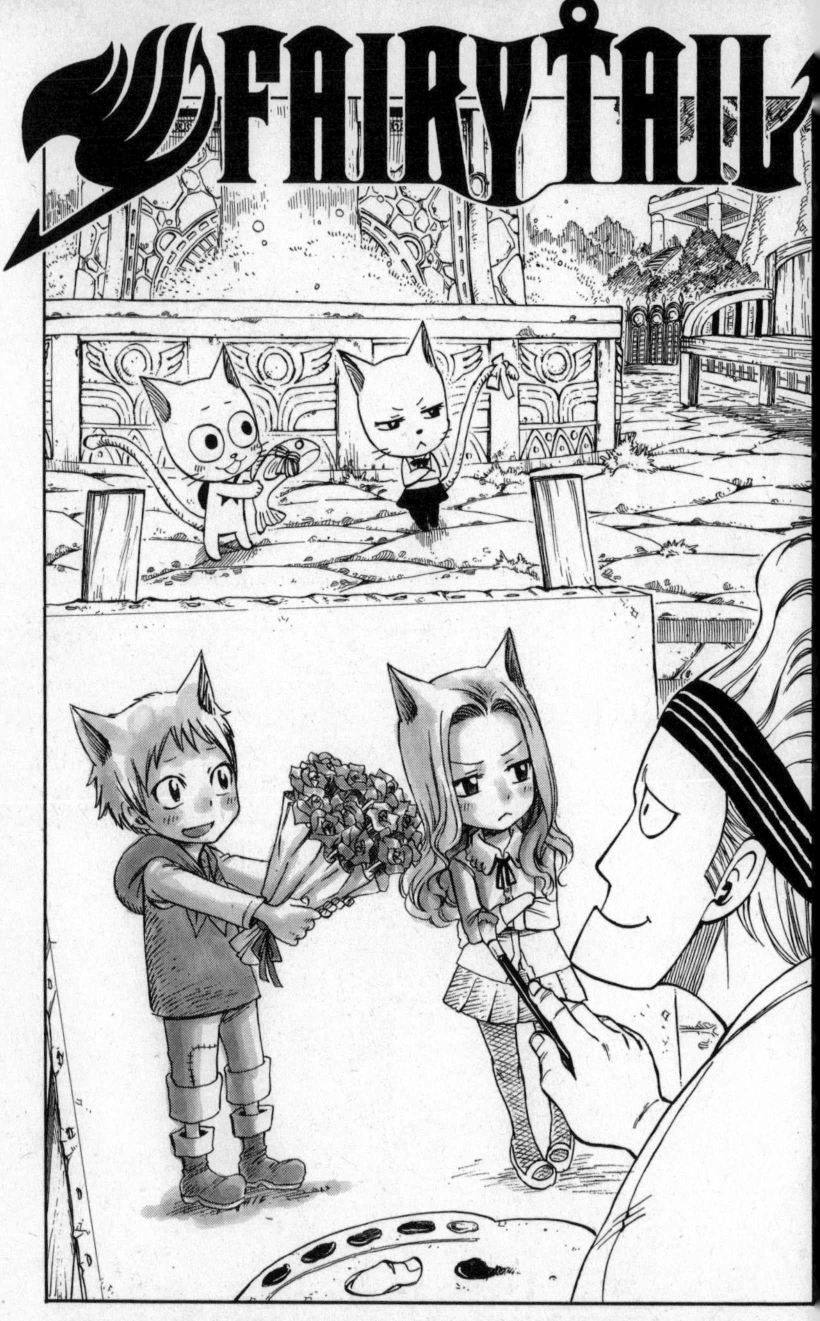
FAIRY TAIL

Chapter 232: The Word I Couldn't Say

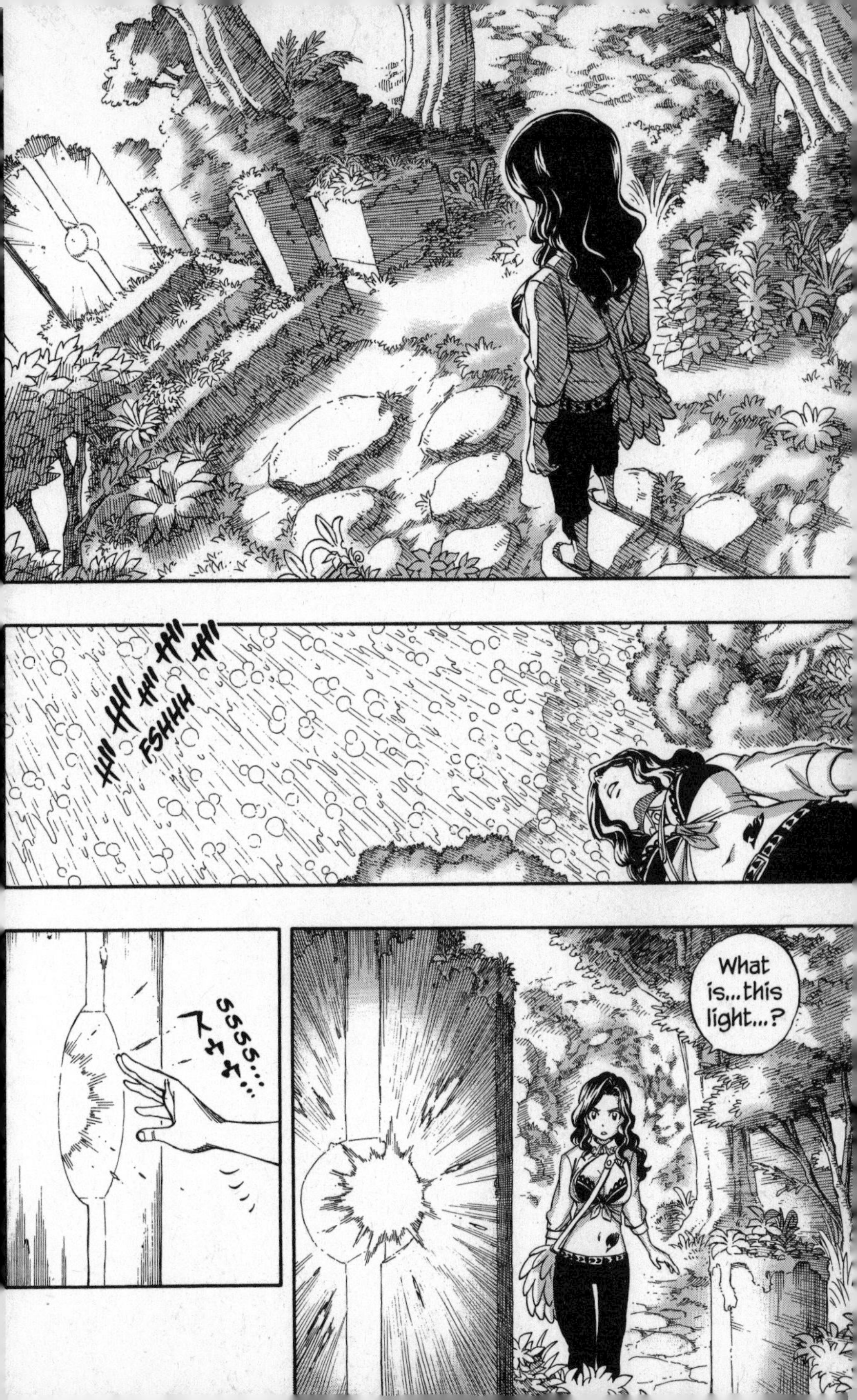
FSHHH
What is...this light...?
SSSS...

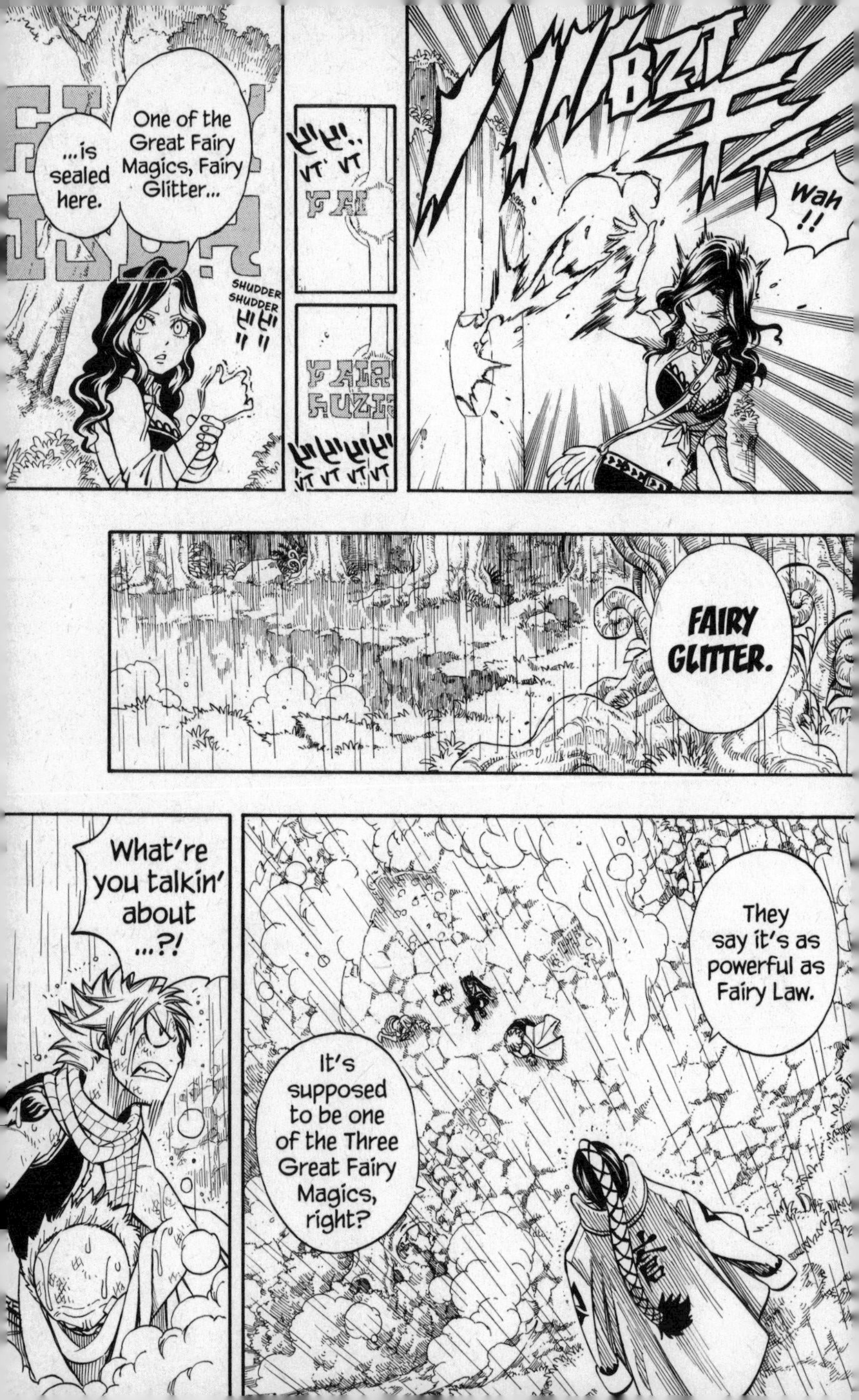
BZZT
Wah!!
VT VT
VT VT VT VT
One of the Great Fairy Magics, Fairy Glitter...
...is sealed here.
SHUDDER SHUDDER
FAIRY GLITTER.
They say it's as powerful as Fairy Law.
It's supposed to be one of the Three Great Fairy Magics, right?
What're you talkin' about ...?!

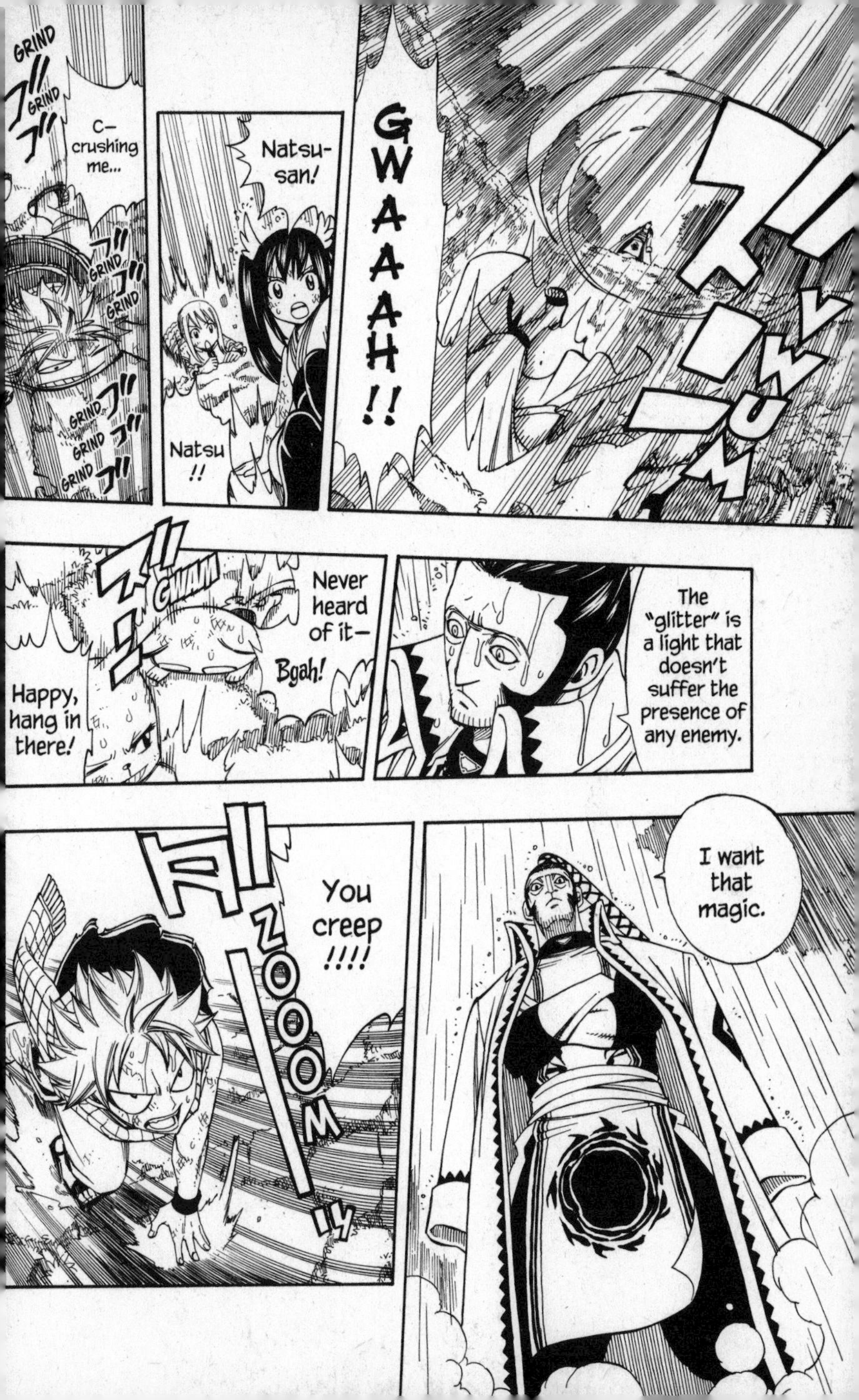
GWAAAH!!
WUM
Natsu-san!
Natsu!!
GRIND GRIND
C—crushing me...
GRIND GRIND
GRIND GRIND GRIND
The "glitter" is a light that doesn't suffer the presence of any enemy.
GWAM
Never heard of it—
Bgah!
Happy, hang in there!
I want that magic.
ZOOOOM
You creep!!!!

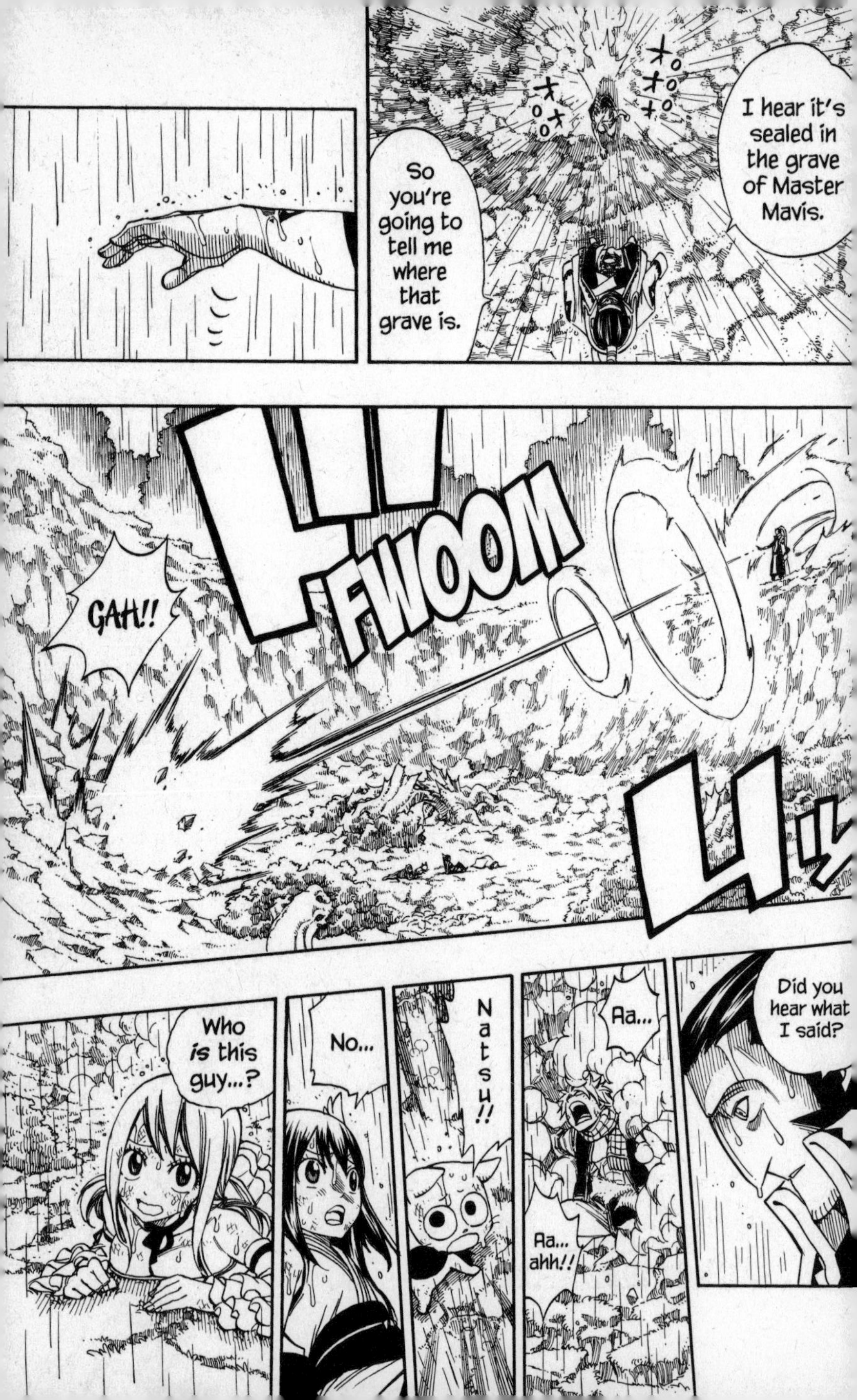
I hear it's sealed in the grave of Master Mavis.
So you're going to tell me where that grave is.
FWOOM
GAH!!
Did you hear what I said?
Aa...
Aa... ahh!!
Natsu!!
No...
Who *is* this guy...?

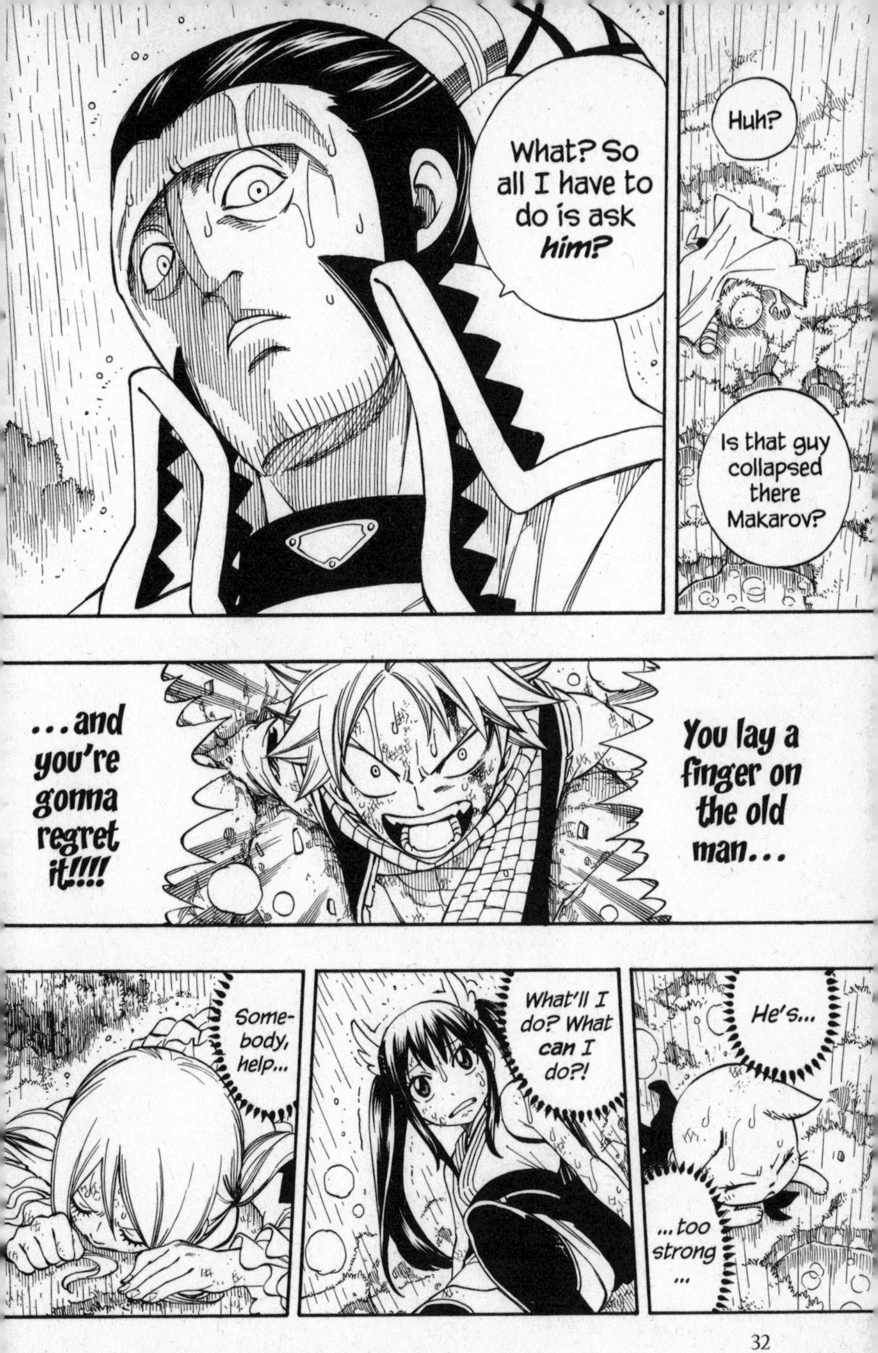
Huh?
Is that guy collapsed there Makarov?
What? So all I have to do is ask *him*?
You lay a finger on the old man...
...and you're gonna regret it!!!!
He's...
...too strong...
What'll I do? What can I do?!
Some-body, help...

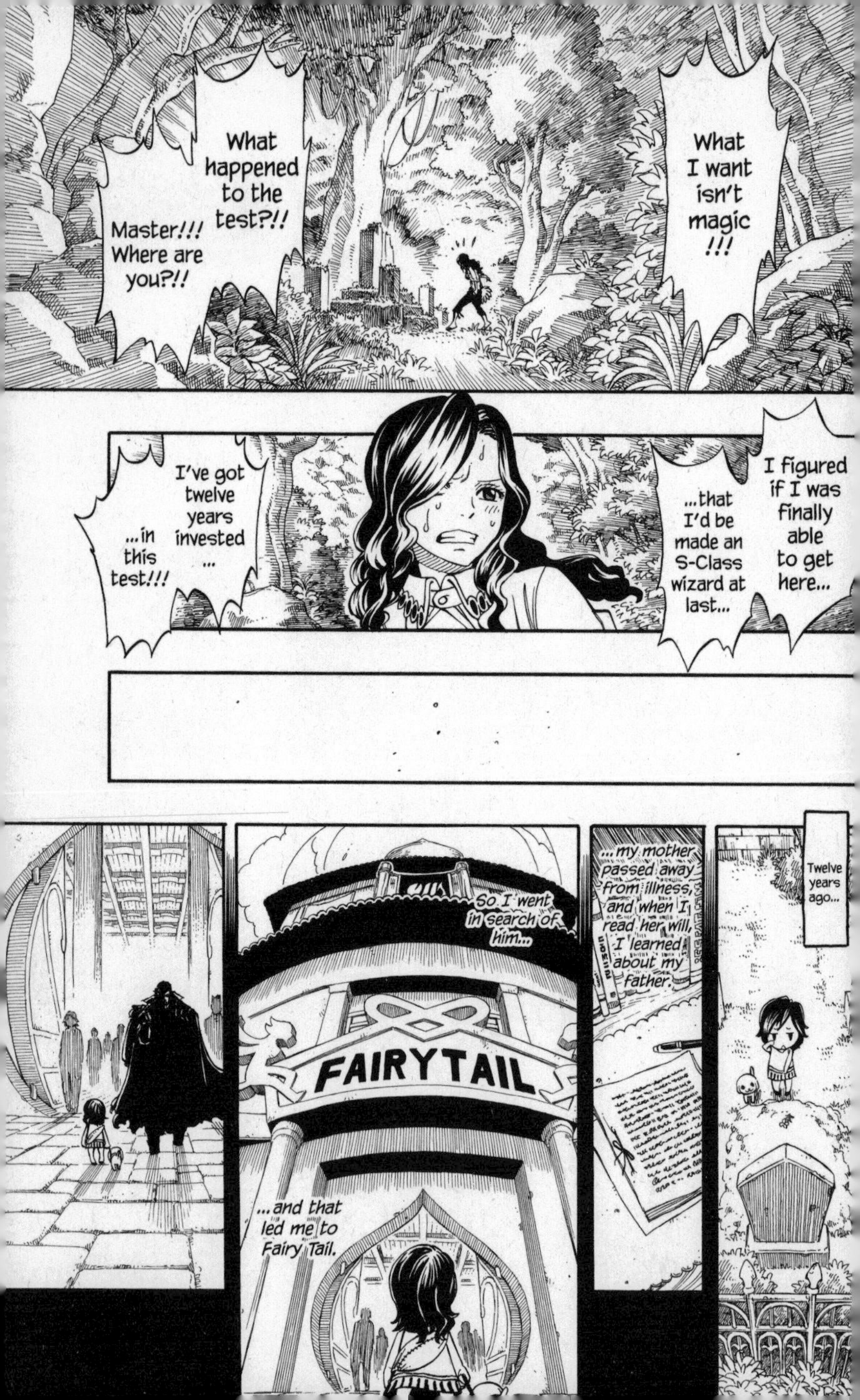
What I want isn't magic!!!
What happened to the test?!!
Master!!! Where are you?!!
I figured if I was finally able to get here...
...that I'd be made an S-Class wizard at last...
I've got twelve years invested...
...in this test!!!
Twelve years ago...
...my mother passed away from illness, and when I read her will, I learned about my father.
So I went in search of him...
FAIRY TAIL
...and that led me to Fairy Tail.

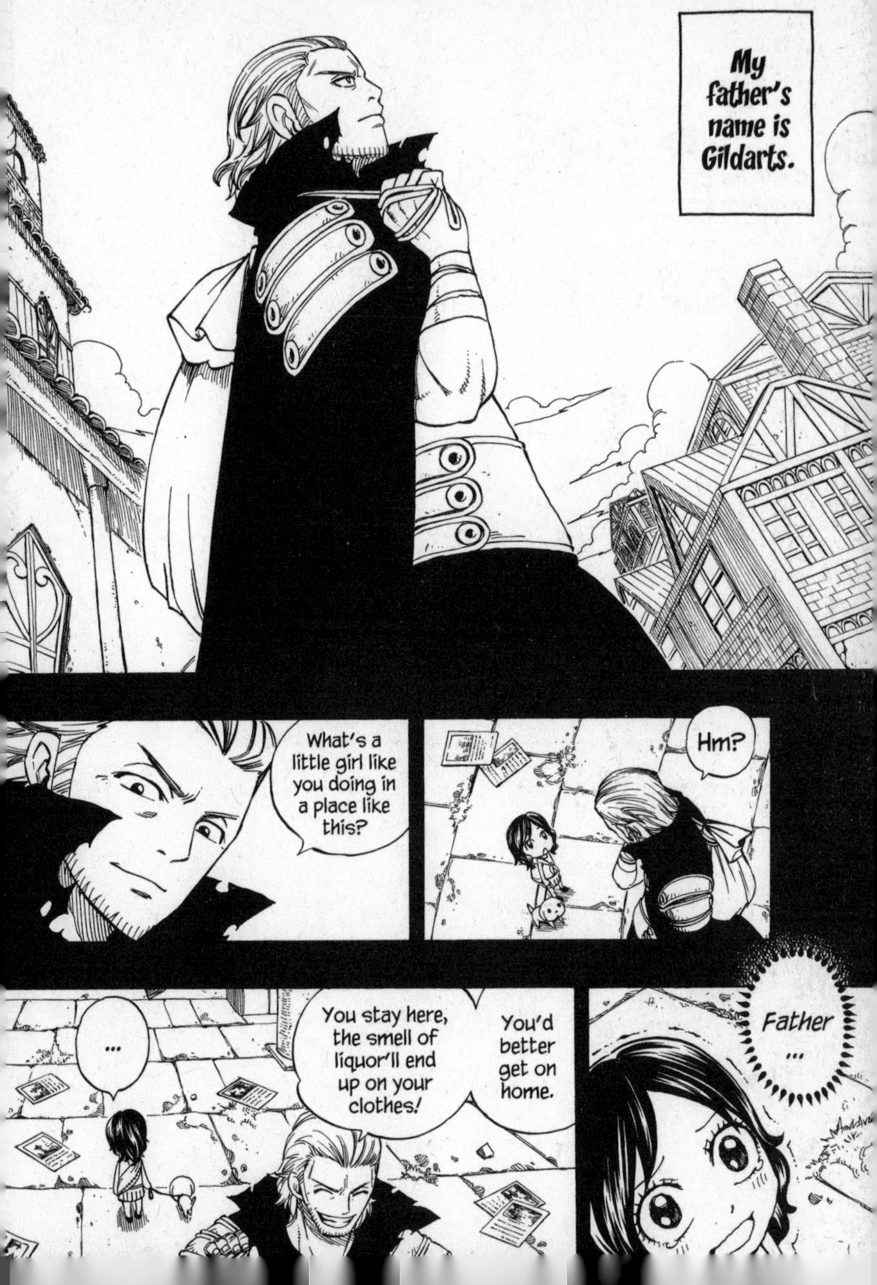

My father's name is Gildarts.
Hm?
What's a little girl like you doing in a place like this?
Father ...
You'd better get on home.
You stay here, the smell of liquor'll end up on your clothes!
...

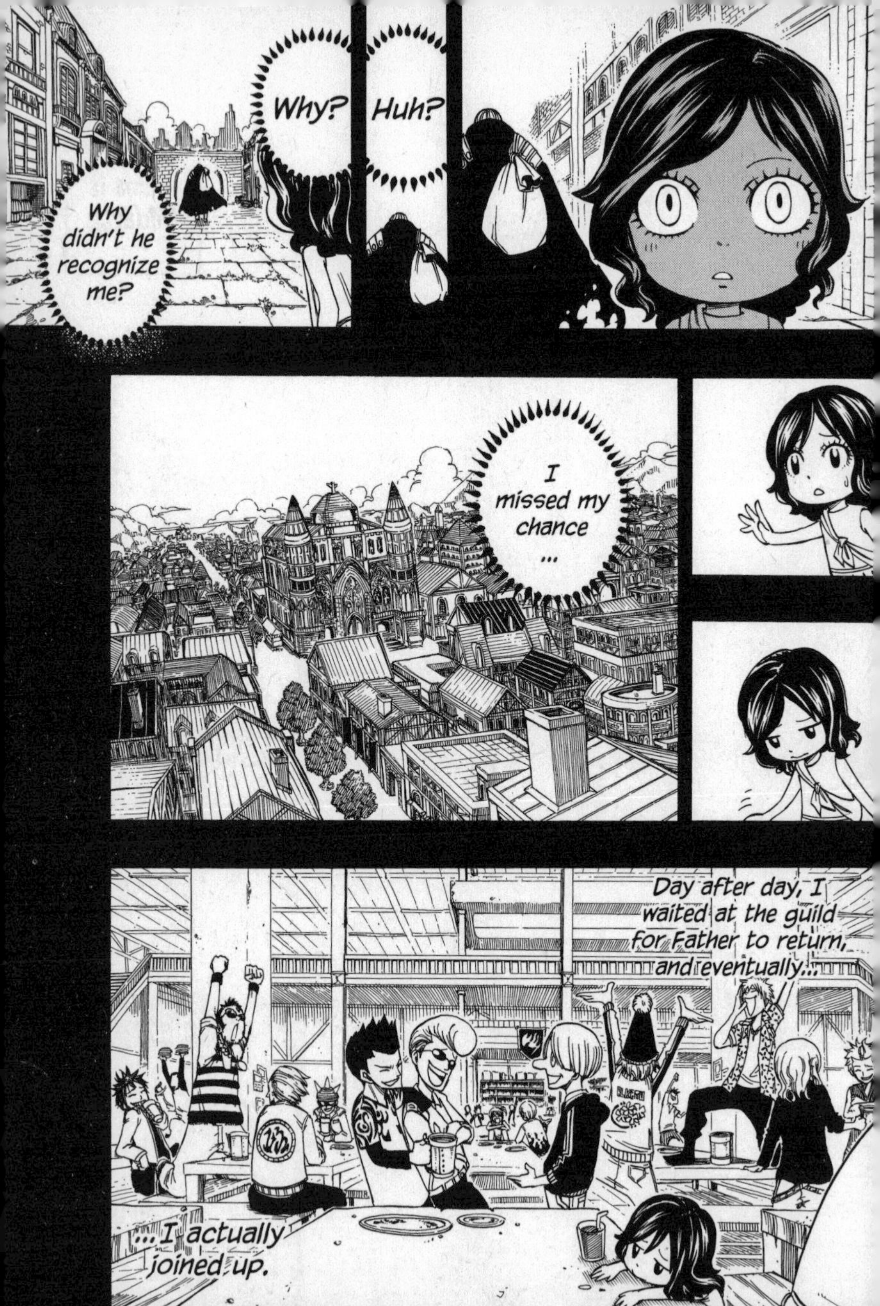
Huh?
Why?
Why didn't he recognize me?
I missed my chance ...
Day after day, I waited at the guild for Father to return, and eventually...
...I actually joined up.

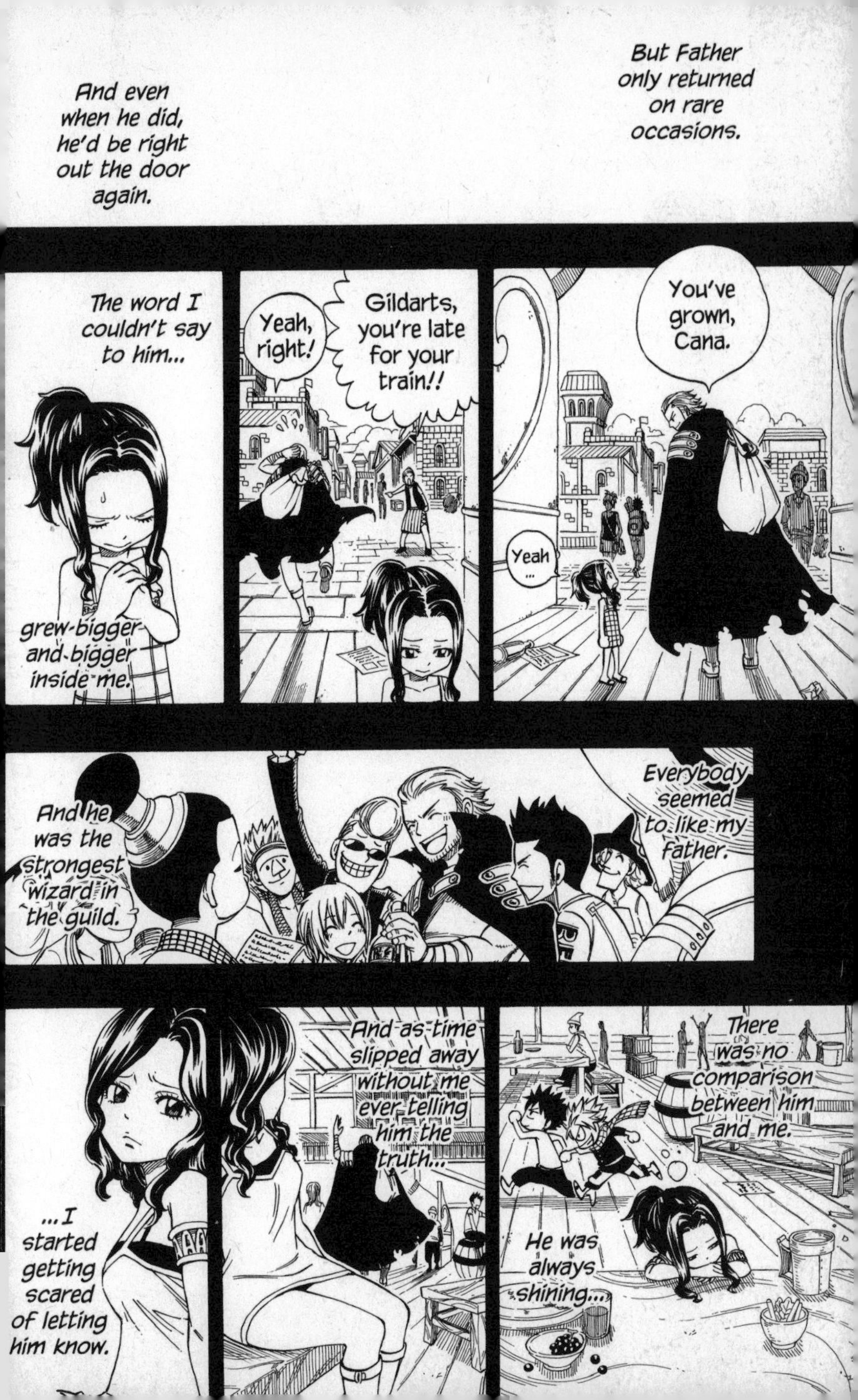
But Father only returned on rare occasions.
And even when he did, he'd be right out the door again.
You've grown, Cana.
Yeah ...
Gildarts, you're late for your train!!
Yeah, right!
The word I couldn't say to him...
grew bigger and bigger inside me.
Everybody seemed to like my father.
And he was the strongest wizard in the guild.
There was no comparison between him and me.
He was always shining...
And as time slipped away without me ever telling him the truth...
...I started getting scared of letting him know.

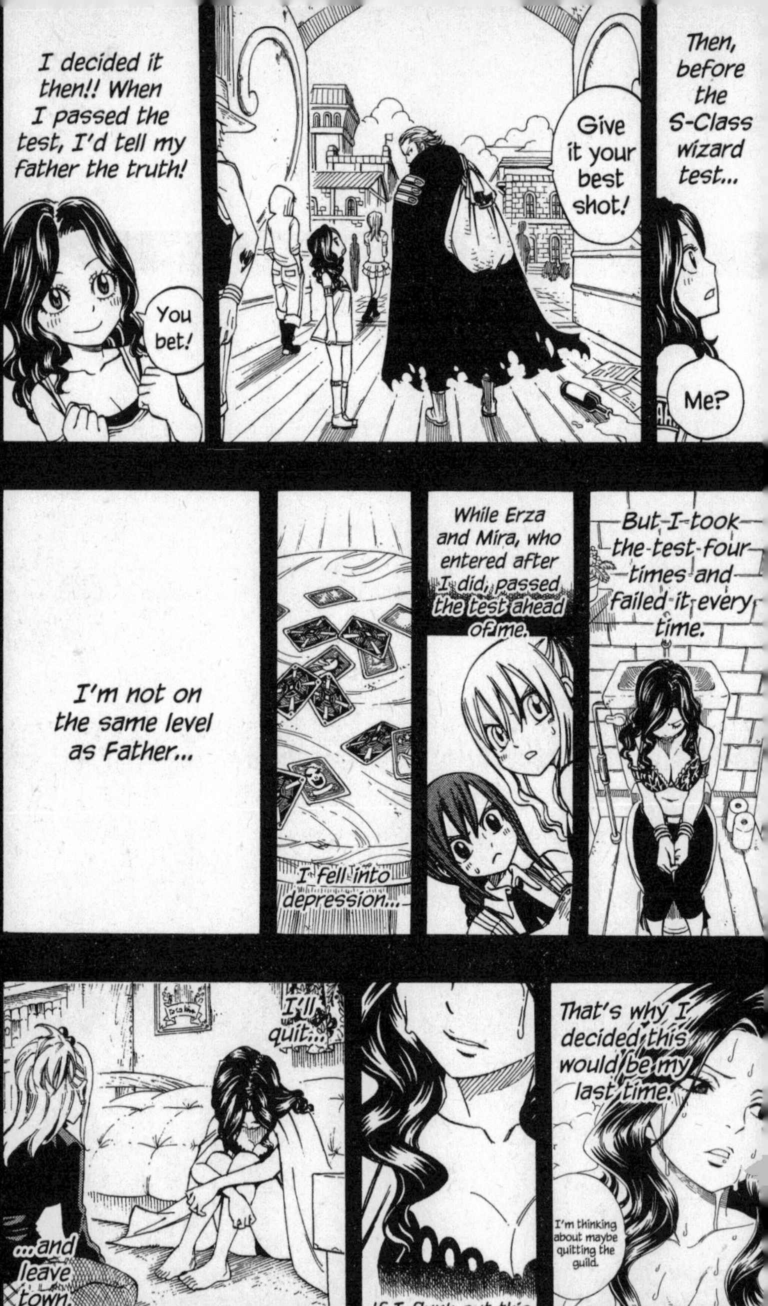
Then, before the S-Class wizard test...
Me?
Give it your best shot!
I decided it then!! When I passed the test, I'd tell my father the truth!
You bet!
But I took the test four times and failed it every time.
While Erza and Mira, who entered after I did, passed the test ahead of me.
I fell into depression...
I'm not on the same level as Father...
That's why I decided this would be my last time.
I'm thinking about maybe quitting the guild.
If I flunk out this
I'll quit...
...and leave town.

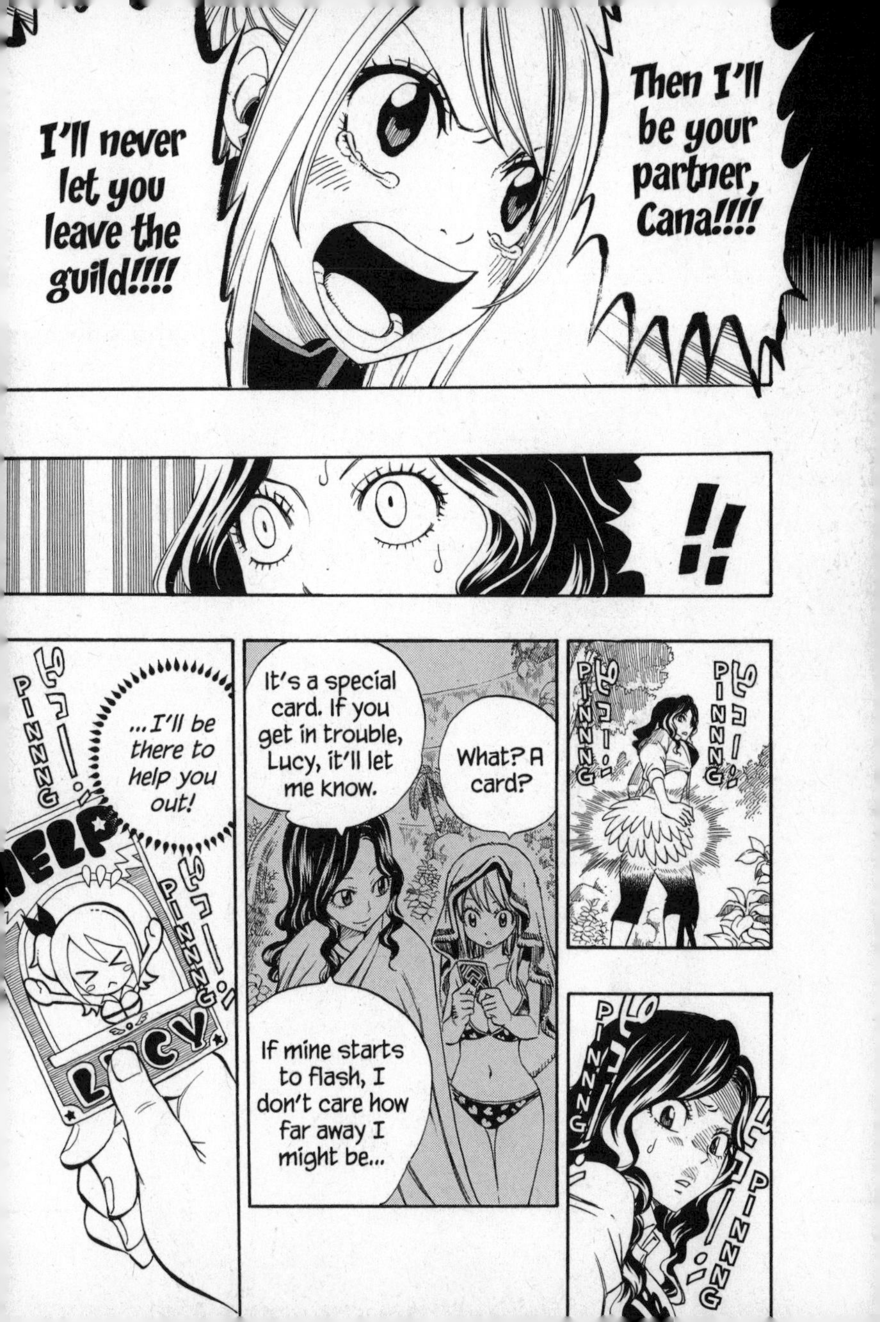
Then I'll be your partner, Cana!!!!
I'll never let you leave the guild!!!!
!!
PINNNG
PINNNG
PINNNG
PINNNG
What? A card?
It's a special card. If you get in trouble, Lucy, it'll let me know.
If mine starts to flash, I don't care how far away I might be...
PINNNG
...I'll be there to help you out!
HELP
LUCY
PINNNG

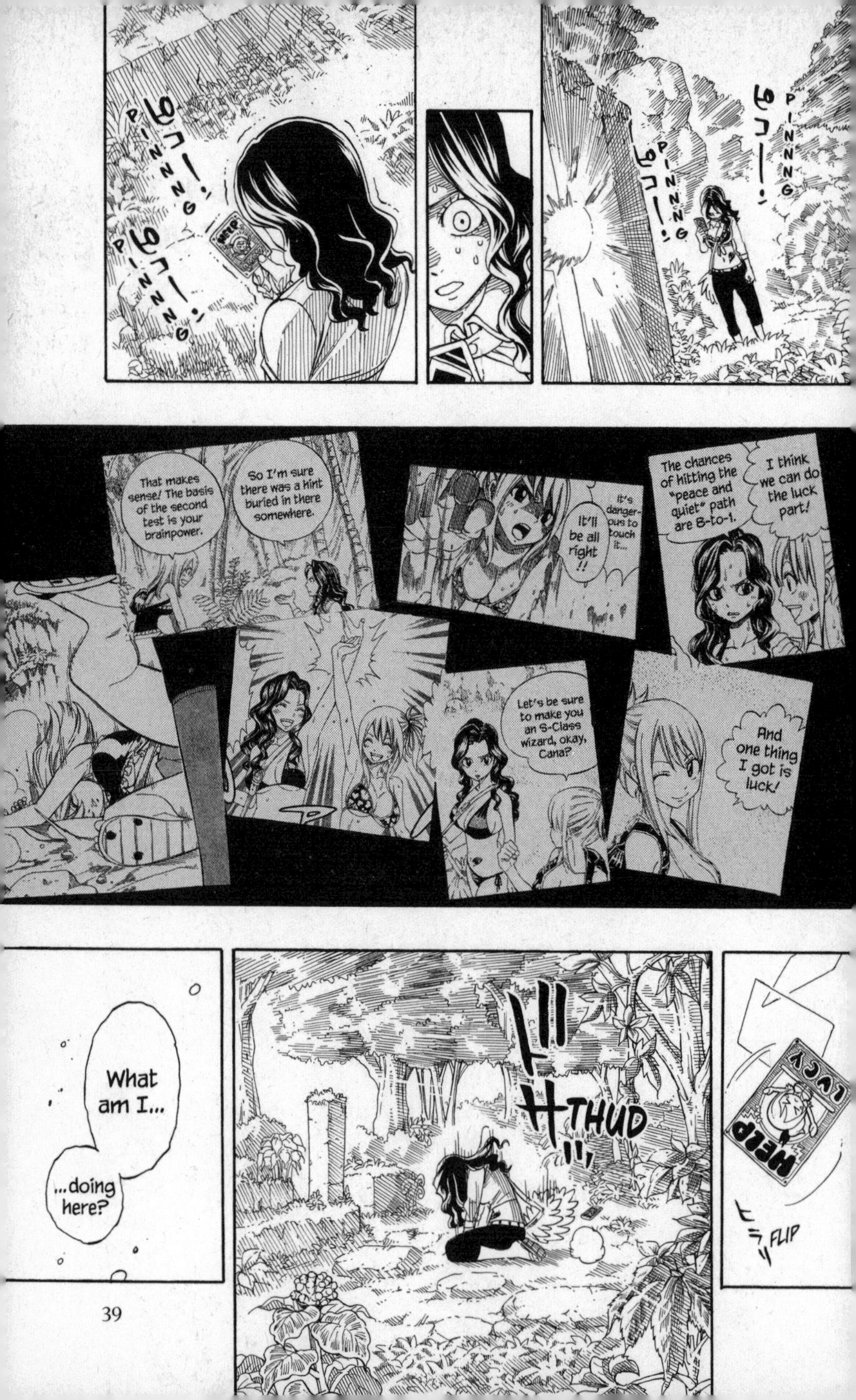
PINNNG
PINNNG
PINNNG
PINNNG
The chances of hitting the "peace and quiet" path are 8-to-1.
I think we can do the luck part!
It's dangerous to touch it...
It'll be all right!!
So I'm sure there was a hint buried in there somewhere.
That makes sense! The basis of the second test is your brainpower.
And one thing I got is luck!
Let's be sure to make you an S-Class wizard, okay, Cana?
HELP LUCY
FLIP
THUD
What am I...
...doing here?

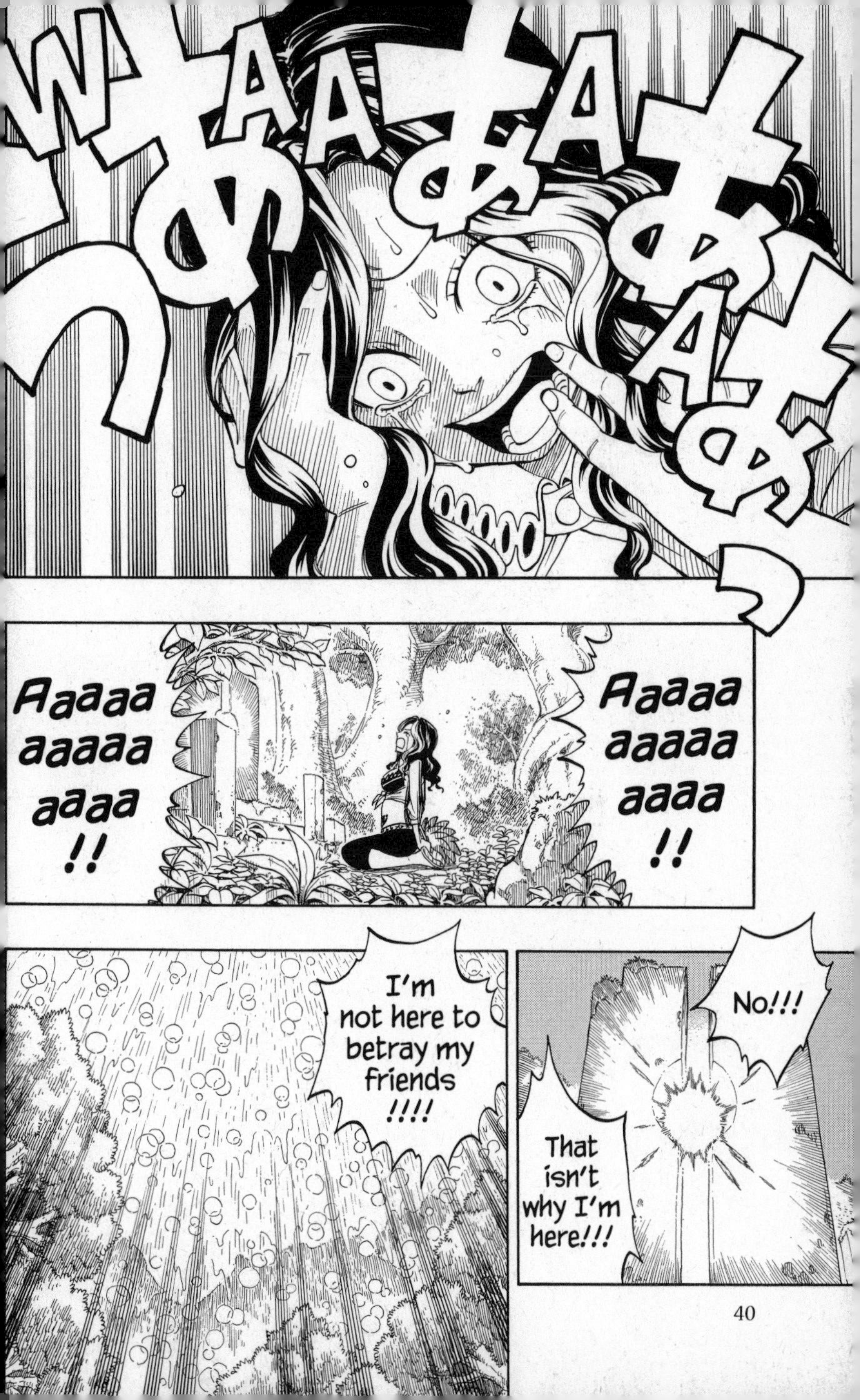

Aaaaaaaaaaaaaa!!
Aaaaaaaaaaaaaa!!
No!!!
That isn't why I'm here!!!
I'm not here to betray my friends!!!!

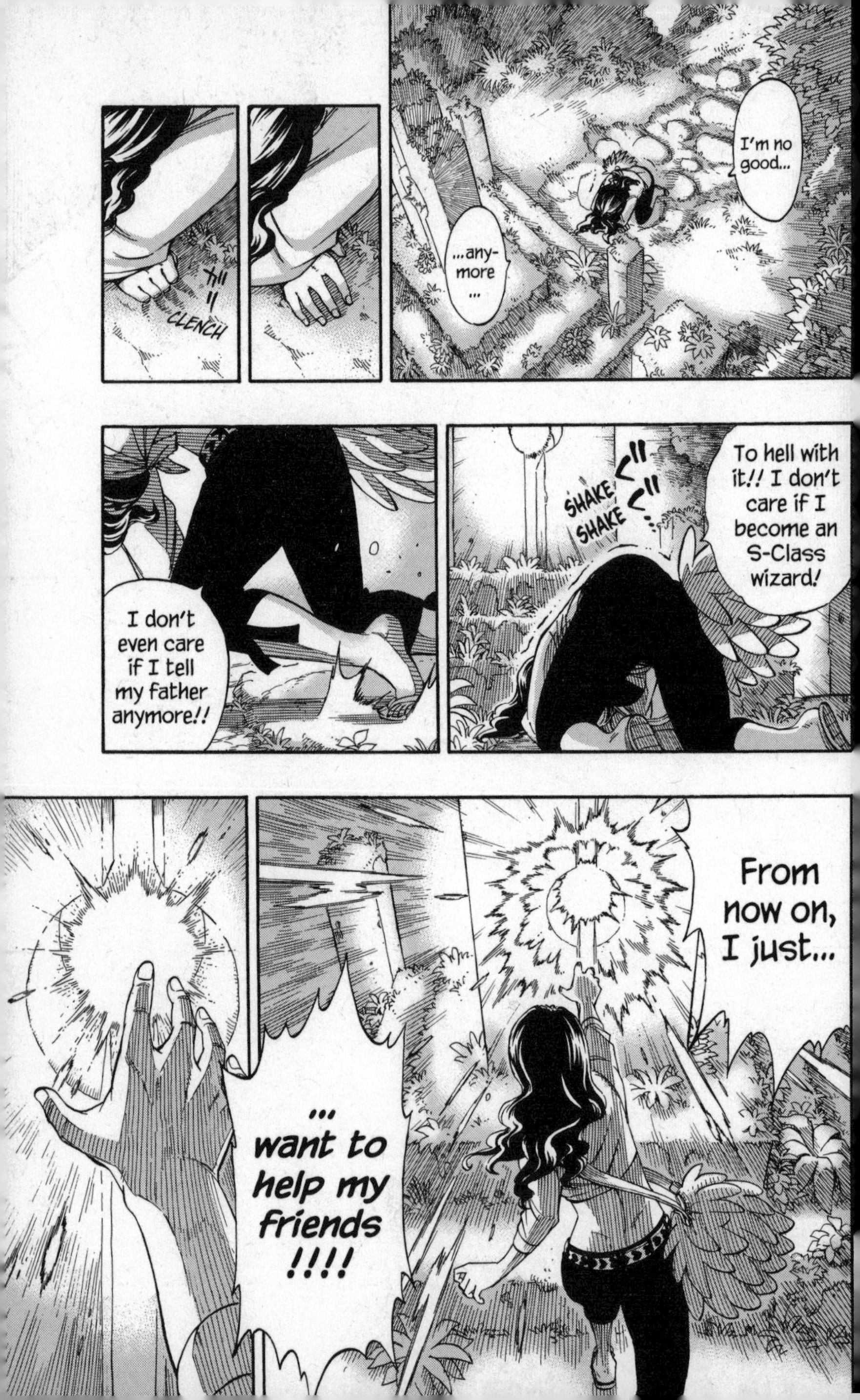
I'm no good...
...any-more...
CLENCH
To hell with it!! I don't care if I become an S-Class wizard!
SHAKE SHAKE
I don't even care if I tell my father anymore!!
From now on, I just...
...want to help my friends!!!!

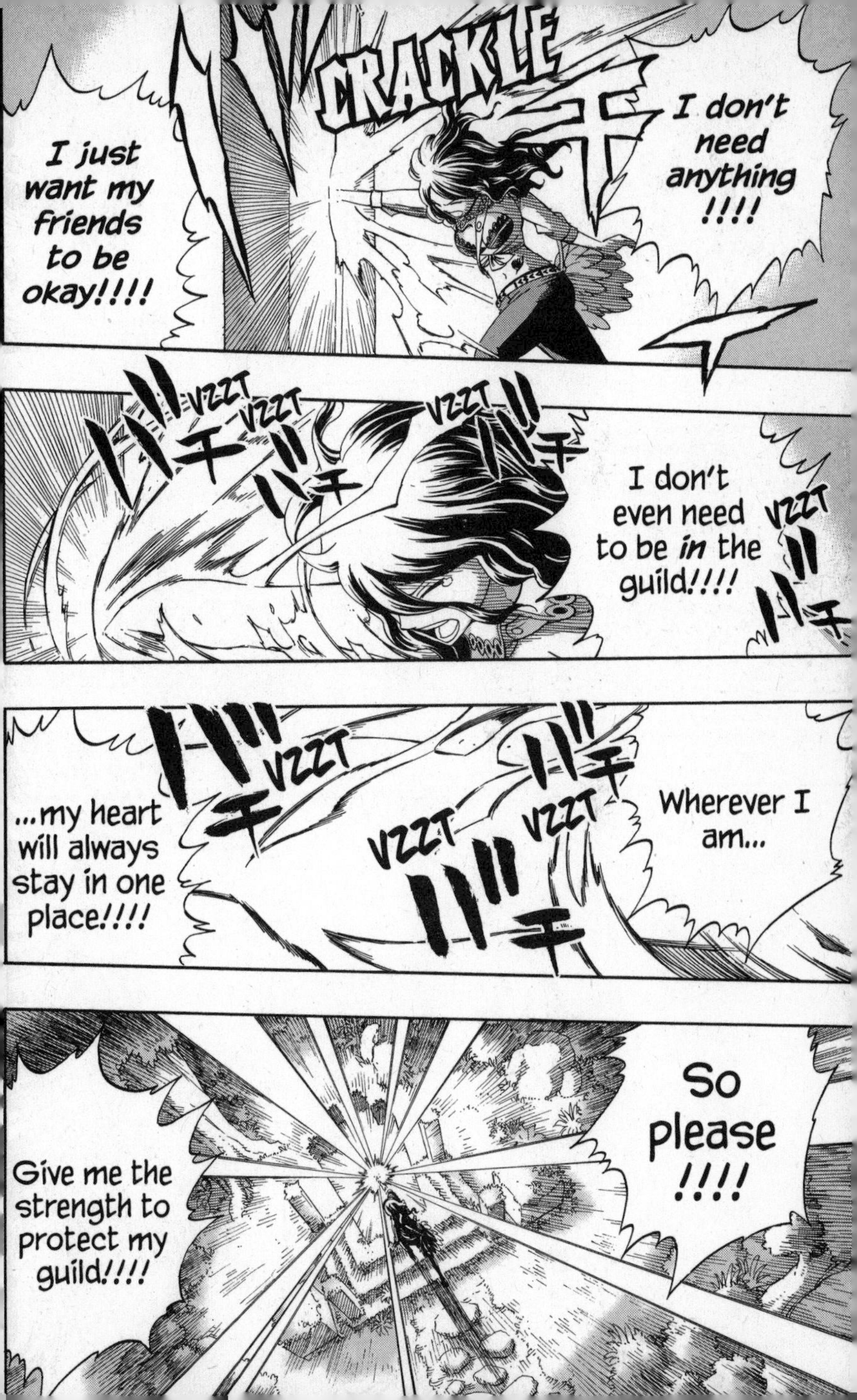
CRACKLE
I don't need anything!!!!
I just want my friends to be okay!!!!
VZZT
VZZT
VZZT
VZZT
I don't even need to be *in* the guild!!!!
Wherever I am...
VZZT
VZZT
VZZT
...my heart will always stay in one place!!!!
So please!!!!
Give me the strength to protect my guild!!!!

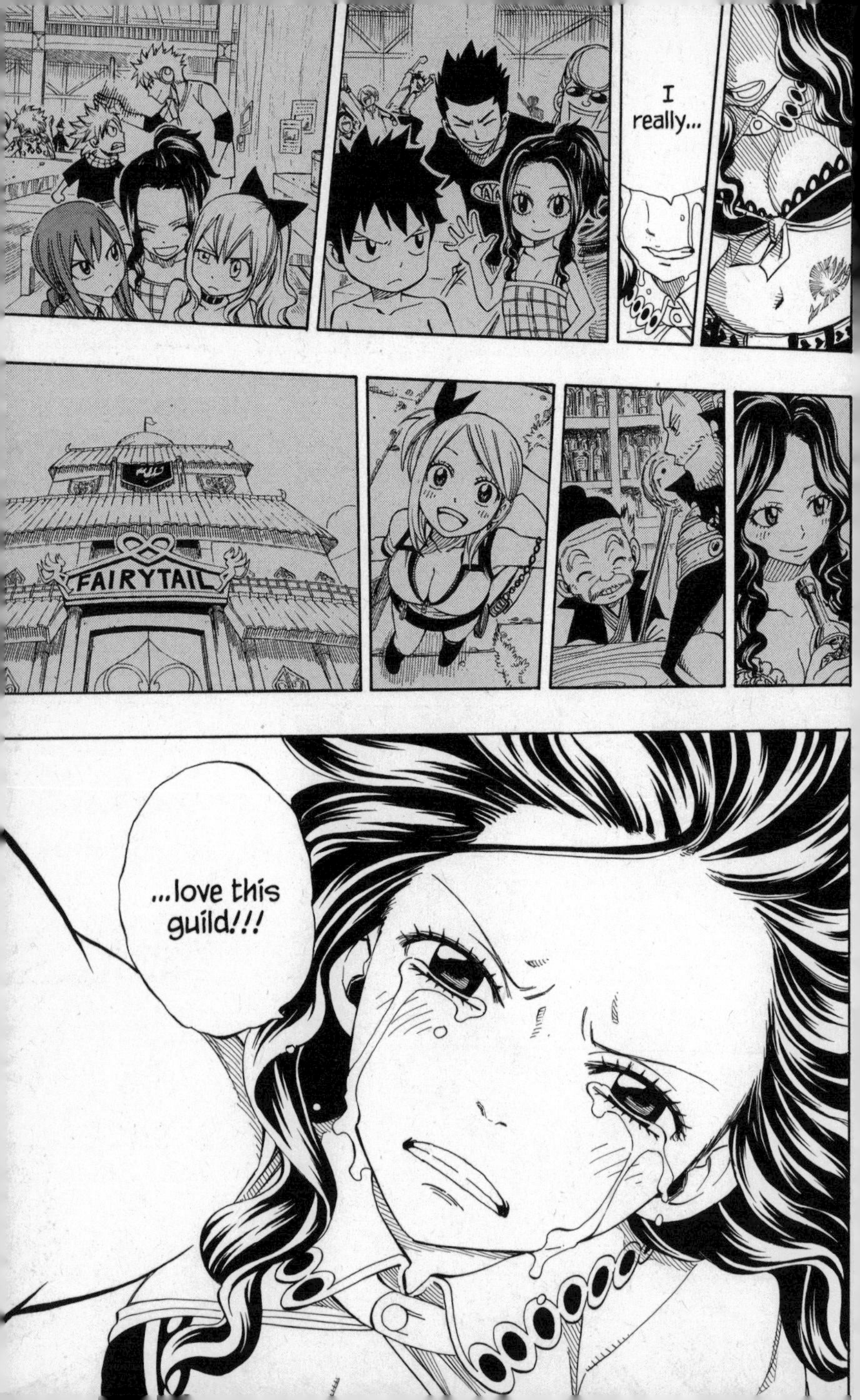
I really...
FAIRYTAIL
...love this guild!!!

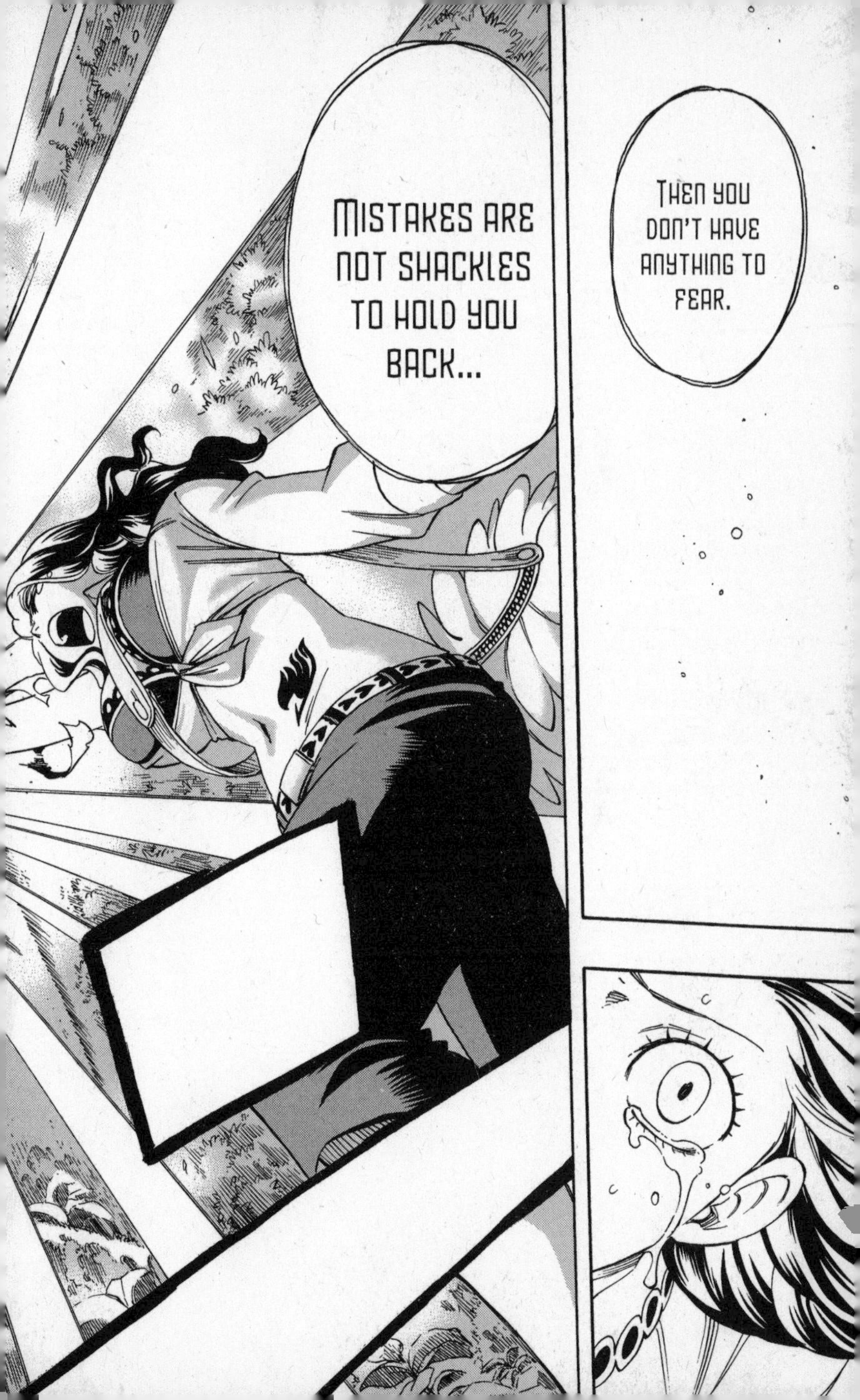
THEN YOU DON'T HAVE ANYTHING TO FEAR.
MISTAKES ARE NOT SHACKLES TO HOLD YOU BACK...

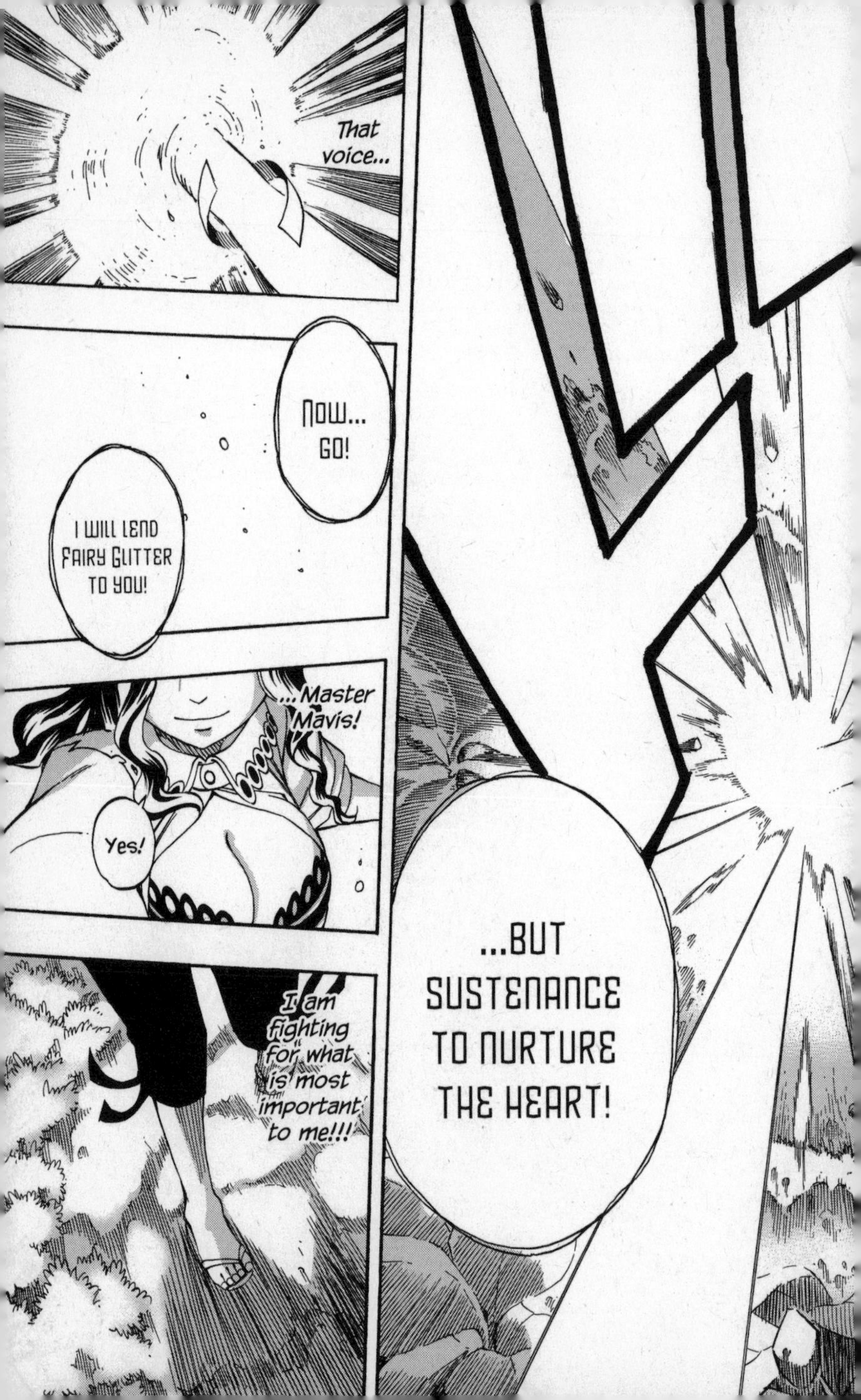
...BUT SUSTENANCE TO NURTURE THE HEART!
That voice...
NOW... GO!
I WILL LEND FAIRY GLITTER TO YOU!
...Master Mavis!
Yes!
I am fighting for what is most important to me!!!

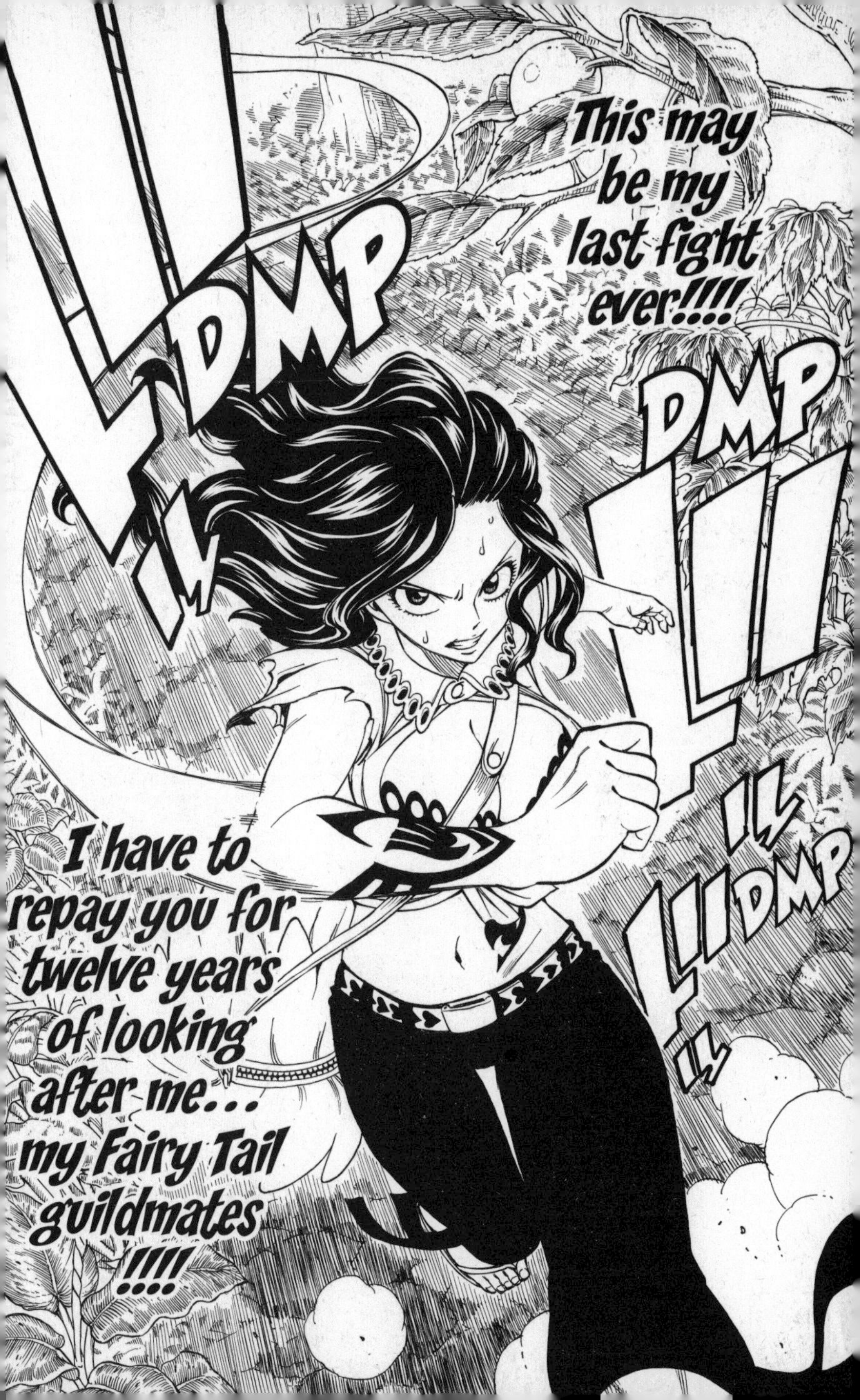
This may be my last fight ever!!!!
DMP
DMP
DMP
I have to repay you for twelve years of looking after me... my Fairy Tail guildmates !!!!

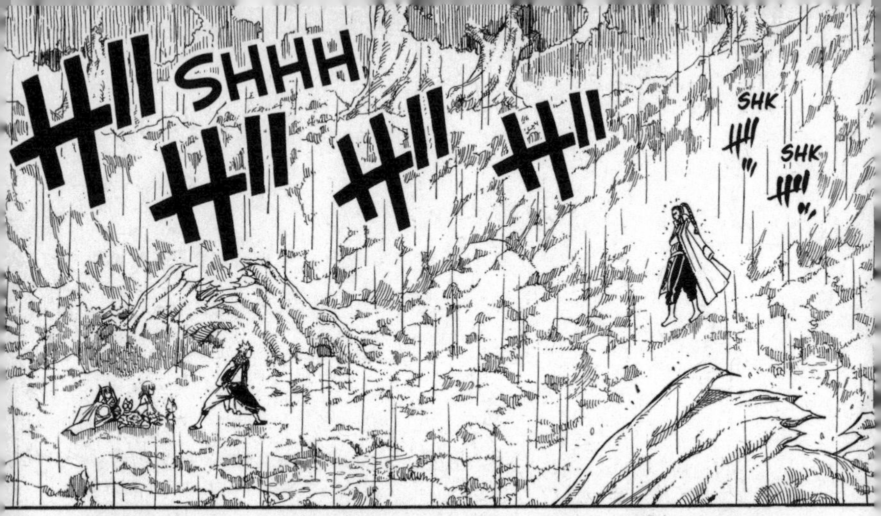
SHHH
SHK
SHK

FAIRY TAIL

Chapter 233: Fairy Glitter

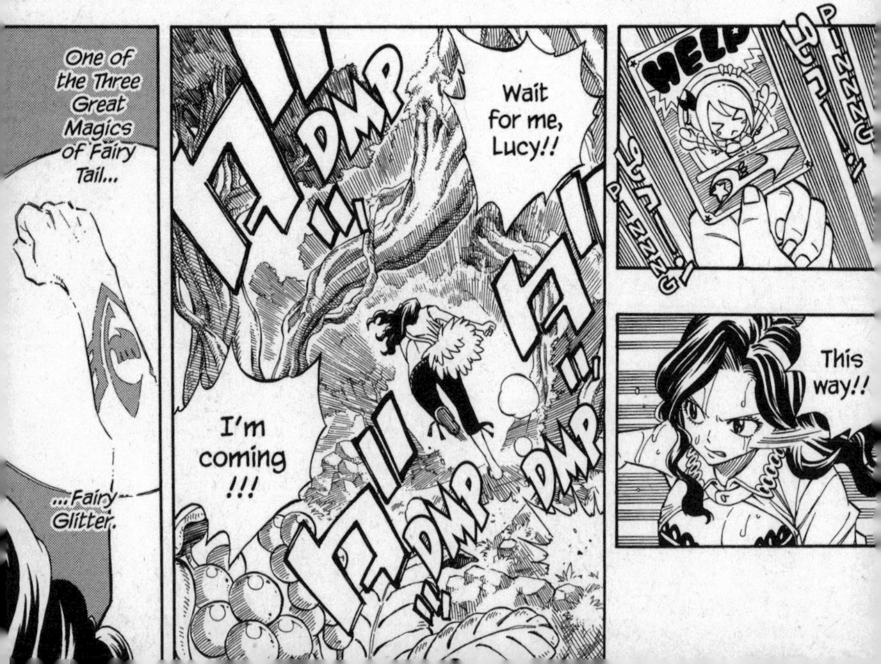
HELP
P-ZZZZG
P-ZZZZG!
This way!!
Wait for me, Lucy!!
DMP
DMP
I'm coming!!!
DMP
DMP
One of the Three Great Magics of Fairy Tail...
...Fairy Glitter.

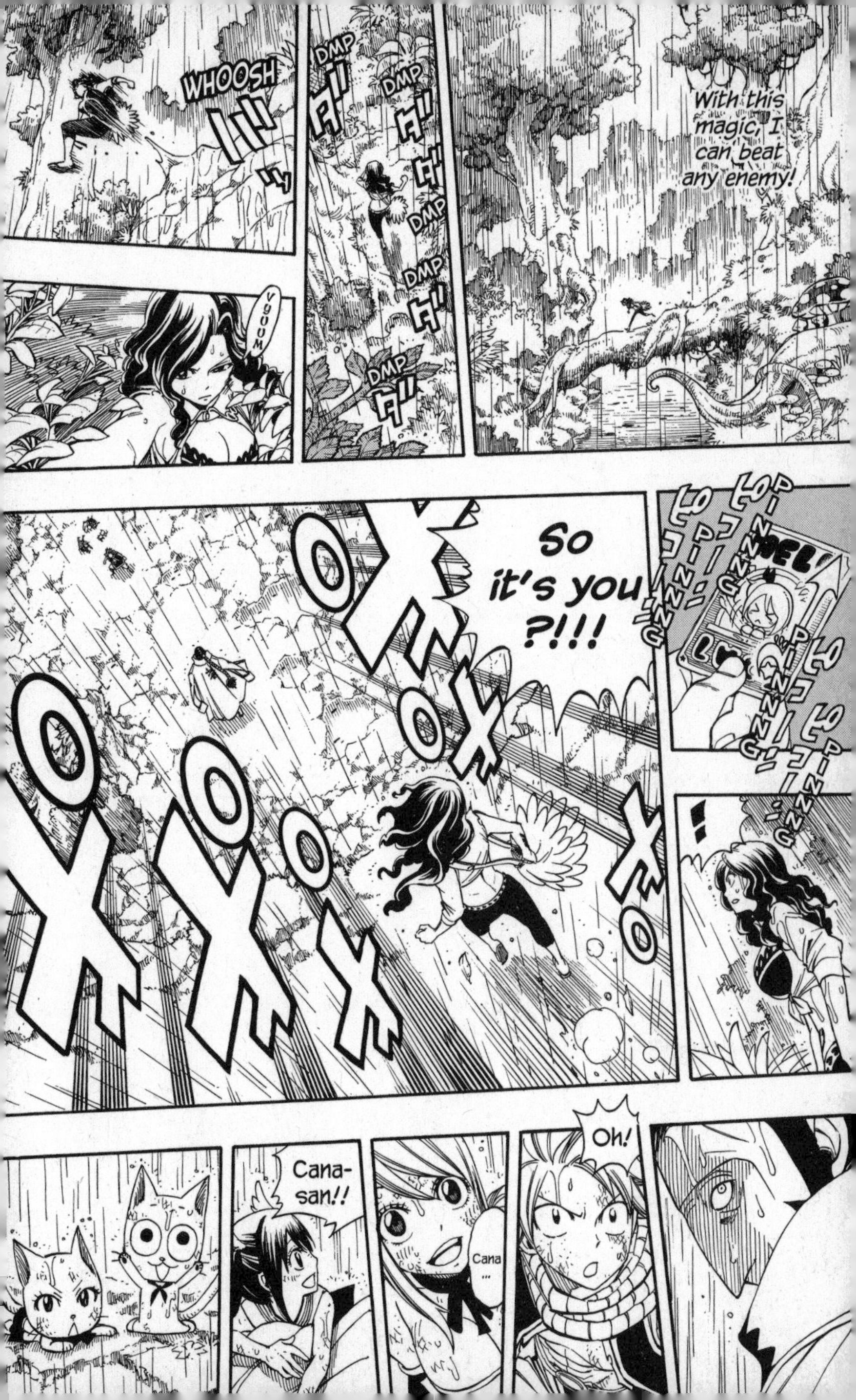

With this magic, I can beat any enemy!
DMP
DMP
DMP
DMP
DMP
WHOOSH
VYUUM
PINNNG
PI-NNNG!
PINNNG!
PI-NNNG!
!!
So it's you?!!!
Oh!
Cana...
Cana-san!!

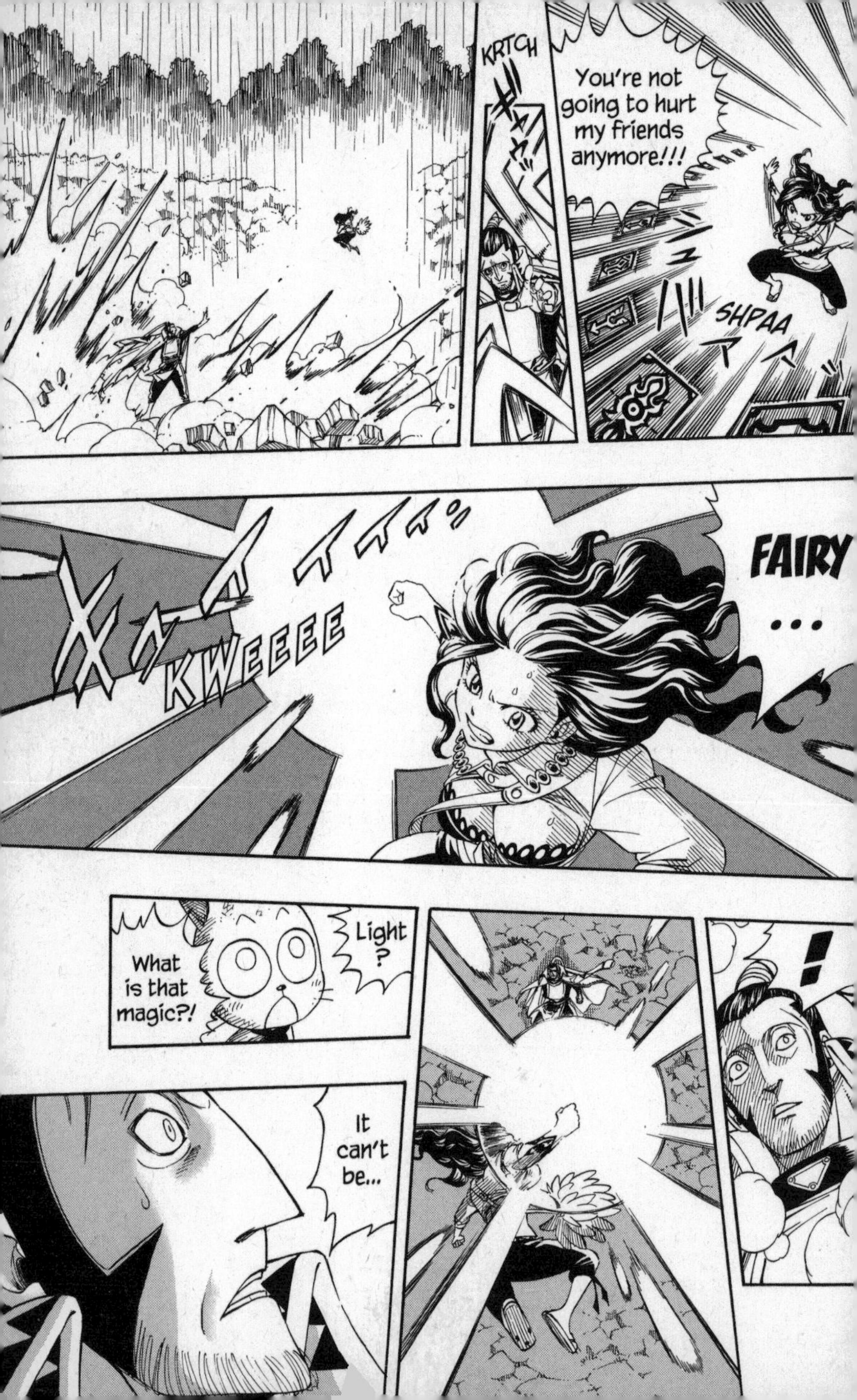
You're not going to hurt my friends anymore!!!
KRTCH
SHPAA
FAIRY
...
KWEEEE
!
Light?
What is that magic?!
It can't be...

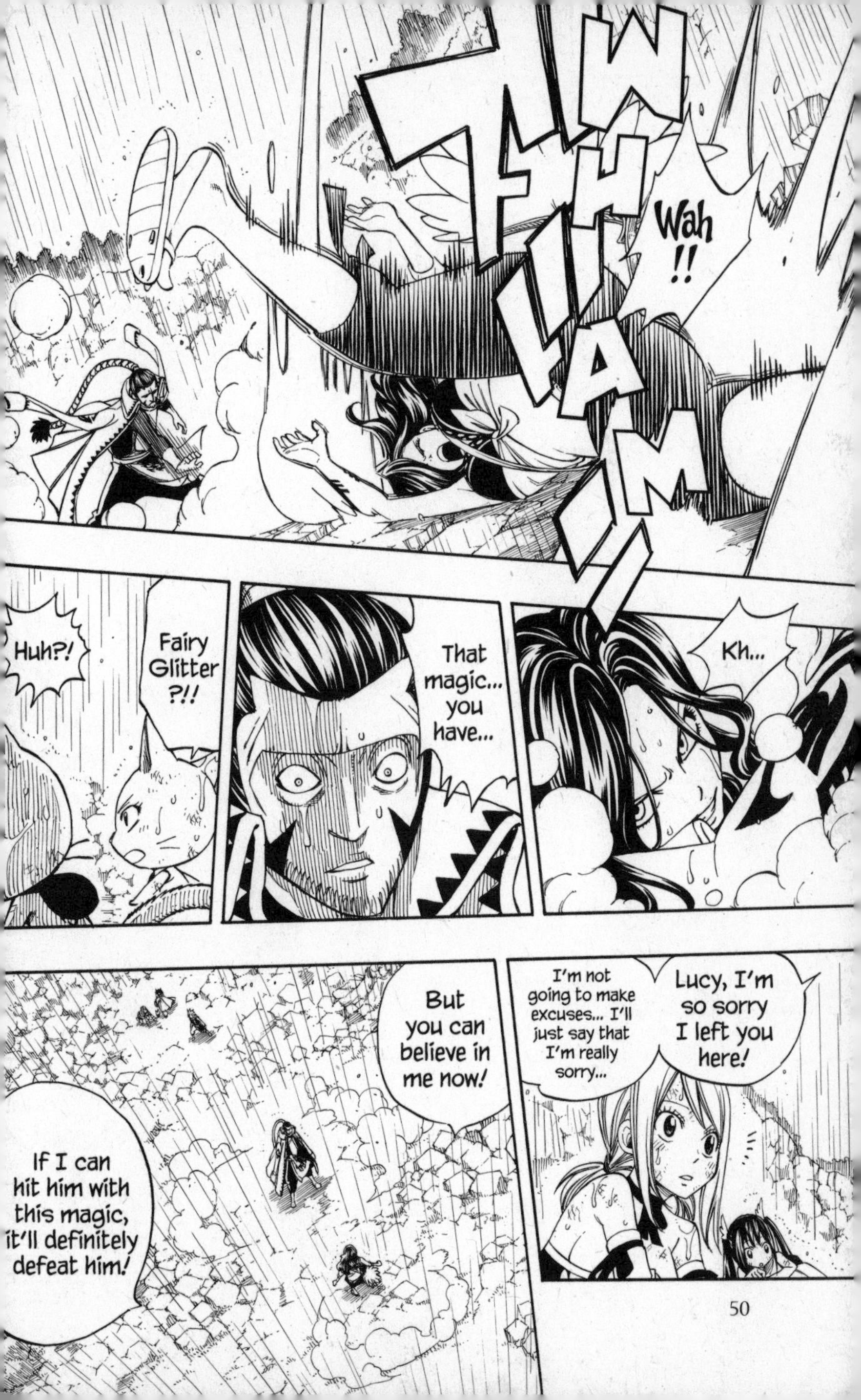
WHHAM
Wah!!
Kh...
That magic... you have...
Fairy Glitter?!!
Huh?!
Lucy, I'm so sorry I left you here!
I'm not going to make excuses... I'll just say that I'm really sorry...
But you can believe in me now!
If I can hit him with this magic, it'll definitely defeat him!

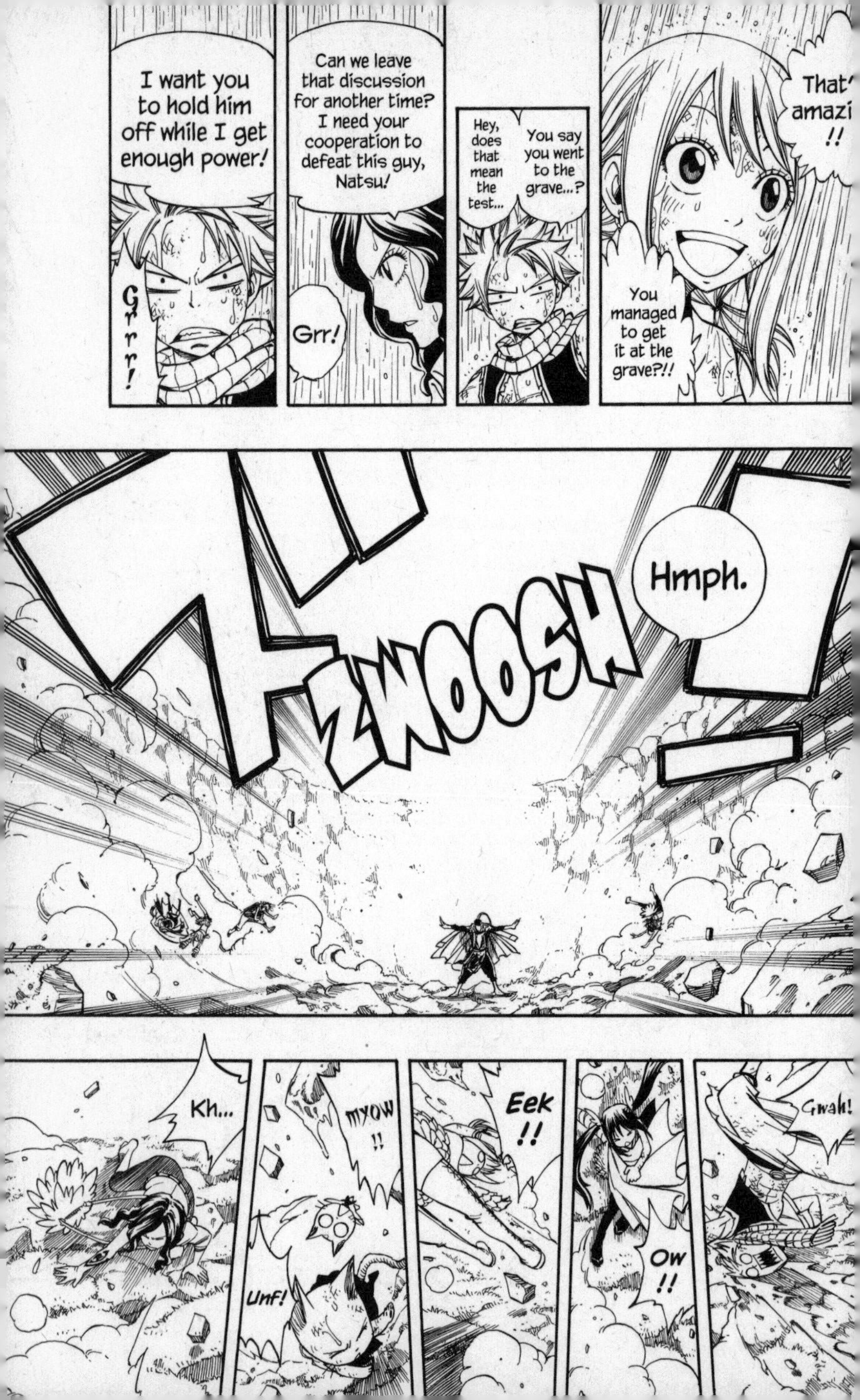
That' amazi !!
You managed to get it at the grave?!!
You say you went to the grave...?
Hey, does that mean the test...
Can we leave that discussion for another time? I need your cooperation to defeat this guy, Natsu!
Grr!
I want you to hold him off while I get enough power!
Grrr!
Hmph.
ZWOOSH
Gwah!
Ow !!
Eek !!
myow !!
Unf!
Kh...

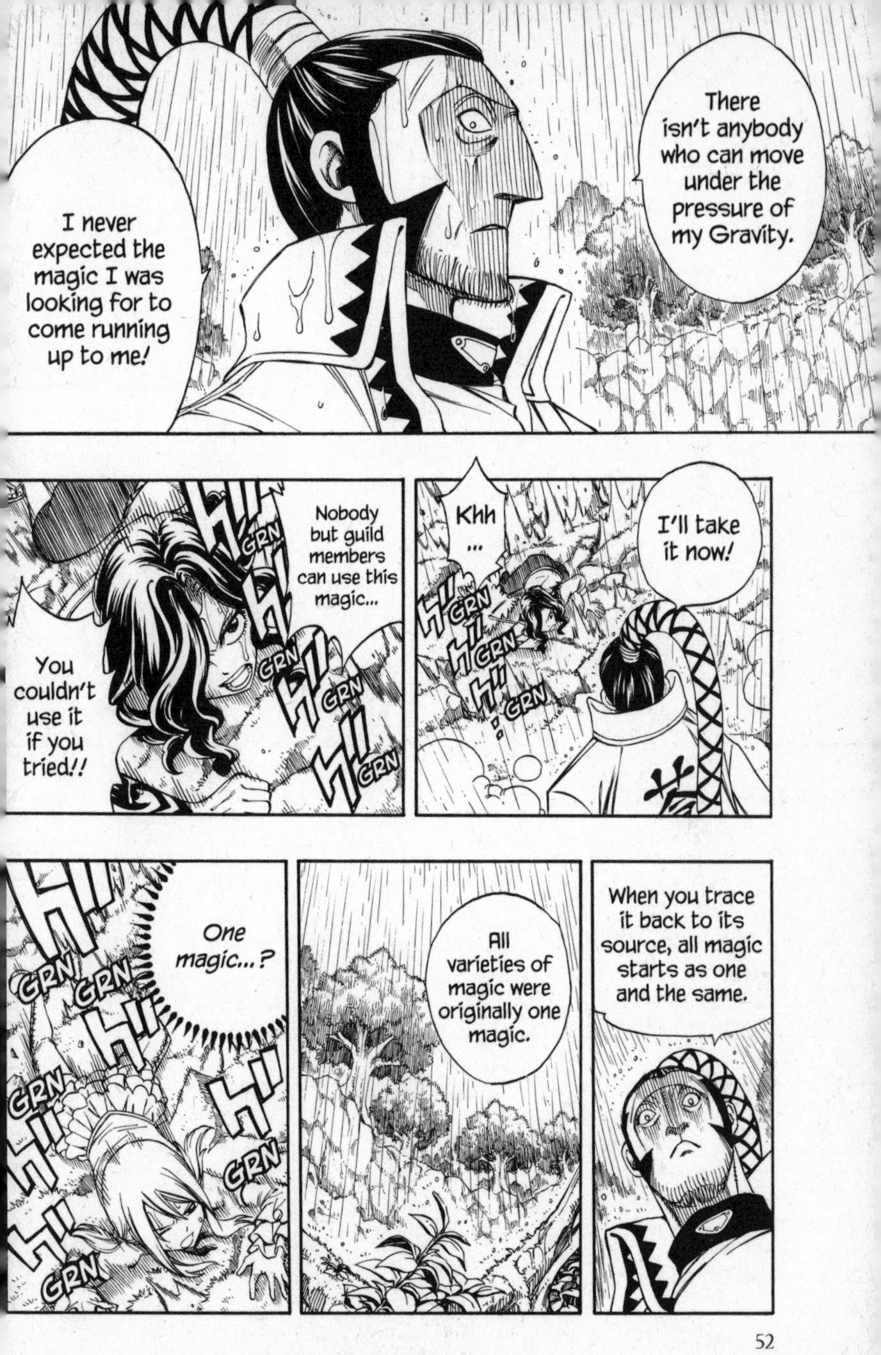
There isn't anybody who can move under the pressure of my Gravity.
I never expected the magic I was looking for to come running up to me!
I'll take it now!
Khh...
GRN
GRN
GRN
Nobody but guild members can use this magic...
You couldn't use it if you tried!!
GRN
GRN
GRN
GRN
When you trace it back to its source, all magic starts as one and the same.
All varieties of magic were originally one magic.
One magic...?
GRN
GRN
GRN
GRN
GRN

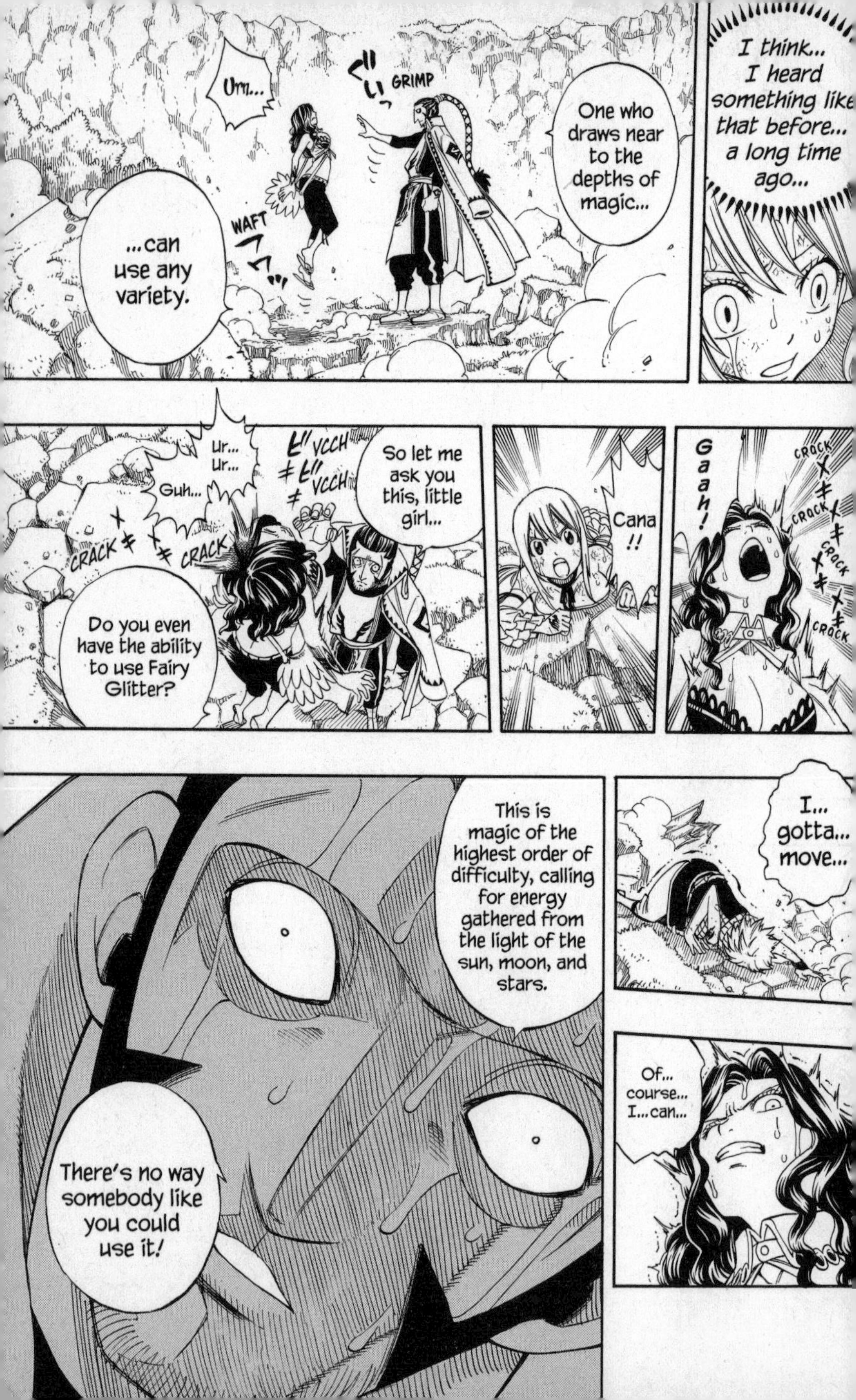
I think... I heard something like that before... a long time ago...
One who draws near to the depths of magic...
GRIMP
Um...
WAFT
...can use any variety.
Gaah!
CRACK
CRACK
CRACK
CRACK
Cana!!
So let me ask you this, little girl...
VCCH
VCCH
Ur... Ur...
Guh...
CRACK
CRACK
Do you even have the ability to use Fairy Glitter?
I... gotta... move...
Of... course... I...can...
This is magic of the highest order of difficulty, calling for energy gathered from the light of the sun, moon, and stars.
There's no way somebody like you could use it!

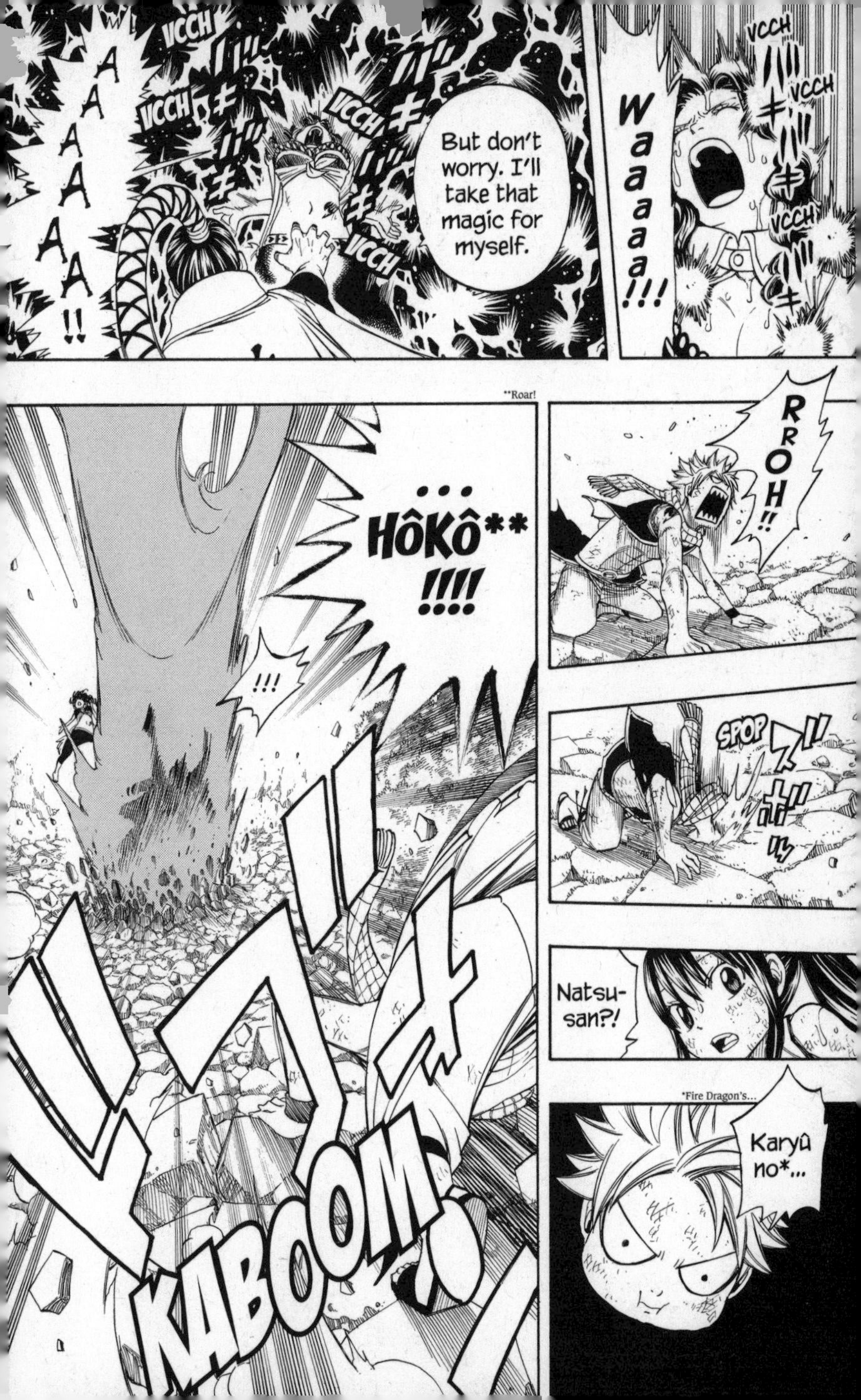
VCCH
VCCH
VCCH
Waaaaaa!!!
VCCH
VCCH
VCCH
VCCH
AAAAAA!!
But don't worry. I'll take that magic for myself.
RROH!!
SPOP
Natsu-san?!
Karyû no*...
...HÔKÔ**!!!!
!!!
KABOOM

**Roar!

*Fire Dragon's...

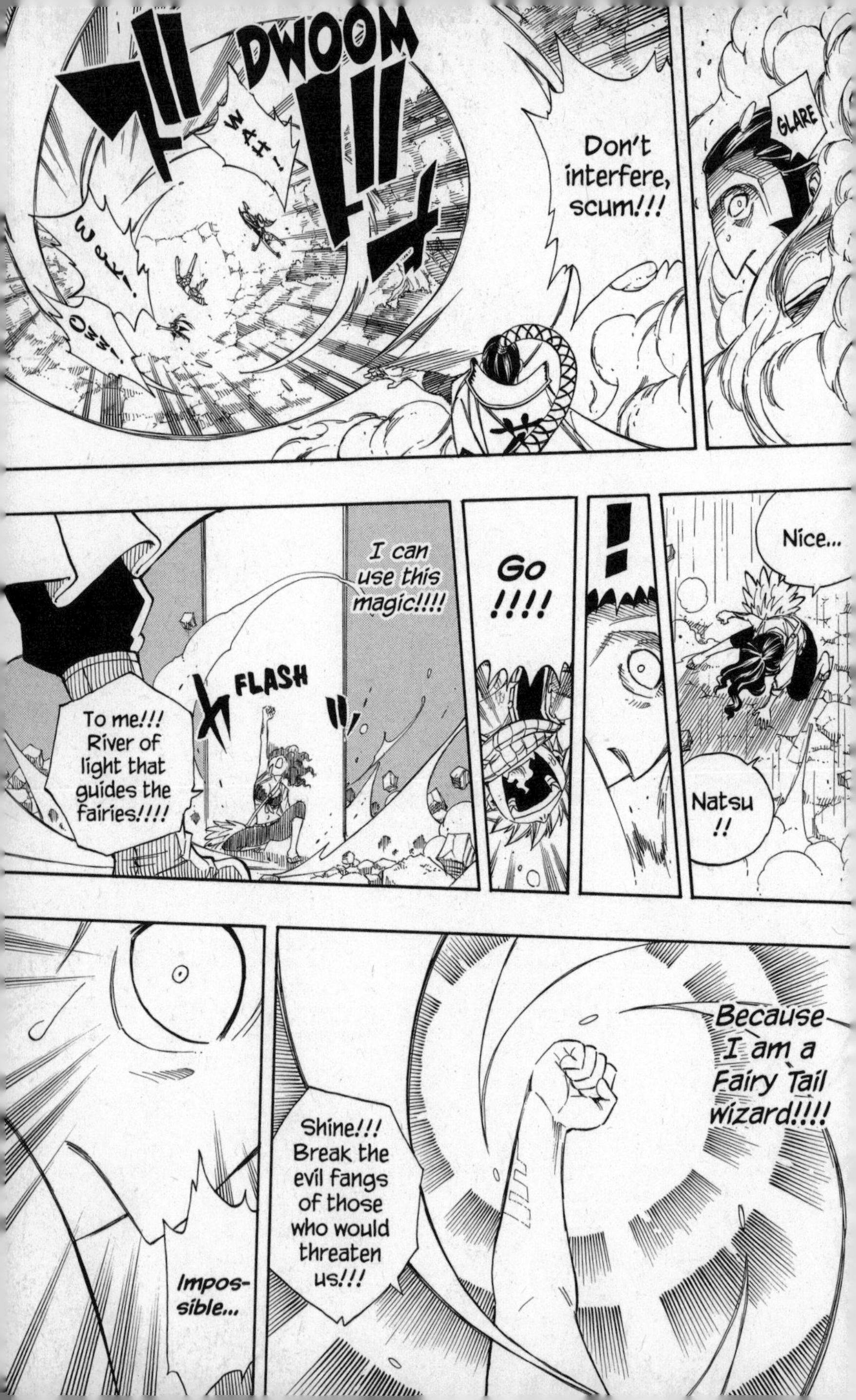
GLARE
Don't interfere, scum!!!
DWOOM
Wait!
Nice...
Natsu!!
!
Go!!!!
I can use this magic!!!!
FLASH
To me!!! River of light that guides the fairies!!!!
Because I am a Fairy Tail wizard!!!!!
Shine!!! Break the evil fangs of those who would threaten us!!!
Impossible...

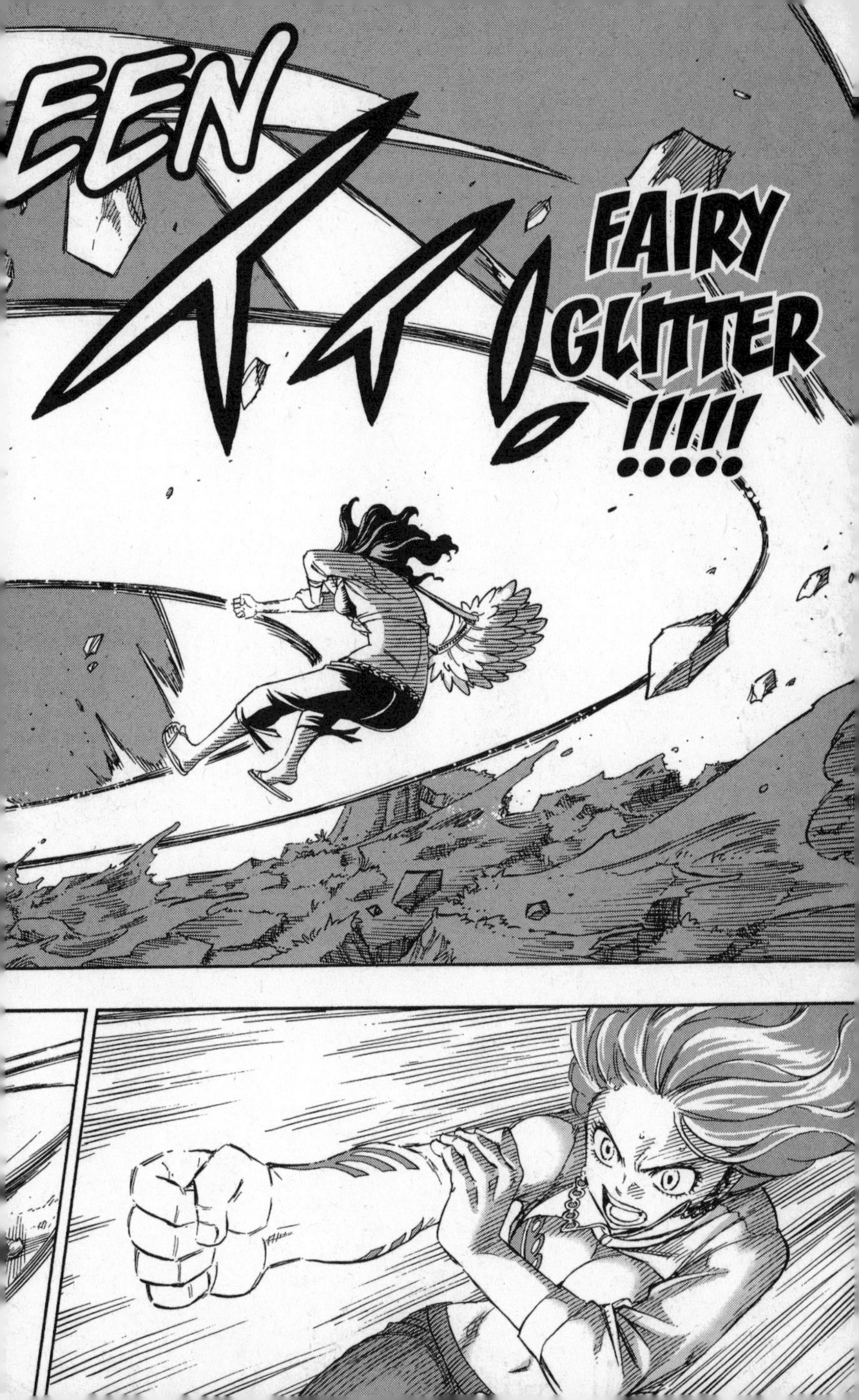
FAIRY GLITTER !!!!!
EEN

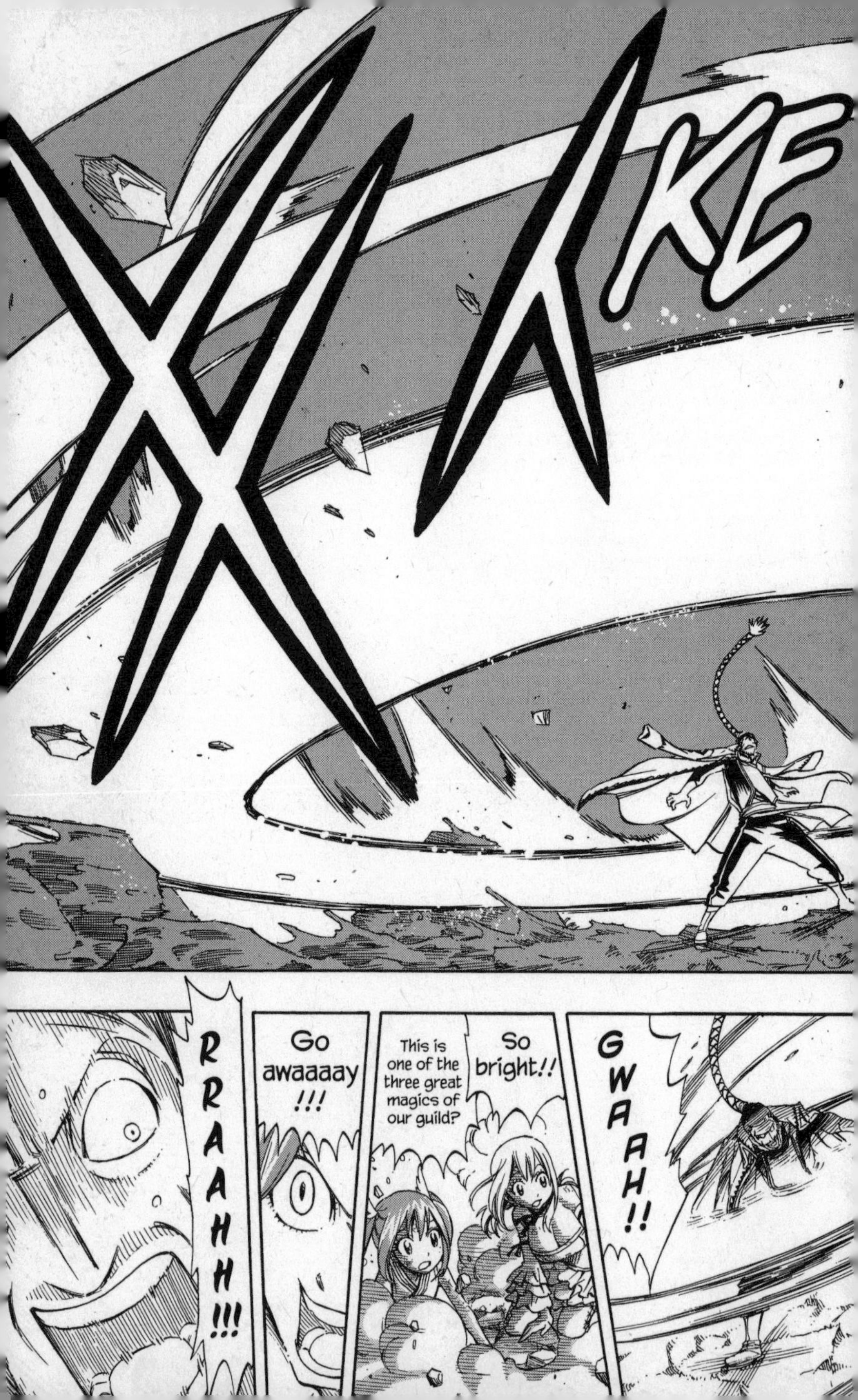
GWAAAH!!
So bright!!
This is one of the three great magics of our guild?
Go awaaaay!!!
RRAAHH!!!

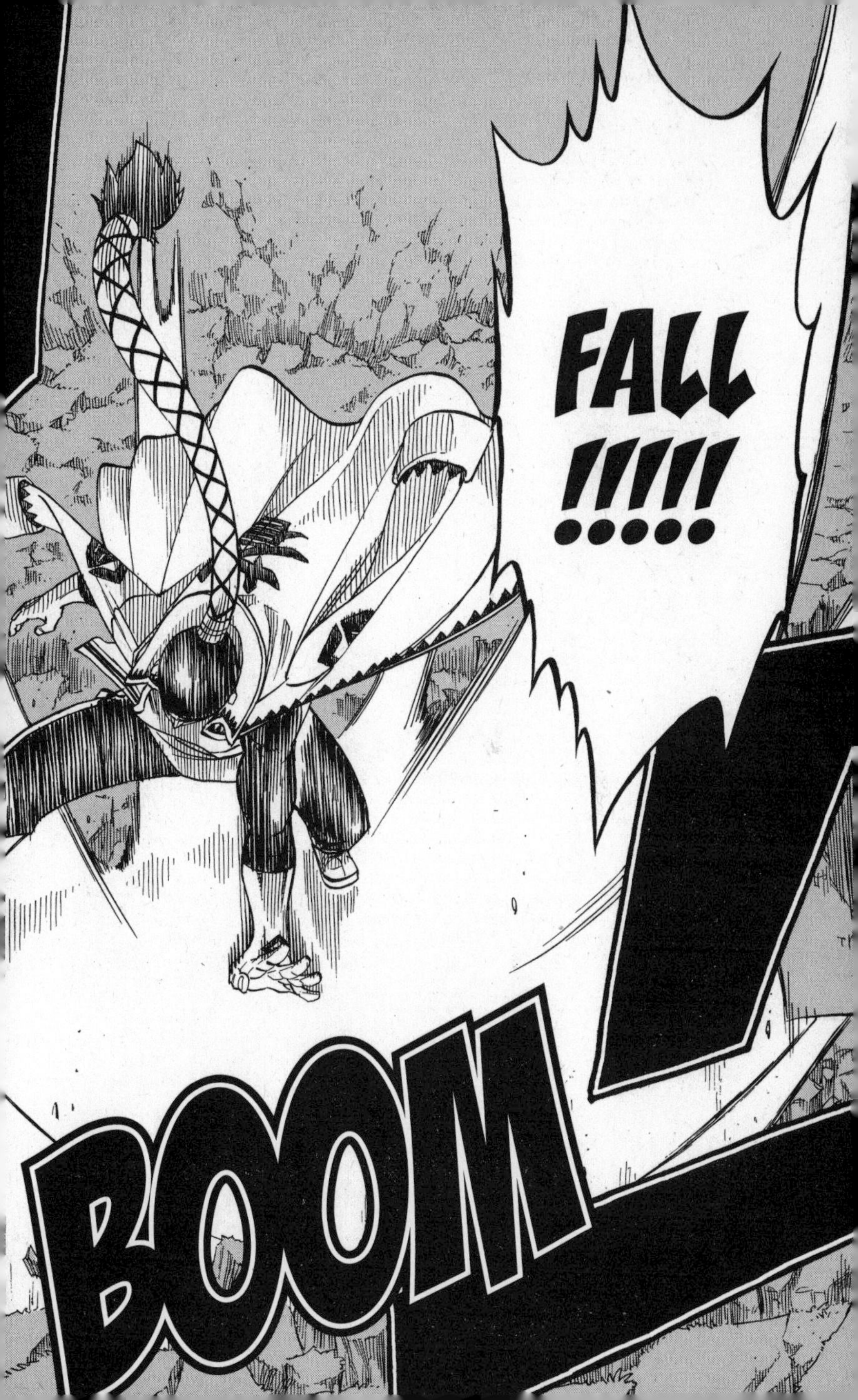
FALL
!!!!!
BOOM

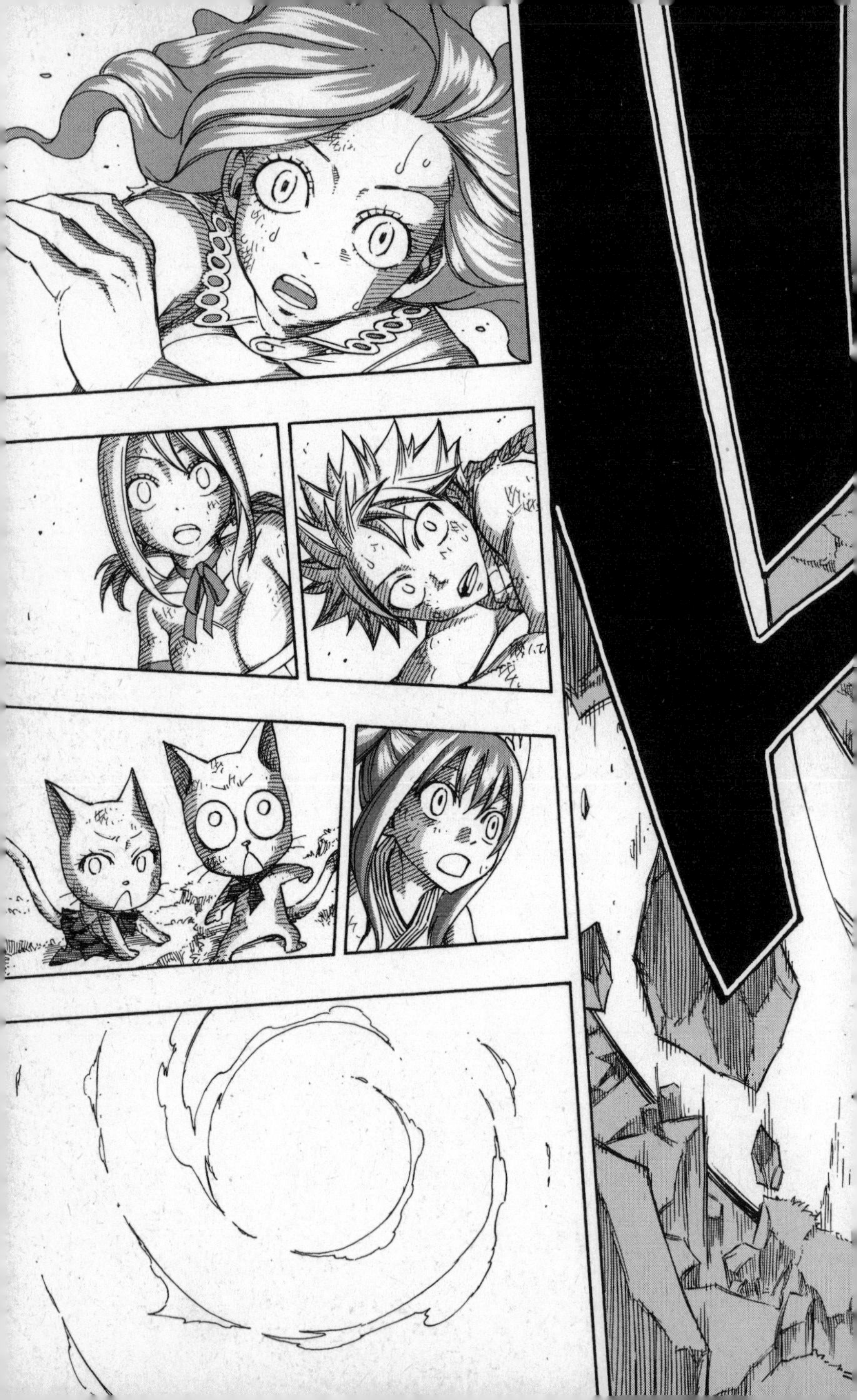

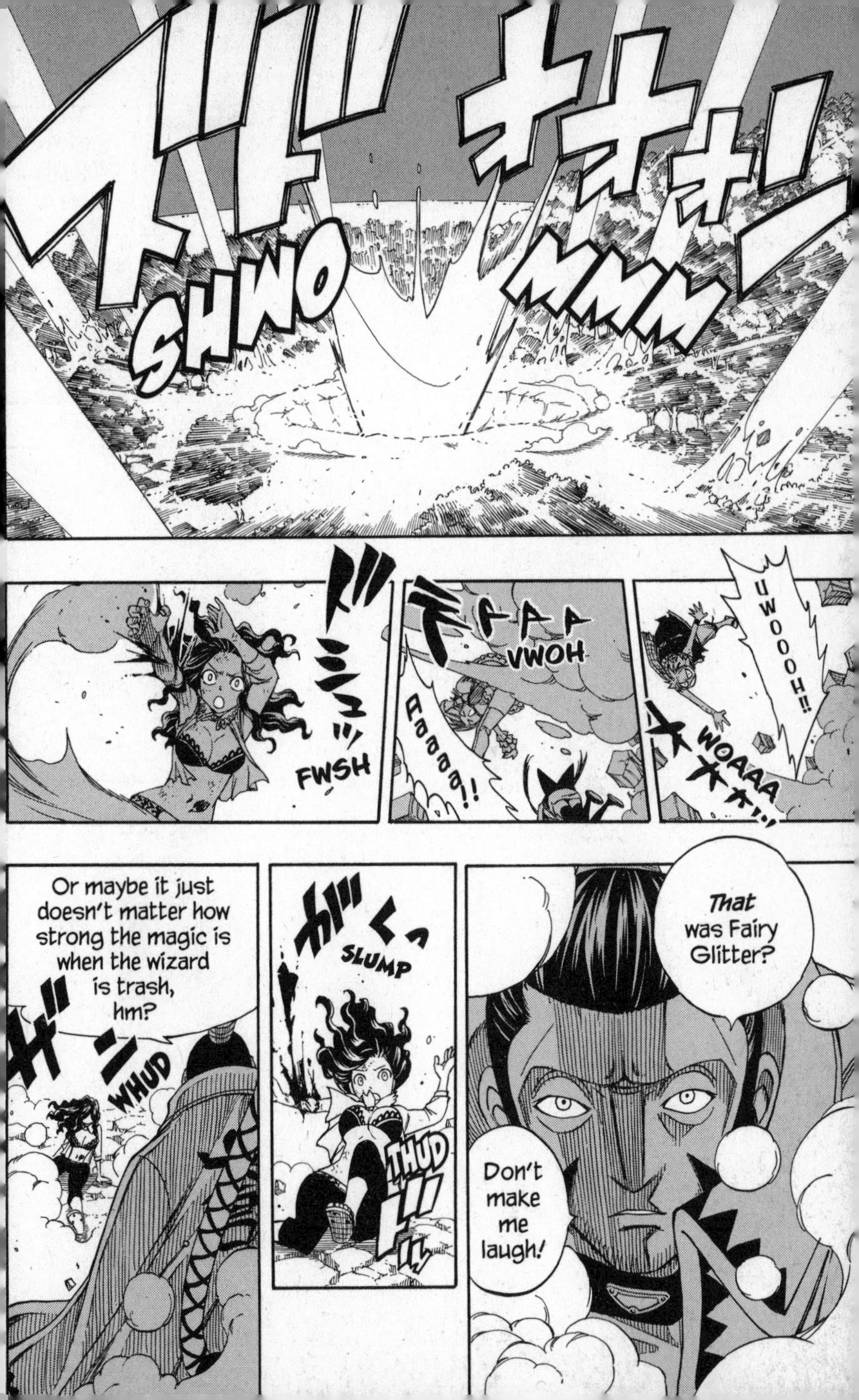
SHWOMMM
UWOOOOH!!
WOAAA!!
VWOH
Aaaaaa!!
FWSH
That was Fairy Glitter?
Don't make me laugh!
SLUMP
THUD
Or maybe it just doesn't matter how strong the magic is when the wizard is trash, hm?
WHUD

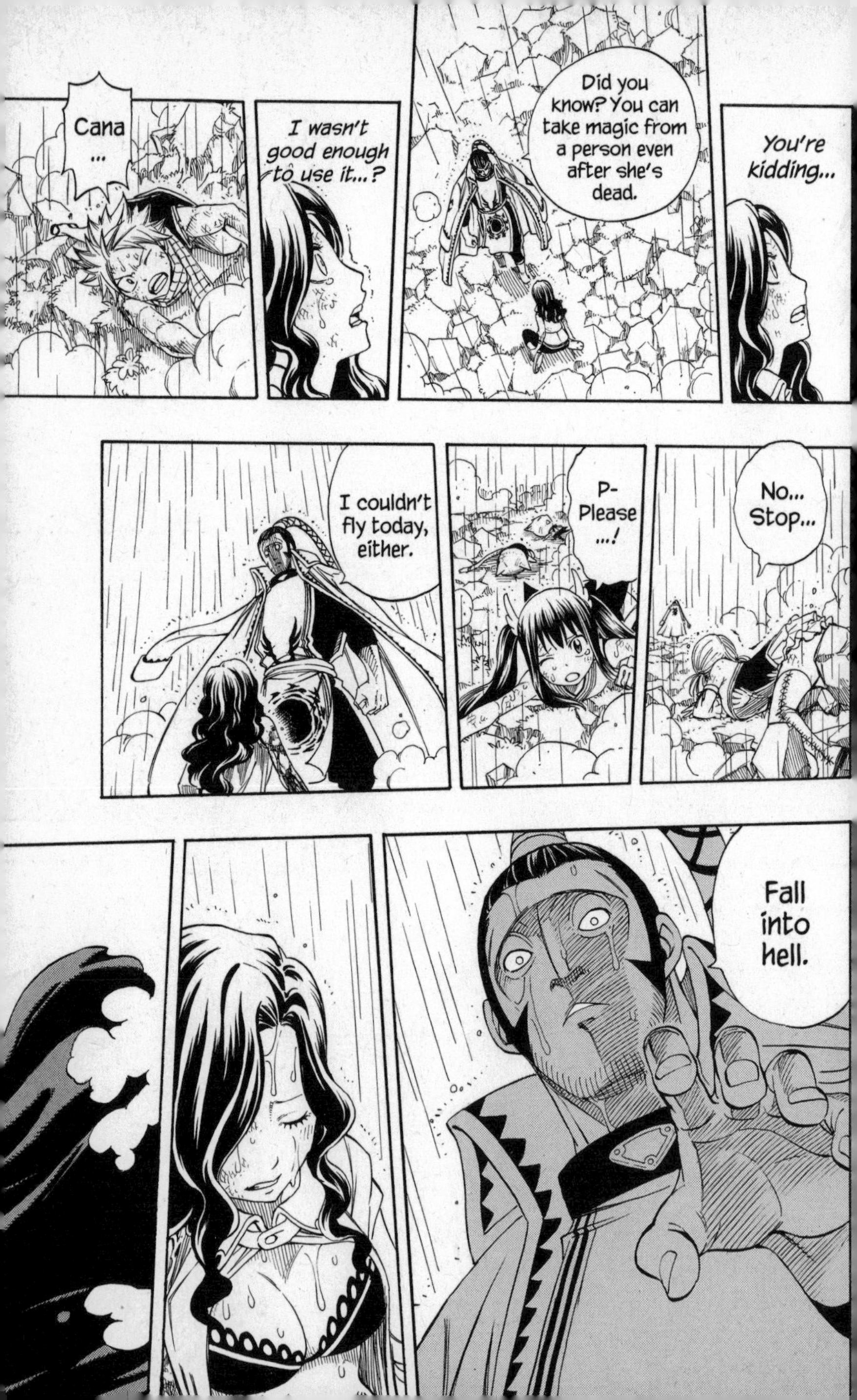
You're kidding...
Did you know? You can take magic from a person even after she's dead.
I wasn't good enough to use it...?
Cana ...
No... Stop...
P- Please ...!
I couldn't fly today, either.
Fall into hell.

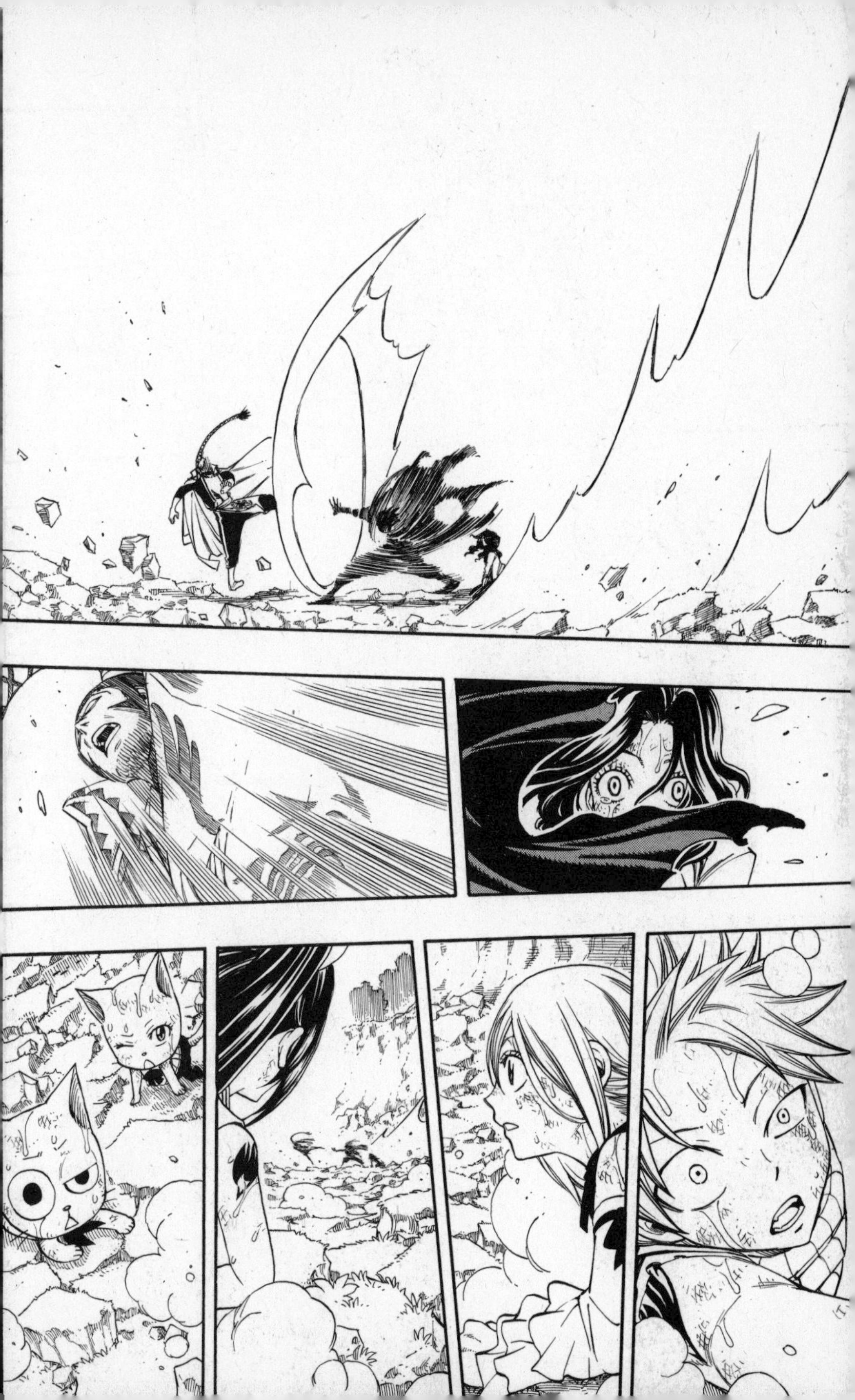

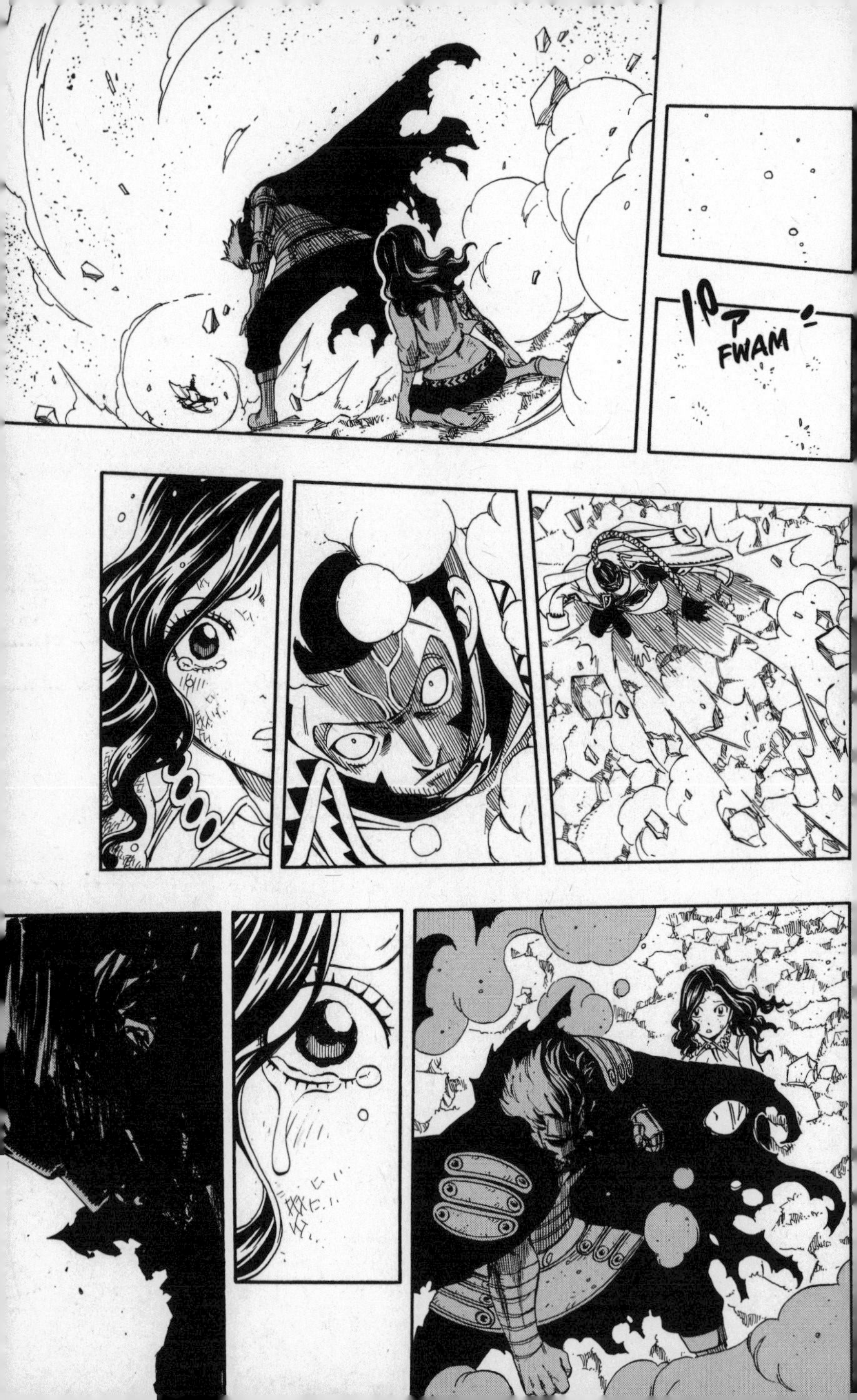
FWAM

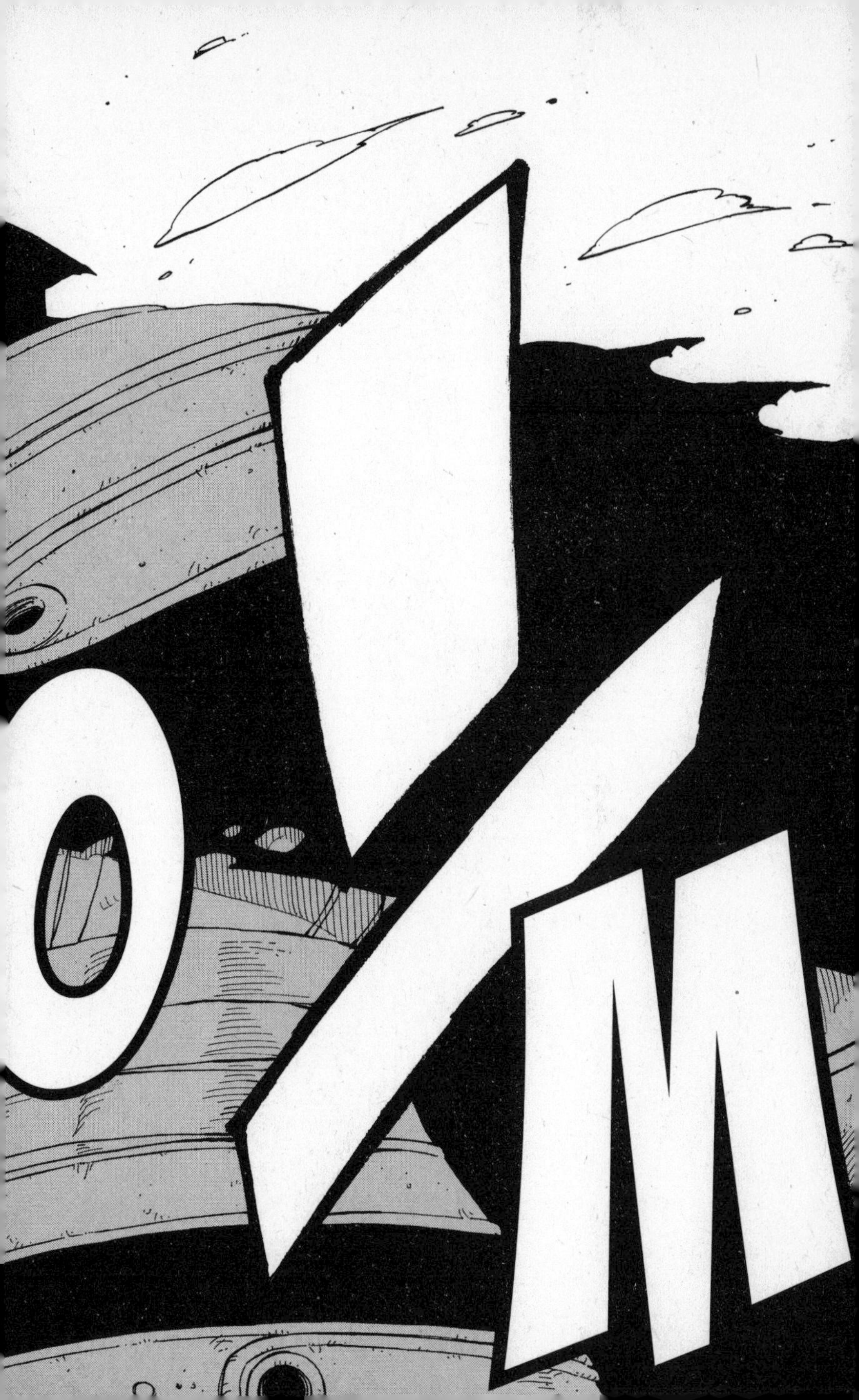

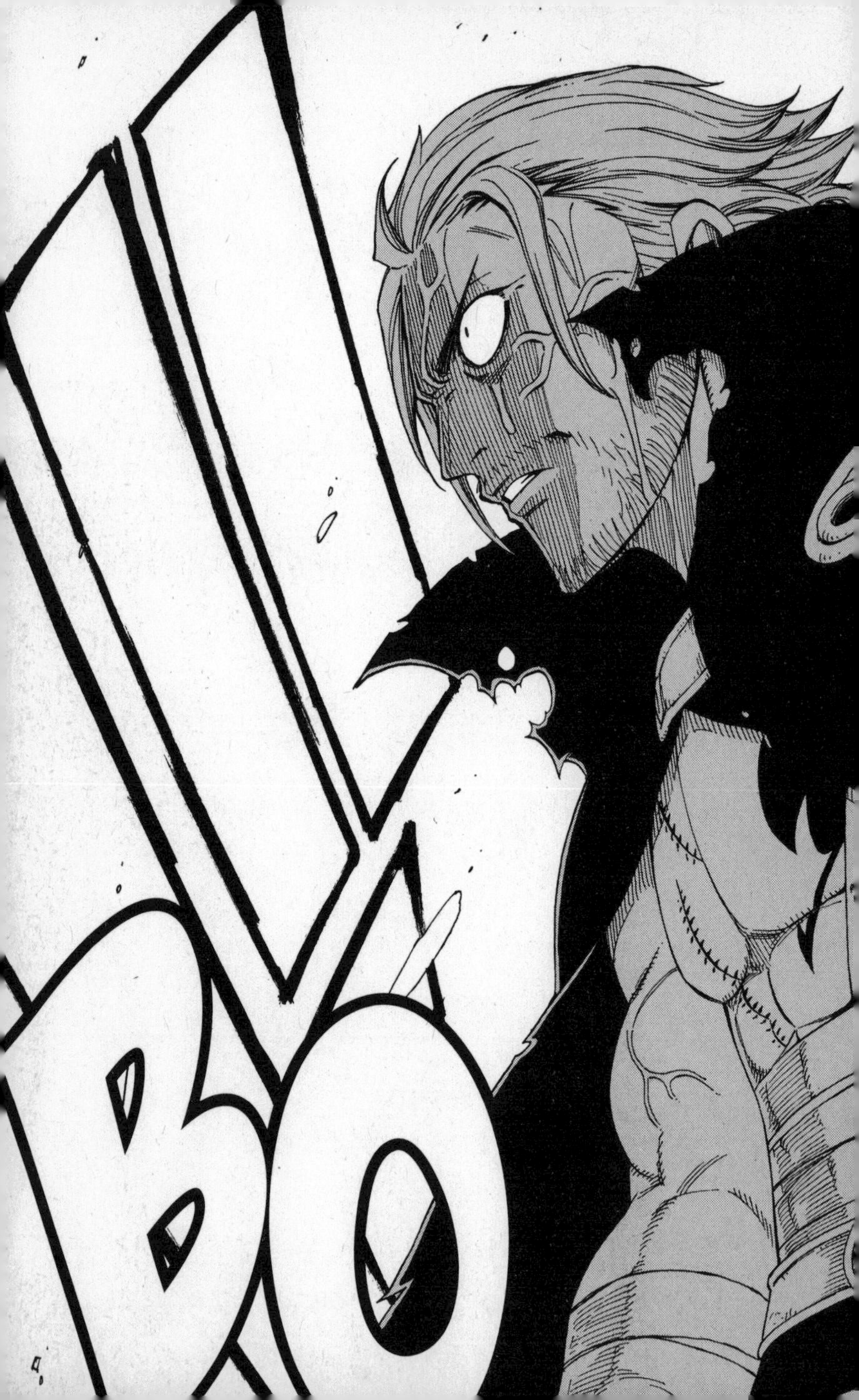
BO

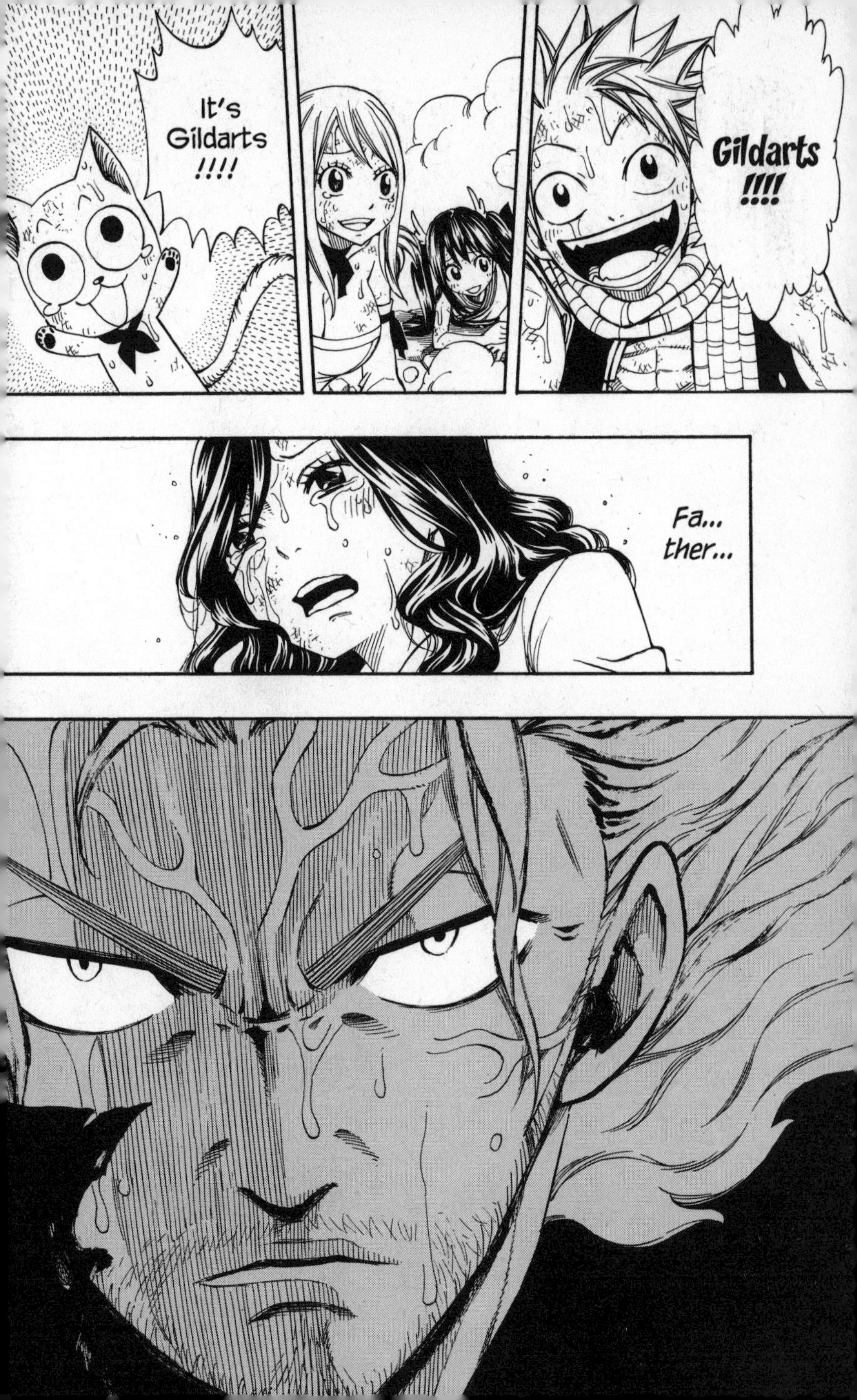
Gildarts !!!!
It's Gildarts !!!!
Fa... ther...

FAIRY TAIL

フェアリーテイル

Chapter 234: The Boy Who Watches the Se

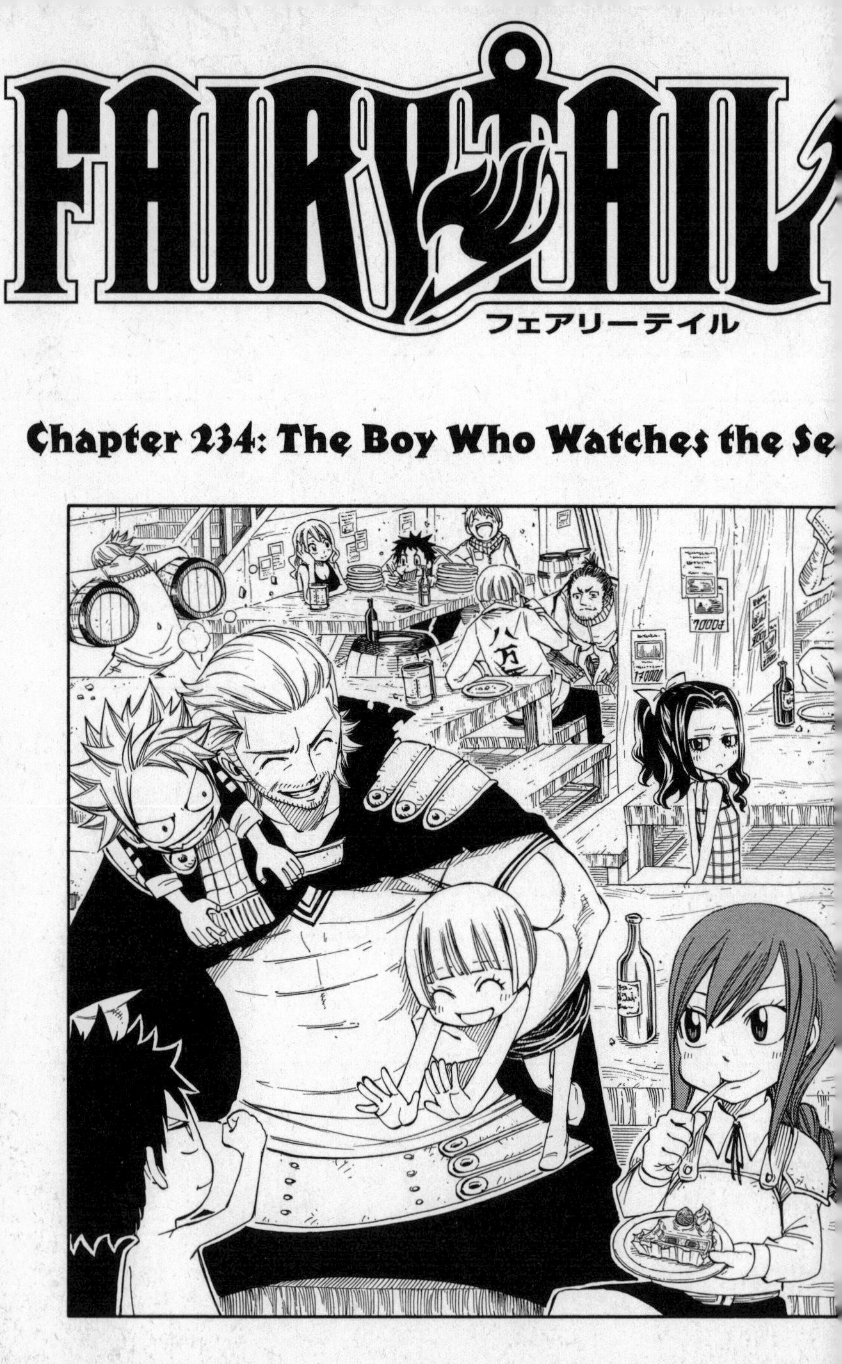

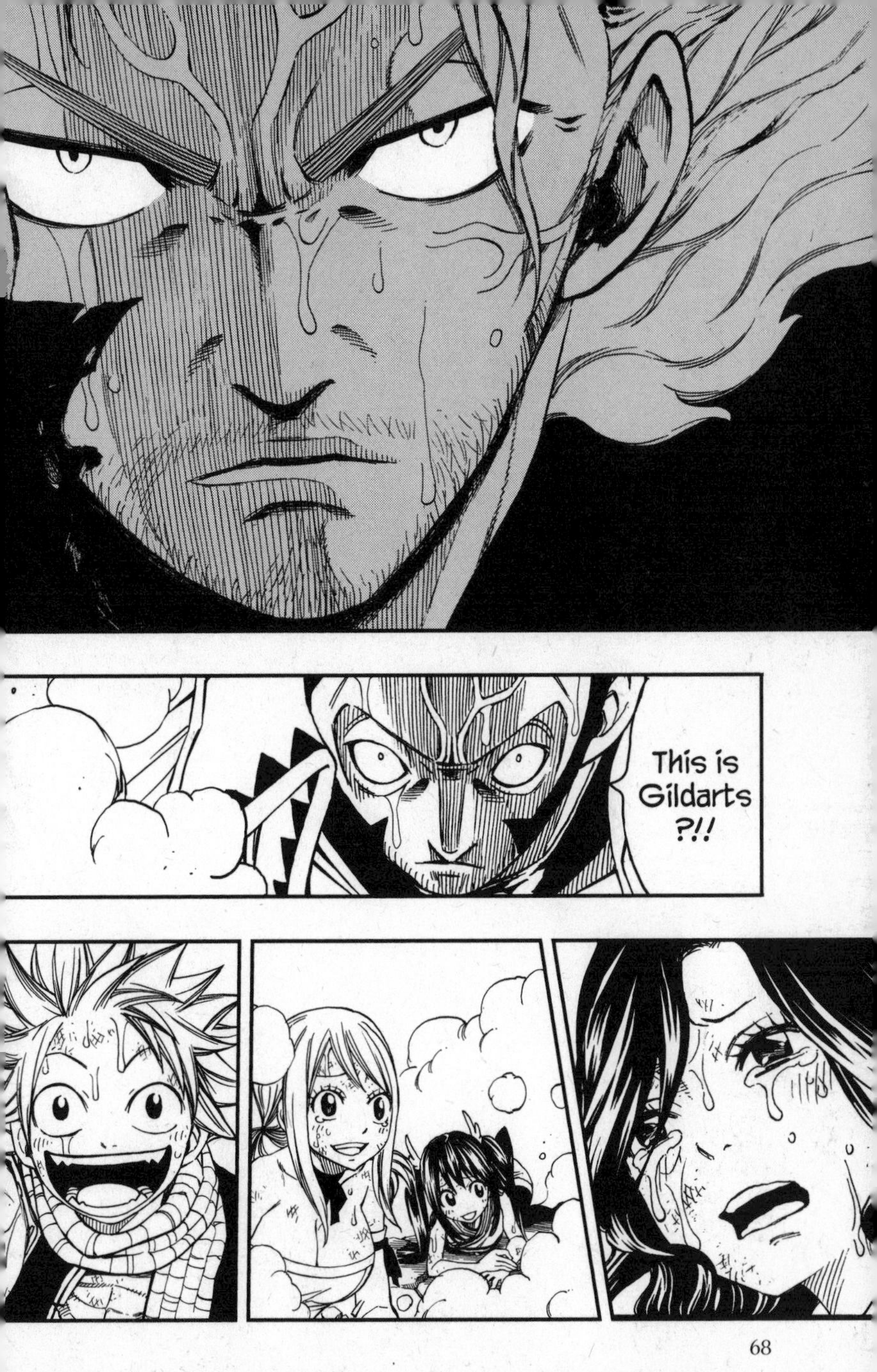
This is Gildarts ?!!

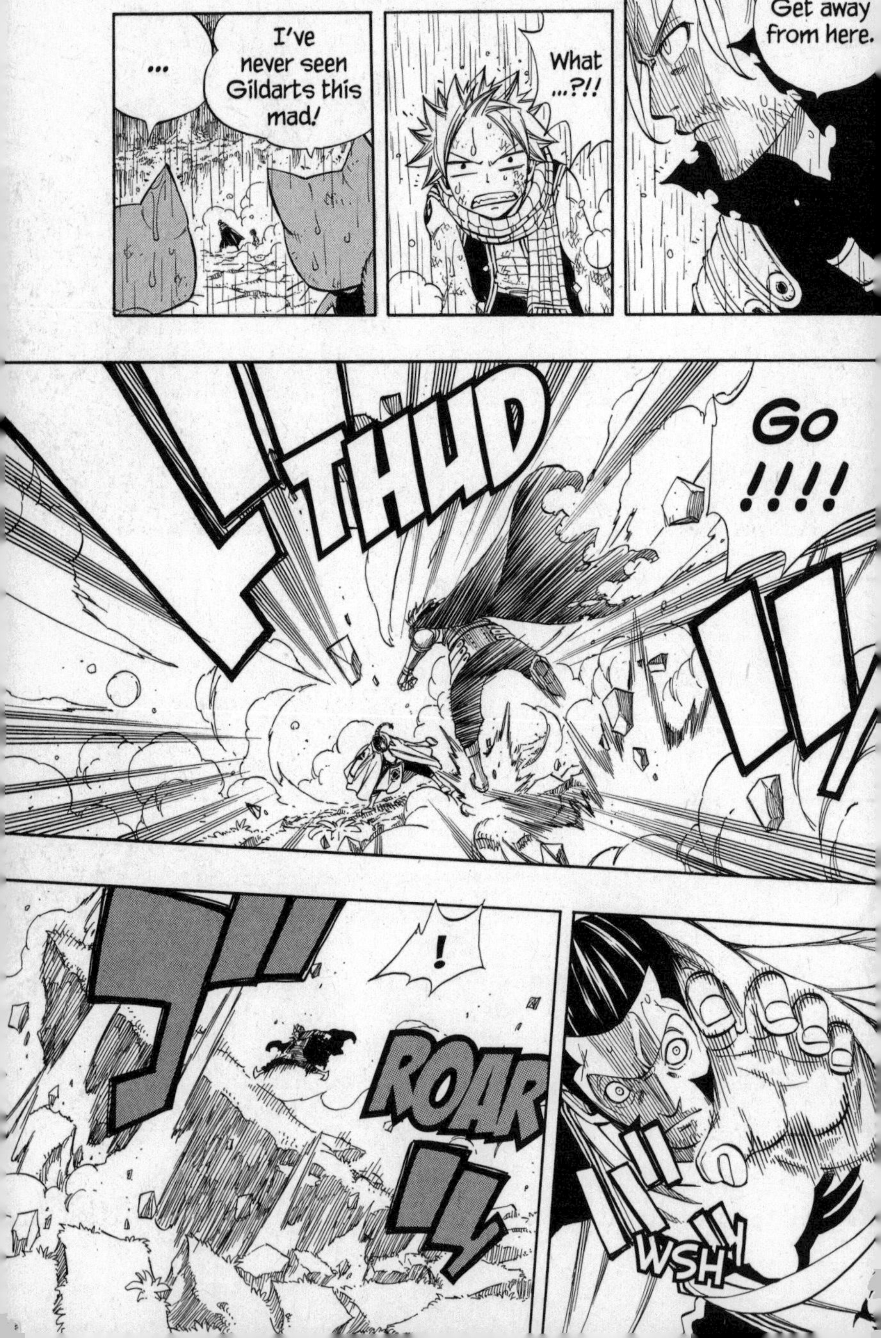
Get away from here.
What ...?!!
I've never seen Gildarts this mad!
...
Go !!!!
THUD
WSH
!
ROAR

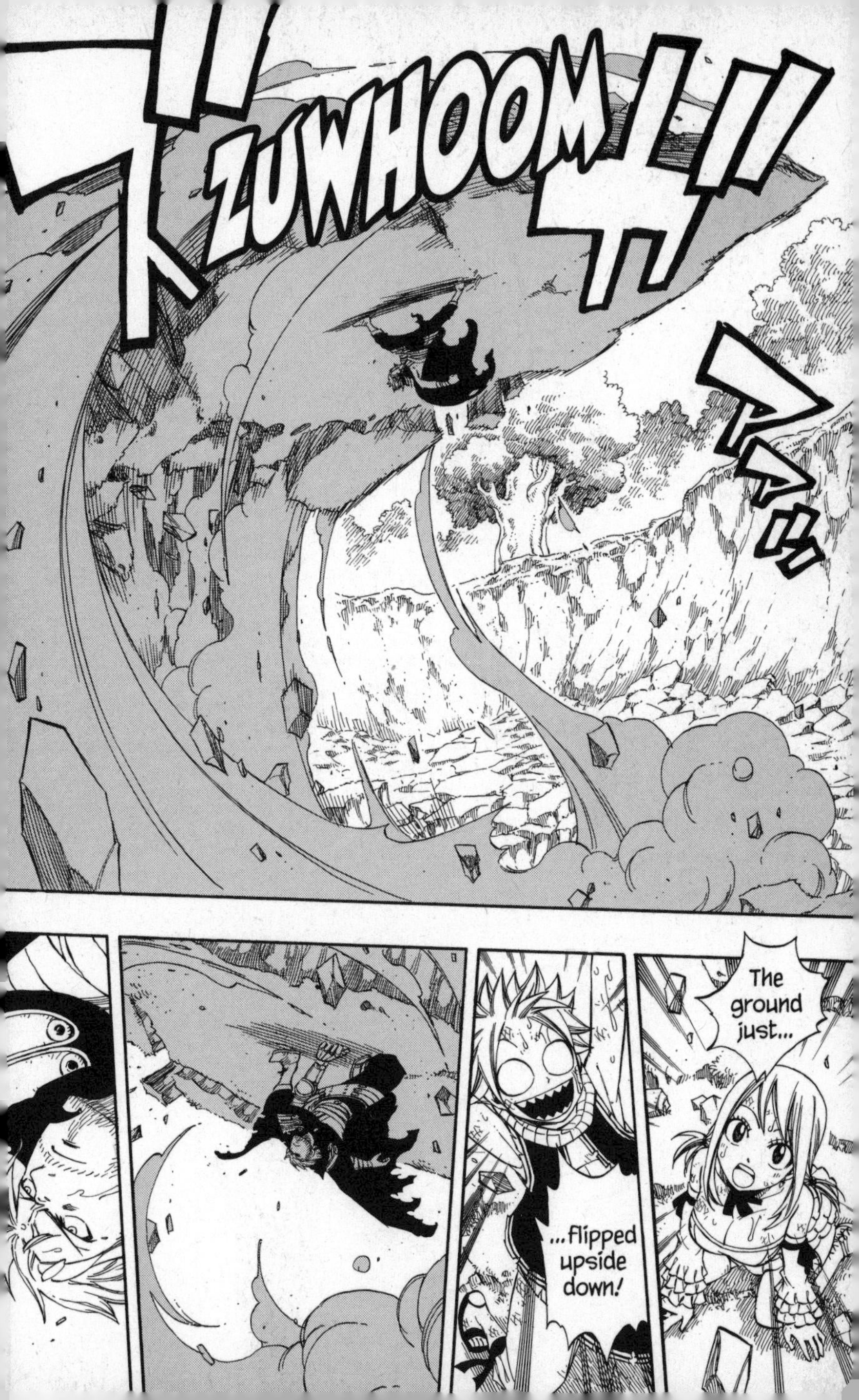
ZUWHOOM!!
The ground just...
...flipped upside down!

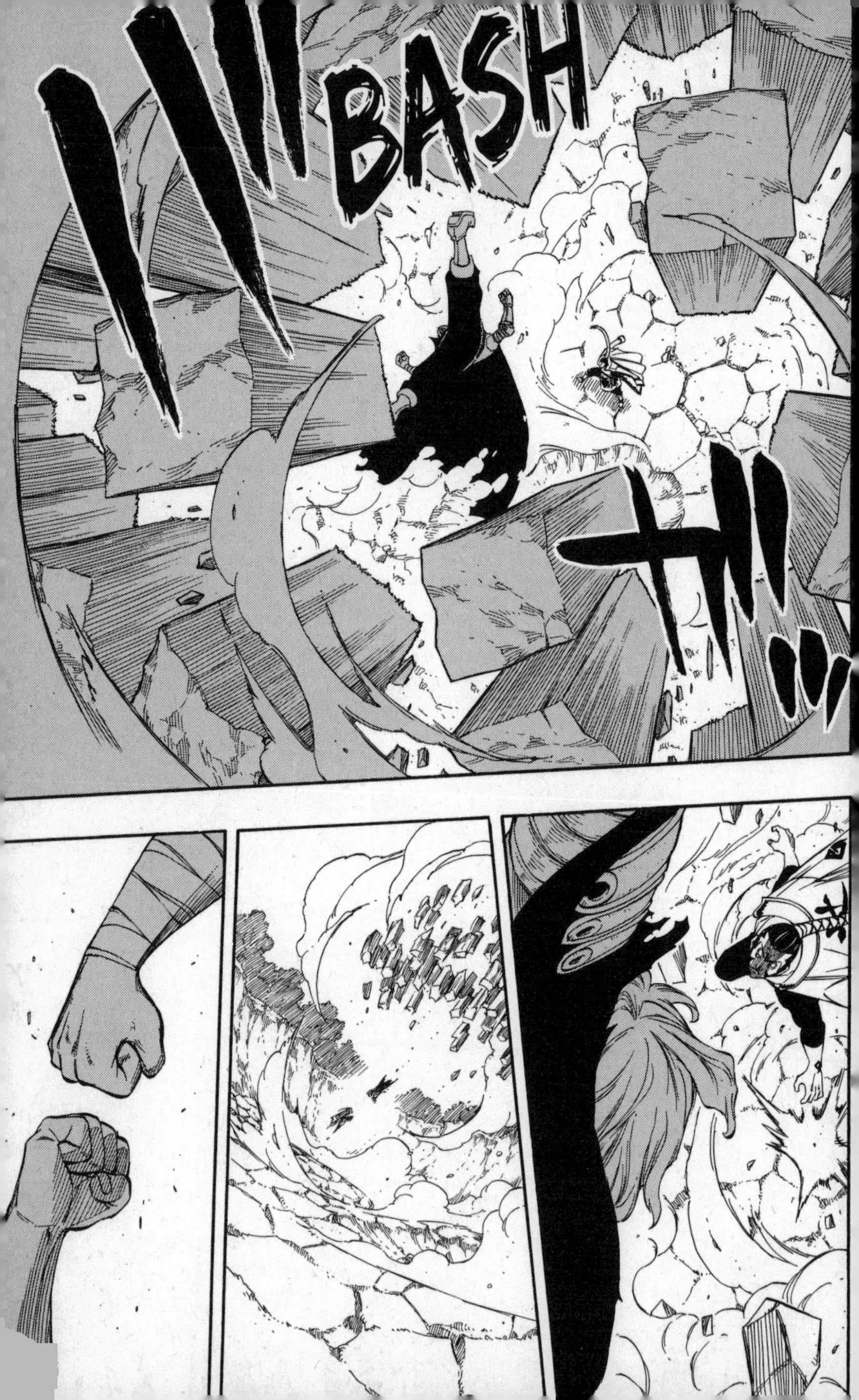
BASH

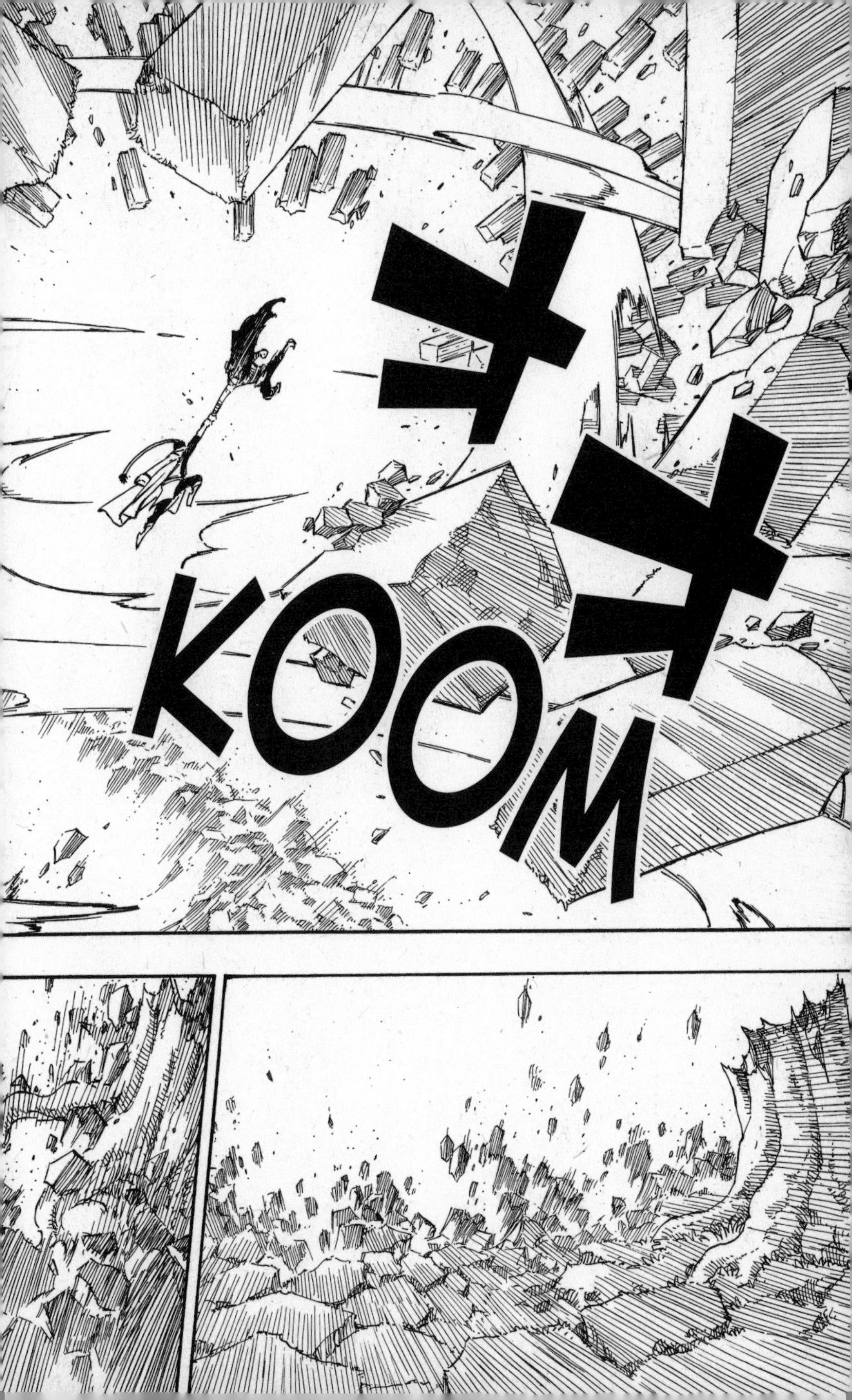
KOOM

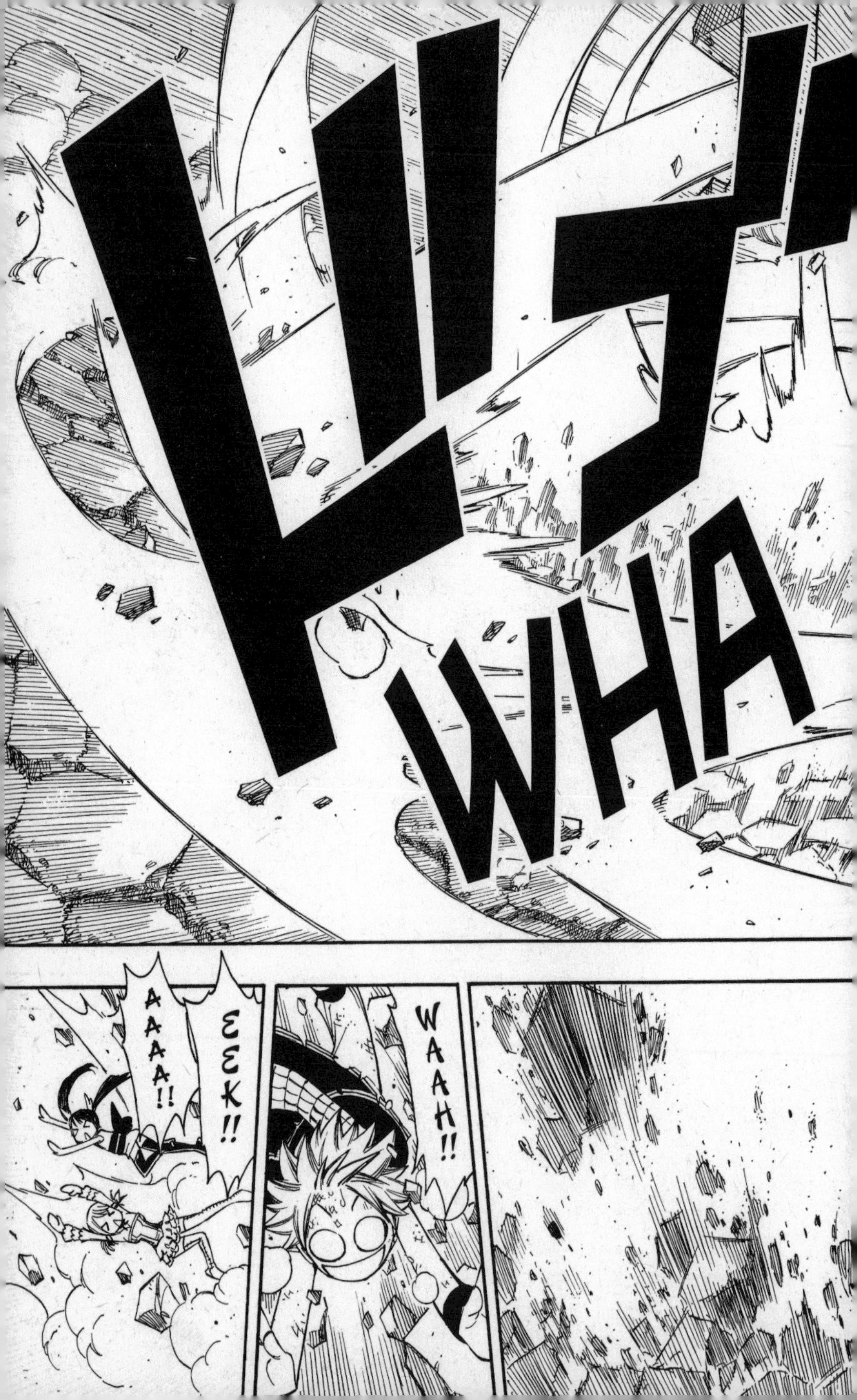
WHA
WAAH!!
EEK!!
AAAA!!

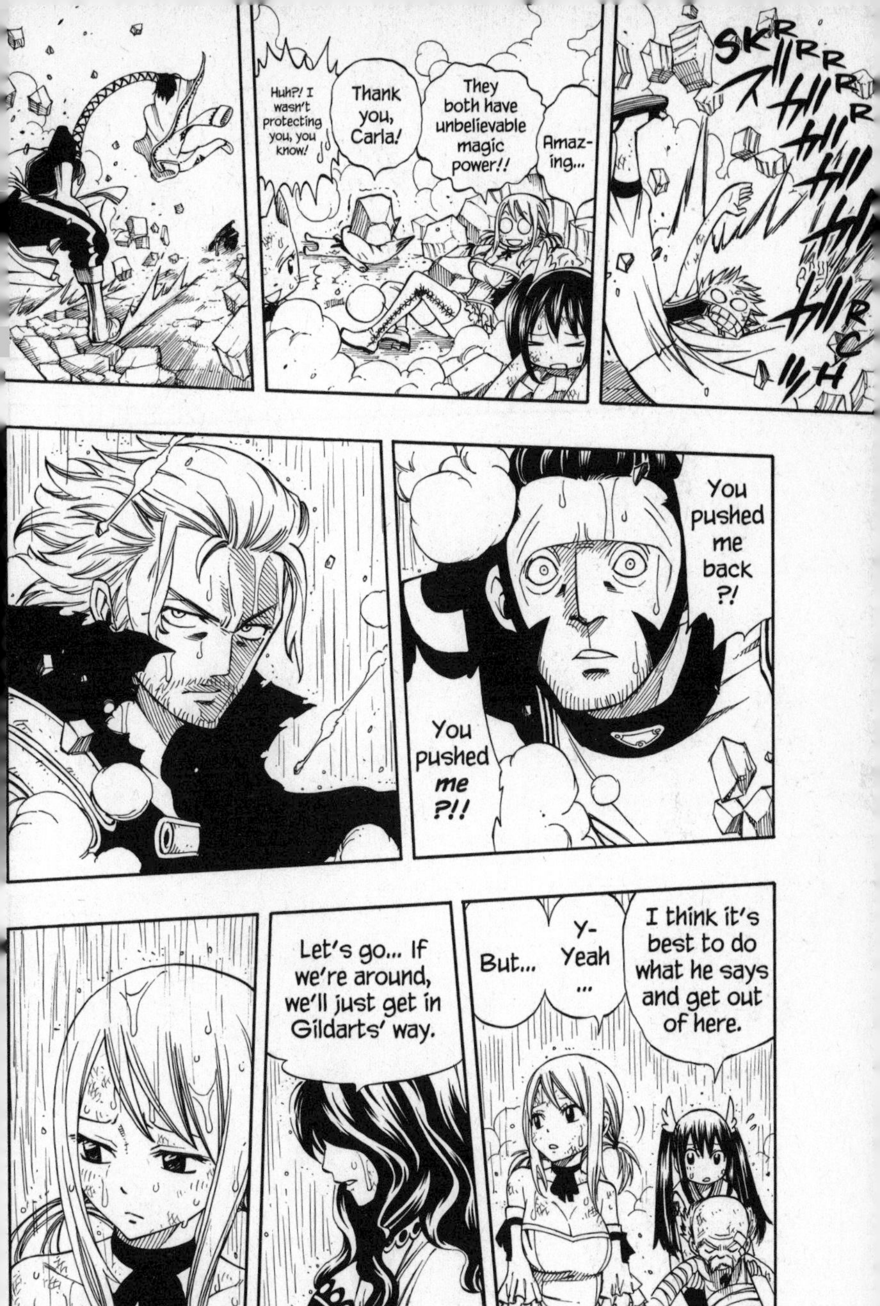
SKRRRRRRCH
Amaz-ing...
They both have unbelievable magic power!!
Thank you, Carla!
Huh?! I wasn't protecting you, you know!
You pushed me back?!
You pushed me?!!
I think it's best to do what he says and get out of here.
Y-Yeah...
But...
Let's go... If we're around, we'll just get in Gildarts' way.

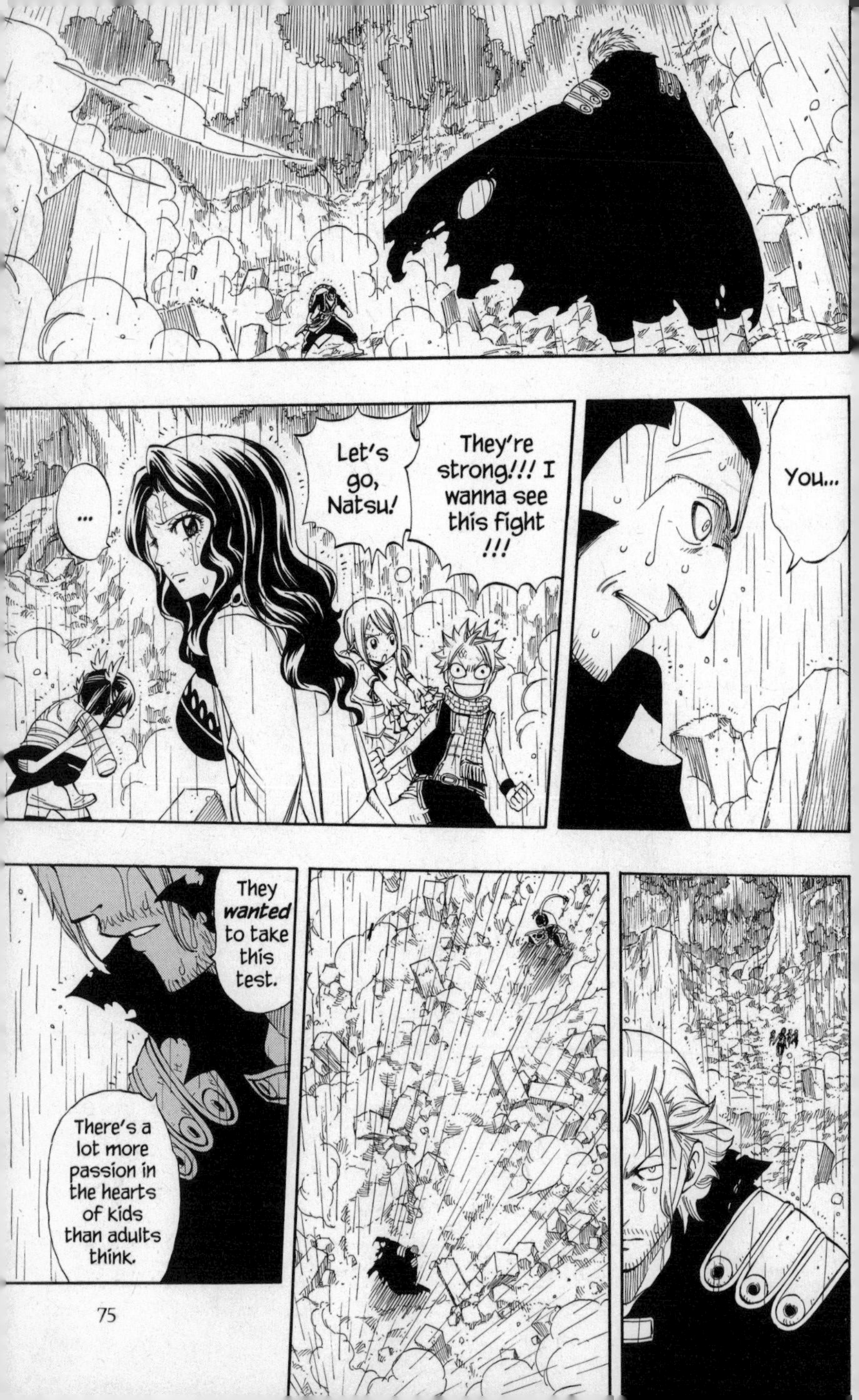
You...
They're strong!!! I wanna see this fight!!!
Let's go, Natsu!
...
They *wanted* to take this test.
There's a lot more passion in the hearts of kids than adults think.

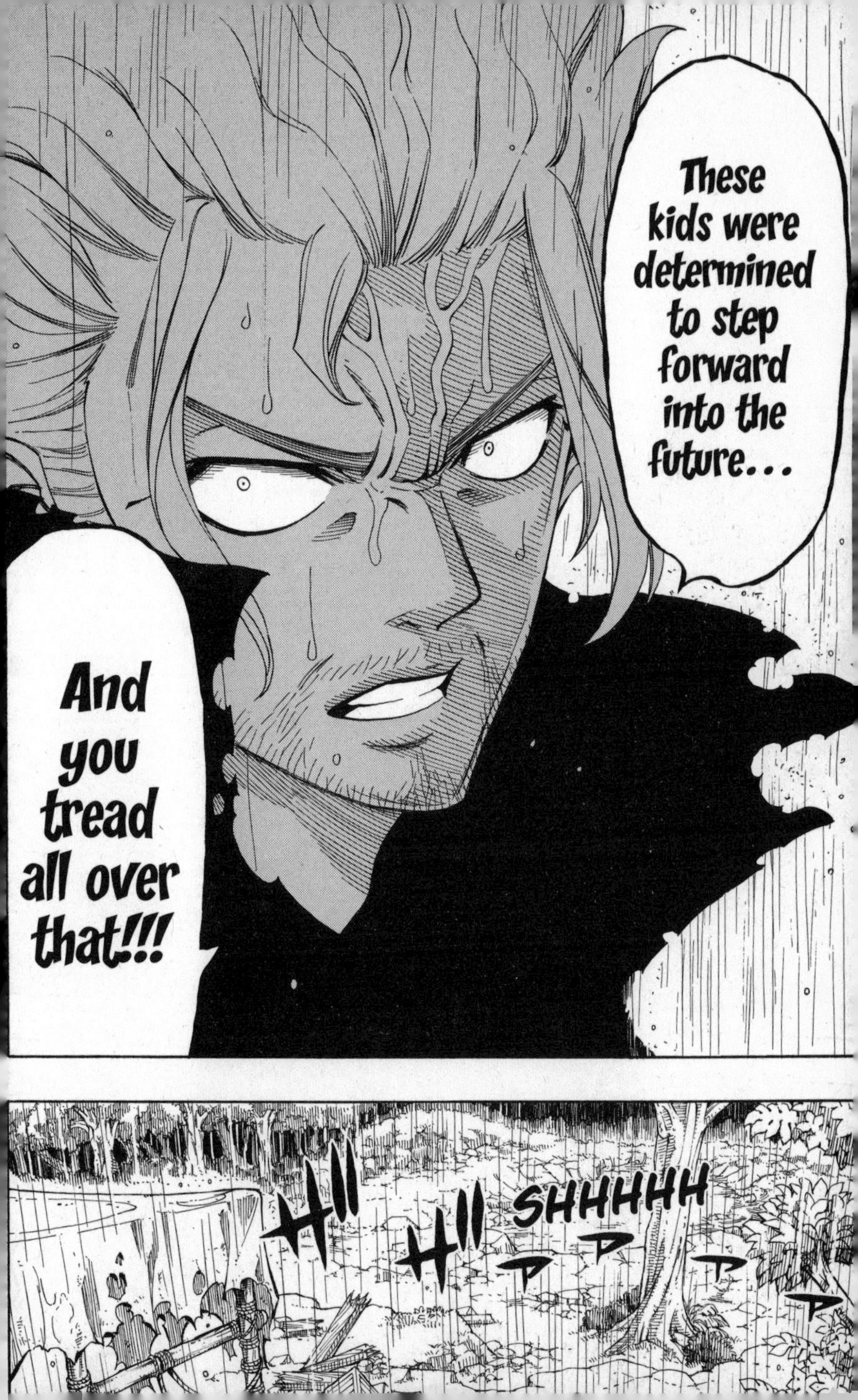
These kids were determined to step forward into the future...
And you tread all over that!!!
SHHHHH
P P P P
H!! H!!

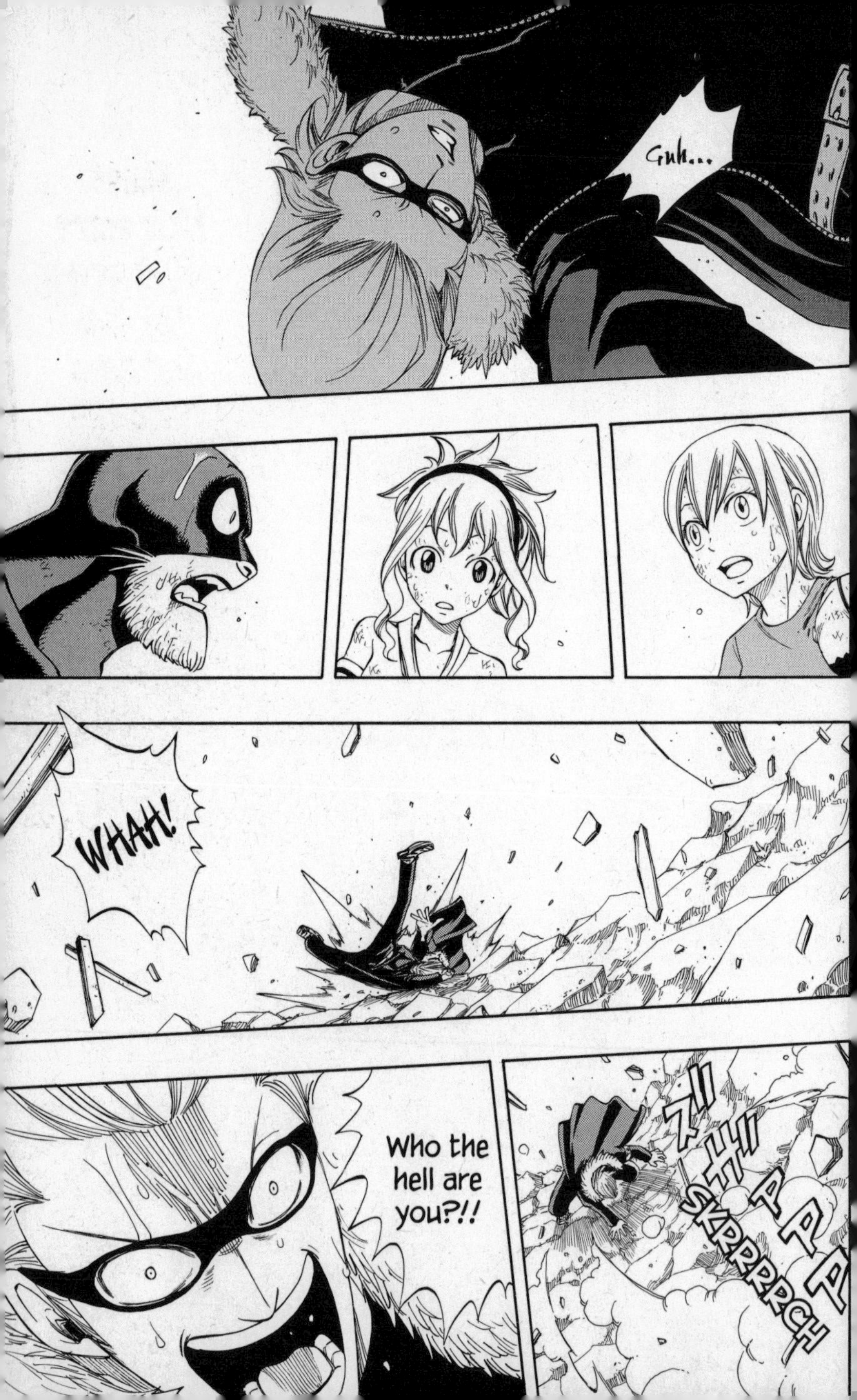
Guh...
WHAH!
SKRRRCH
Who the hell are you?!!

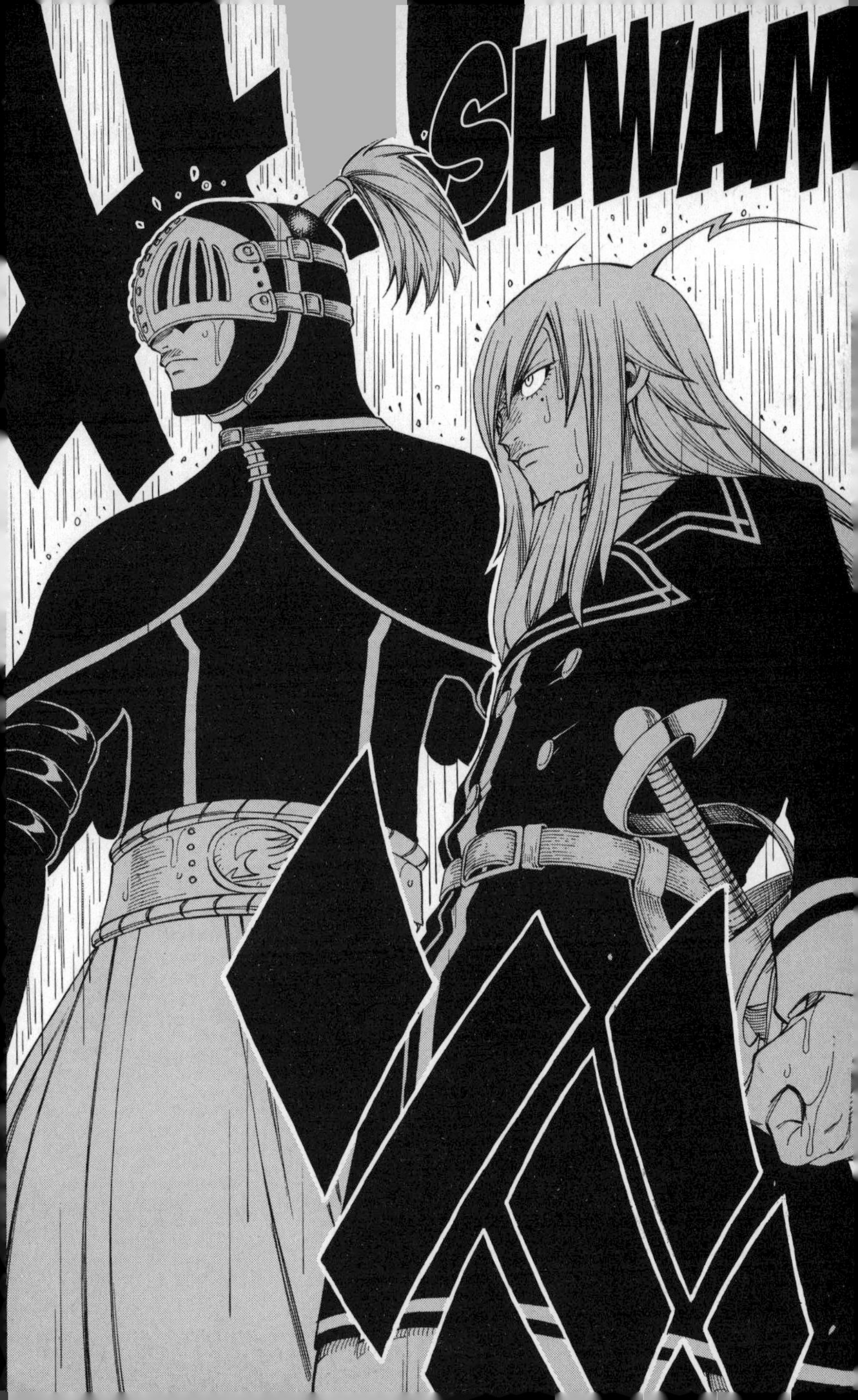
SHWAM

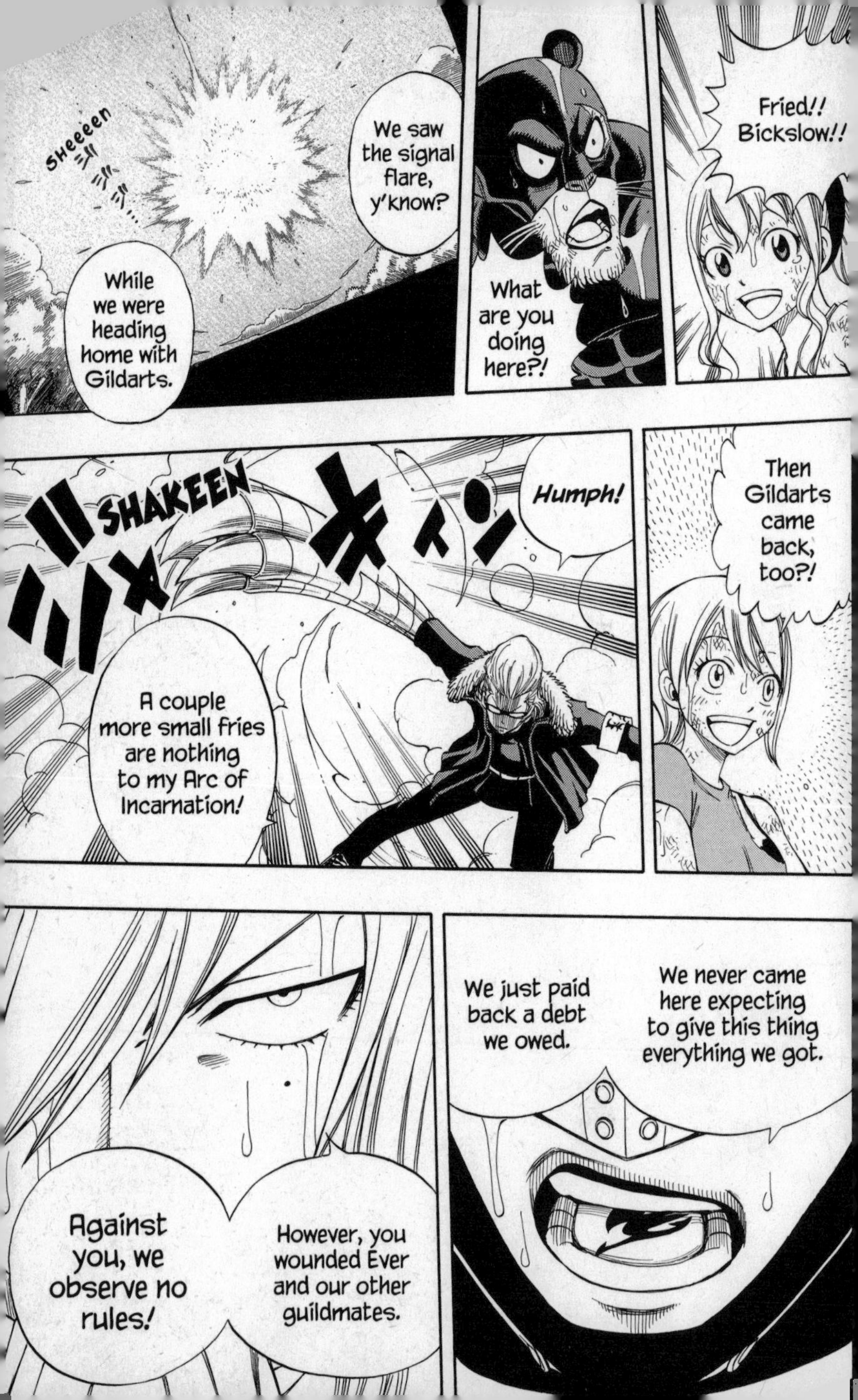
Fried!! Bickslow!!
What are you doing here?!
We saw the signal flare, y'know?
While we were heading home with Gildarts.
Sheeeen
Then Gildarts came back, too?!
Humph!
SHAKEEN
A couple more small fries are nothing to my Arc of Incarnation!
We never came here expecting to give this thing everything we got.
We just paid back a debt we owed.
However, you wounded Ever and our other guildmates.
Against you, we observe no rules!

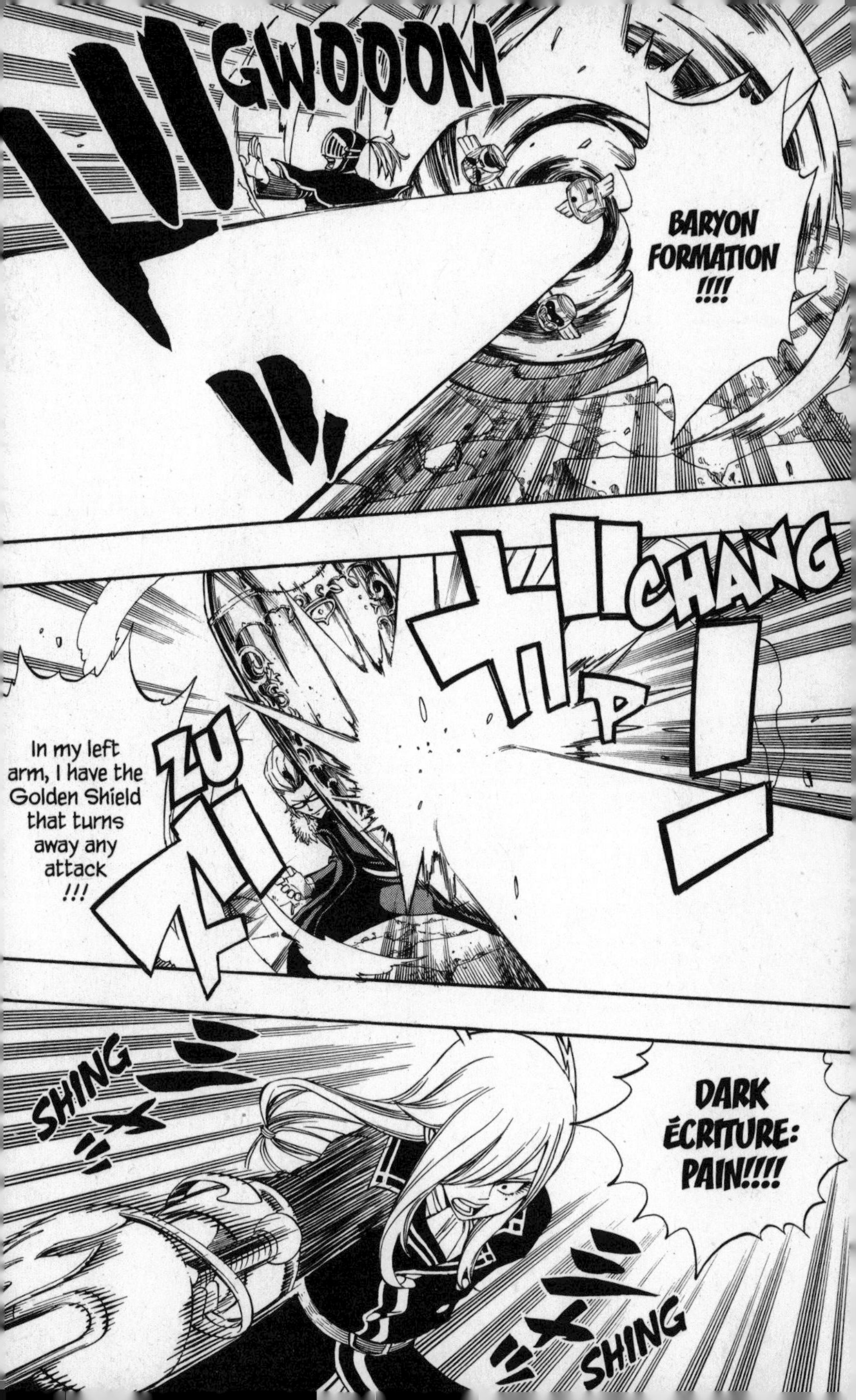
GWOOOM
BARYON FORMATION !!!!
CHANG
ZU
In my left arm, I have the Golden Shield that turns away any attack !!!
DARK ÉCRITURE: PAIN!!!!
SHING
SHING

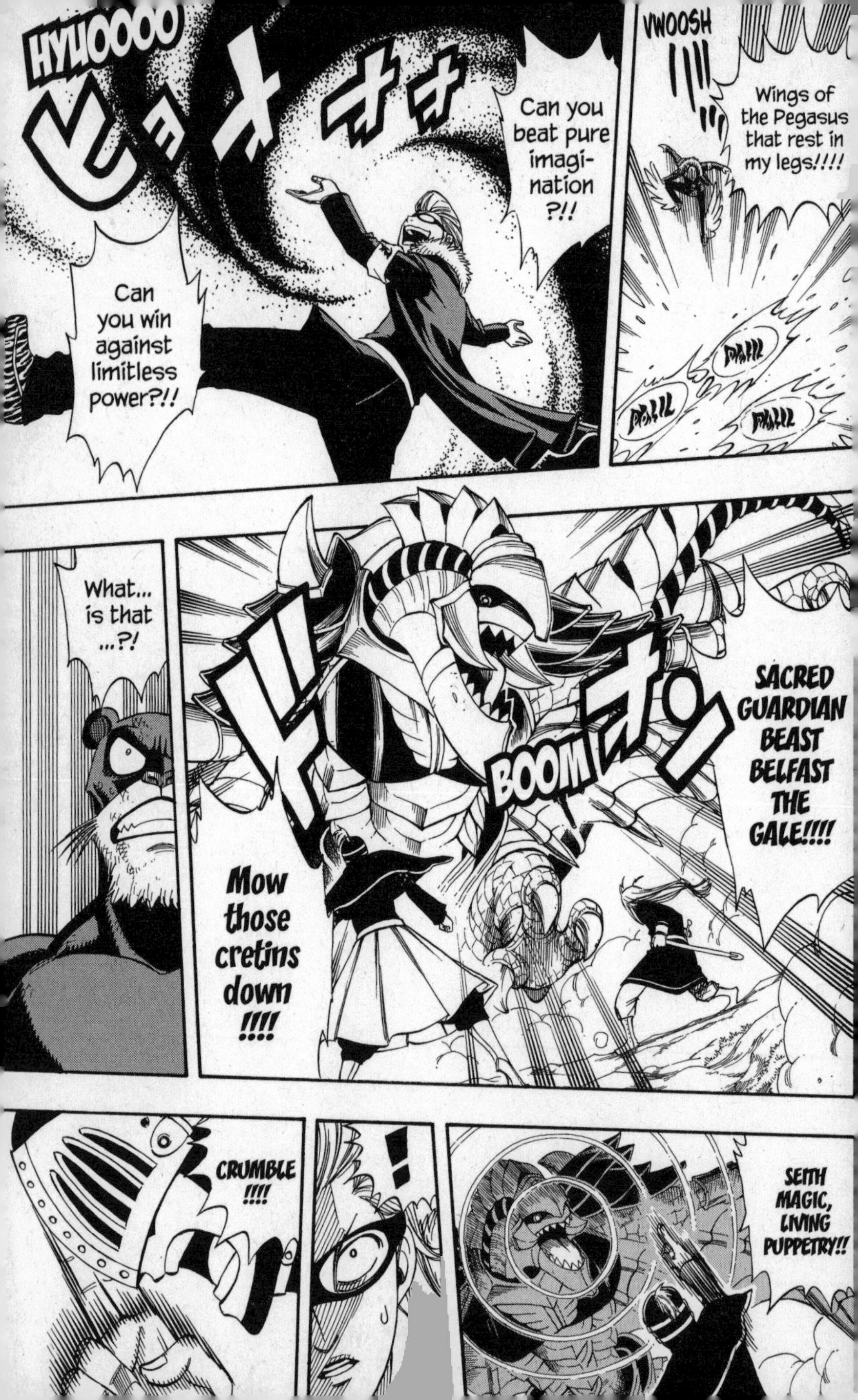
VWOOSH
Wings of the Pegasus that rest in my legs!!!!
HYUOOO
Can you beat pure imagination?!!
Can you win against limitless power?!!
SACRED GUARDIAN BEAST BELFAST THE GALE!!!!
BOOM
Mow those cretins down!!!!
What... is that ...?!
SEITH MAGIC, LIVING PUPPETRY!!
!
CRUMBLE!!!!

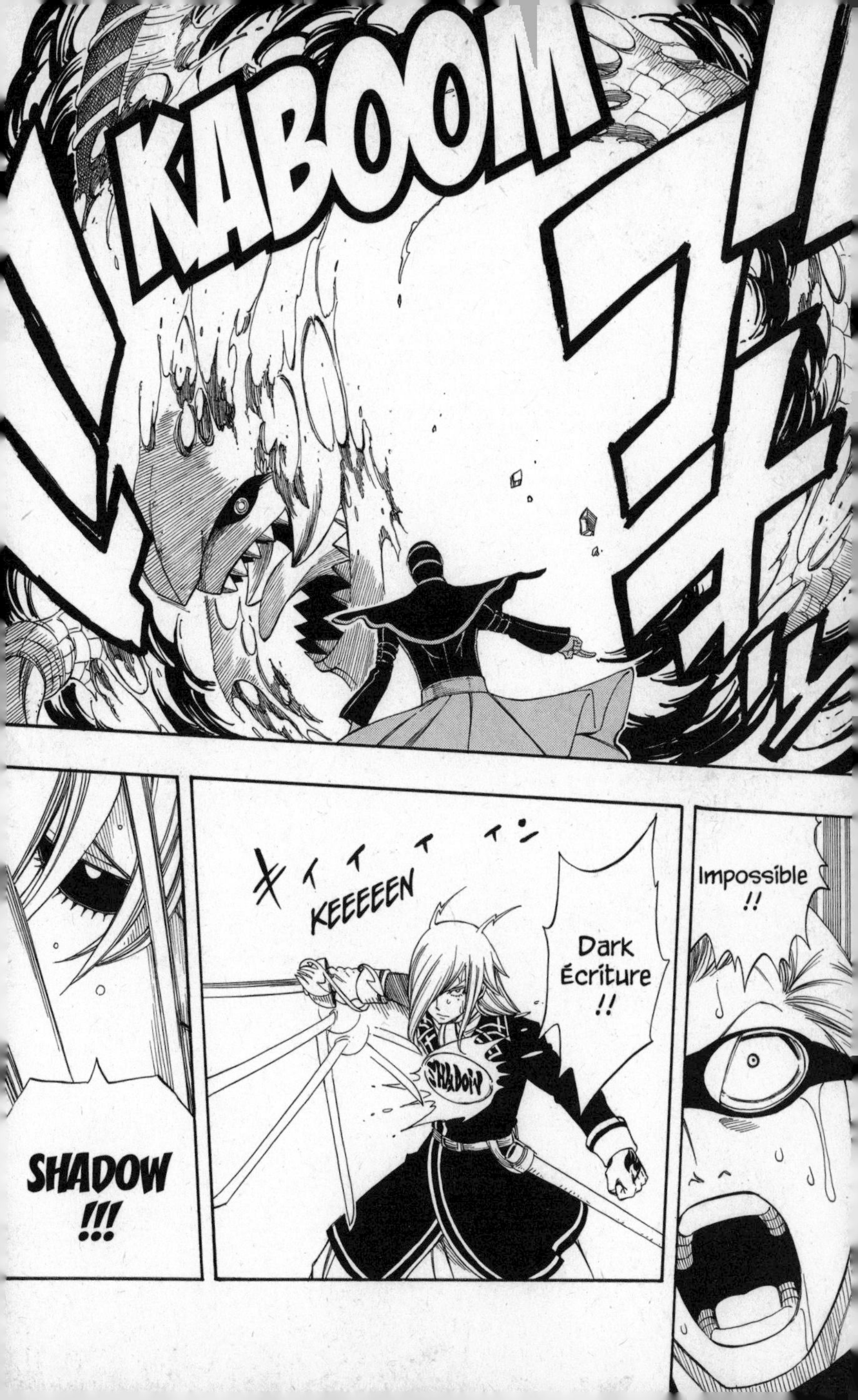
KABOOM
Impossible !!
Dark Écriture !!
キイイイイン
KEEEEEN
SHADOW
SHADOW !!!

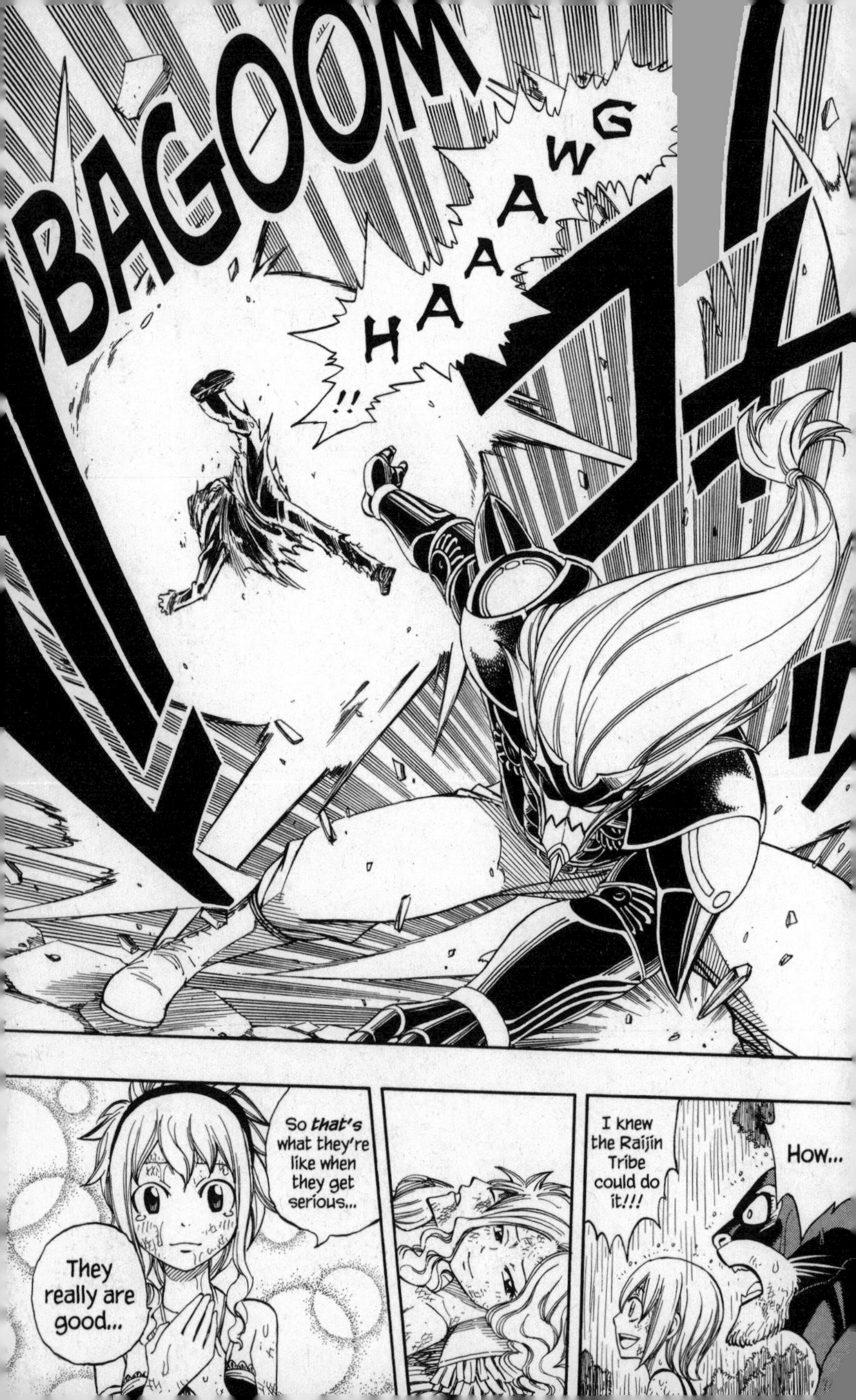
BAGOOM
HAAAWG!!
How...
I knew the Raijin Tribe could do it!!!
So *that's* what they're like when they get serious...
They really are good...

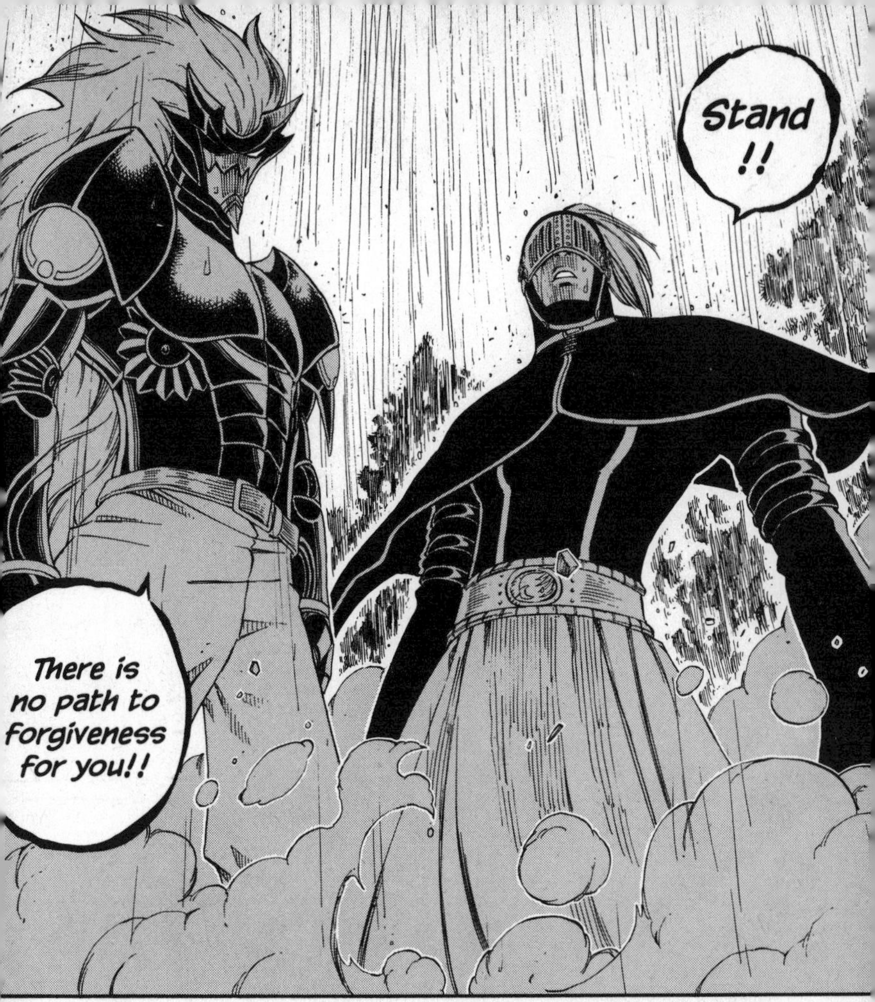
Stand !!
There is no path to forgiveness for you!!

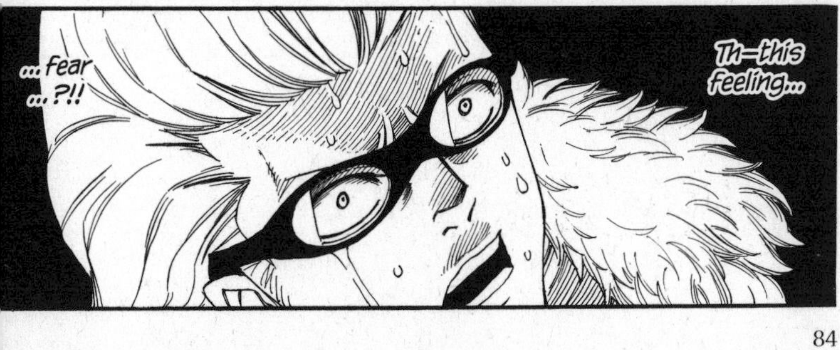
Th—this feeling...
...fear ...?!!

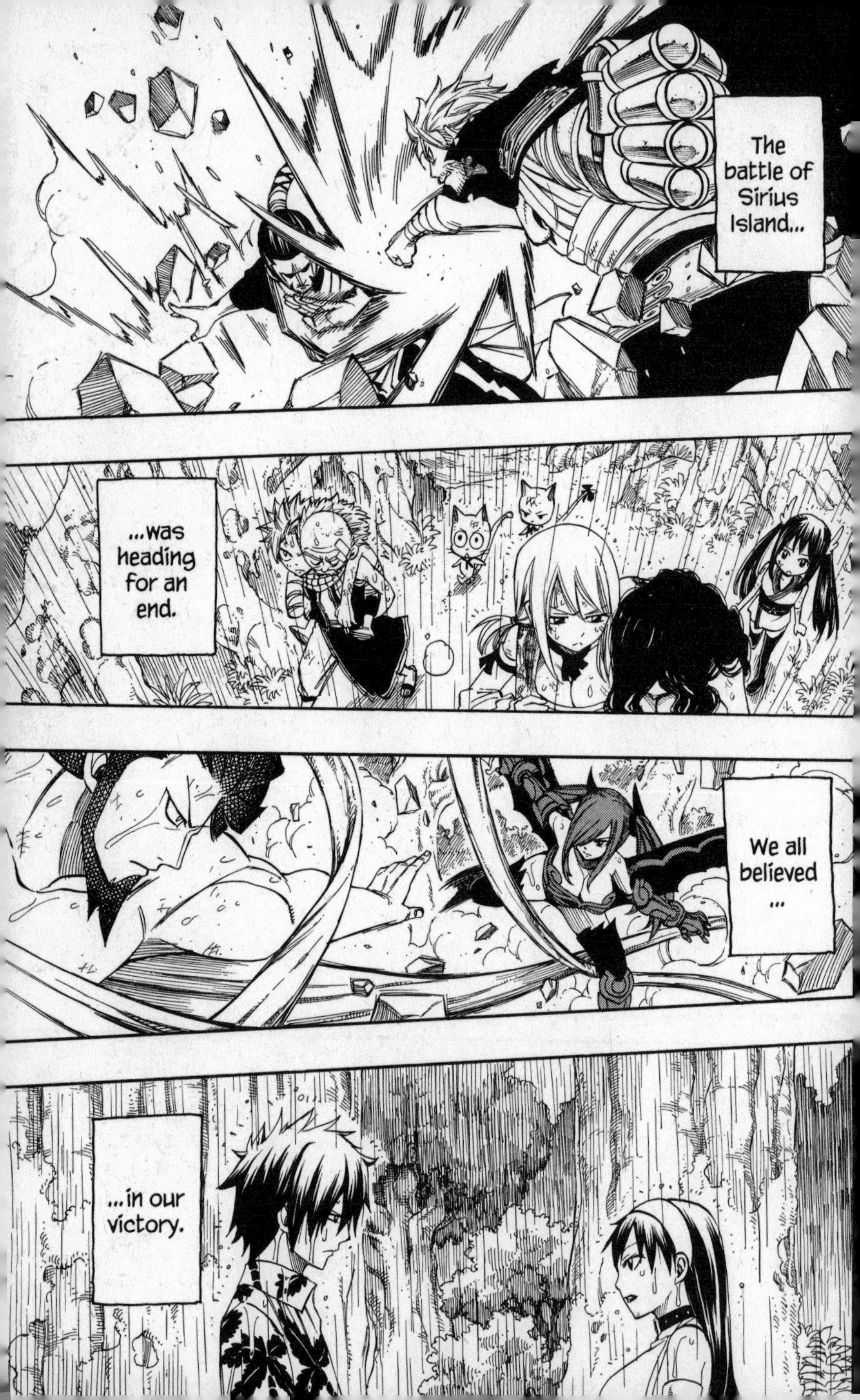
The battle of Sirius Island...
...was heading for an end.
We all believed ...
...in our victory.

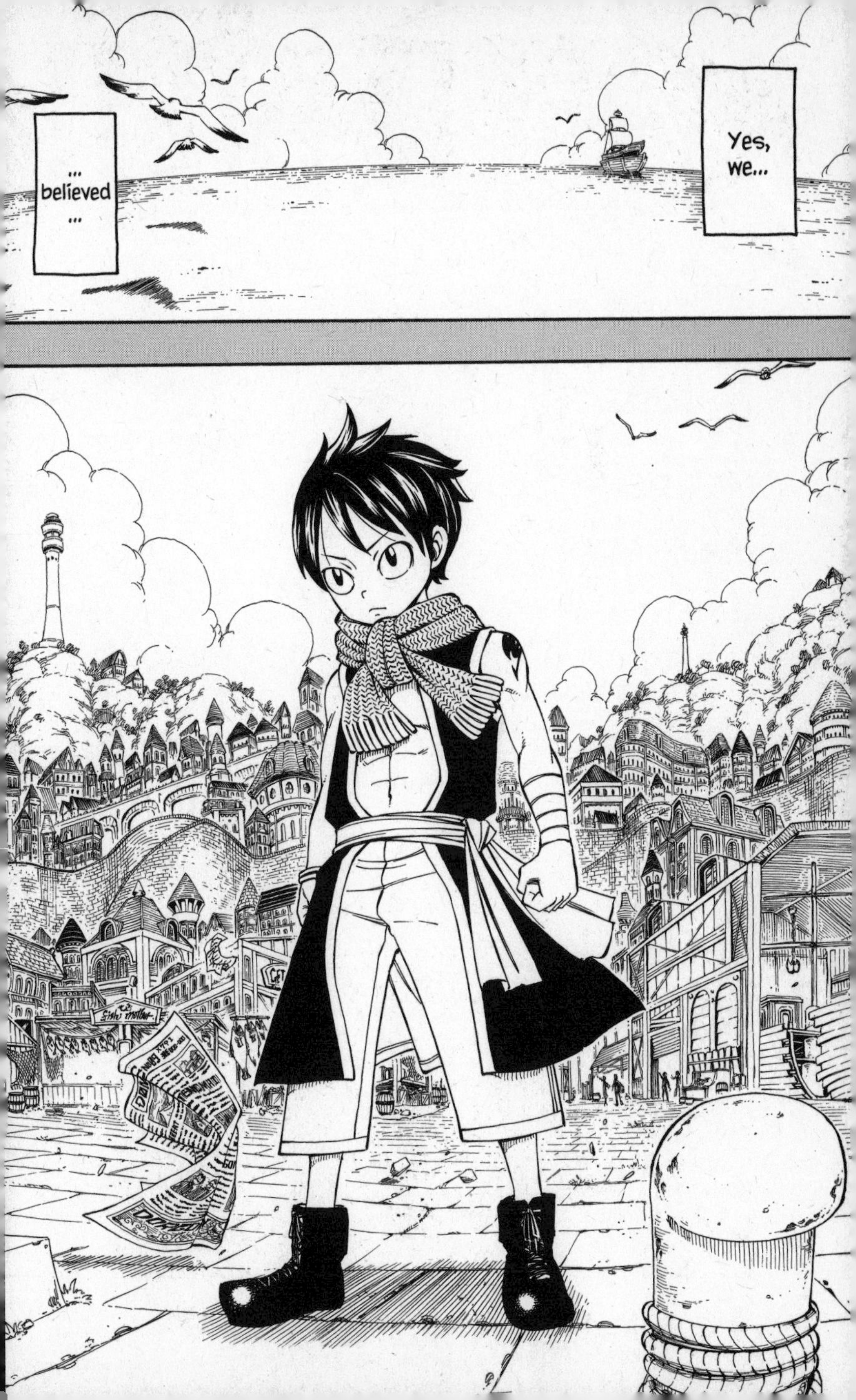
Yes, we...
... believed ...

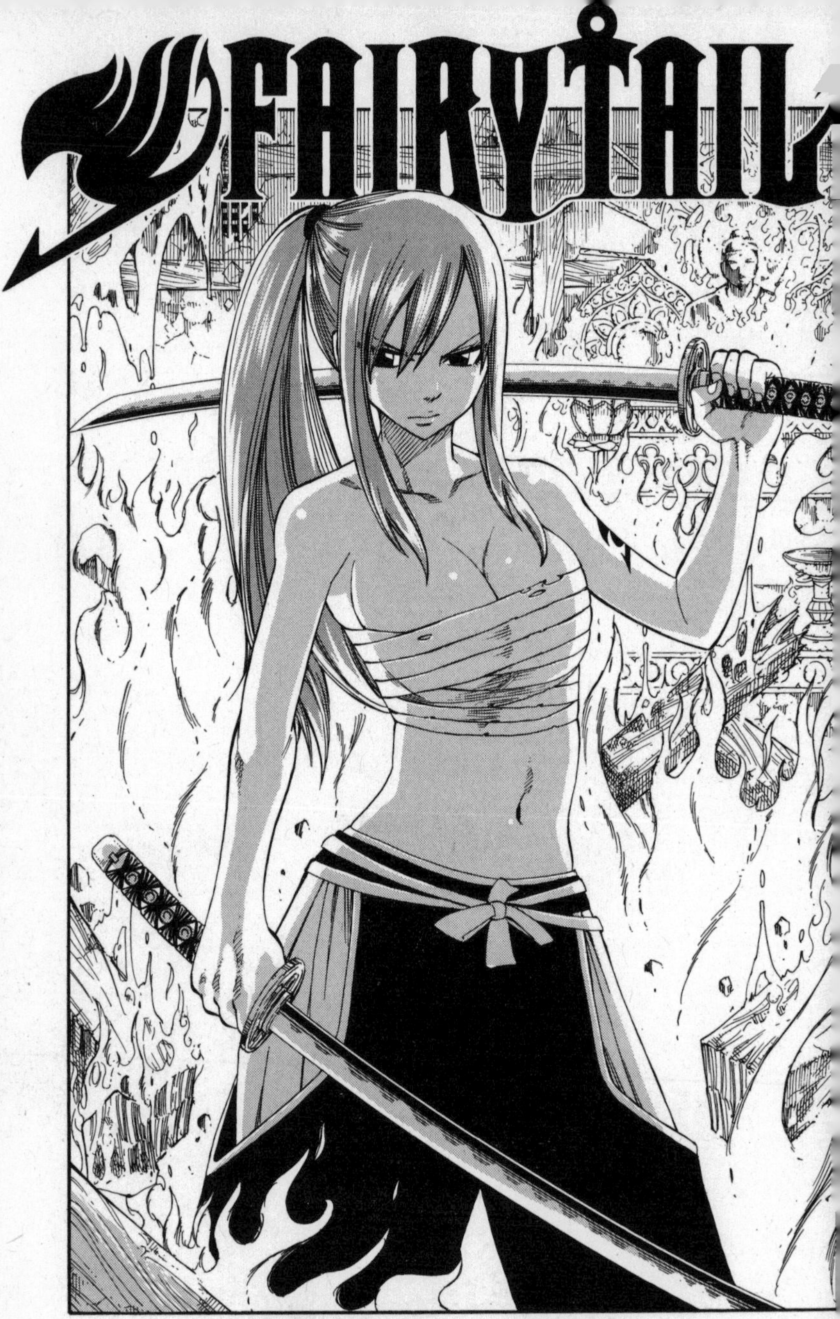
FAIRY TAIL

Chapter 235: Sirius Tree

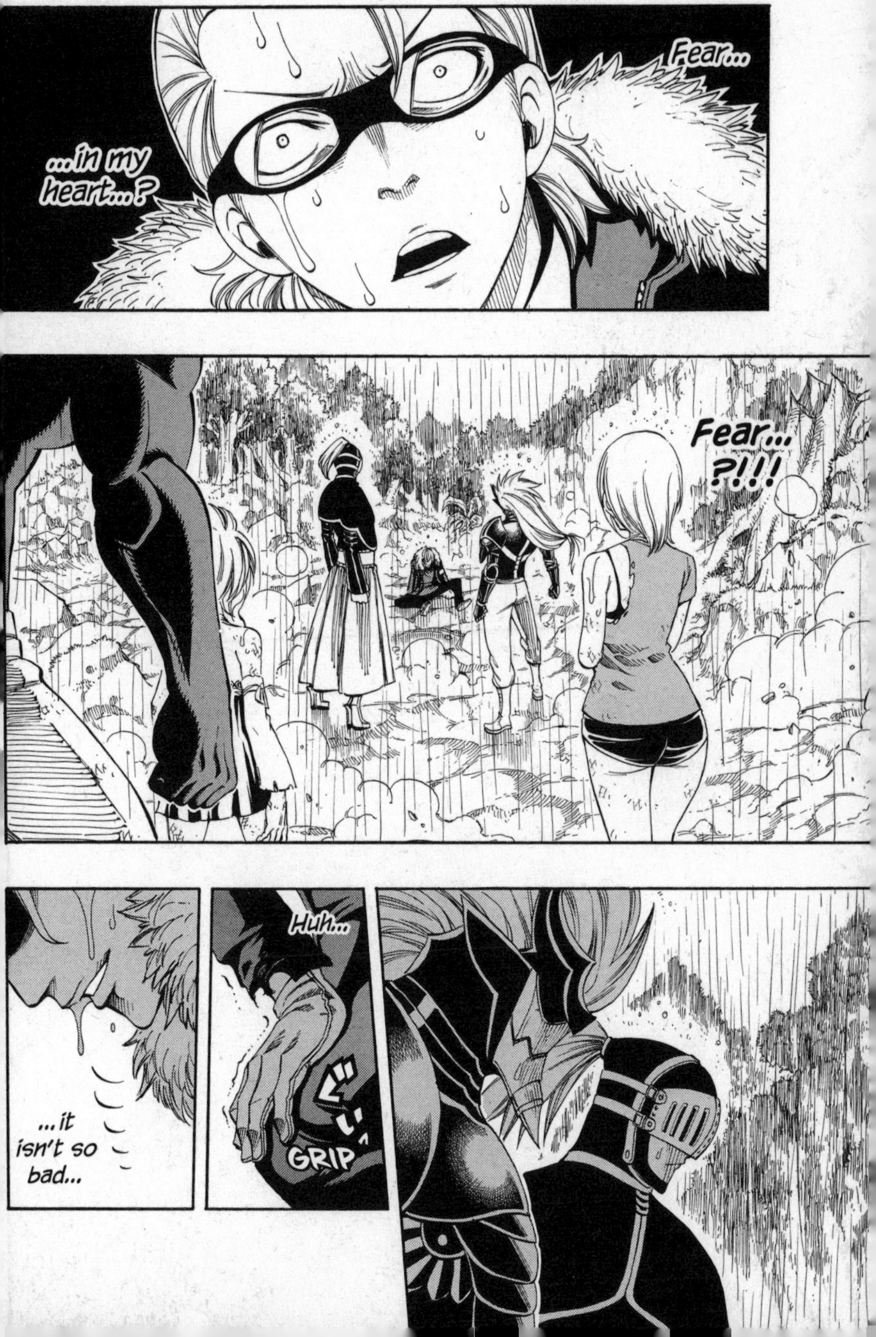
Fear...
...in my heart...?
Fear...?!!!
Huh...
GRIP
...it isn't so bad...

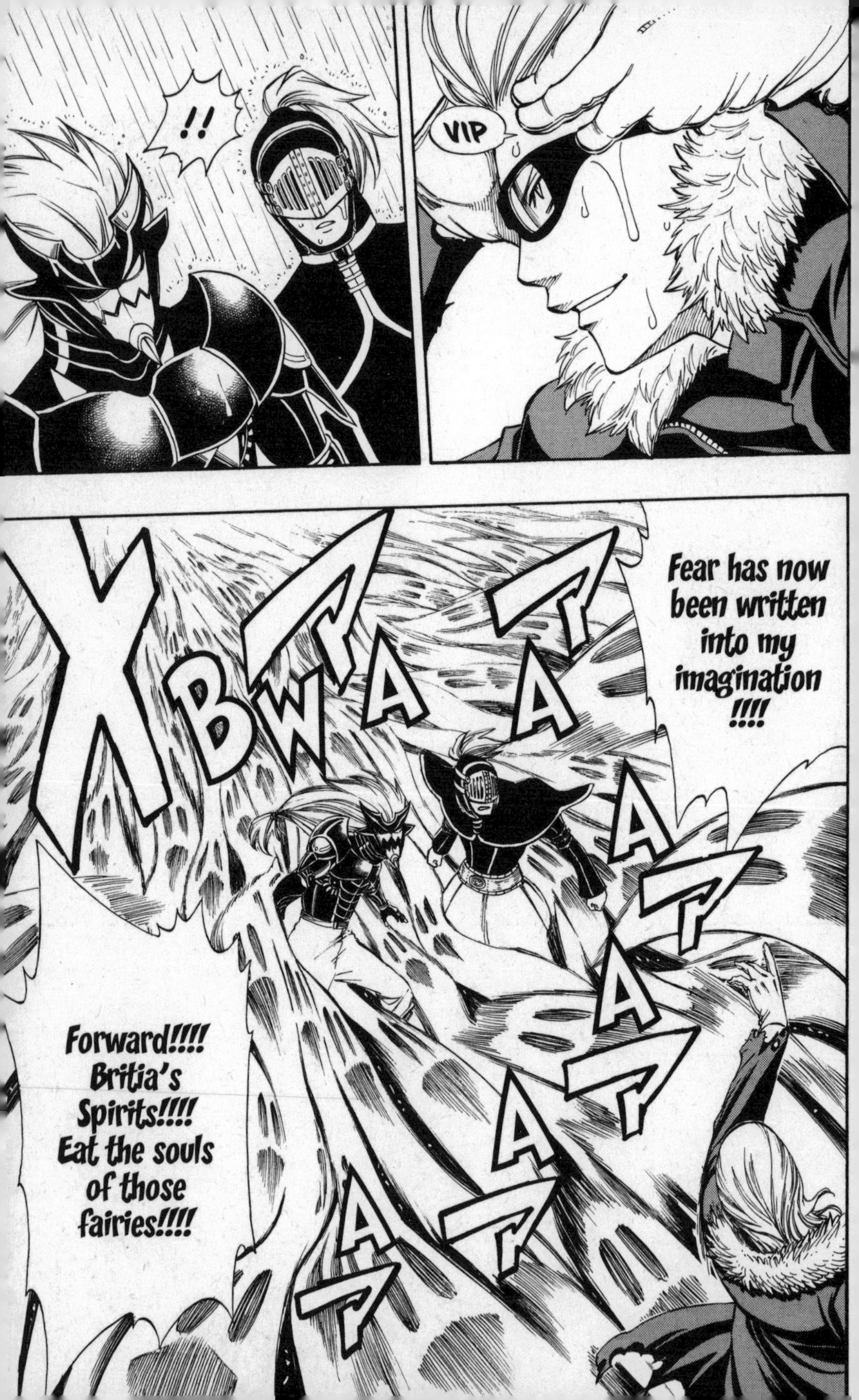
VIP
!!
Fear has now been written into my imagination !!!!
Forward!!!! Britia's Spirits!!!! Eat the souls of those fairies!!!!

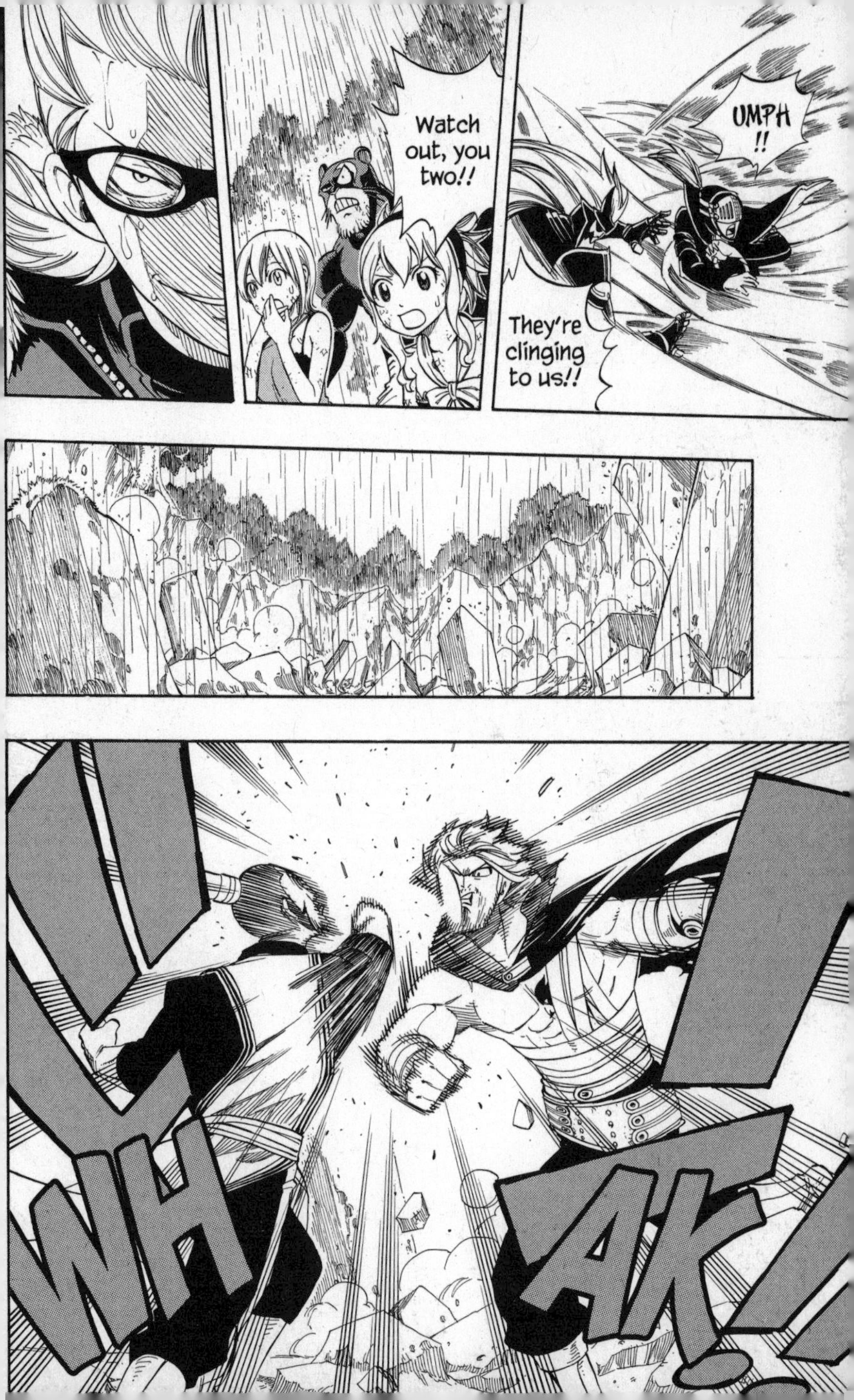
UMPH!!
They're clinging to us!!
Watch out, you two!!
WHAK!!

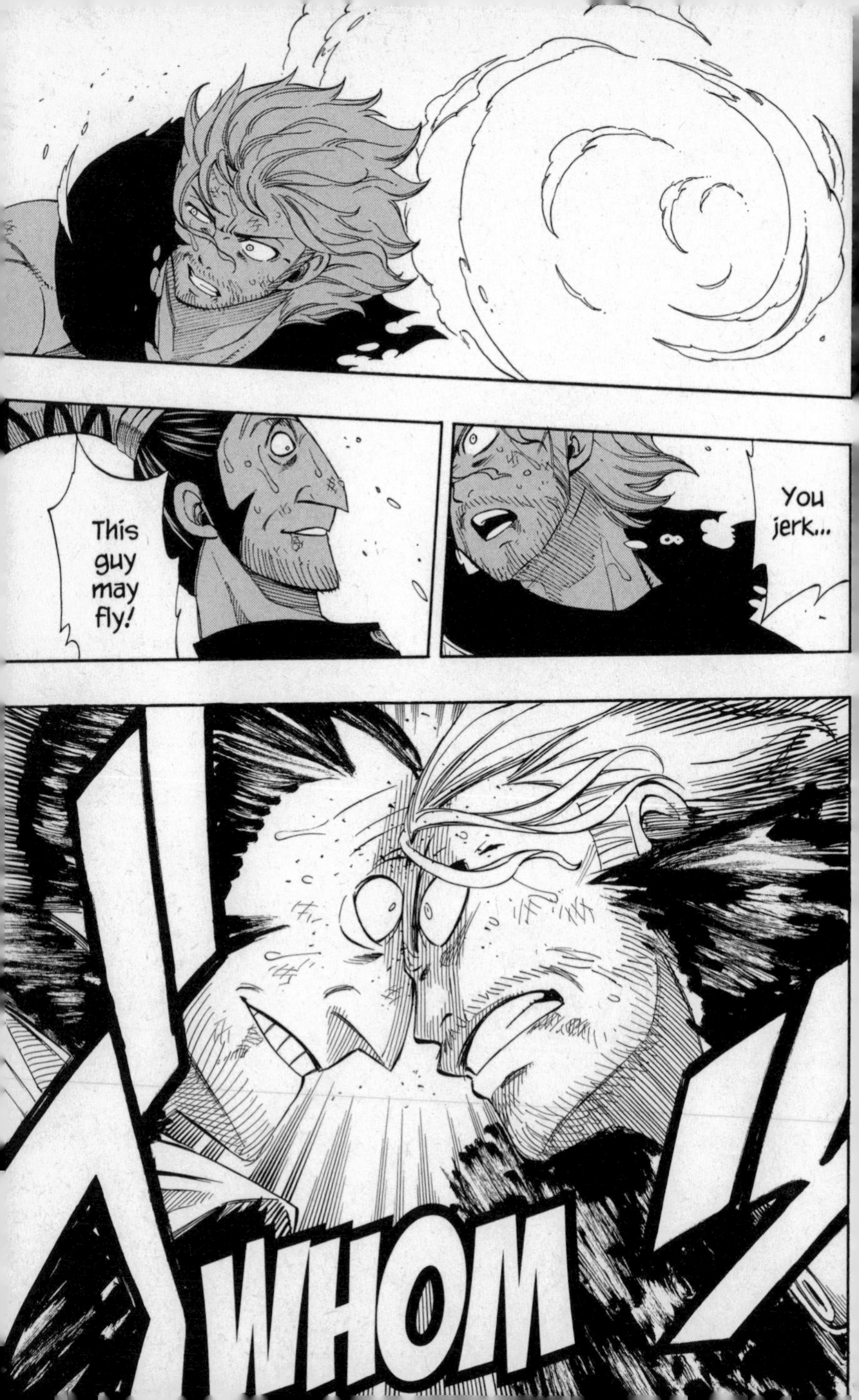
You jerk...
This guy may fly!
WHOM

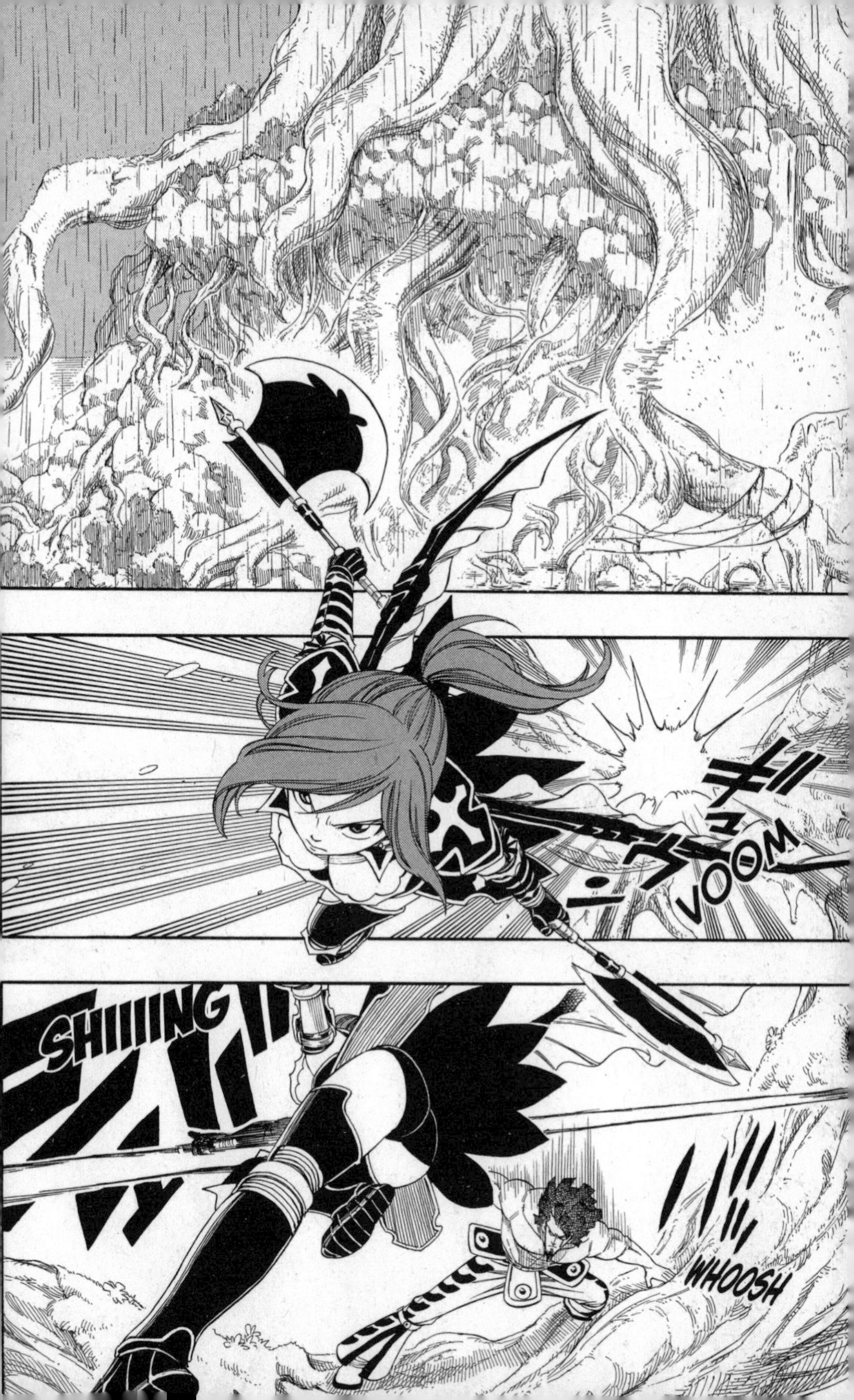
VOOM
SHIIIING
WHOOSH

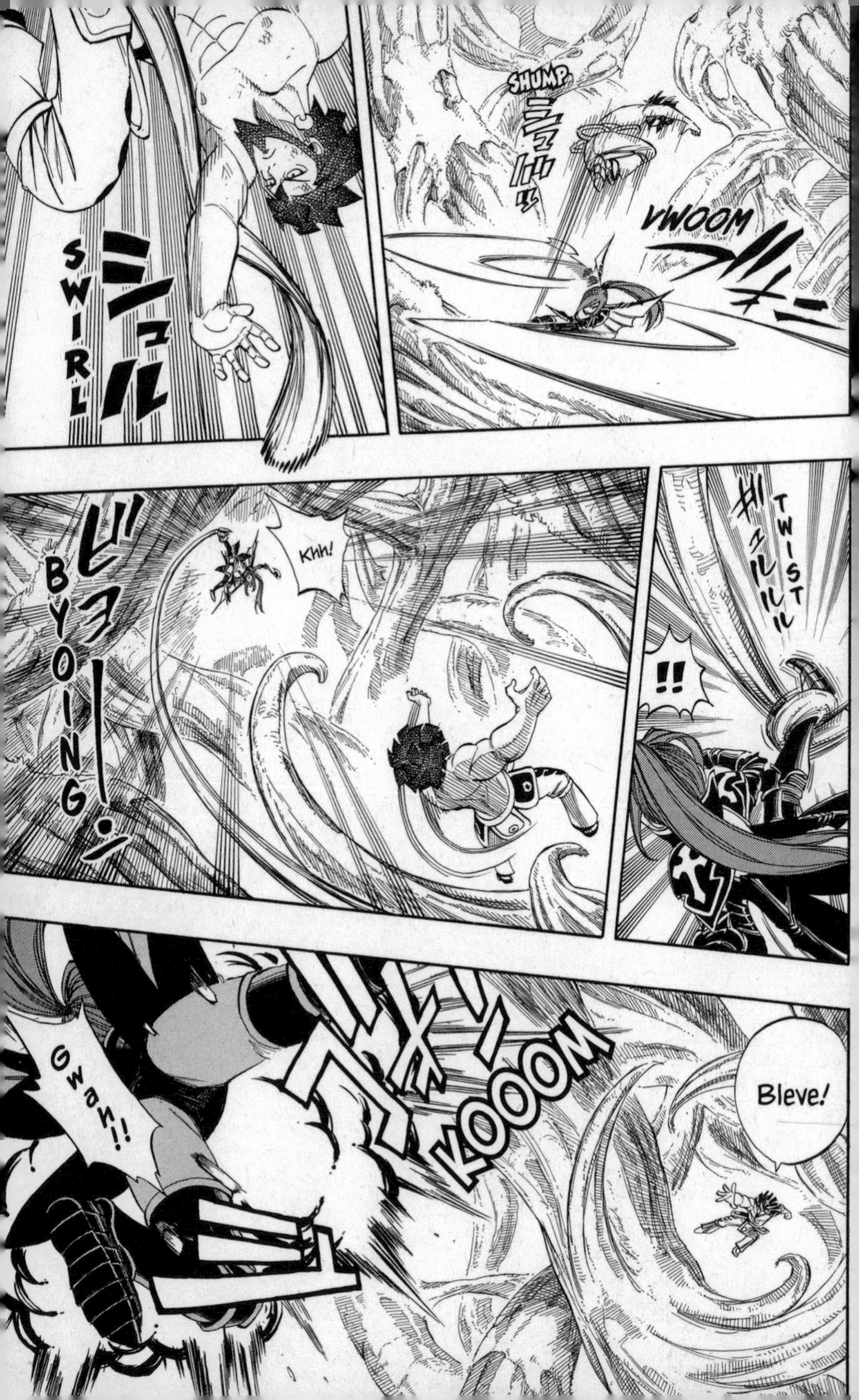
SHUMP
VWOOM
SWIRL
TWIST
!!
Khh!
BYOING
Bleve!
KOOOM
Gwah!!

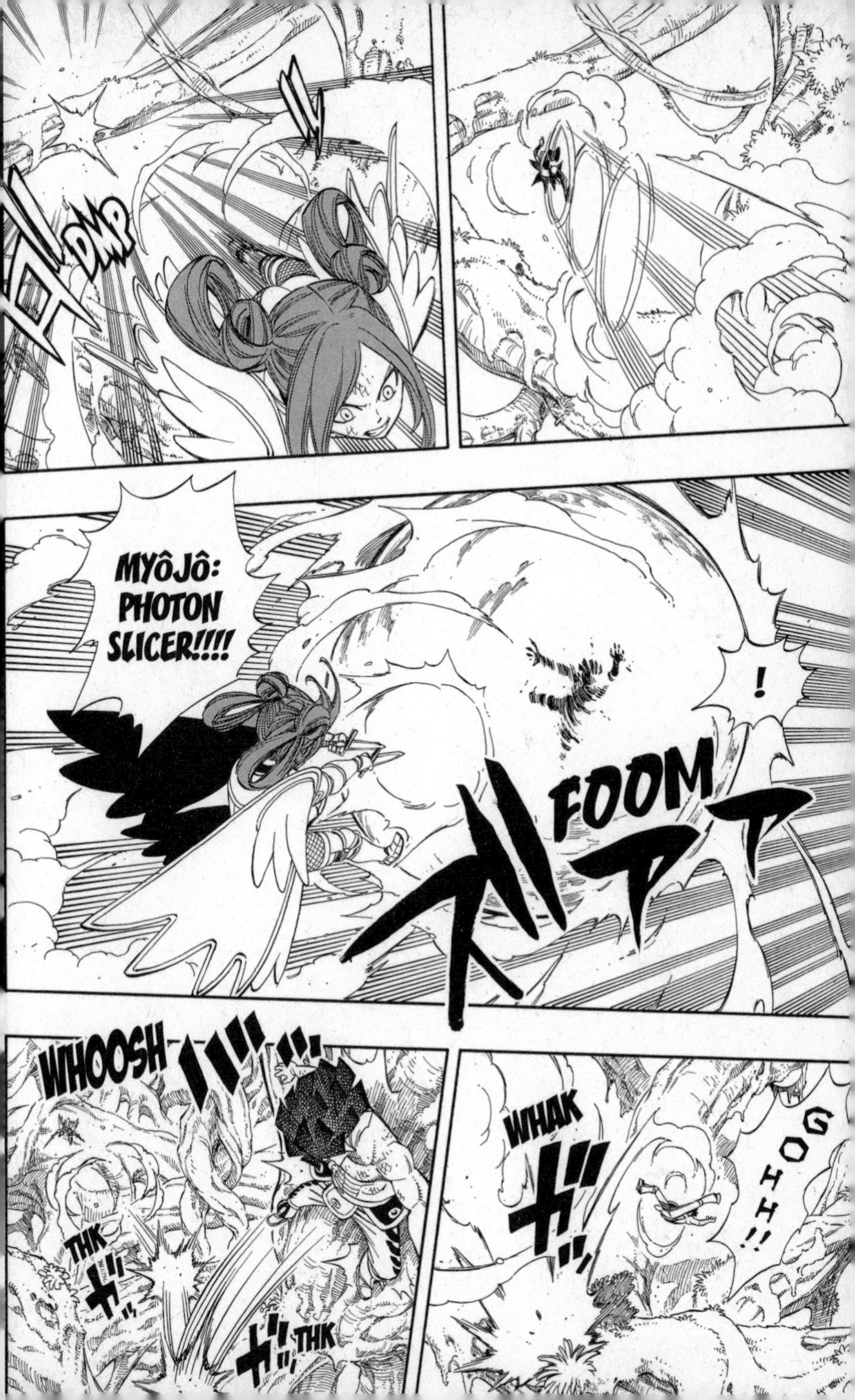
DMP
MYÔJÔ: PHOTON SLICER!!!!
!
FOOM
WHAK
GOHH!!
WHOOSH
THK
THK

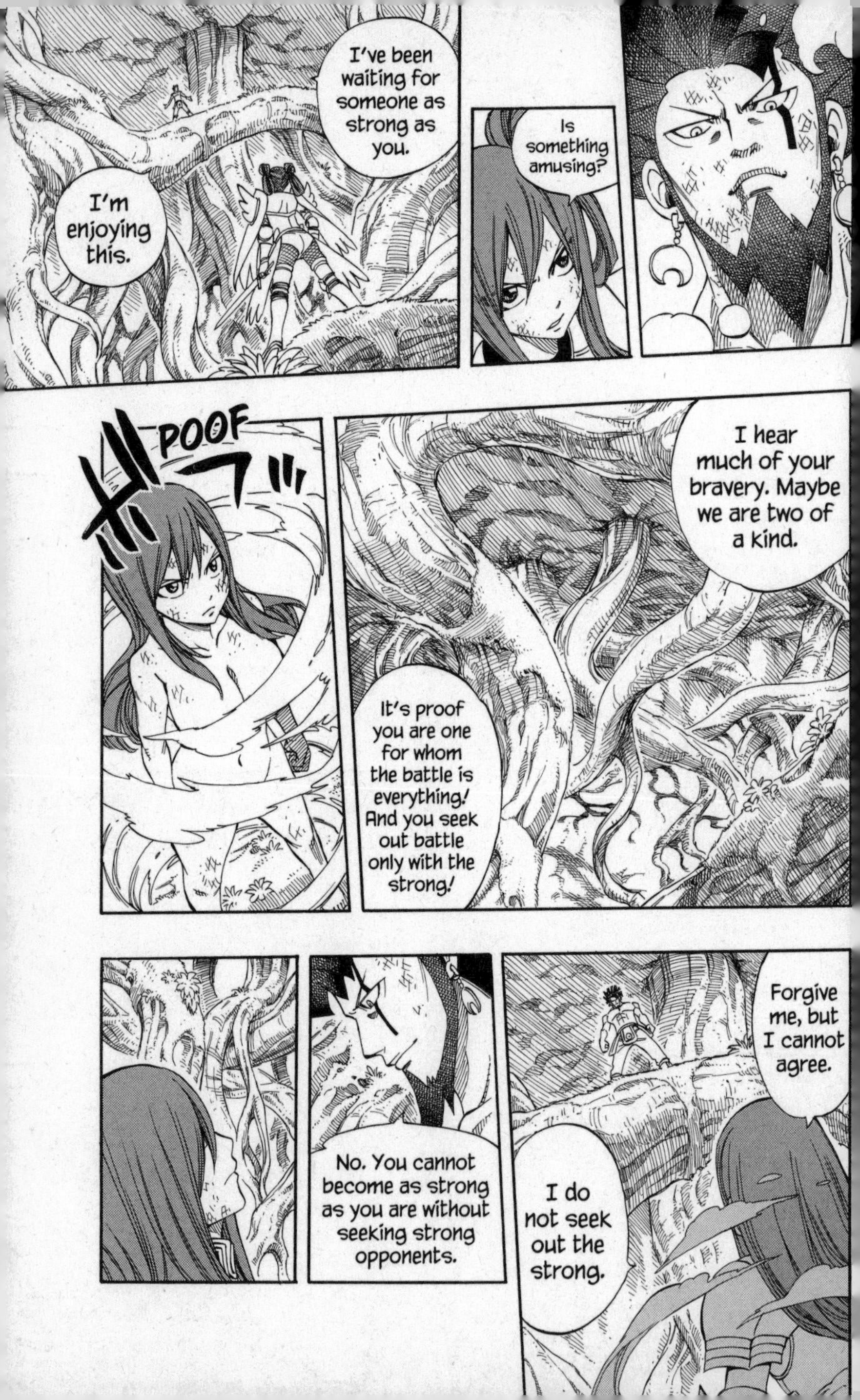
Is something amusing?
I've been waiting for someone as strong as you.
I'm enjoying this.
I hear much of your bravery. Maybe we are two of a kind.
It's proof you are one for whom the battle is everything! And you seek out battle only with the strong!
POOF
Forgive me, but I cannot agree.
I do not seek out the strong.
No. You cannot become as strong as you are without seeking strong opponents.

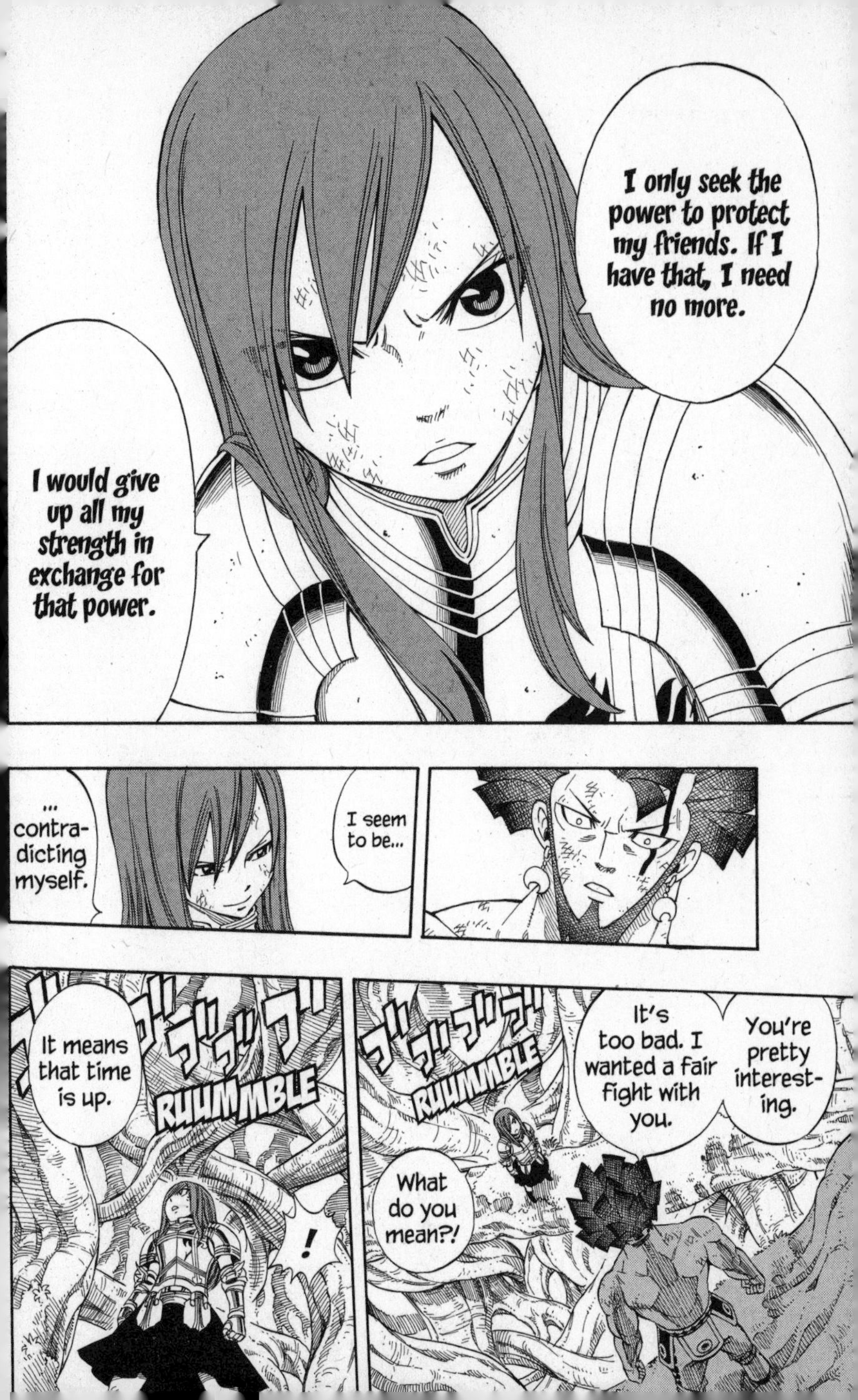
I only seek the power to protect my friends. If I have that, I need no more.
I would give up all my strength in exchange for that power.
I seem to be...
... contra-dicting myself.
You're pretty interest-ing.
It's too bad. I wanted a fair fight with you.
RUUMMBLE
What do you mean?!
It means that time is up.
RUUMMBLE
!

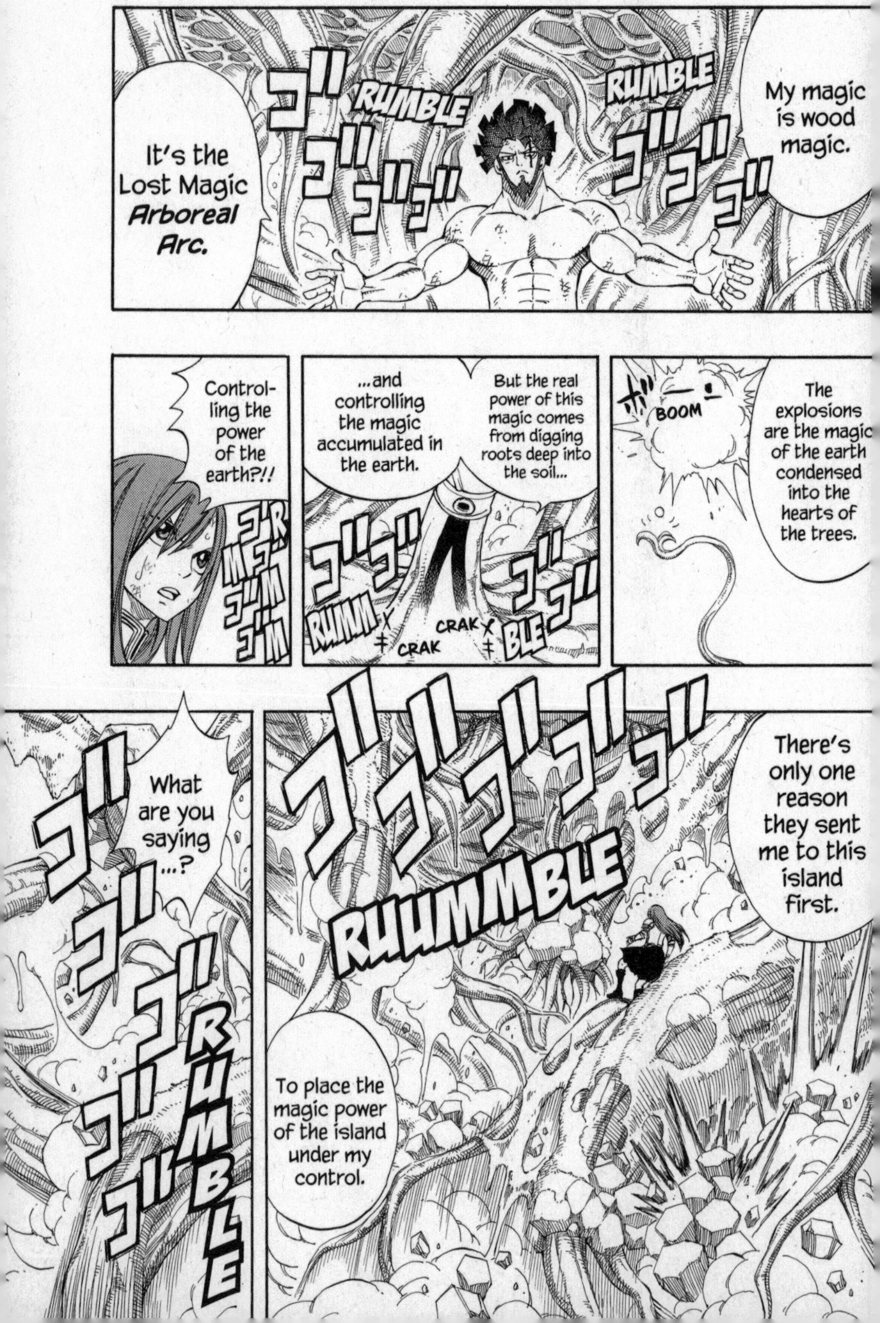

My magic is wood magic.
RUMBLE
RUMBLE
It's the Lost Magic *Arboreal Arc.*
The explosions are the magic of the earth condensed into the hearts of the trees.
BOOM
But the real power of this magic comes from digging roots deep into the soil...
...and controlling the magic accumulated in the earth.
RUMMBLE
CRAK
CRAK
Controlling the power of the earth?!!
RUMBLE
There's only one reason they sent me to this island first.
RUUMMBLE
To place the magic power of the island under my control.
What are you saying...?
RUMBLE

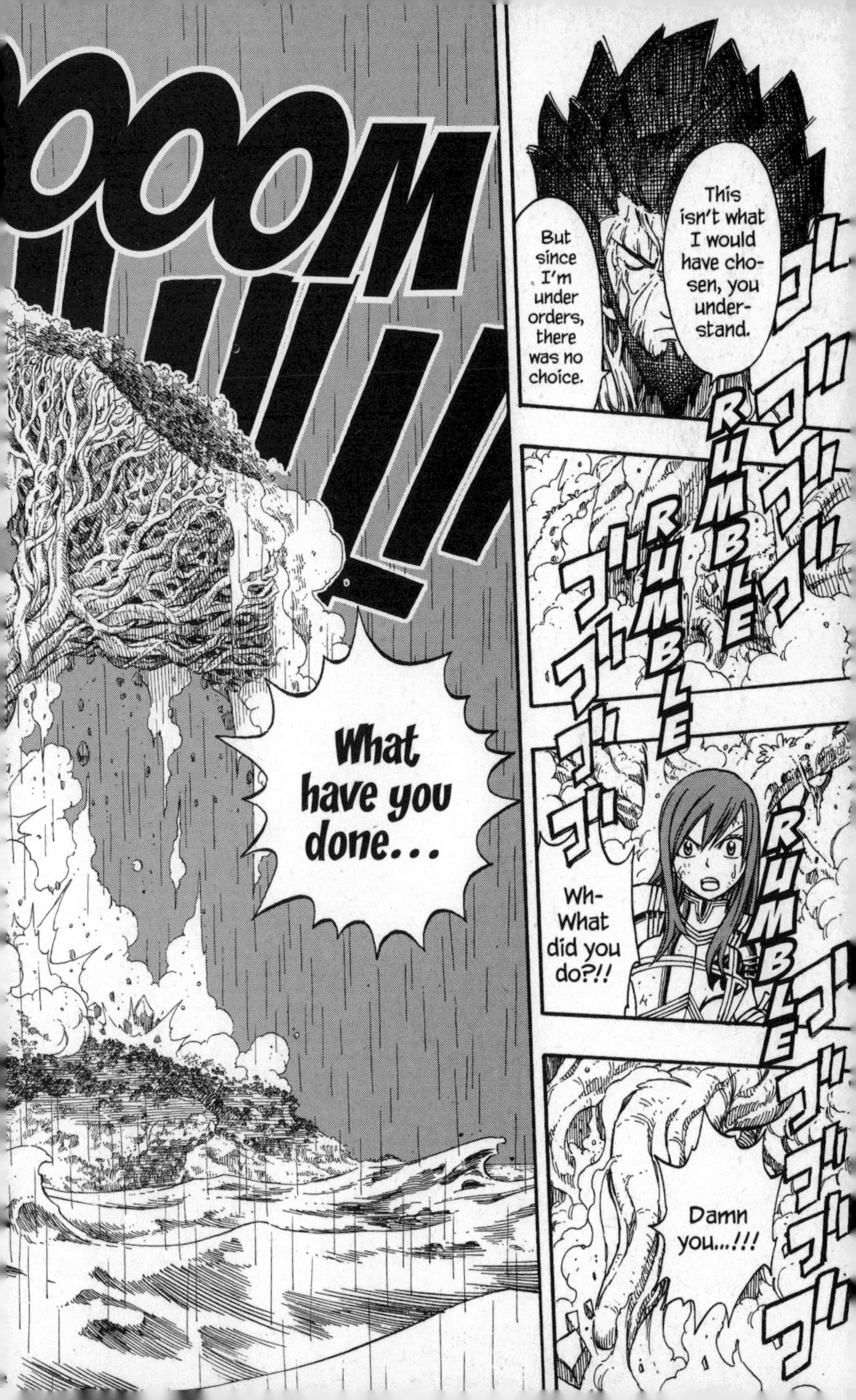
This isn't what I would have cho- sen, you under- stand.
But since I'm under orders, there was no choice.
RUMBLE
RUMBLE
Wh- What did you do?!!
RUMBLE
Damn you...!!!
OOOM!!!!
What have you done...

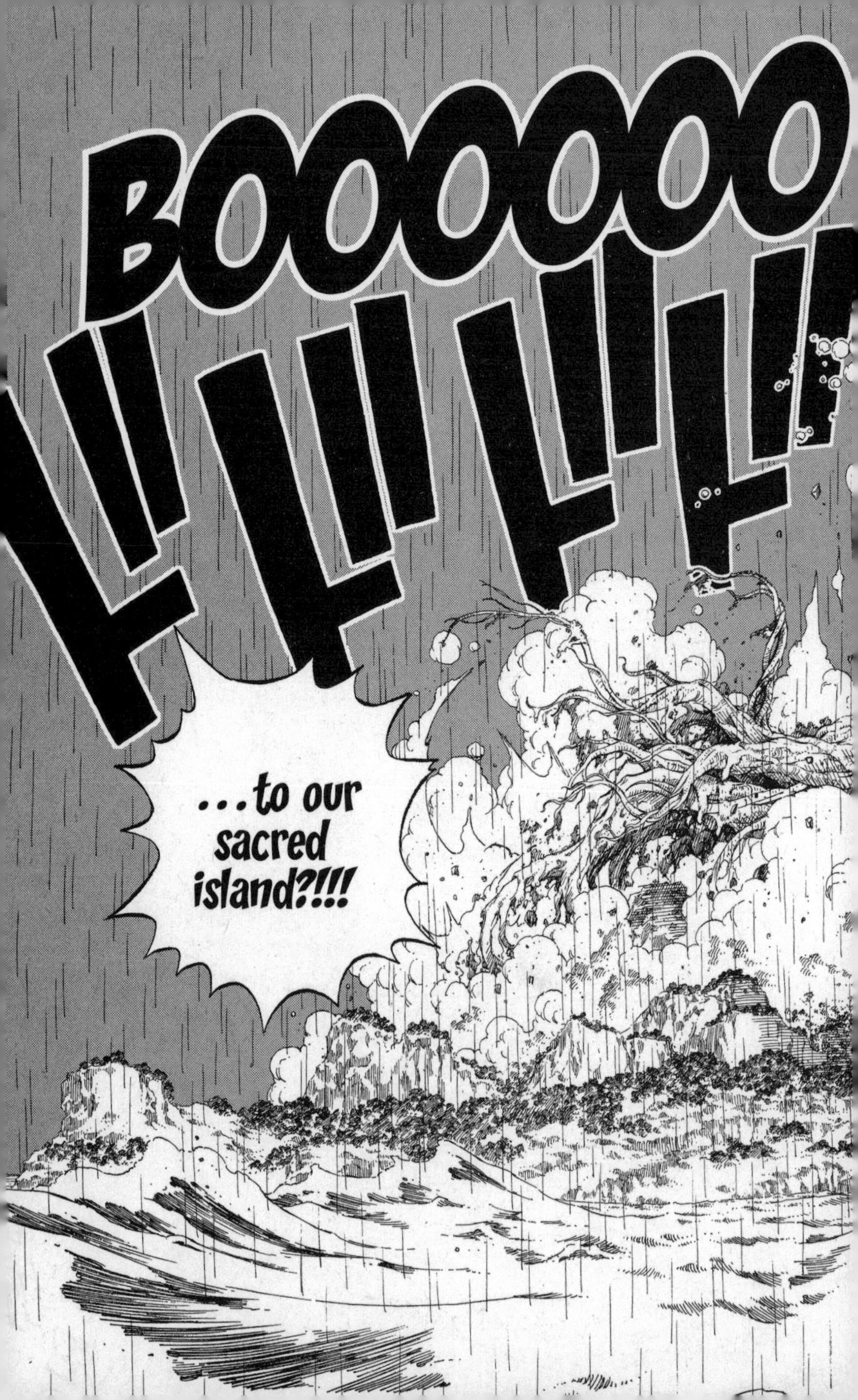
BOOOOOOM!!!!!!
...to our sacred island?!!!

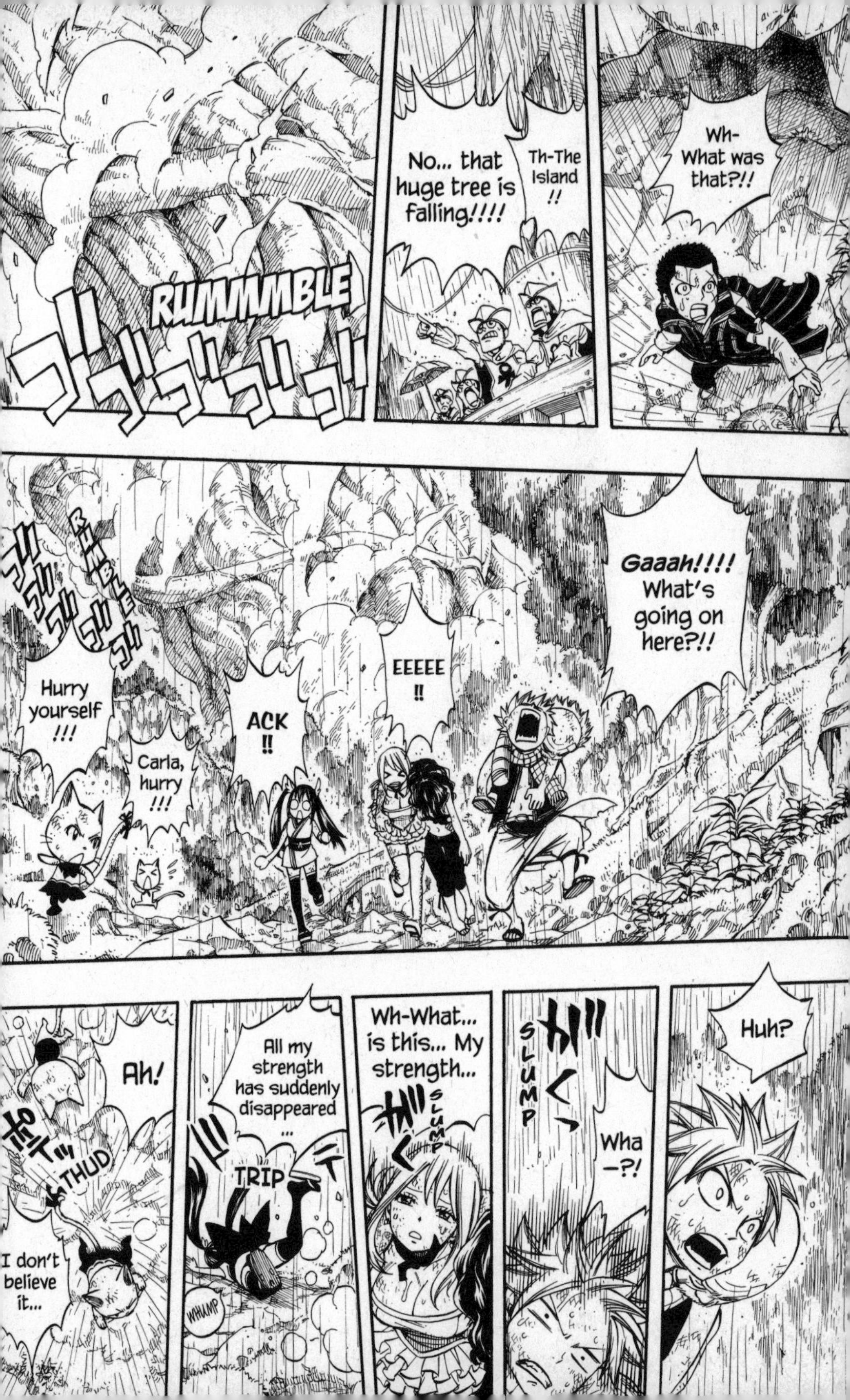
Wh- What was that?!!
Th-The Island !!
No... that huge tree is falling!!!!
RUMMMBLE
Gaaah!!!! What's going on here?!!
EEEEE !!
ACK !!
Carla, hurry !!!
Hurry yourself !!!
RUMBLE
Huh?
Wha -?!
SLUMP
Wh-What... is this... My strength...
SLUMP
All my strength has suddenly disappeared ...
TRIP
WHAMP
Ah!
THUD
I don't believe it...

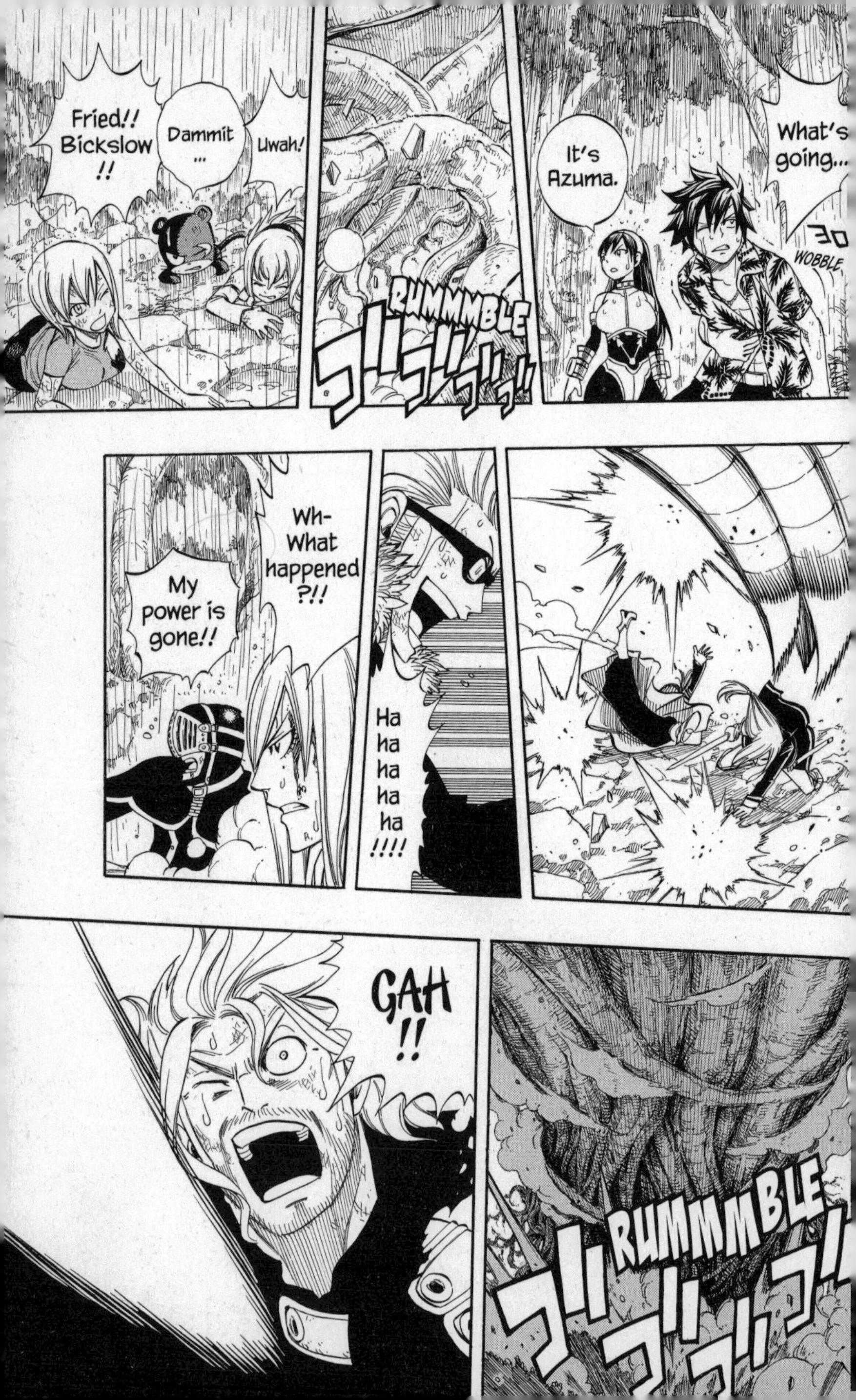
What's going...
It's Azuma.
WOBBLE
RUMMMBLE
Uwah!
Dammit ...
Fried!! Bickslow !!
Ha ha ha ha ha !!!!
Wh- What happened ?!!
My power is gone!!
RUMMMBLE
GAH !!

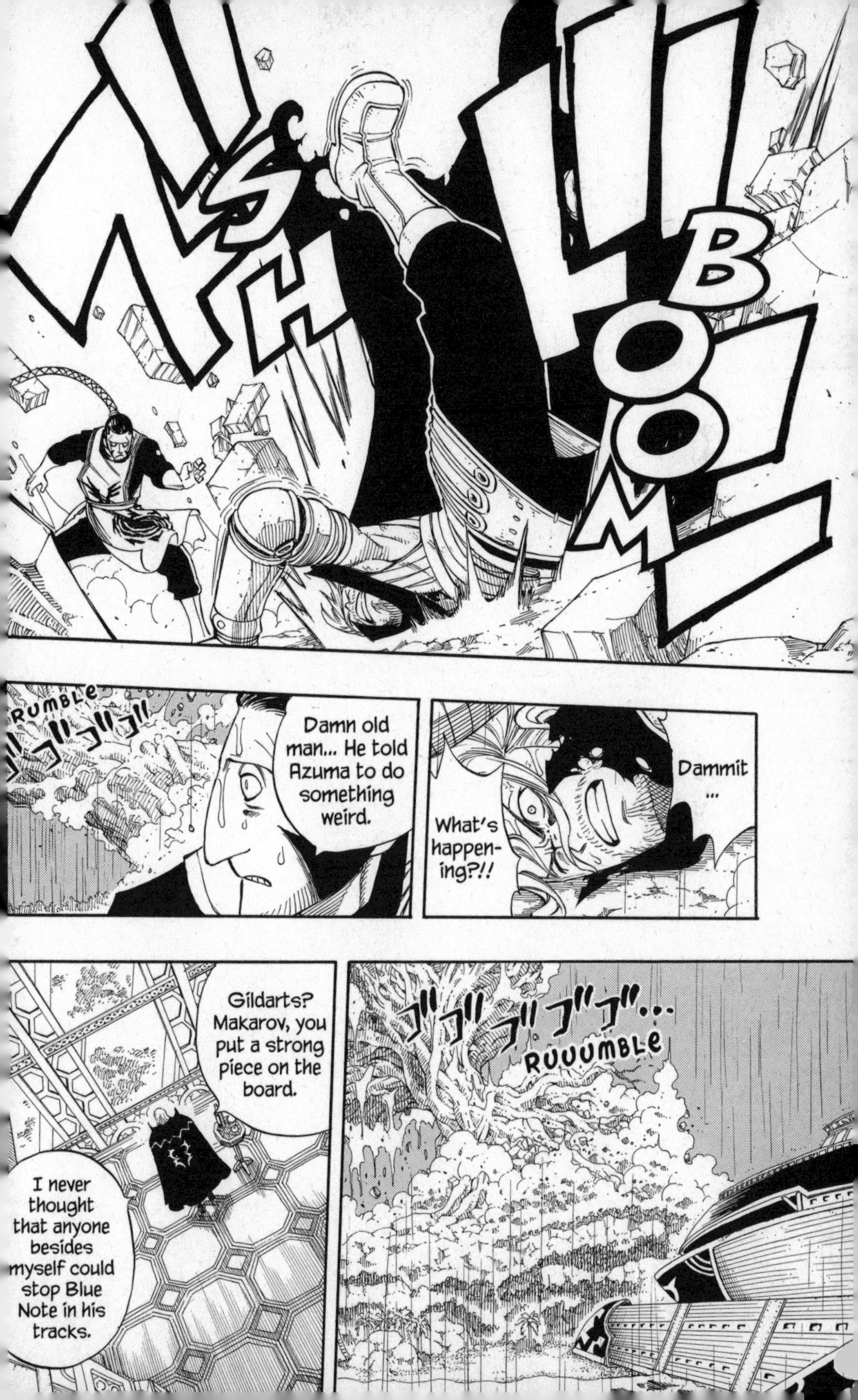
SH
BOOM
Dammit...
What's happening?!!
RUMBLE
Damn old man... He told Azuma to do something weird.
RUUUMBLE
Gildarts? Makarov, you put a strong piece on the board.
I never thought that anyone besides myself could stop Blue Note in his tracks.

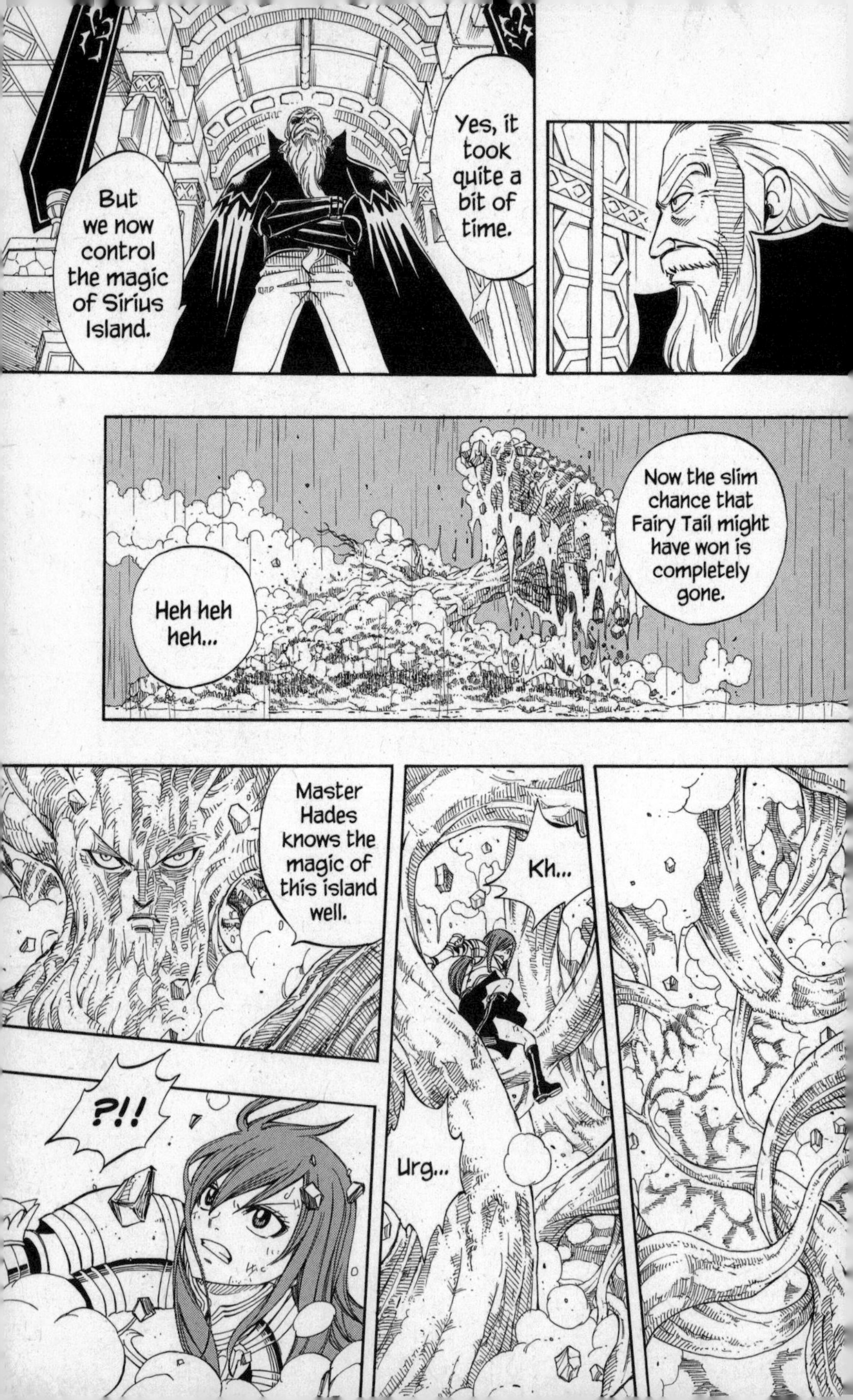
Yes, it took quite a bit of time.
But we now control the magic of Sirius Island.
Now the slim chance that Fairy Tail might have won is completely gone.
Heh heh heh...
Kh...
Urg...
Master Hades knows the magic of this island well.
?!!

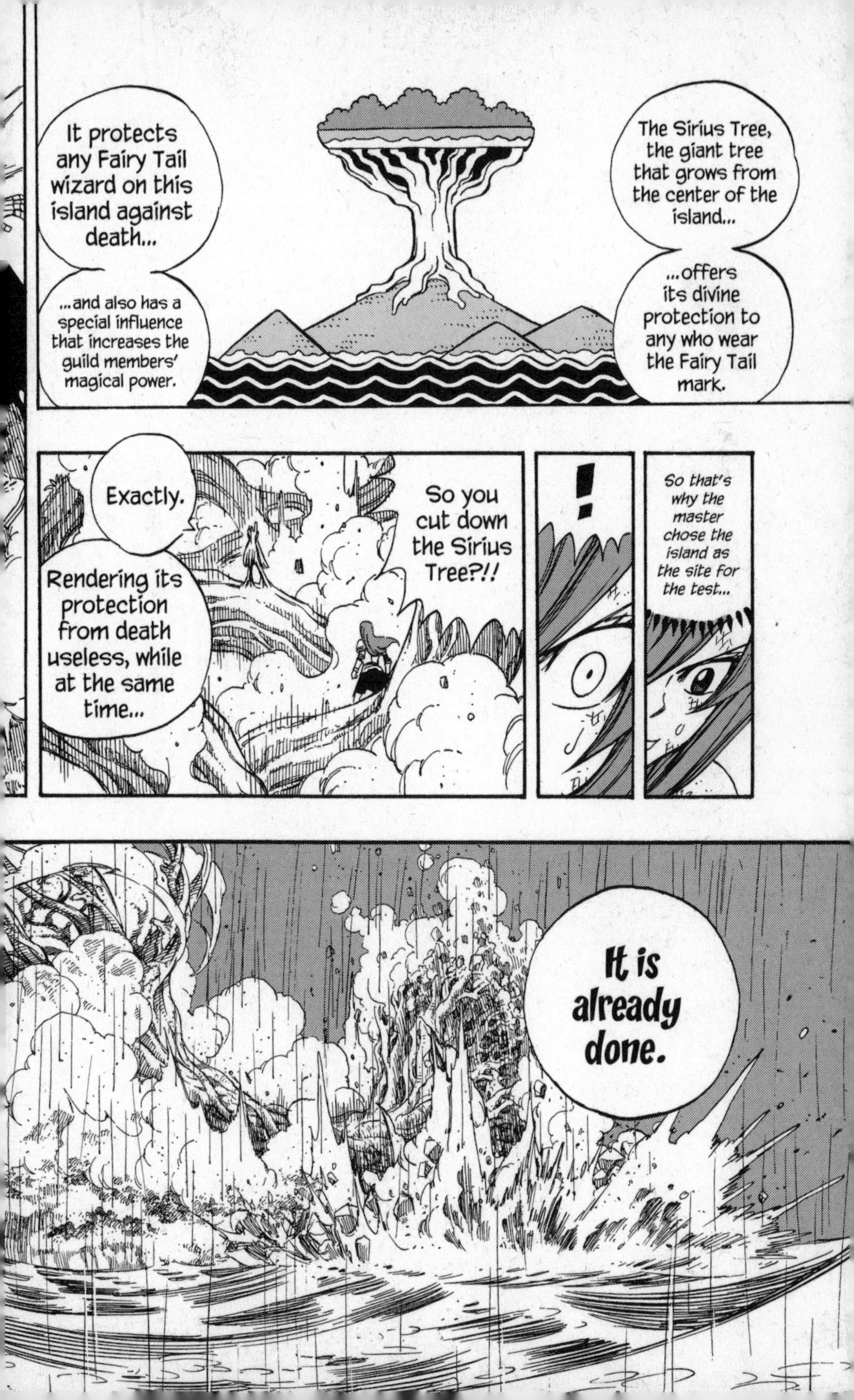
The Sirius Tree, the giant tree that grows from the center of the island...
...offers its divine protection to any who wear the Fairy Tail mark.
It protects any Fairy Tail wizard on this island against death...
...and also has a special influence that increases the guild members' magical power.
So that's why the master chose the island as the site for the test...
!
So you cut down the Sirius Tree?!!
Exactly.
Rendering its protection from death useless, while at the same time...
It is already done.

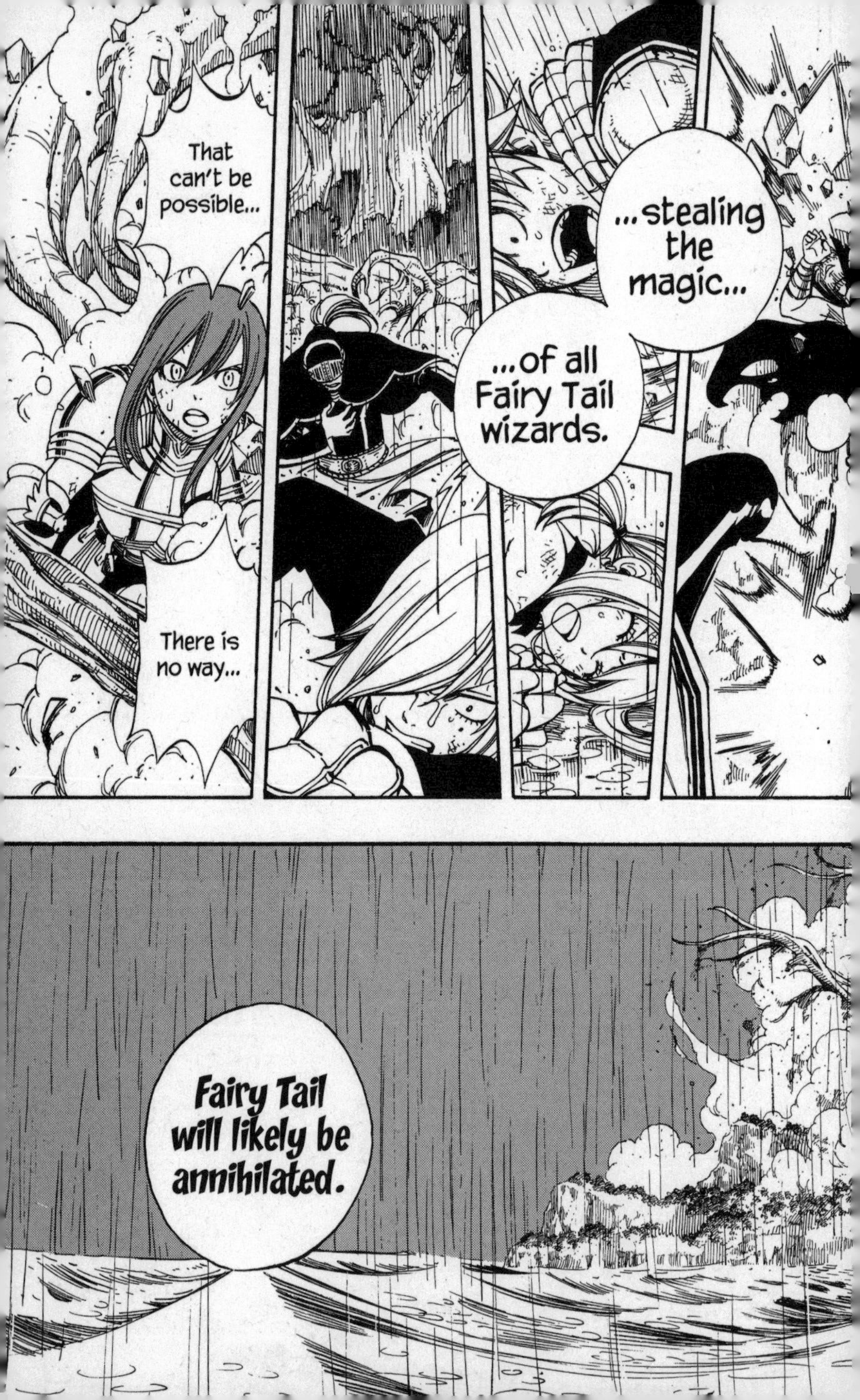
...stealing the magic...
...of all Fairy Tail wizards.
That can't be possible...
There is no way...
Fairy Tail will likely be annihilated.

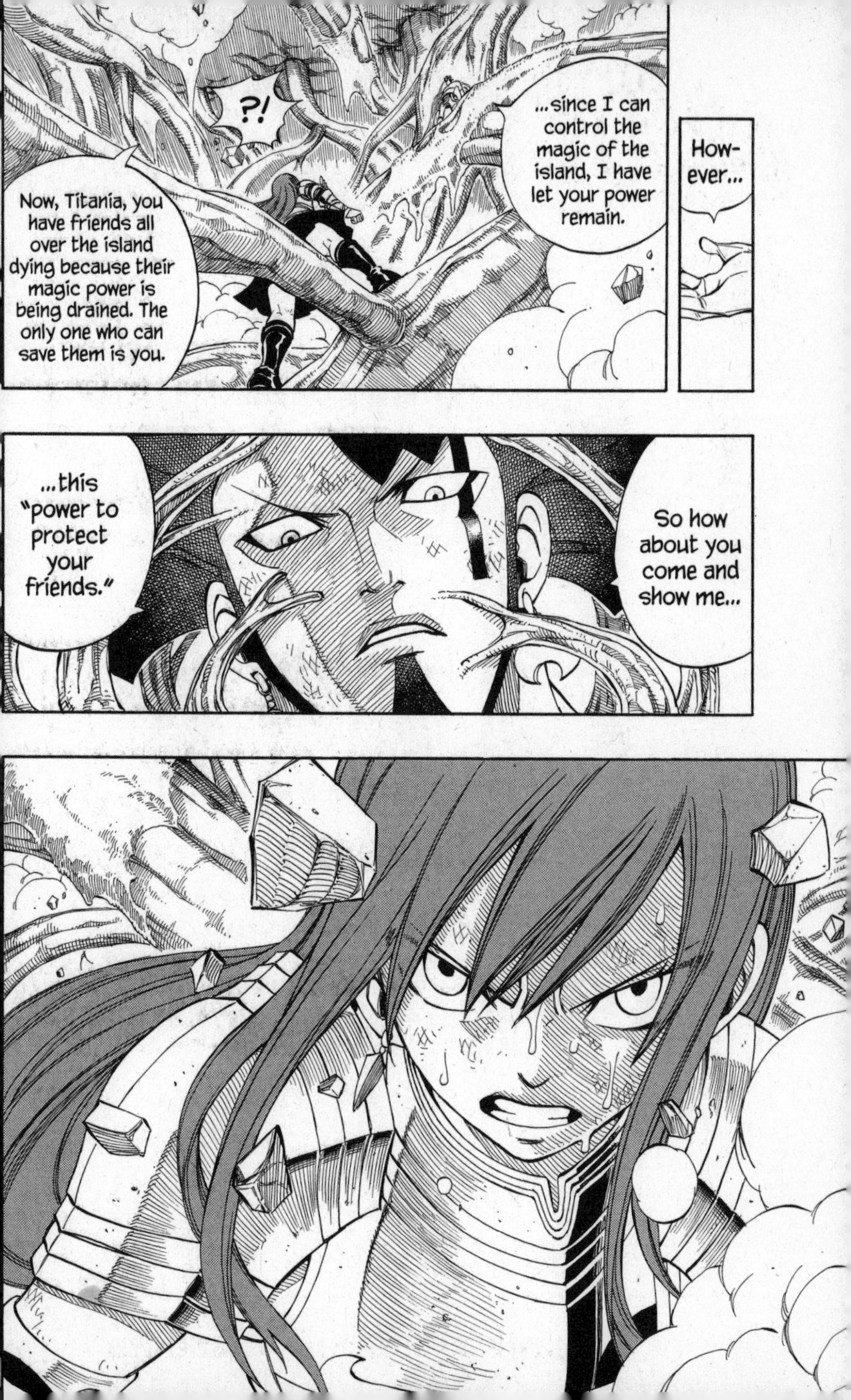
How-ever...
...since I can control the magic of the island, I have let your power remain.
?!
Now, Titania, you have friends all over the island dying because their magic power is being drained. The only one who can save them is you.
So how about you come and show me...
...this "power to protect your friends."

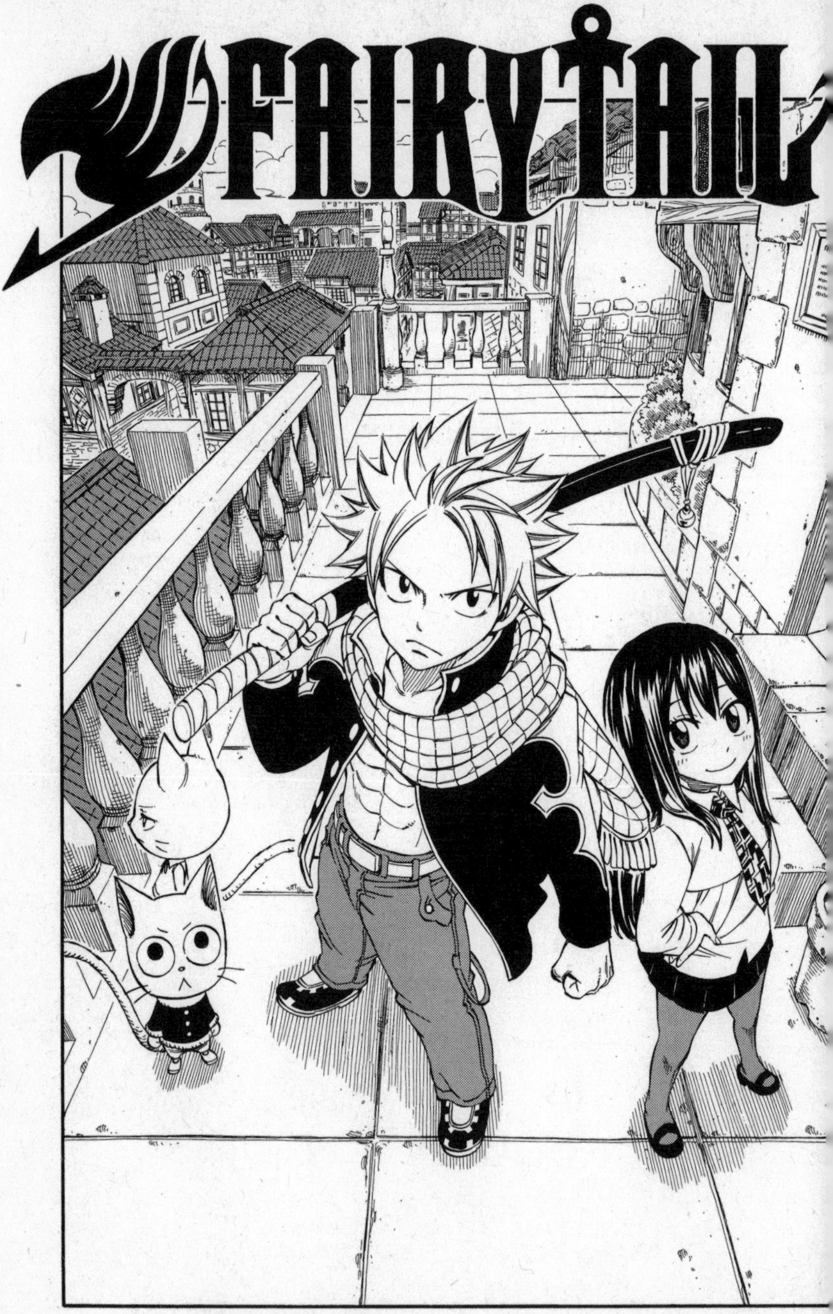
FAIRY TAIL

Chapter 236: Erza vs. Azuma

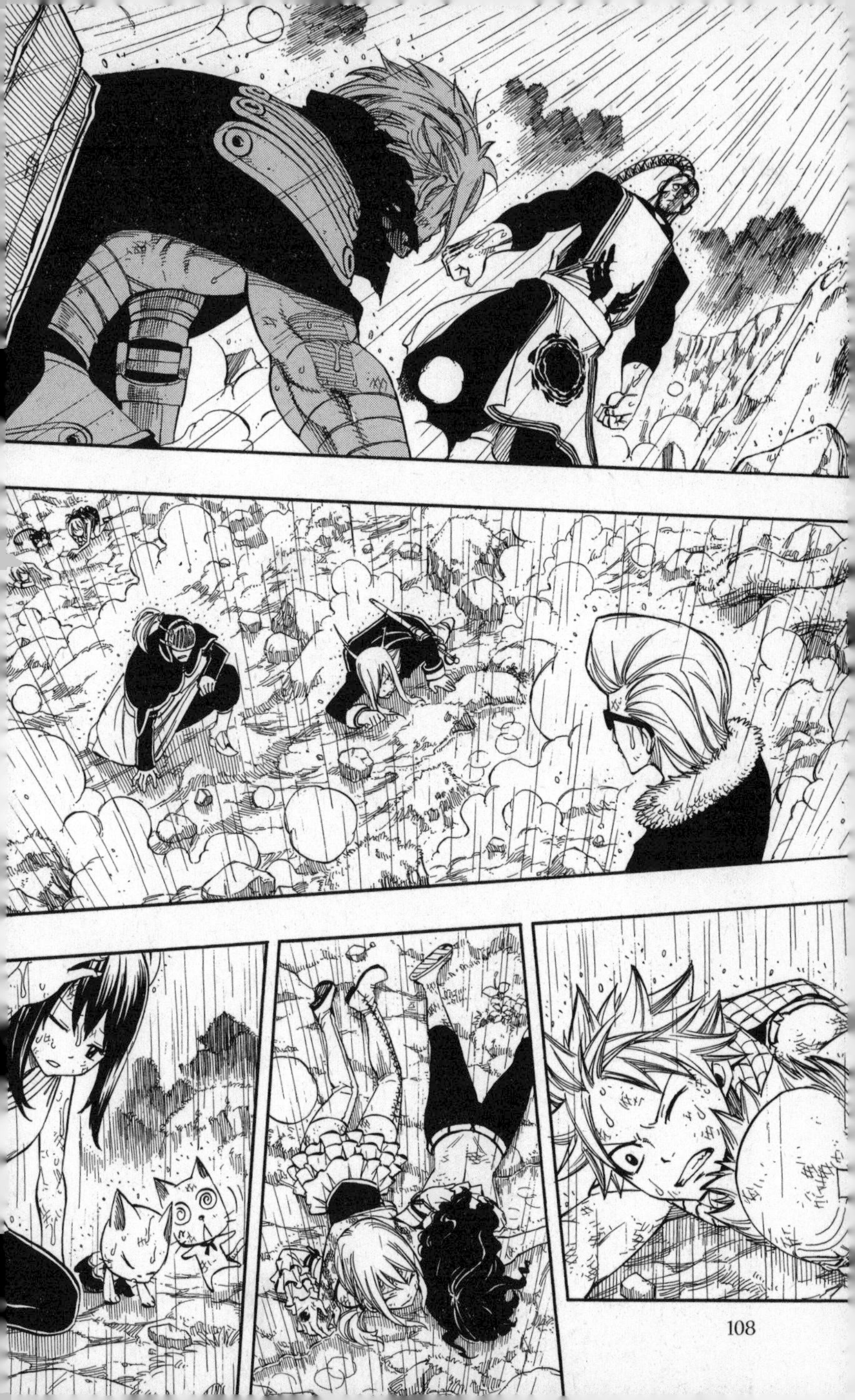

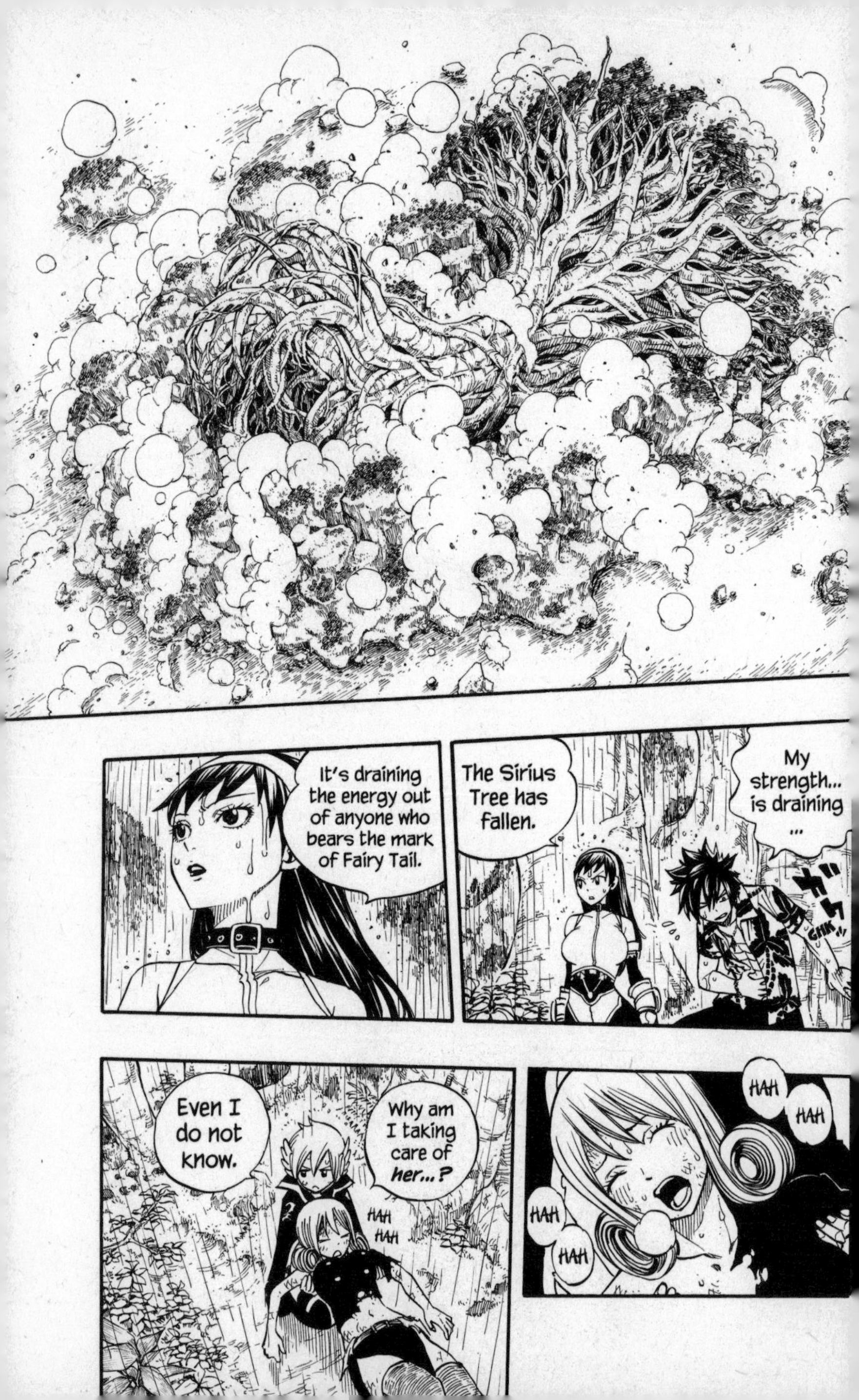
My strength... is draining ...
GHK
The Sirius Tree has fallen.
It's draining the energy out of anyone who bears the mark of Fairy Tail.
HAH
HAH
HAH
HAH
Why am I taking care of *her*...?
Even I do not know.
HAH HAH

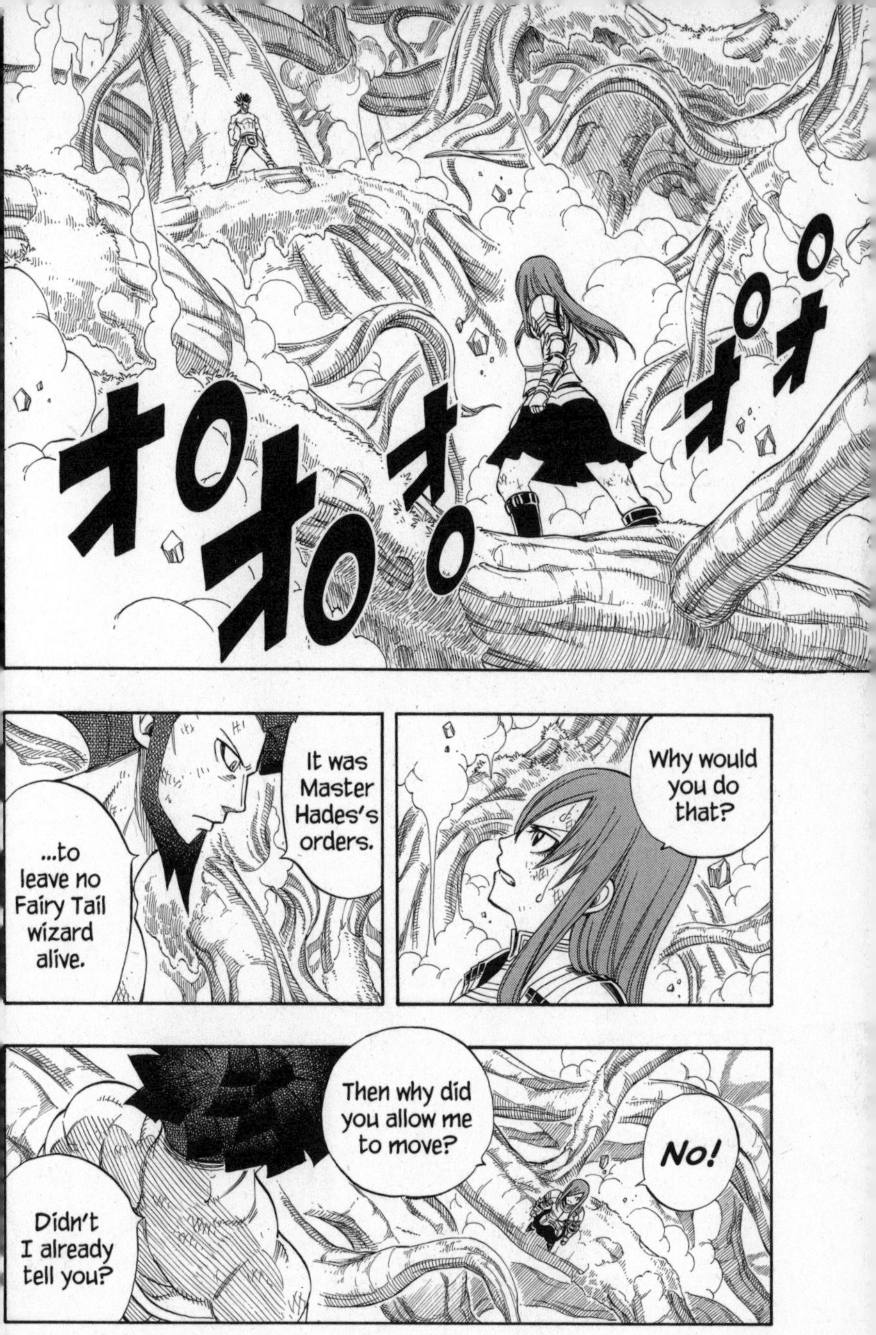
Why would you do that?
It was Master Hades's orders.
...to leave no Fairy Tail wizard alive.
No!
Then why did you allow me to move?
Didn't I already tell you?

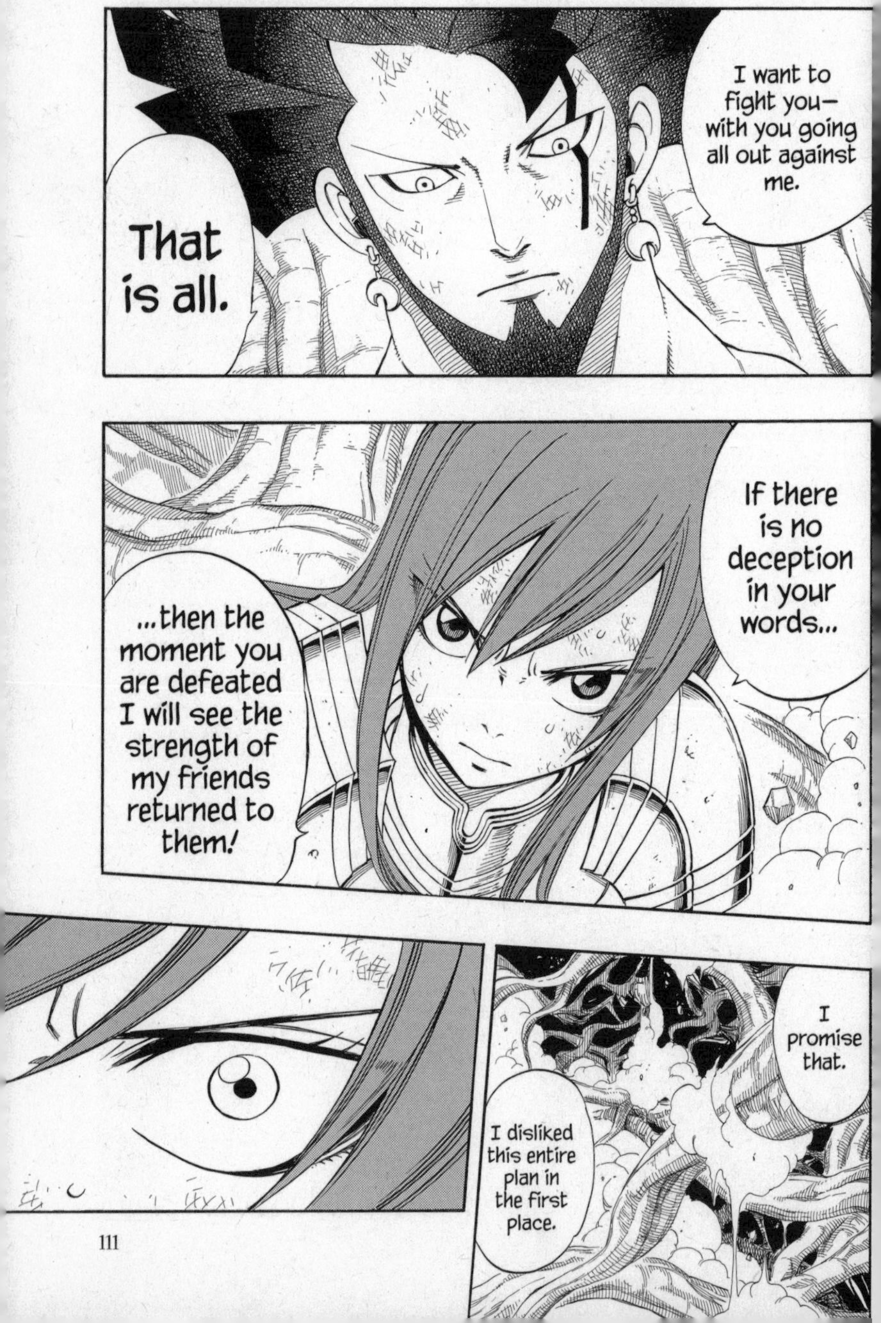
I want to fight you— with you going all out against me.
That is all.
If there is no deception in your words...
...then the moment you are defeated I will see the strength of my friends returned to them!
I promise that.
I disliked this entire plan in the first place.

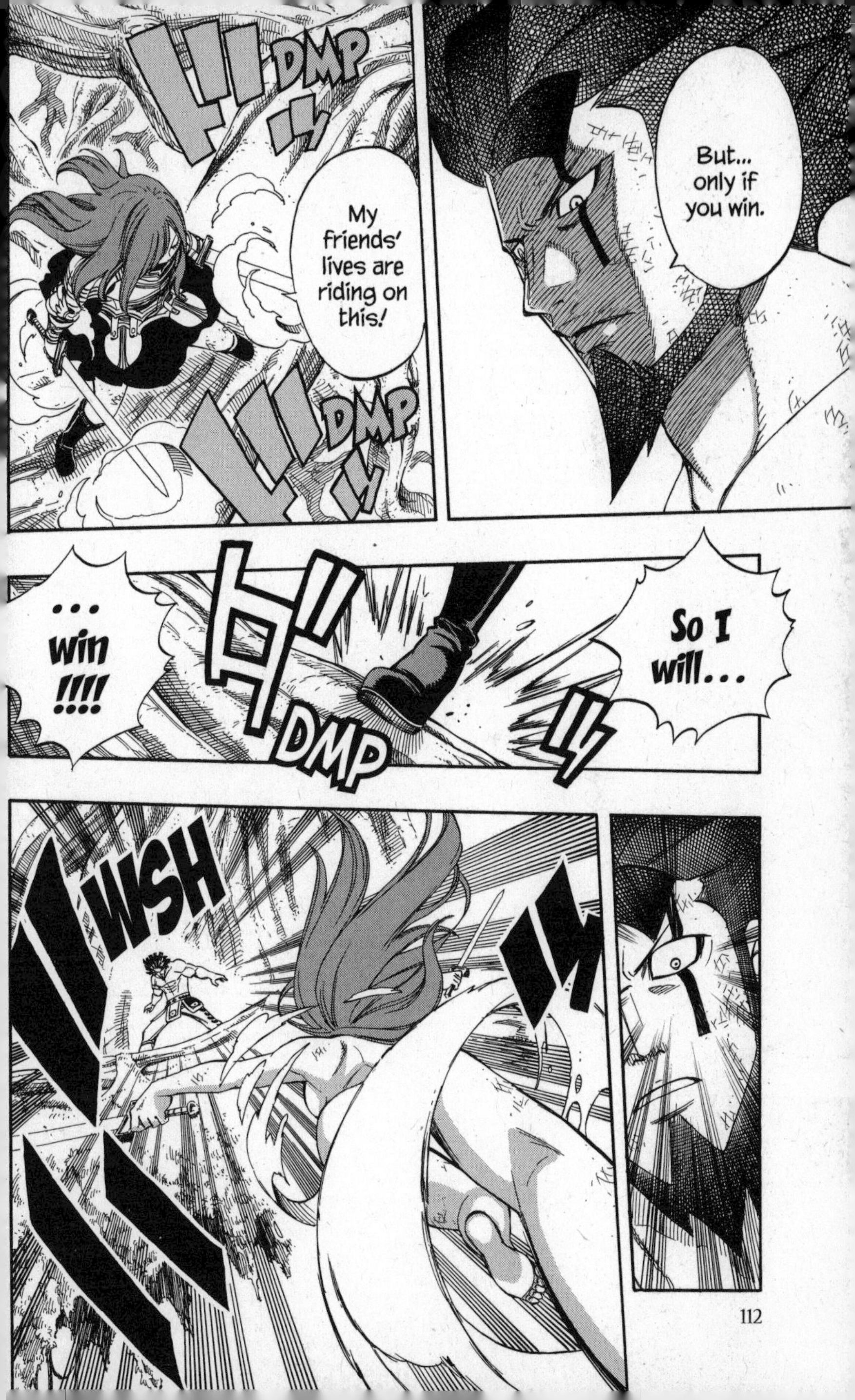
But... only if you win.
My friends' lives are riding on this!
DMP
DMP
So I will...
DMP
... win !!!!
WSH

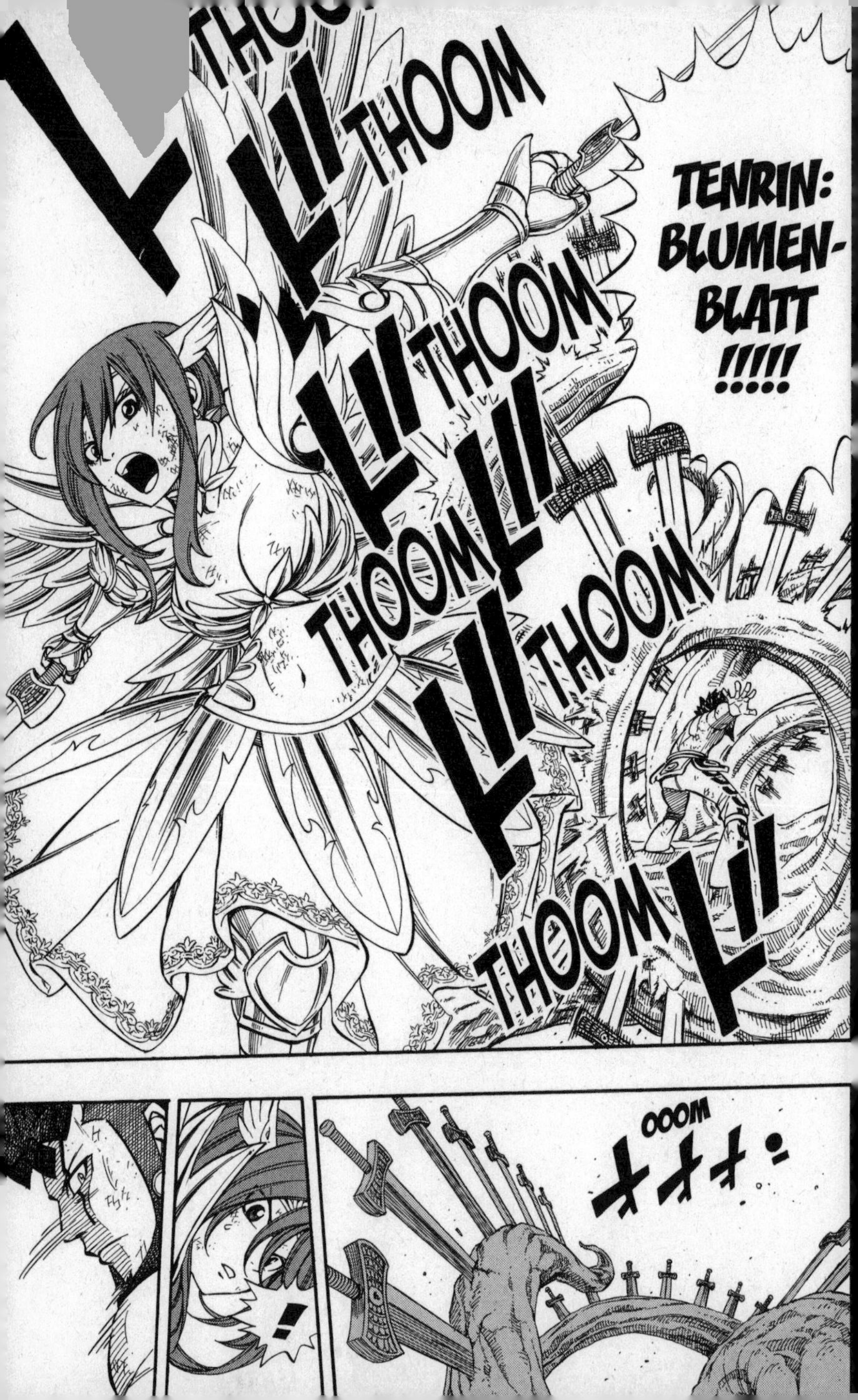
TENRIN: BLUMEN-BLATT !!!!!
THOOM
THOOM
THOOM
THOOM
THOOM
THOOM
OOOM

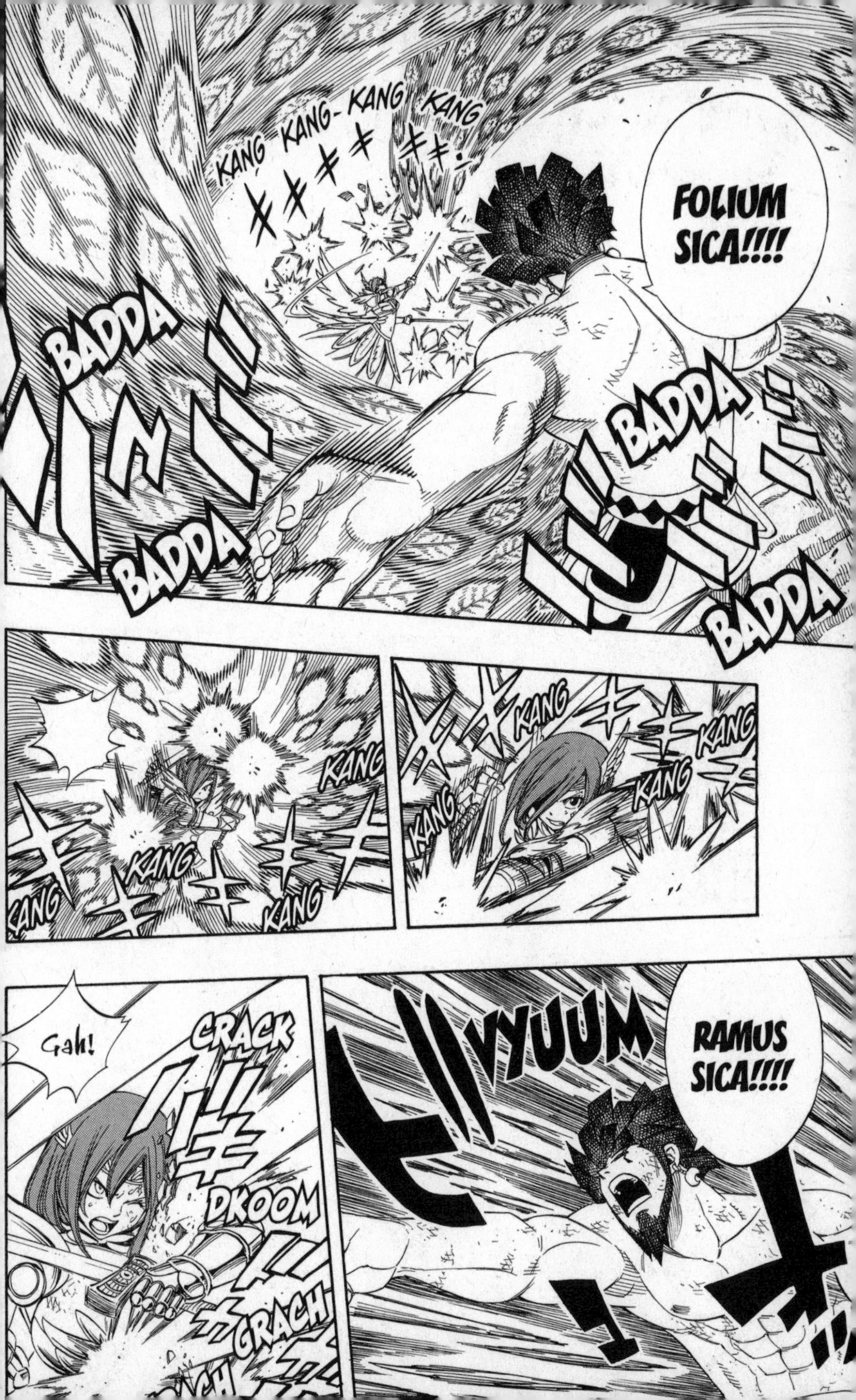
FOLIUM SICA!!!!
BADDA
BADDA
KANG KANG-KANG KANG
BADDA
BADDA
KANG
KANG
KANG
KANG
KANG
KANG
KANG
KANG
RAMUS SICA!!!!
VYUUM
Gah!
CRACK
DKOOM
CRACH

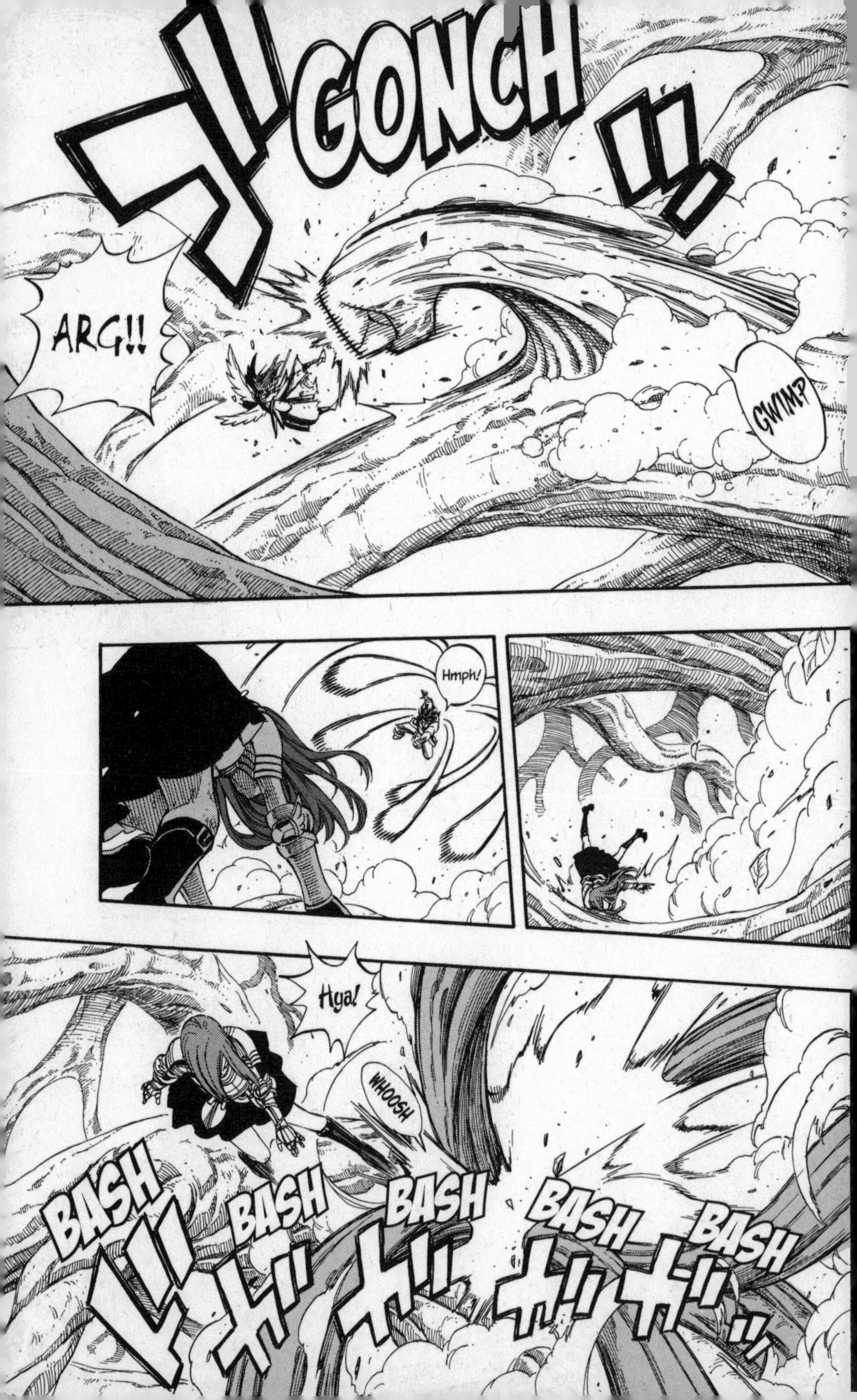
GONCH
GWIMP
ARG!!
Hmph!
Hya!
WHOOSH
BASH
BASH
BASH
BASH
BASH

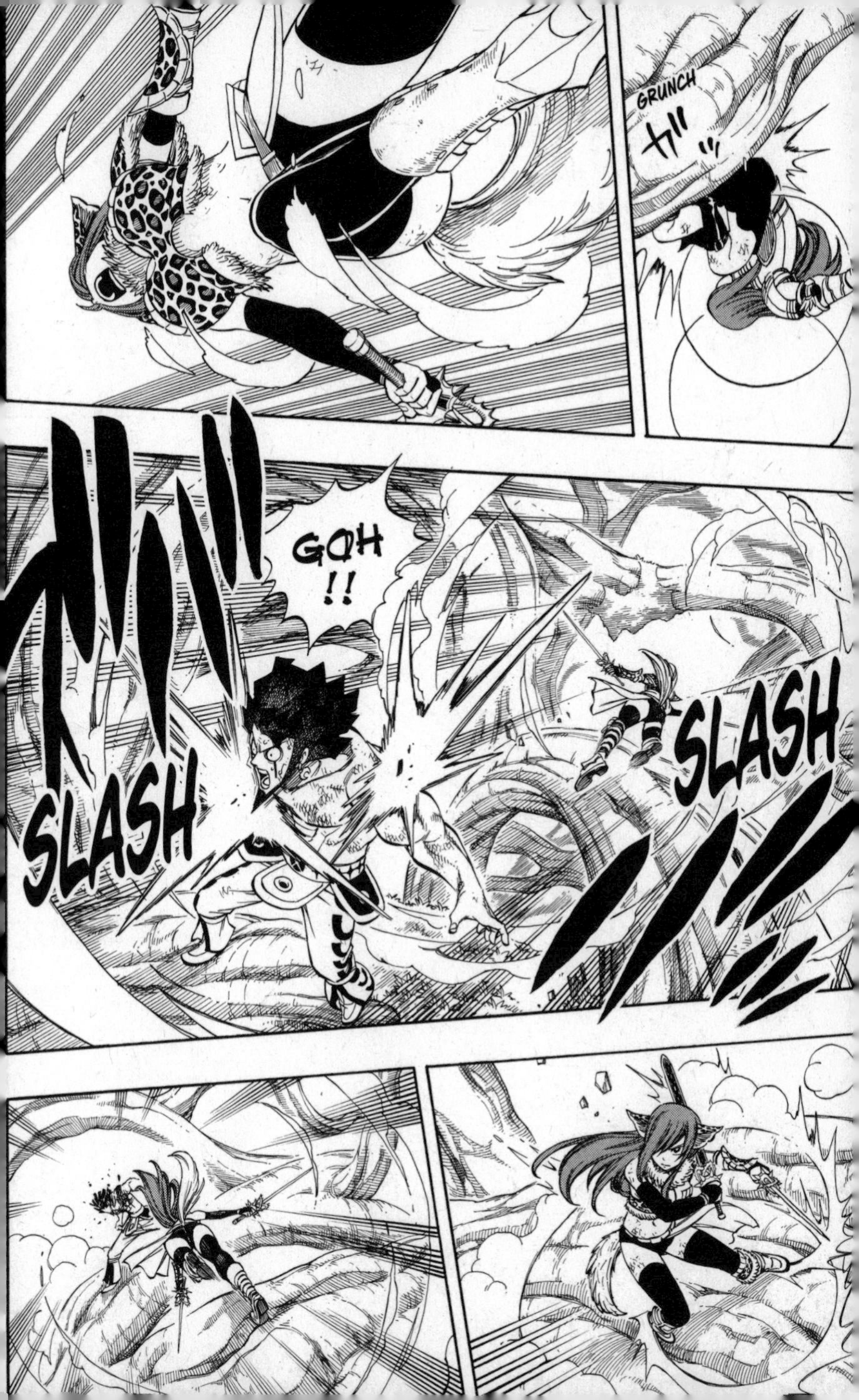
GRUNCH
GOH !!
SLASH
SLASH

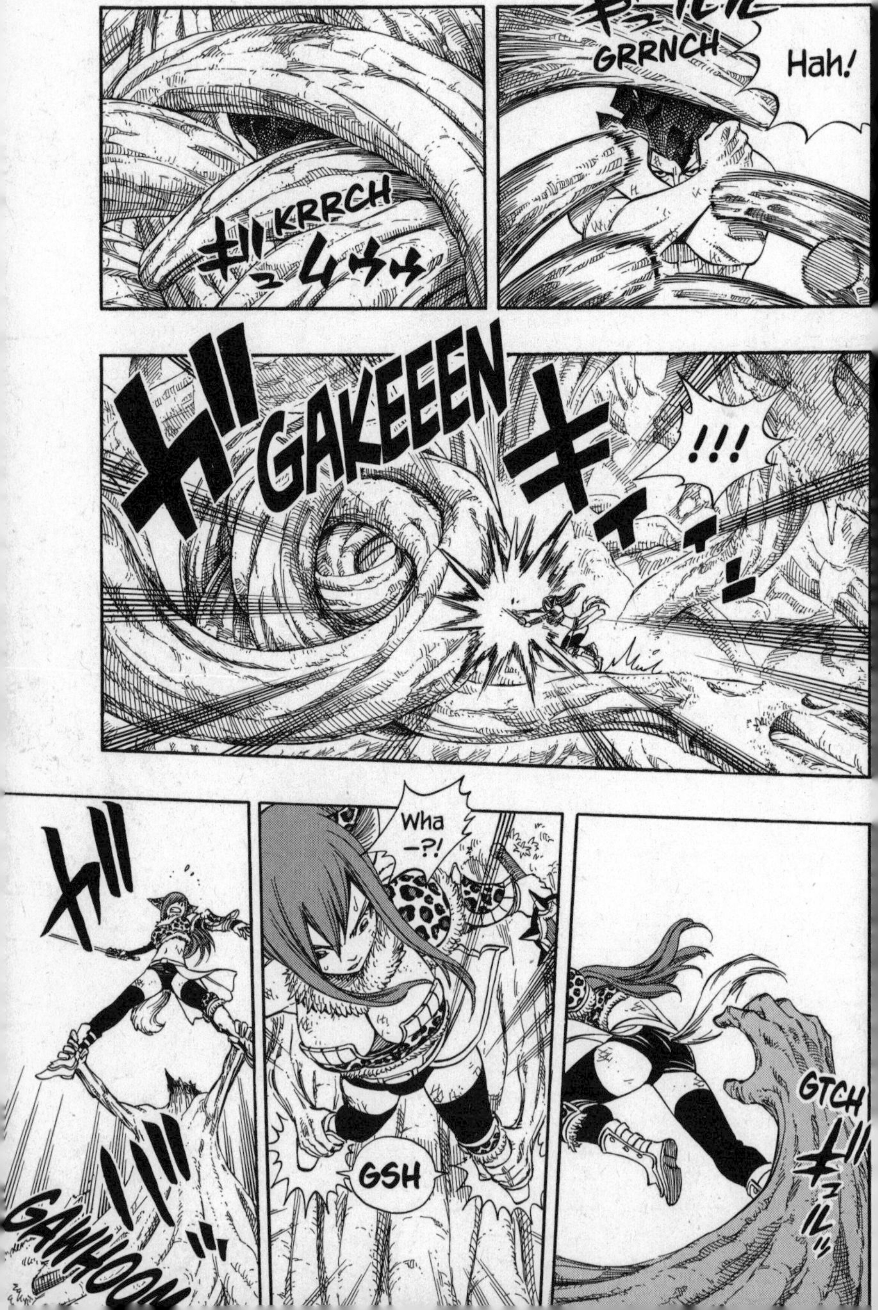

GRRNCH
Hah!
KRRCH
GAKEEN
!!!
GTCH
Wha —?!
GSH
GAWHOOM

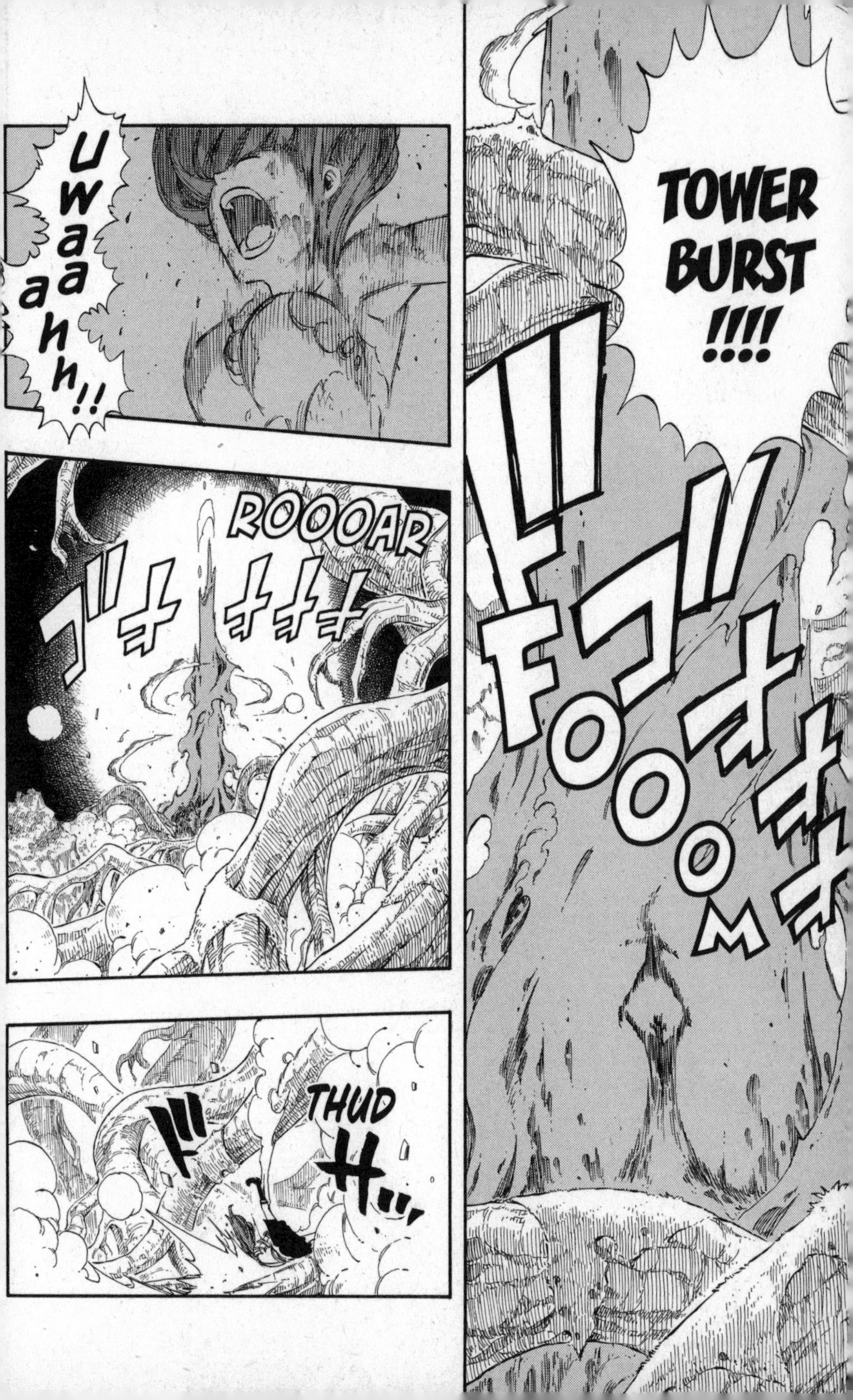
TOWER BURST!!!!
FOOOM
Uwaaahn!!
ROOOAR
THUD

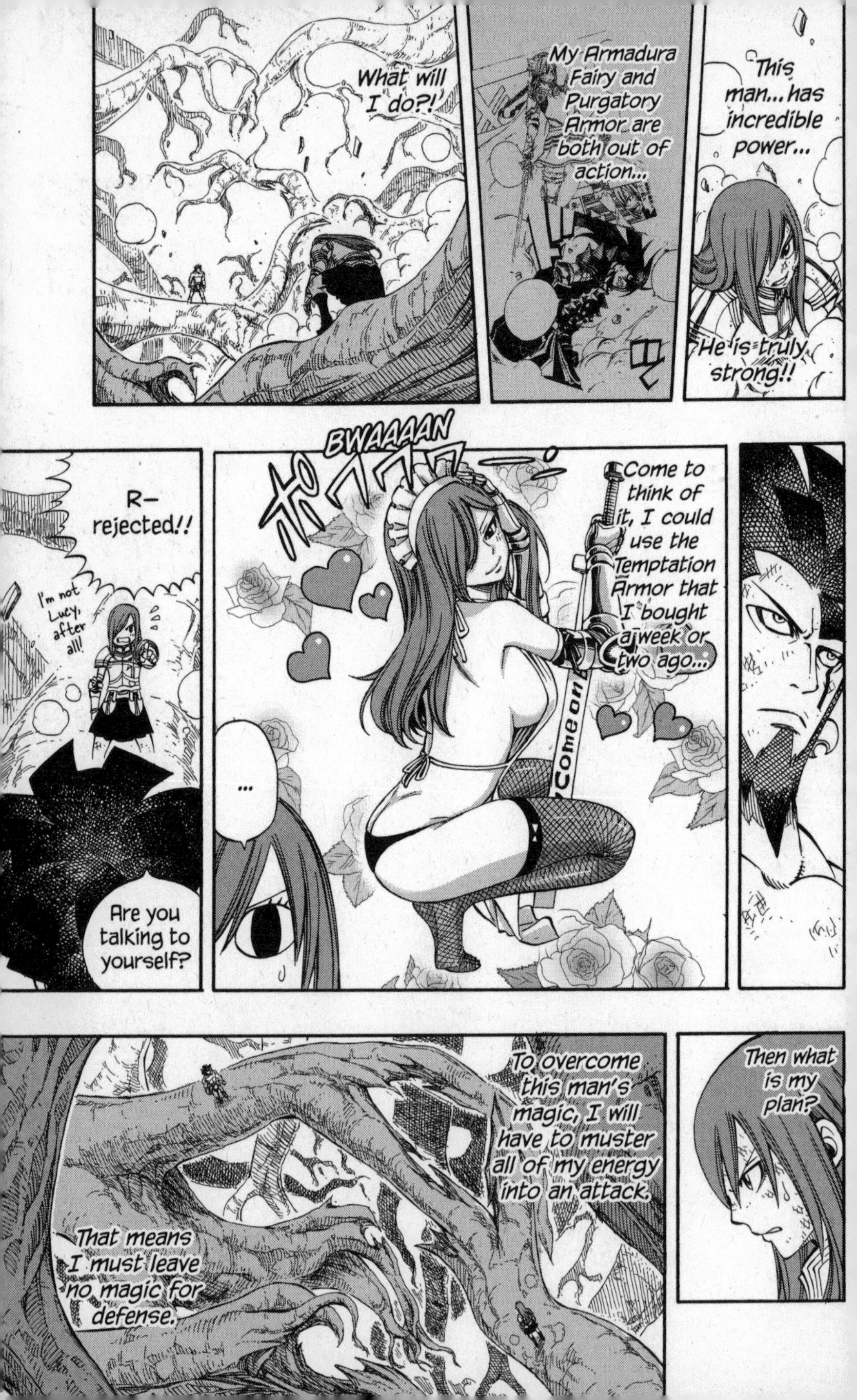
This man... has incredible power...
He is truly strong!!
My Armadura Fairy and Purgatory Armor are both out of action...
What will I do?!
BWAAAAN
Come to think of it, I could use the Temptation Armor that I bought a week or two ago...
Come on
...
R— rejected!!
I'm not Lucy, after all!
Are you talking to yourself?
Then what is my plan?
To overcome this man's magic, I will have to muster all of my energy into an attack.
That means I must leave no magic for defense.

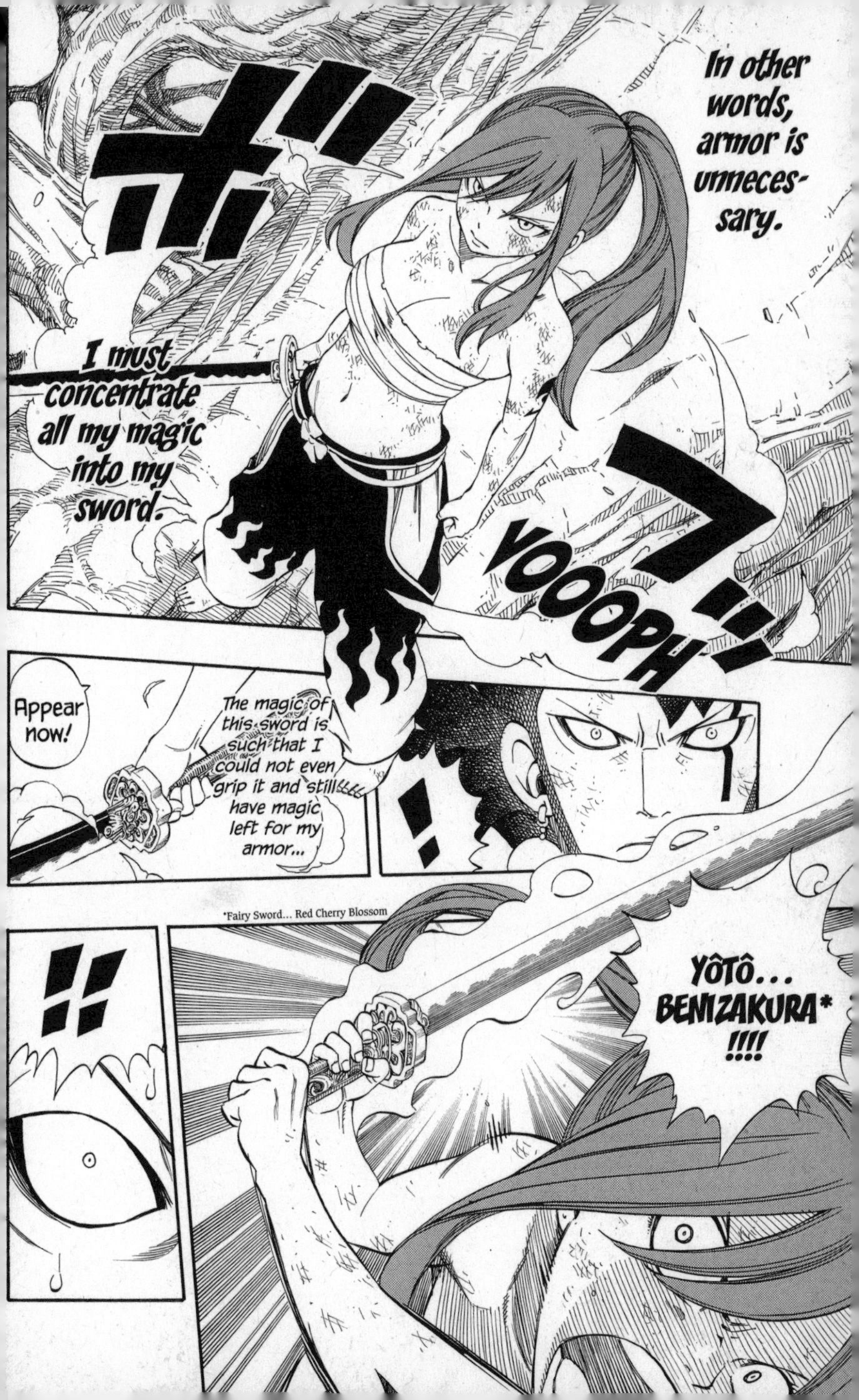
In other words, armor is unneces-sary.
I must concentrate all my magic into my sword.
VOOOPH!!
!
The magic of this sword is such that I could not even grip it and still have magic left for my armor...
Appear now!
YÔTÔ... BENIZAKURA* !!!!
!!
*Fairy Sword... Red Cherry Blossom

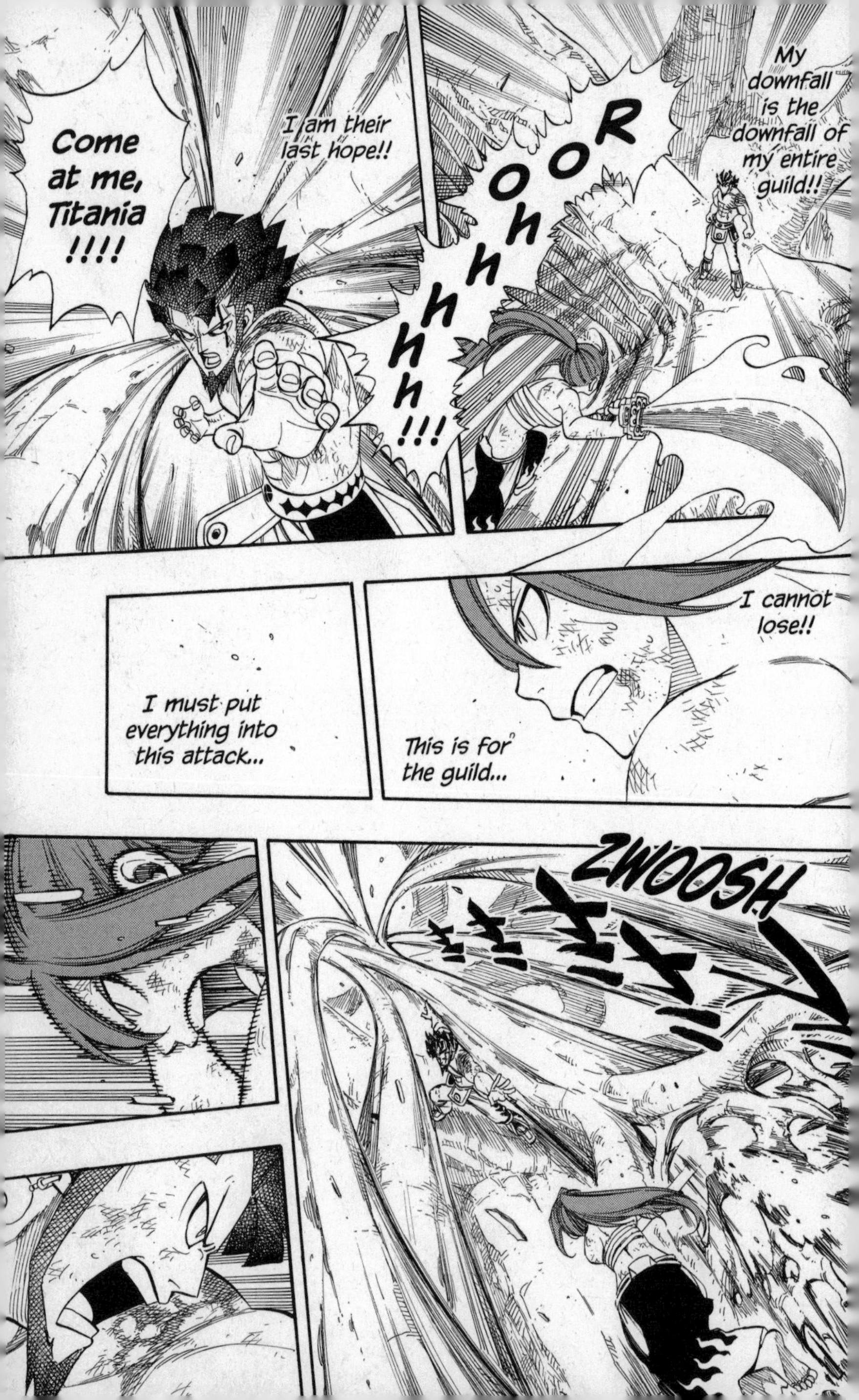

My downfall is the downfall of my entire guild!!
ROOhhhhh!!!
I am their last hope!!
Come at me, Titania!!!!
I cannot lose!!
This is for the guild...
I must put everything into this attack...
ZWOOSH

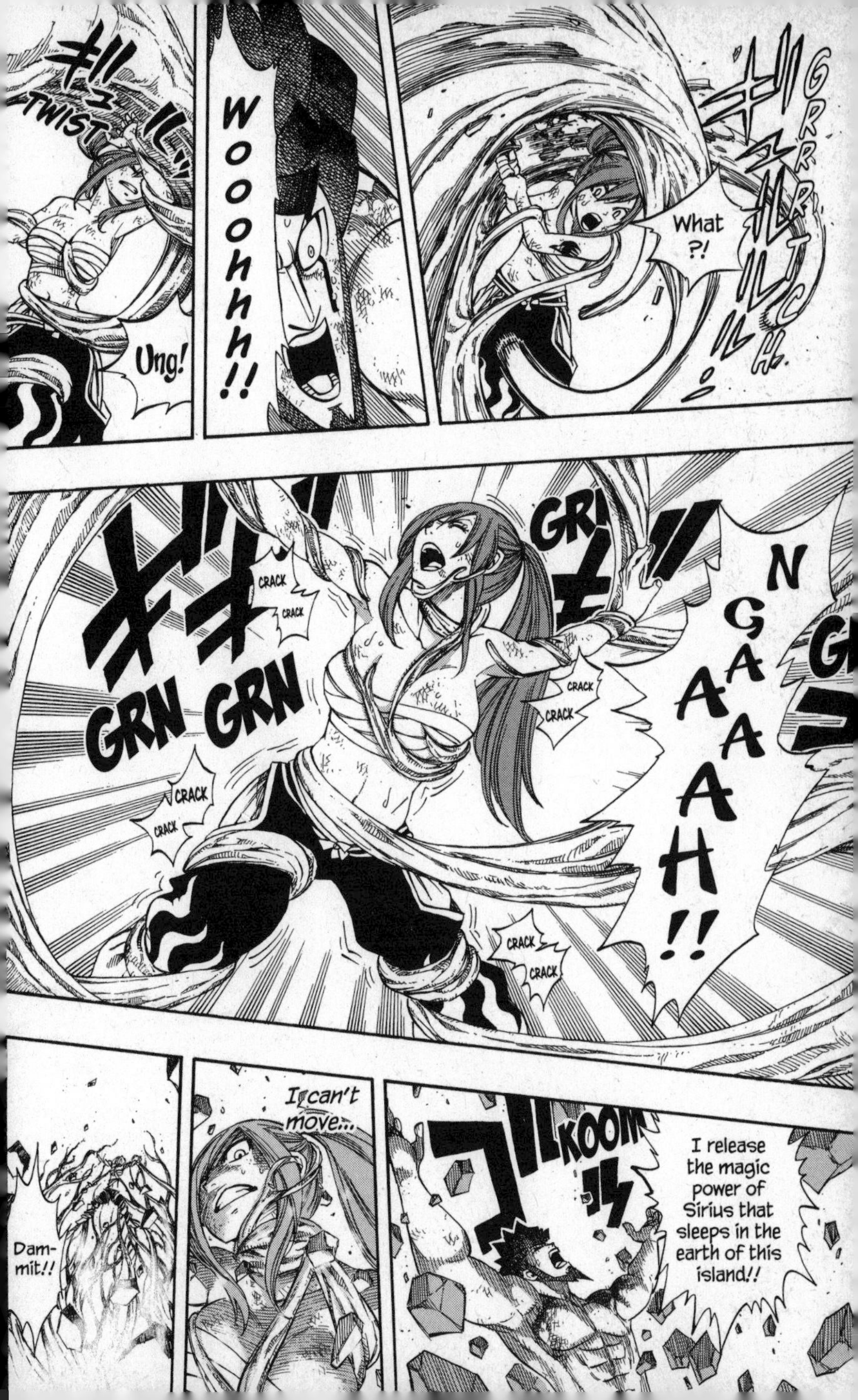
GRRRTCH
What?!
Wooohhhh!!
TWIST
Ung!
NGAAAAAH!!
GRN
CRACK
CRACK
CRACK
CRACK
GRN GRN
CRACK
CRACK
CRACK
CRACK
I release the magic power of Sirius that sleeps in the earth of this island!!
KOOM
I can't move...
Dam-mit!!

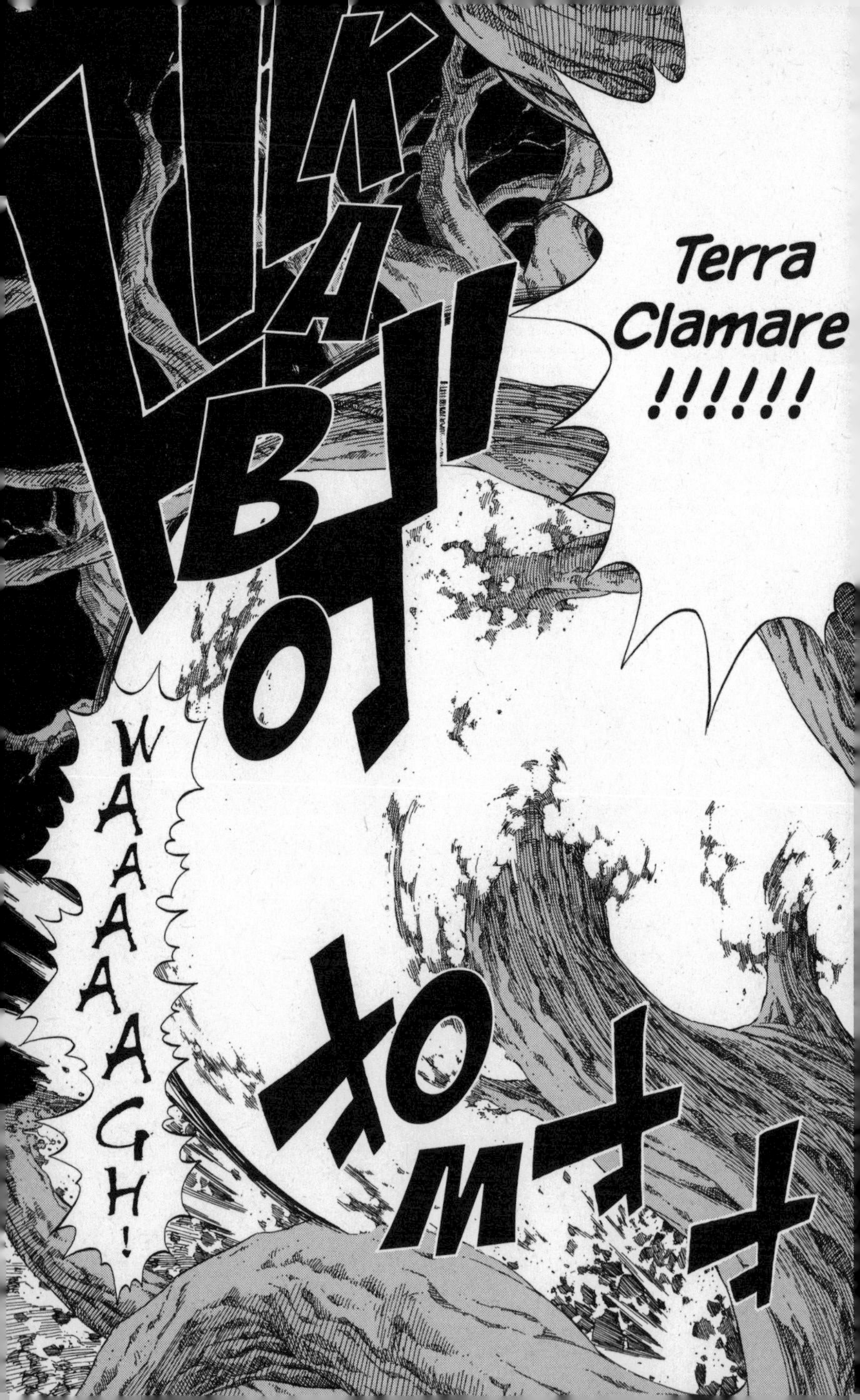
Terra Clamare !!!!!!
KAABOOM
WAAAAAGH!

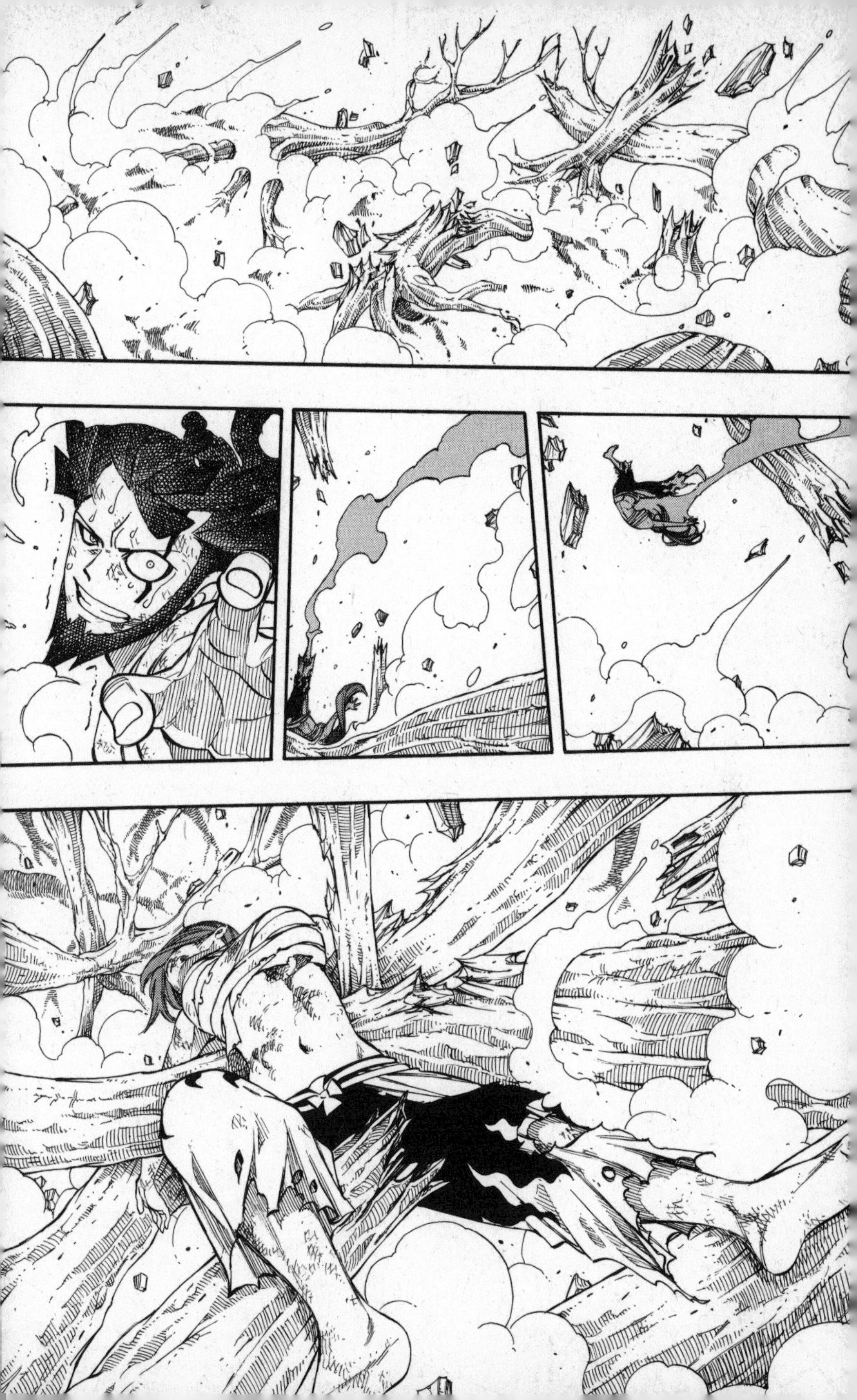

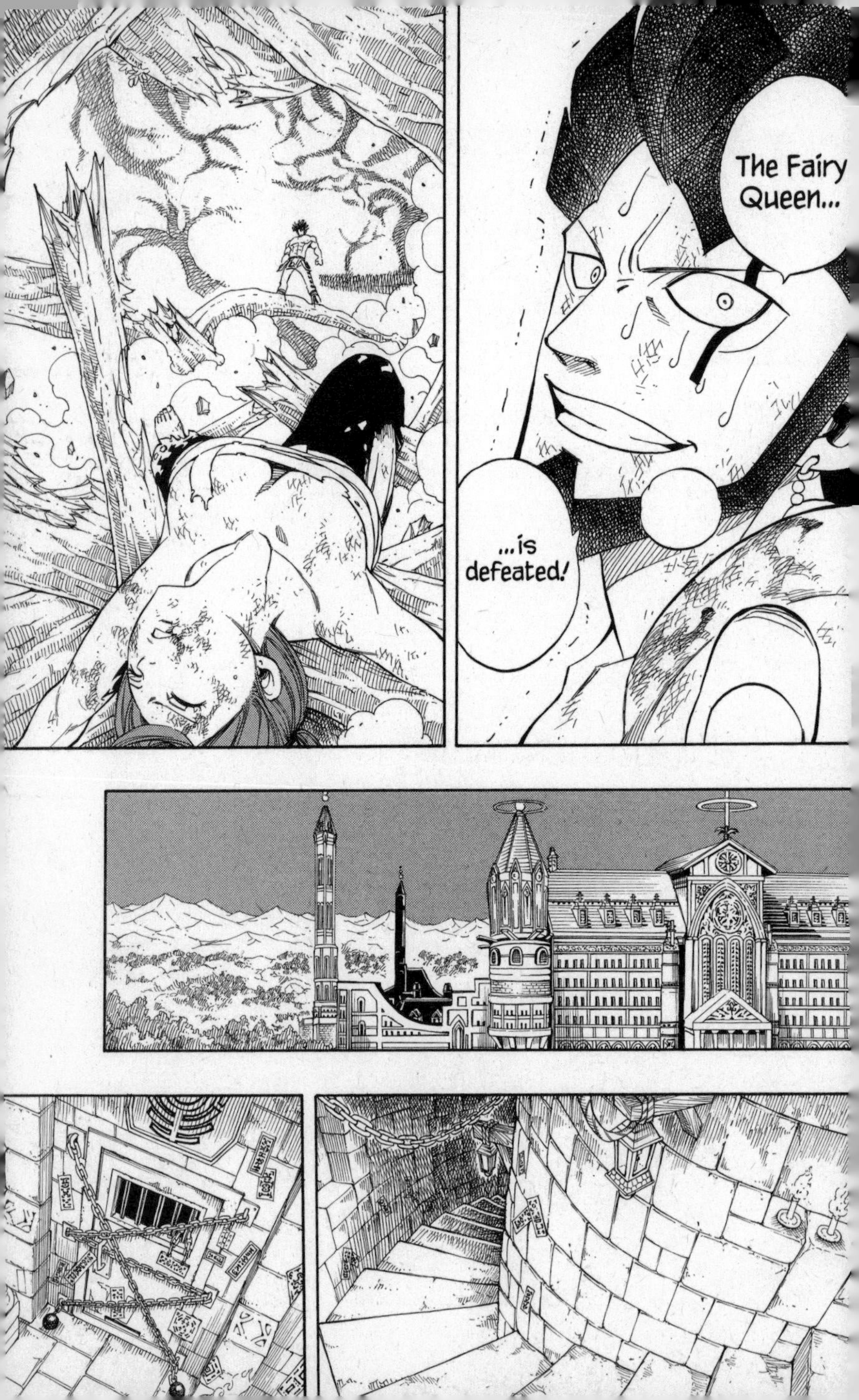
The Fairy Queen...
...is defeated!

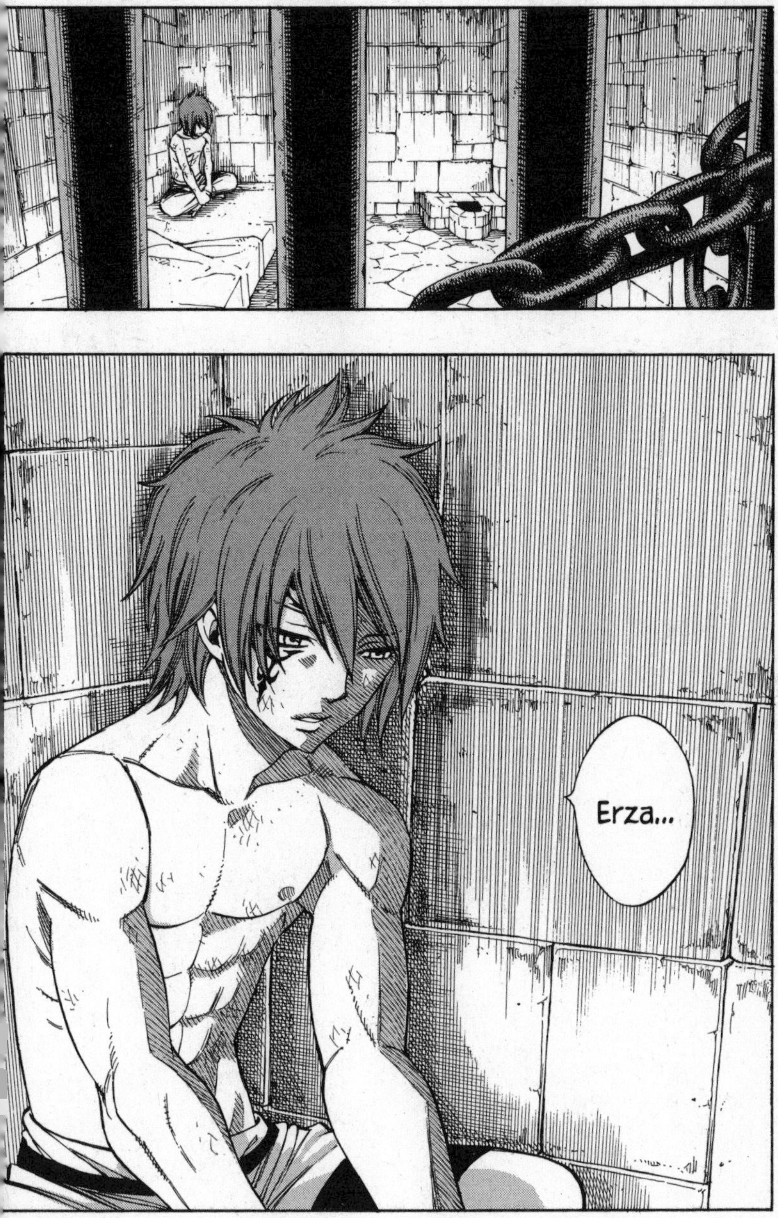
Erza...

FAIRY TAIL
フェアリーテイル

Chapter 237: What Kind of Guild Is This

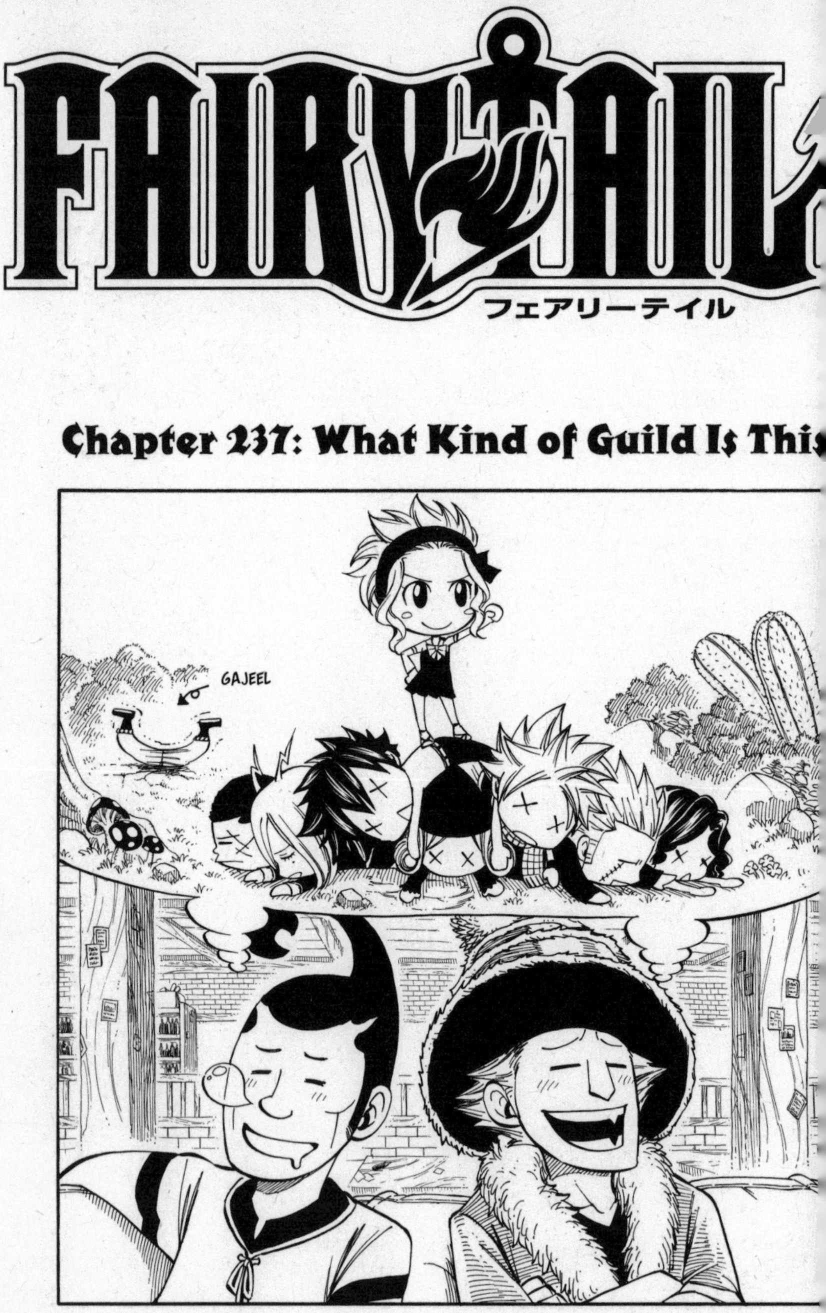
GAJEEL

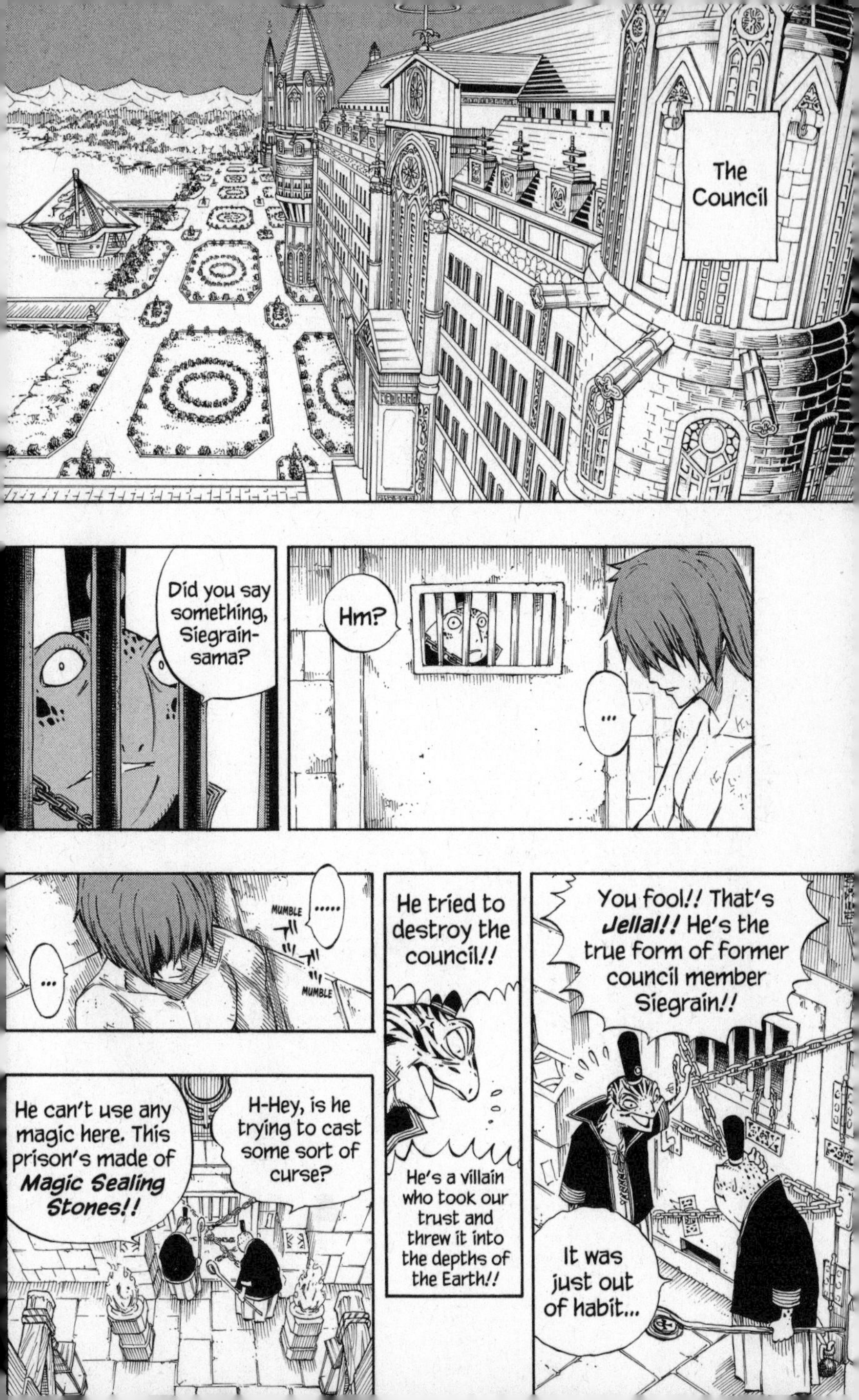

The Council
Hm?
...
Did you say something, Siegrain-sama?
You fool!! That's *Jellal!!* He's the true form of former council member Siegrain!!
It was just out of habit...
He tried to destroy the council!!
He's a villain who took our trust and threw it into the depths of the Earth!!
......
MUMBLE
MUMBLE
...
H-Hey, is he trying to cast some sort of curse?
He can't use any magic here. This prison's made of ***Magic Sealing Stones!!***

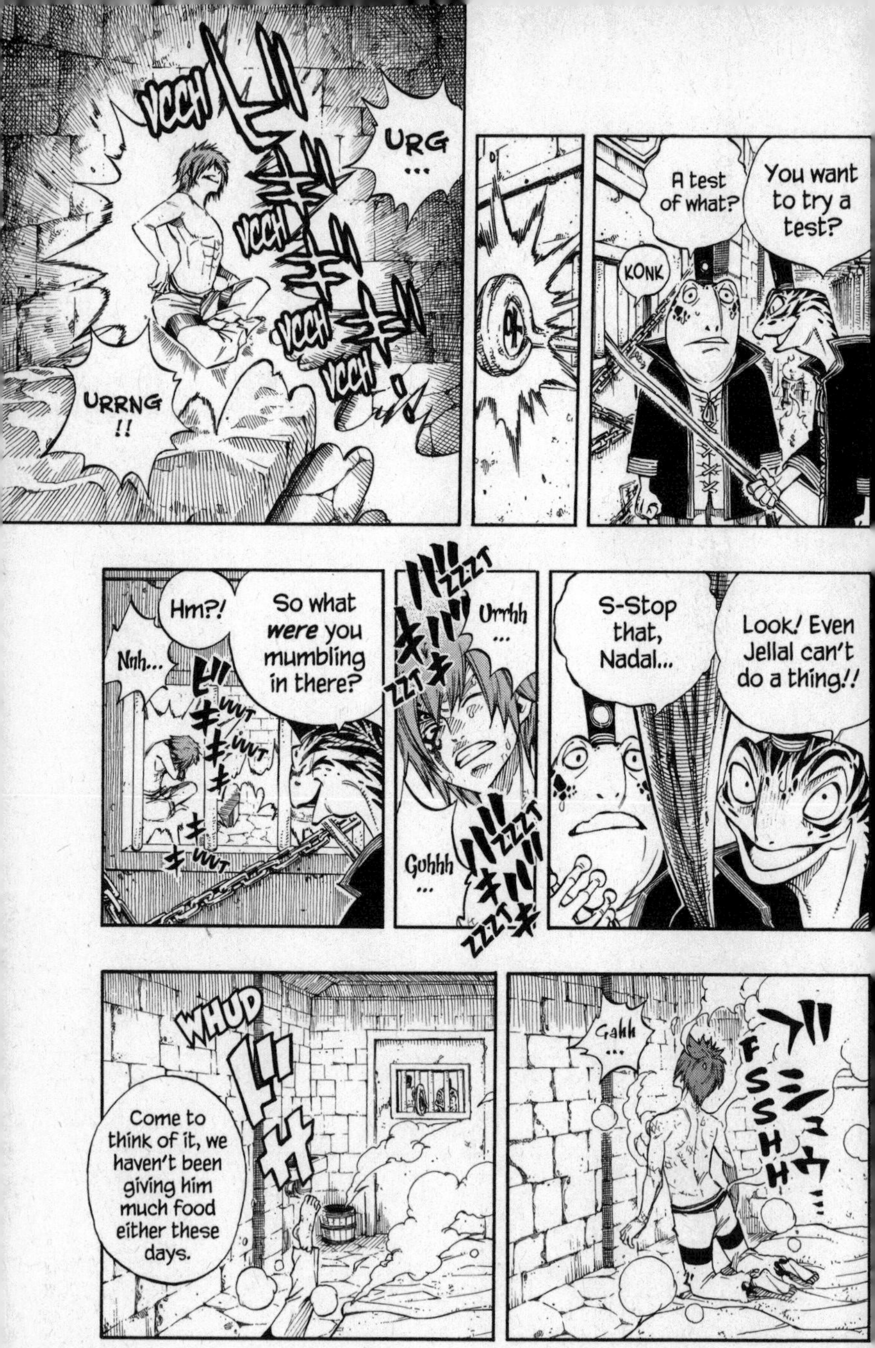
You want to try a test?
A test of what?
KONK
URG...
VCCH
VCCH
VCCH
VCCH
URRNG!!
Look! Even Jellal can't do a thing!!
S-Stop that, Nadal...
ZZZT
Urrhh...
ZZZT
Guhhh...
ZZZT
ZZZT
So what *were* you mumbling in there?
Hm?!
Nnh...
VVVT
VVVT
VVVT
Gahh...
FSSHH
WHUD
Come to think of it, we haven't been giving him much food either these days.

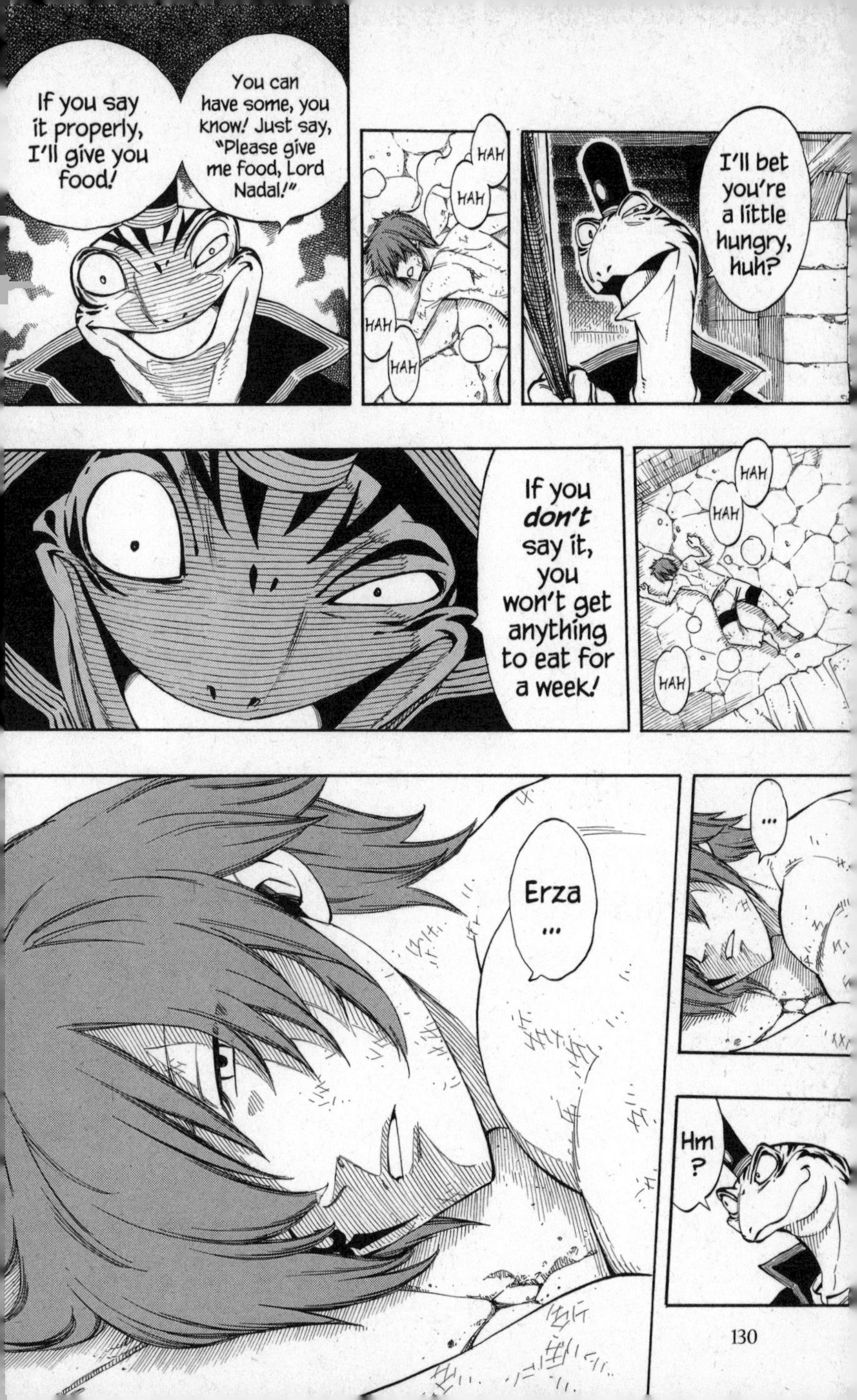
I'll bet you're a little hungry, huh?
HAH
HAH
HAH
HAH
You can have some, you know! Just say, "Please give me food, Lord Nadal!"
If you say it properly, I'll give you food!
HAH
HAH
HAH
If you *don't* say it, you won't get anything to eat for a week!
...
Hm?
Erza ...

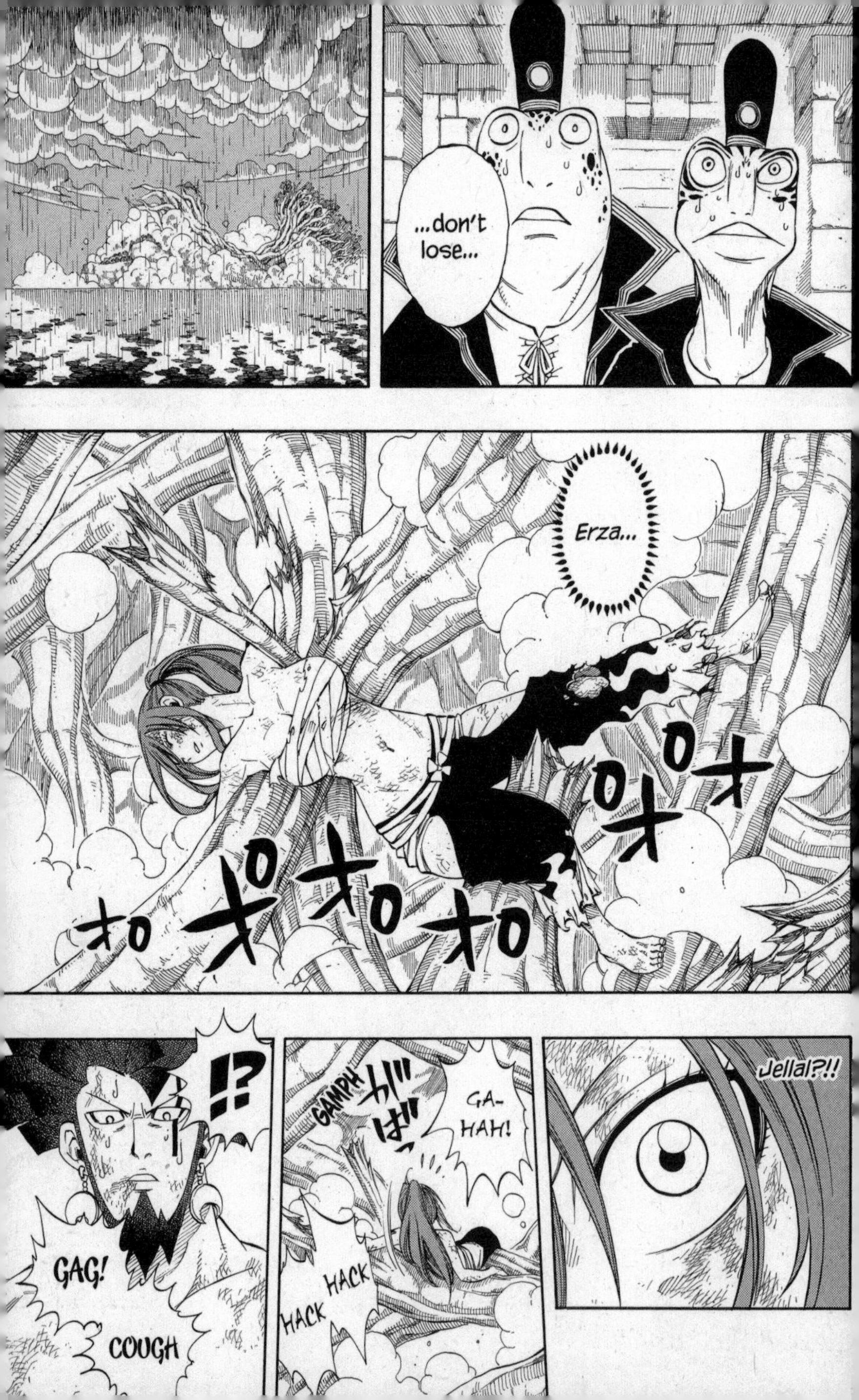

...don't lose...
Erza...
Jellal?!!
GAMPH
がばっ
GA-HAH!
HACK
HACK
!?
GAG!
COUGH

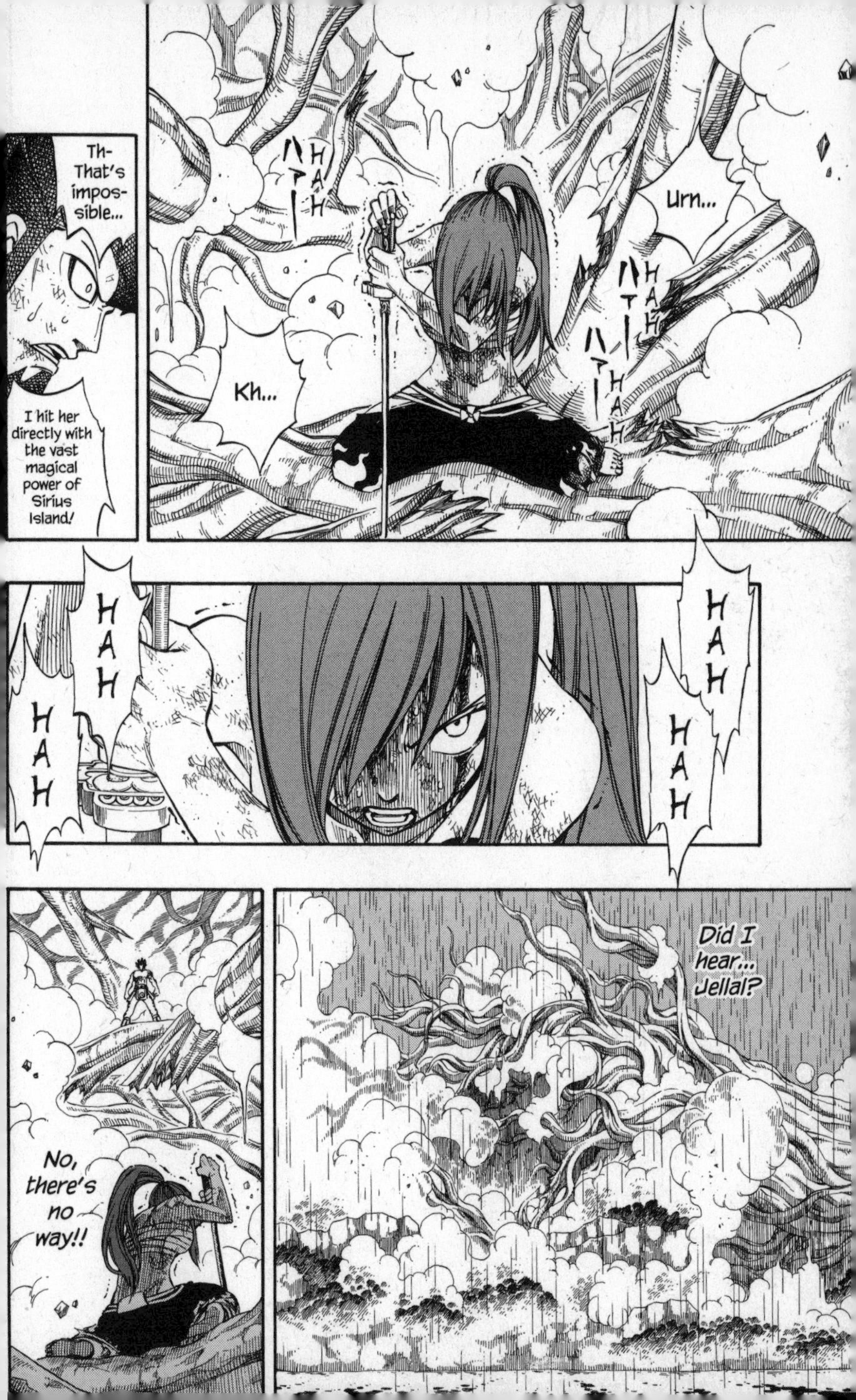
Urn...
HAH HAH
HAH HAH
Kh...
HAH
Th-That's impossible...
I hit her directly with the vast magical power of Sirius Island!
HAH HAH
HAH HAH
Did I hear... Jellal?
No, there's no way!!

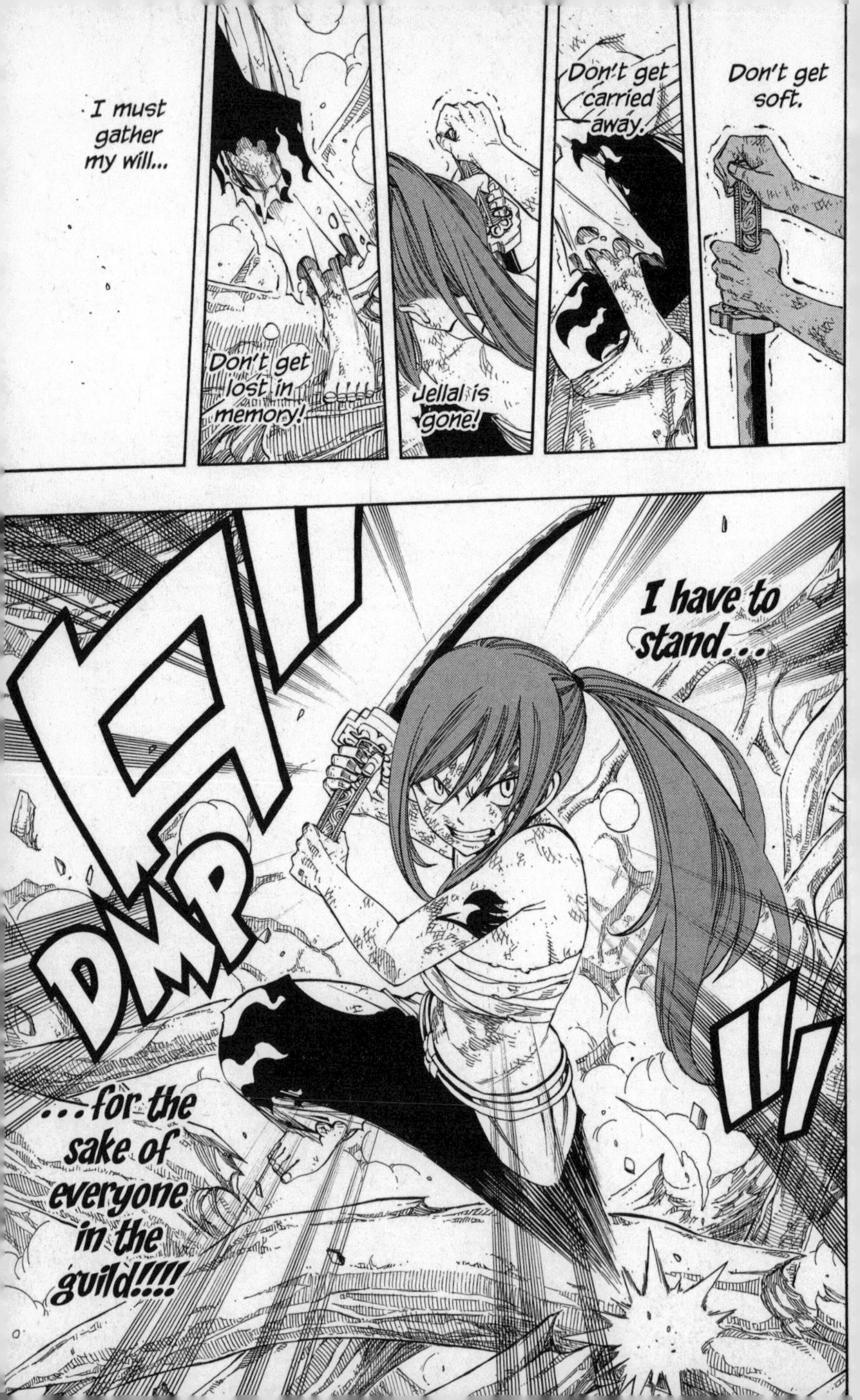
Don't get soft.
Don't get carried away.
Jellal is gone!
Don't get lost in memory!
I must gather my will...
I have to stand...
DMP
...for the sake of everyone in the guild!!!!

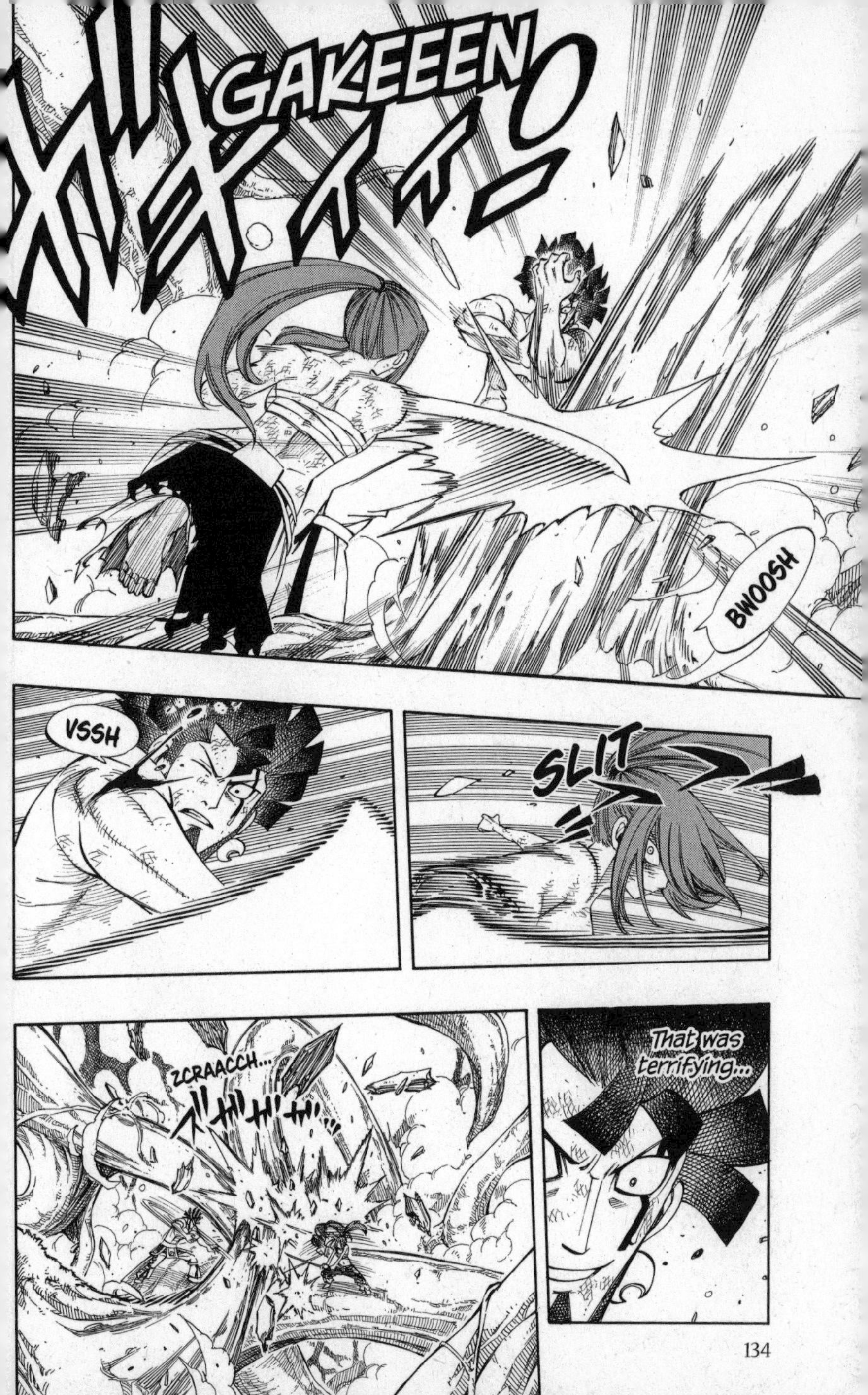
GAKEEEN
BWOOSH
SLIT
VSSH
That was terrifying...
ZCRAACCH...

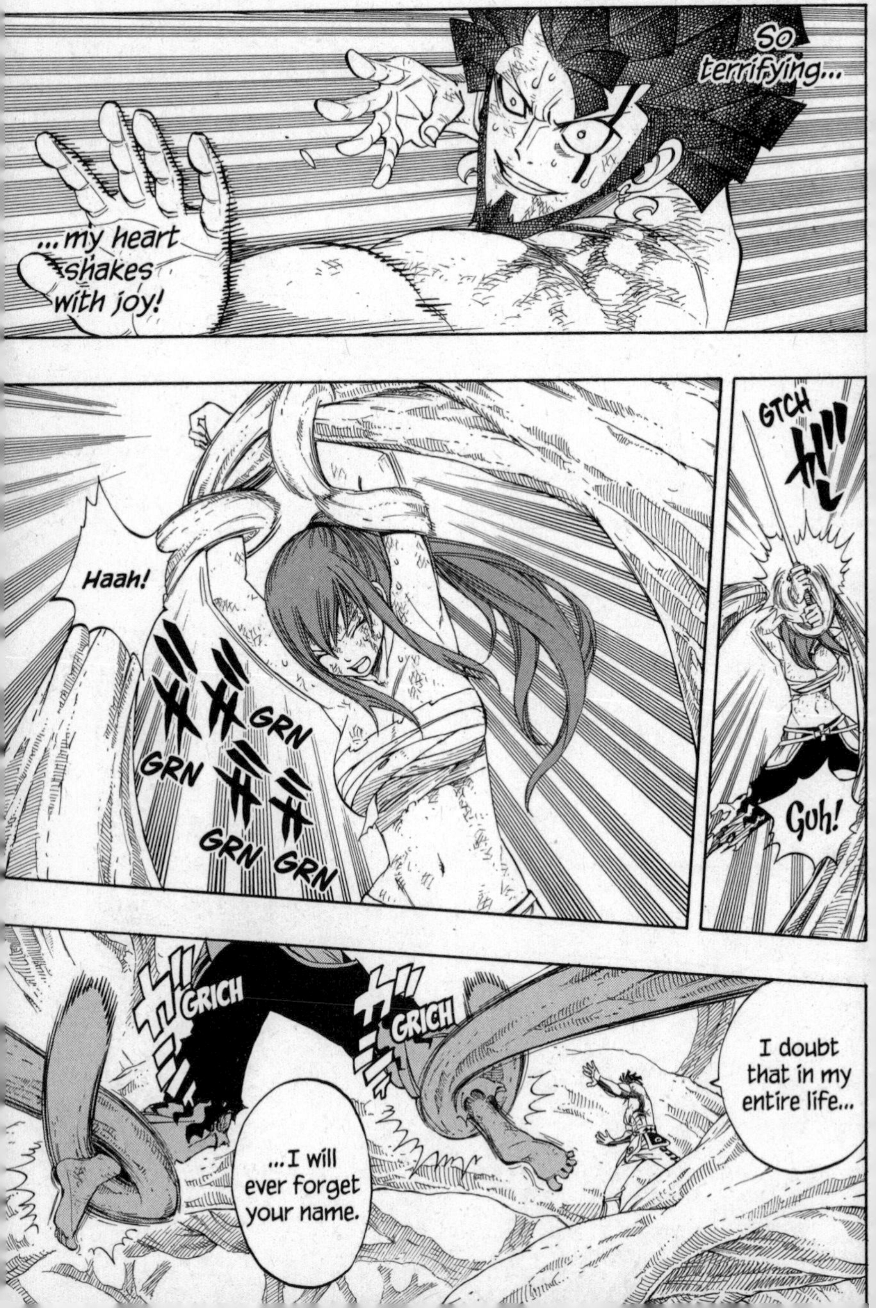
So terrifying...
...my heart shakes with joy!
GTCH
Guh!
Haah!
GRN
GRN
GRN
GRN
I doubt that in my entire life...
GRICH
GRICH
...I will ever forget your name.

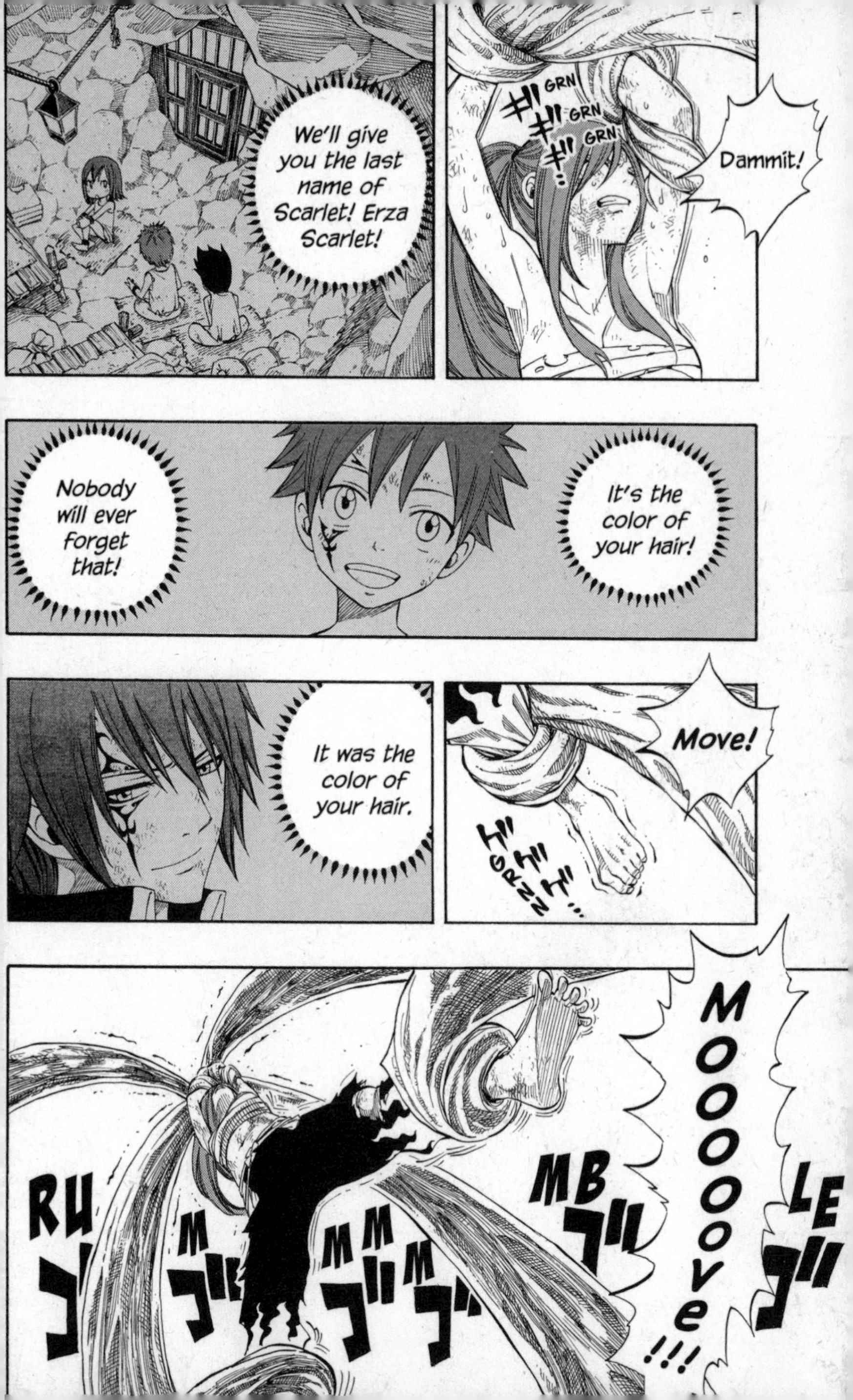

GRN
GRN
GRN
Dammit!
We'll give you the last name of Scarlet! Erza Scarlet!
It's the color of your hair!
Nobody will ever forget that!
Move!
GRNN
It was the color of your hair.
MOOOOOve!!!
RUMMMMBLE

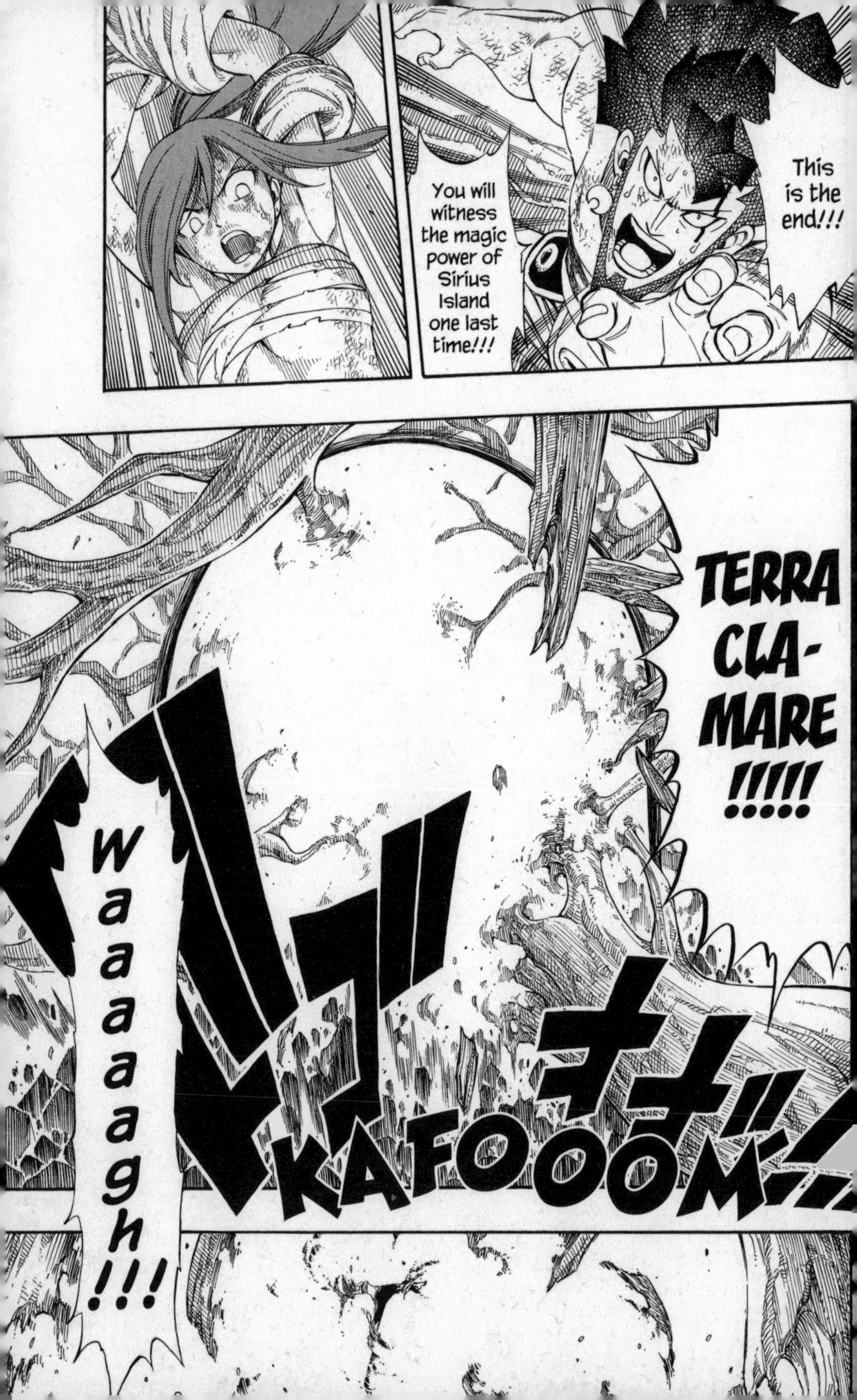
This is the end!!!
You will witness the magic power of Sirius Island one last time!!!
TERRA CLA-MARE!!!!!
KAFOOOM!!
Waaaaaagh!!!

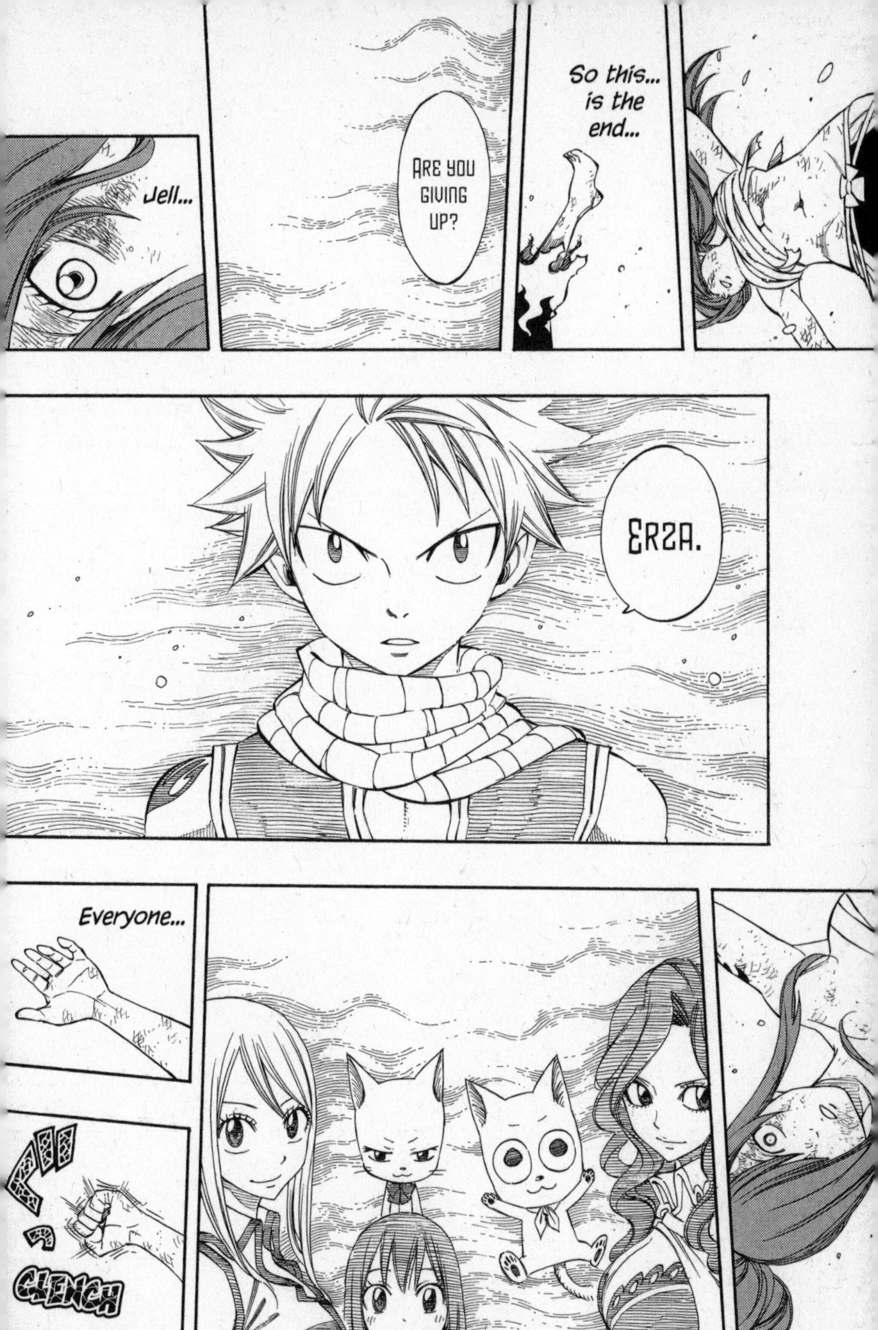
So this... is the end...
Are you giving up?
Jell...
Erza.
Everyone...
CLENCH

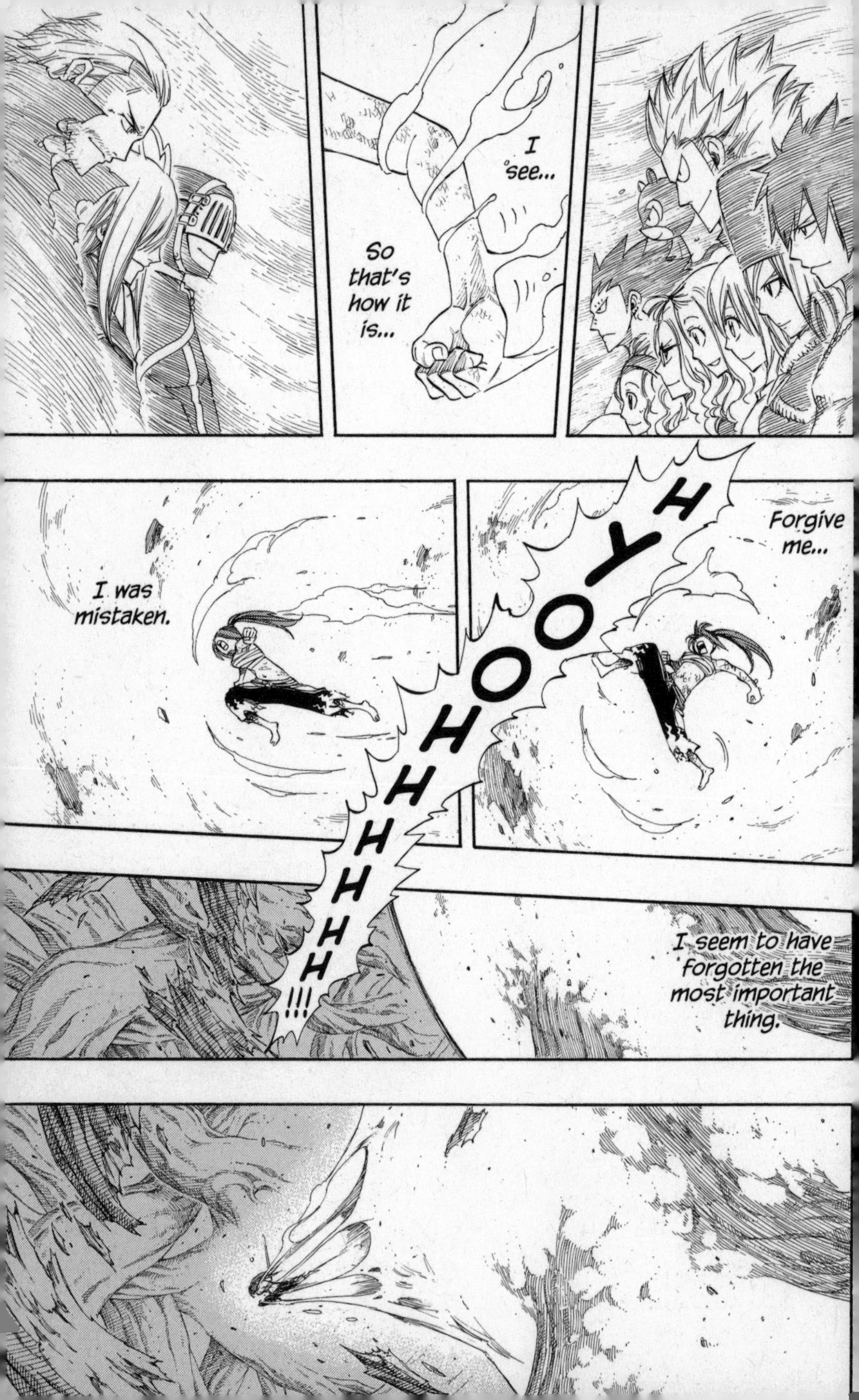
I see...
So that's how it is...
Forgive me...
HYOOHHHHHH!!!
I was mistaken.
I seem to have forgotten the most important thing.

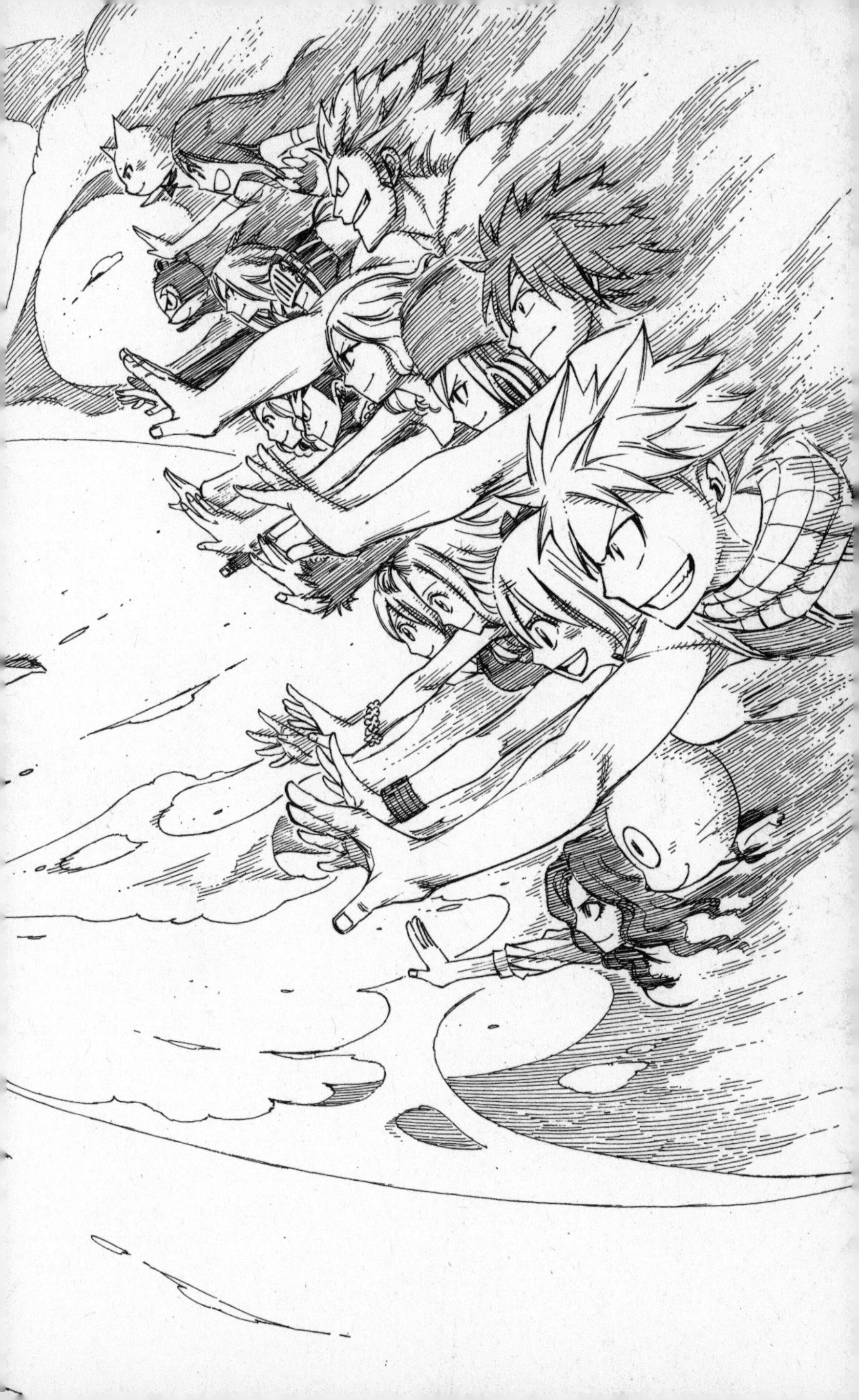

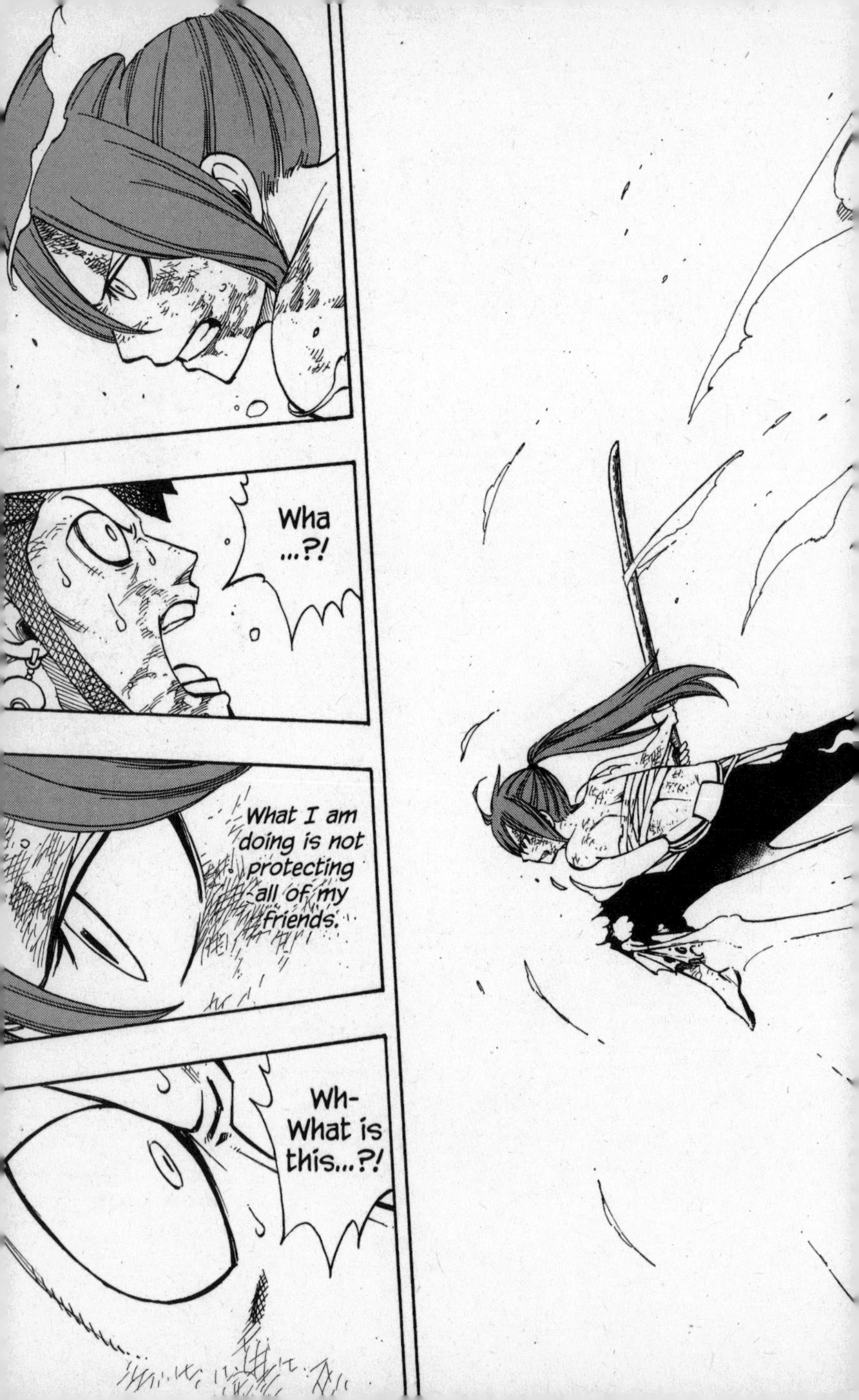
Wha ...?!
What I am doing is not protecting all of my friends.
Wh- What is this...?!

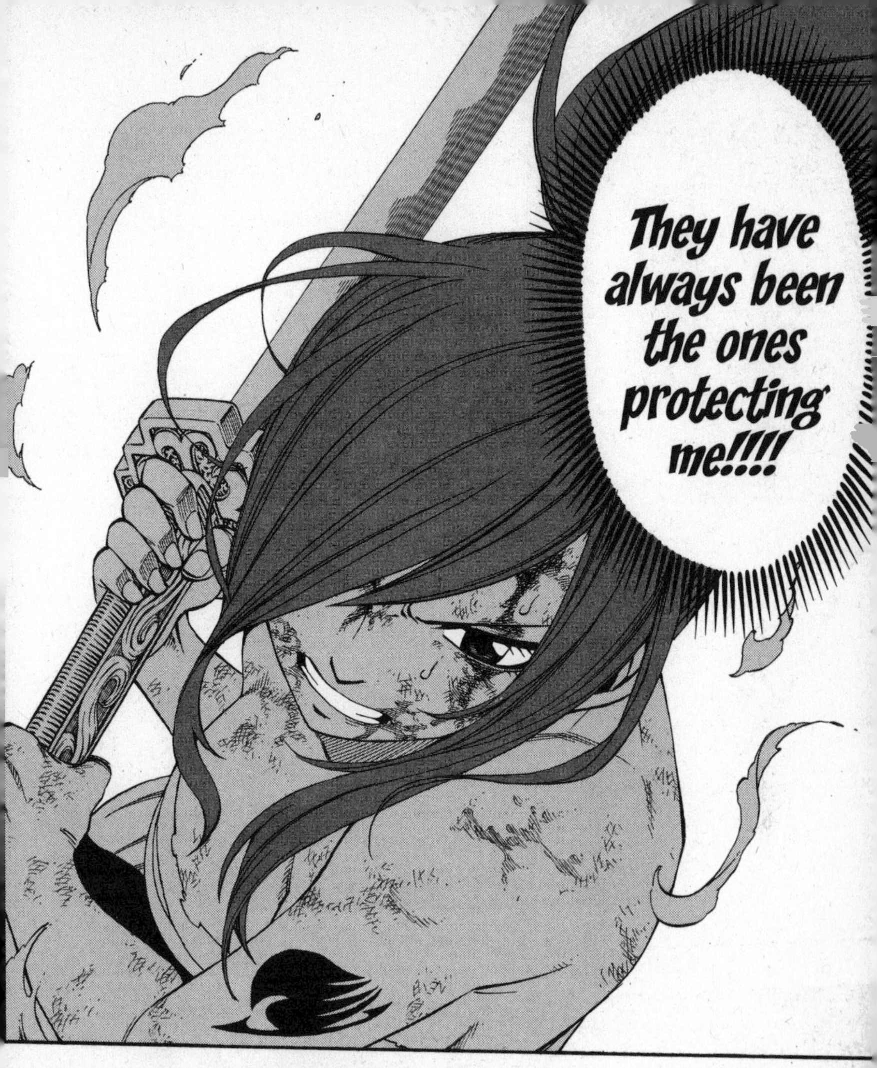
They have always been the ones protecting me!!!!

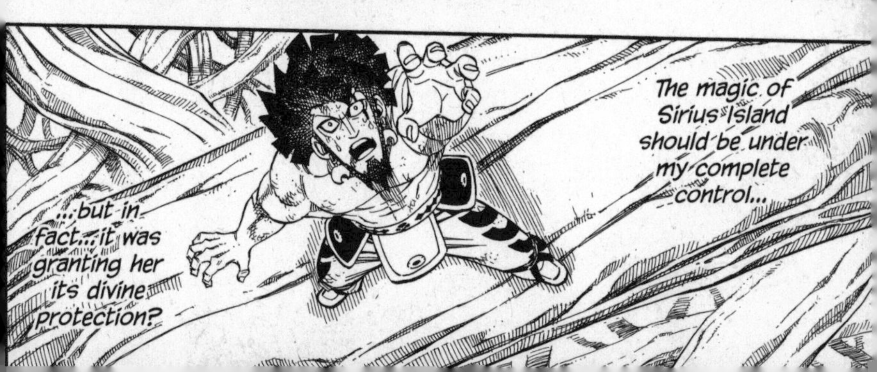
The magic of Sirius Island should be under my complete control...
...but in fact... it was granting her its divine protection?

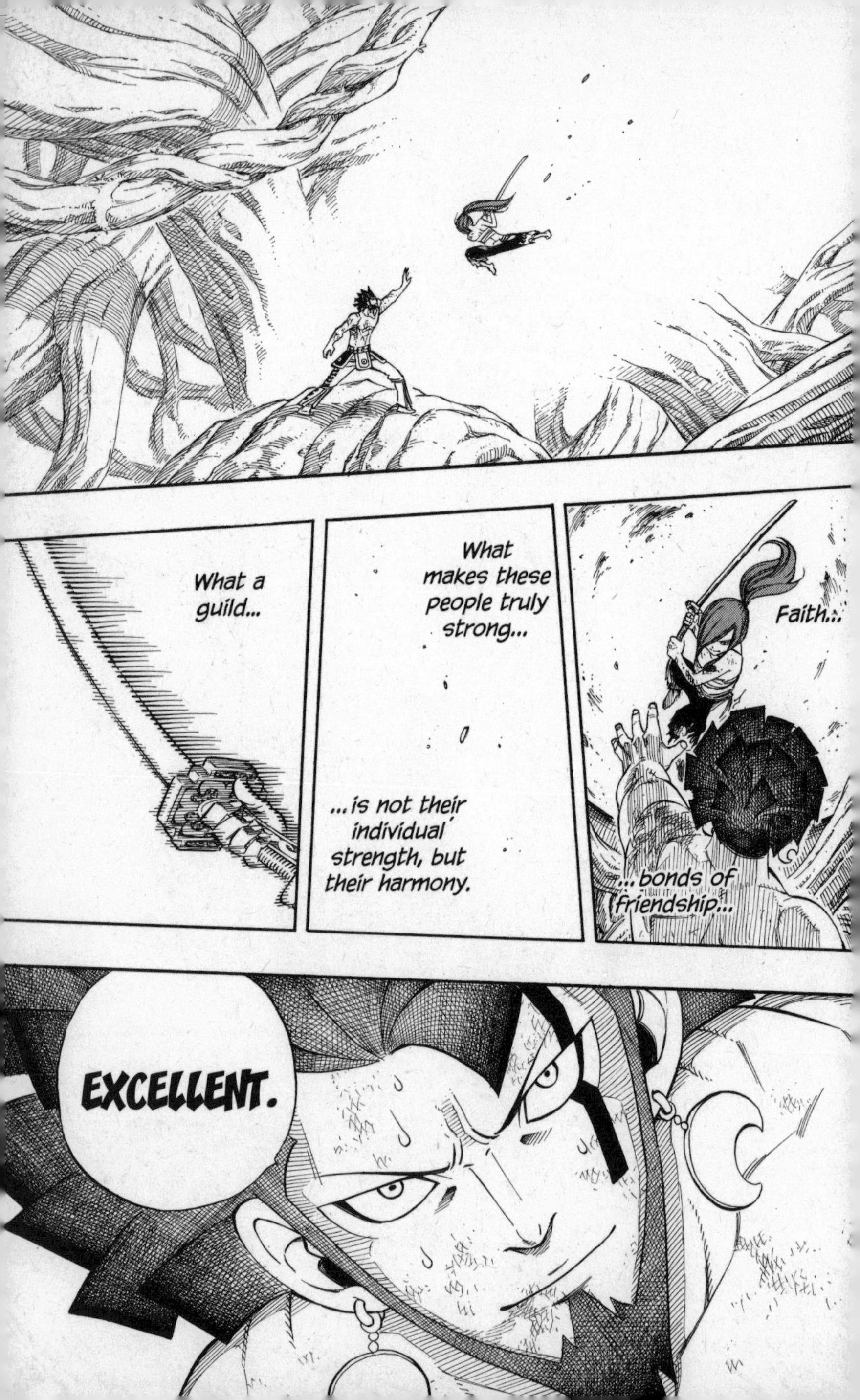
Faith...
...bonds of friendship...
What makes these people truly strong...
...is not their individual strength, but their harmony.
What a guild...
EXCELLENT.

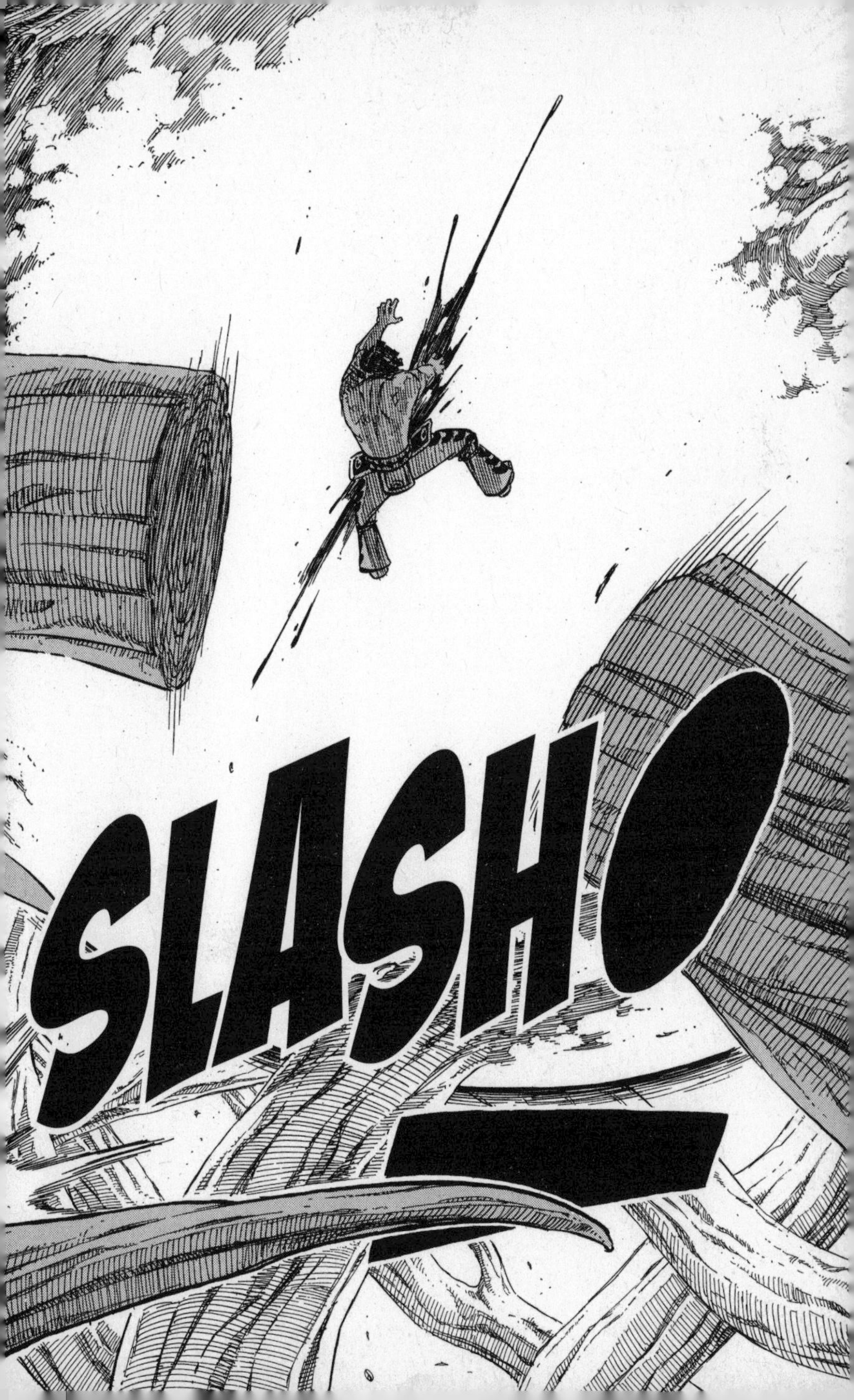
SLASH

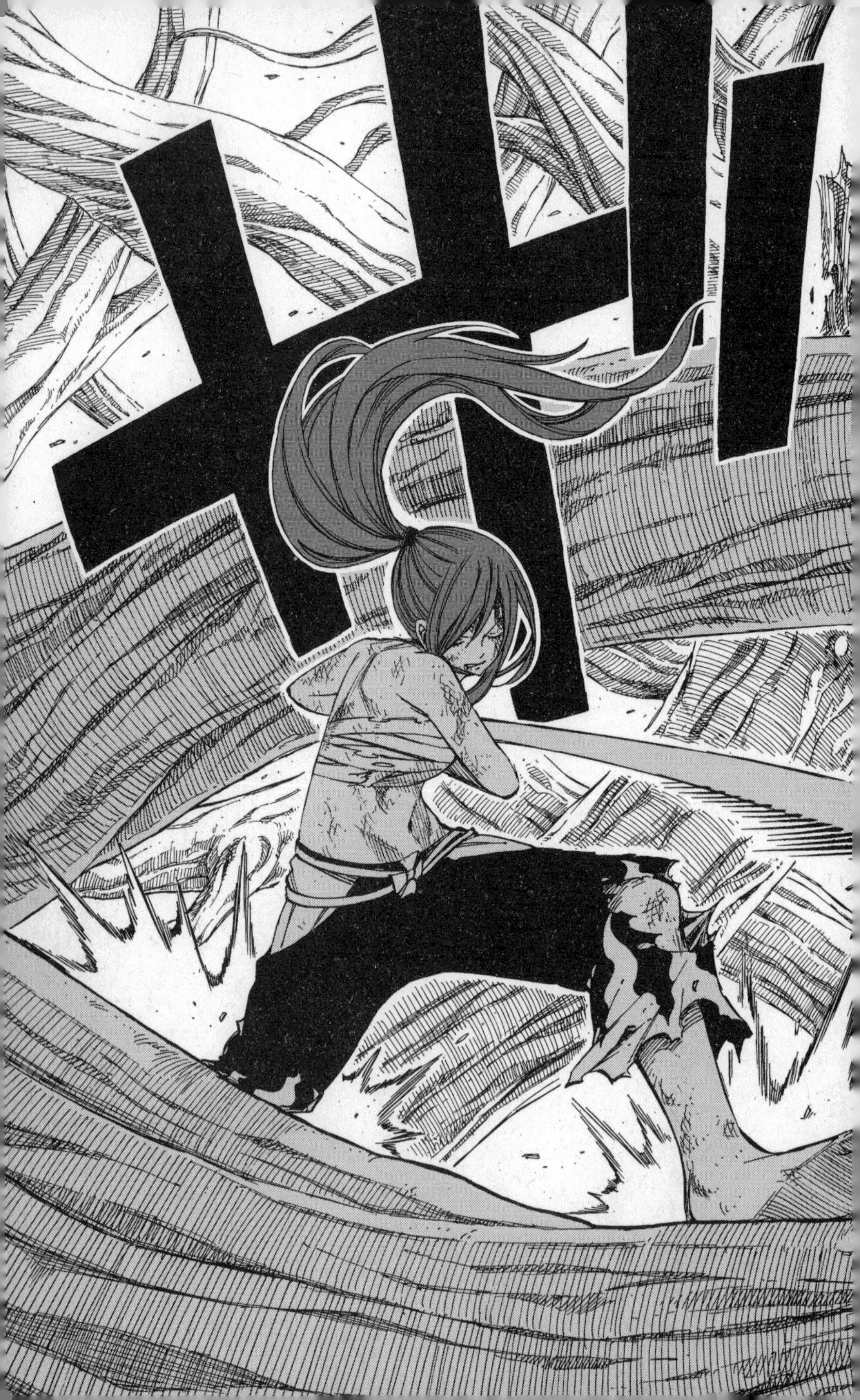

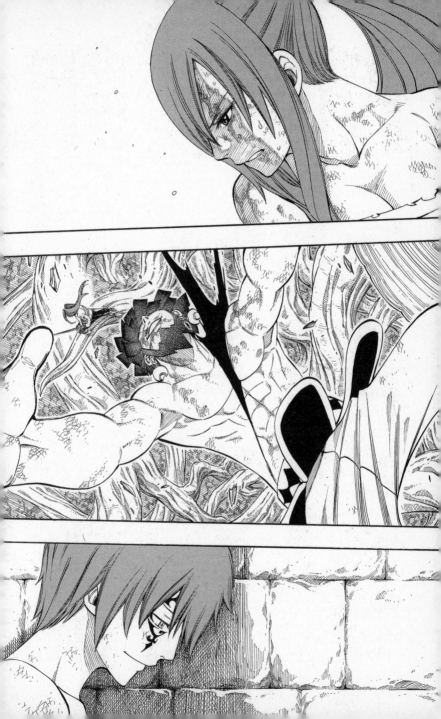

FAIRY TAIL
フェアリーテイル

Chapter 238: At One Time

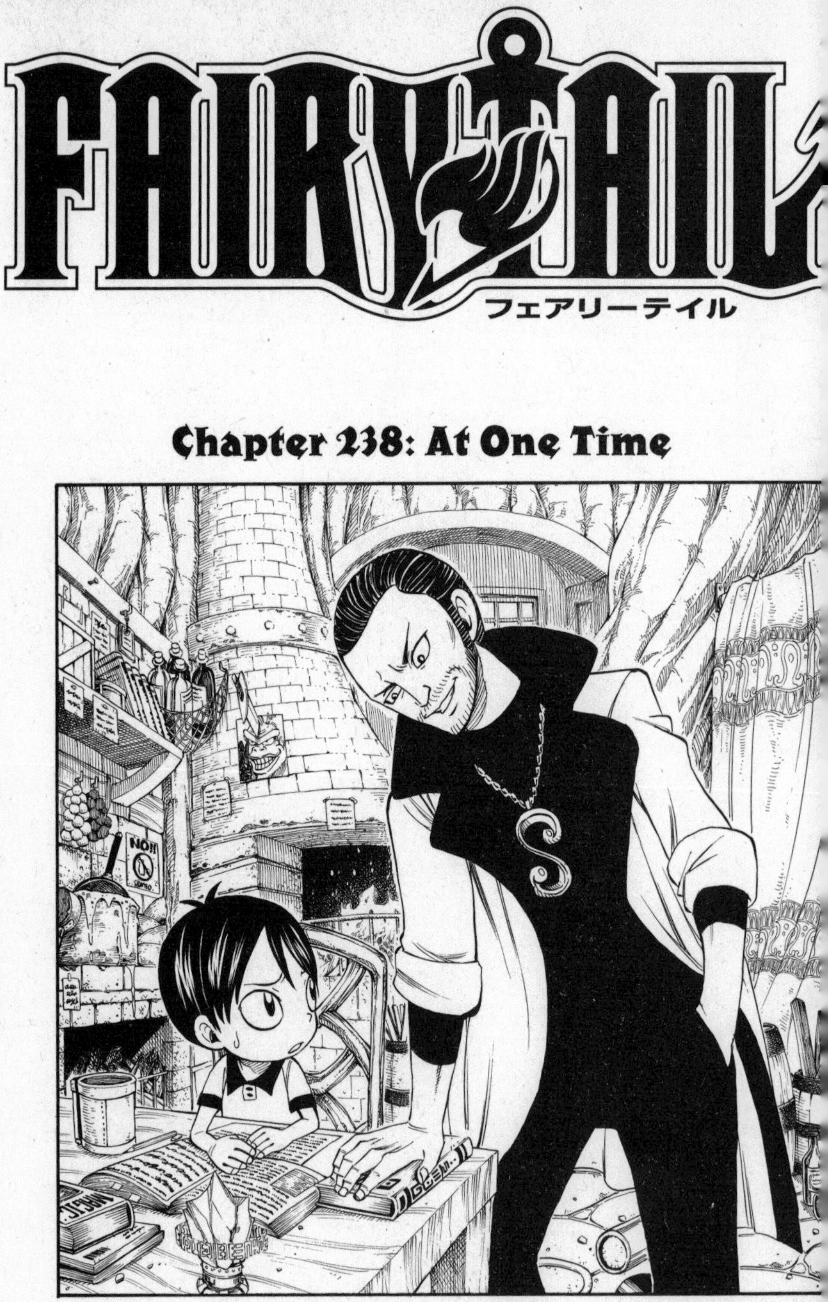
NO!!

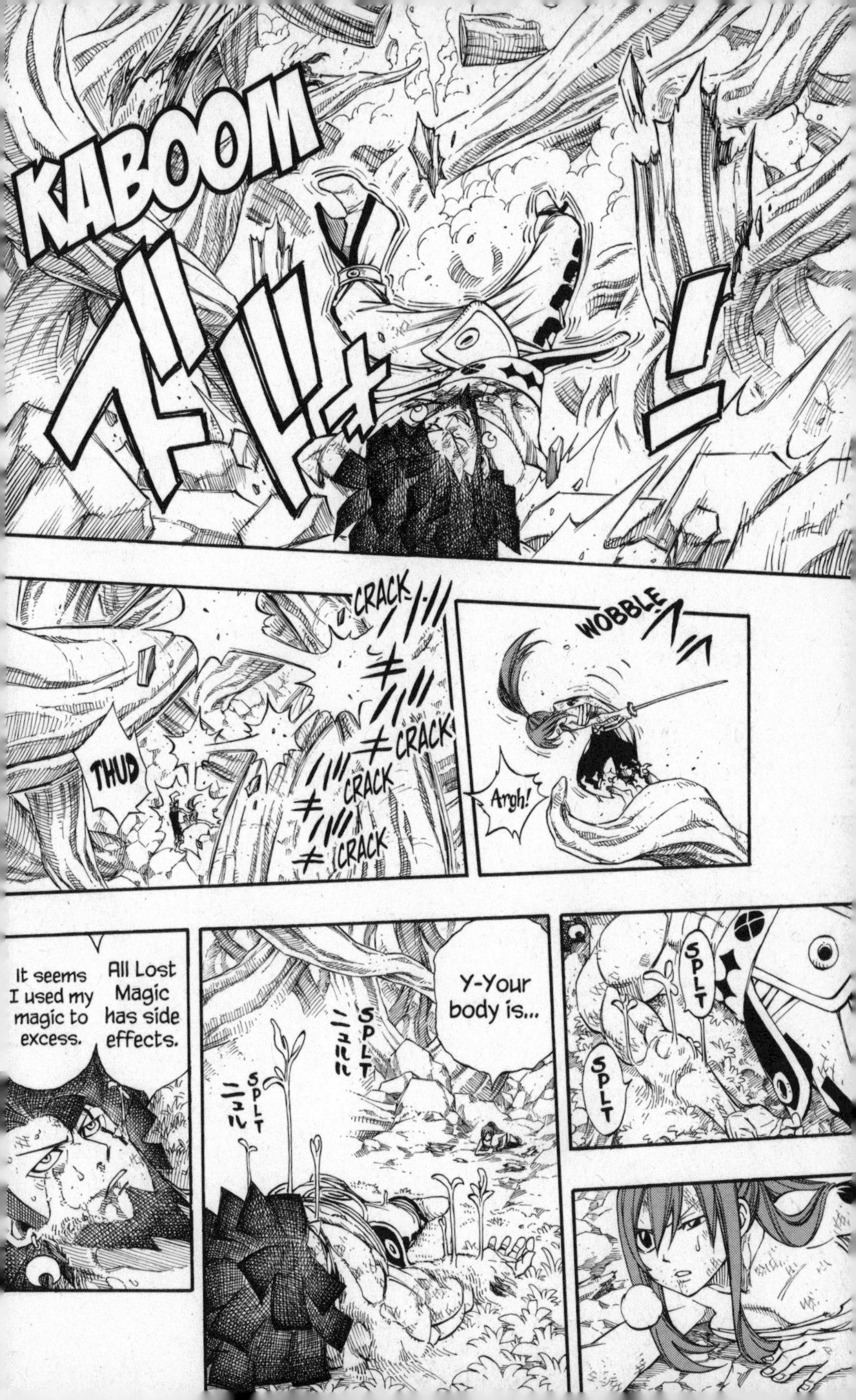
KABOOM
WOBBLE
Argh!
CRACK
CRACK
CRACK
CRACK
THUD
SPLT
SPLT
Y-Your body is...
SPLT
ニュルル
SPLT
ニュル
It seems I used my magic to excess. All Lost Magic has side effects.

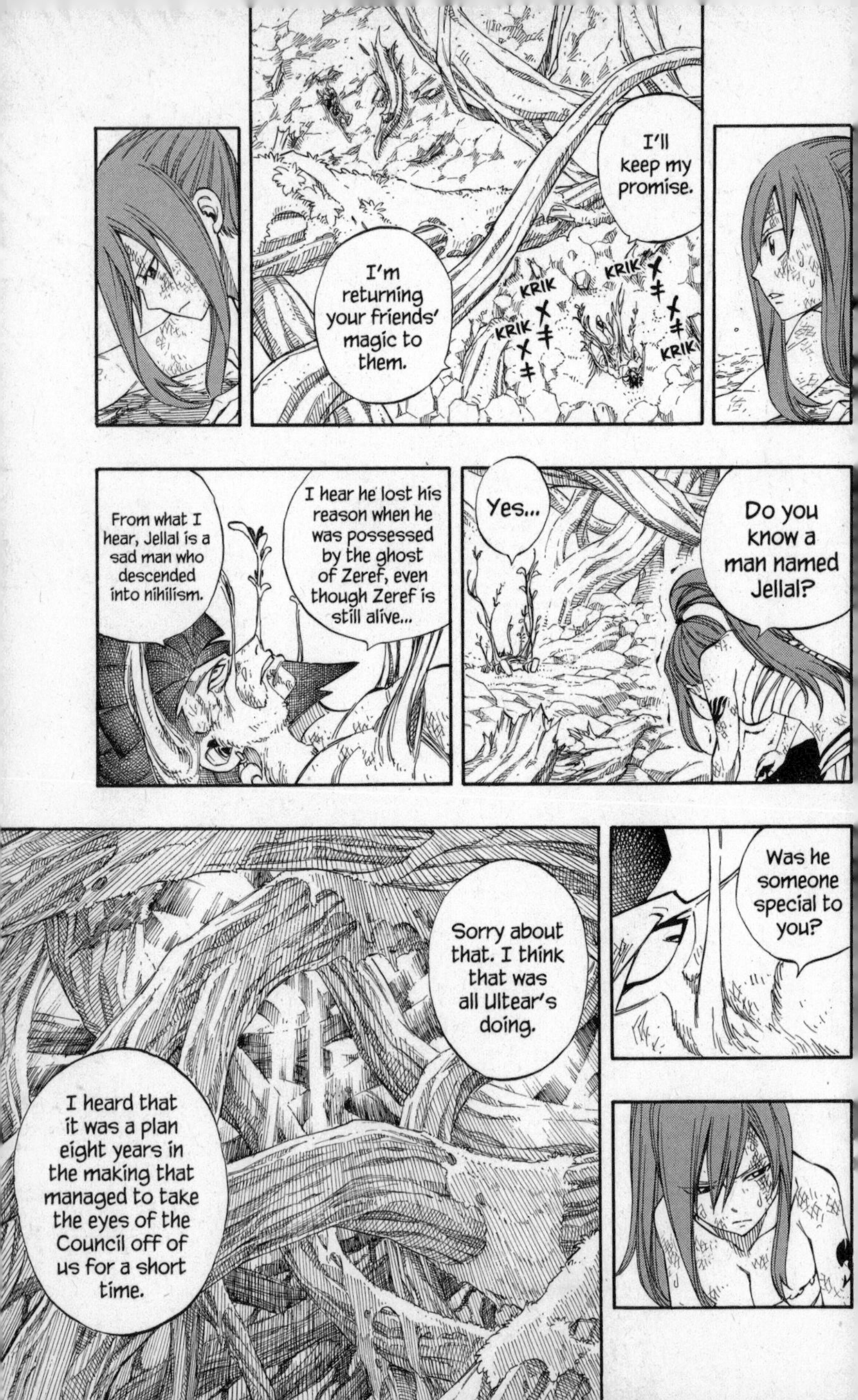
I'll keep my promise.
I'm returning your friends' magic to them.
KRIK
KRIK
KRIK
KRIK
Do you know a man named Jellal?
Yes...
I hear he lost his reason when he was possessed by the ghost of Zeref, even though Zeref is still alive...
From what I hear, Jellal is a sad man who descended into nihilism.
Was he someone special to you?
Sorry about that. I think that was all Ultear's doing.
I heard that it was a plan eight years in the making that managed to take the eyes of the Council off of us for a short time.

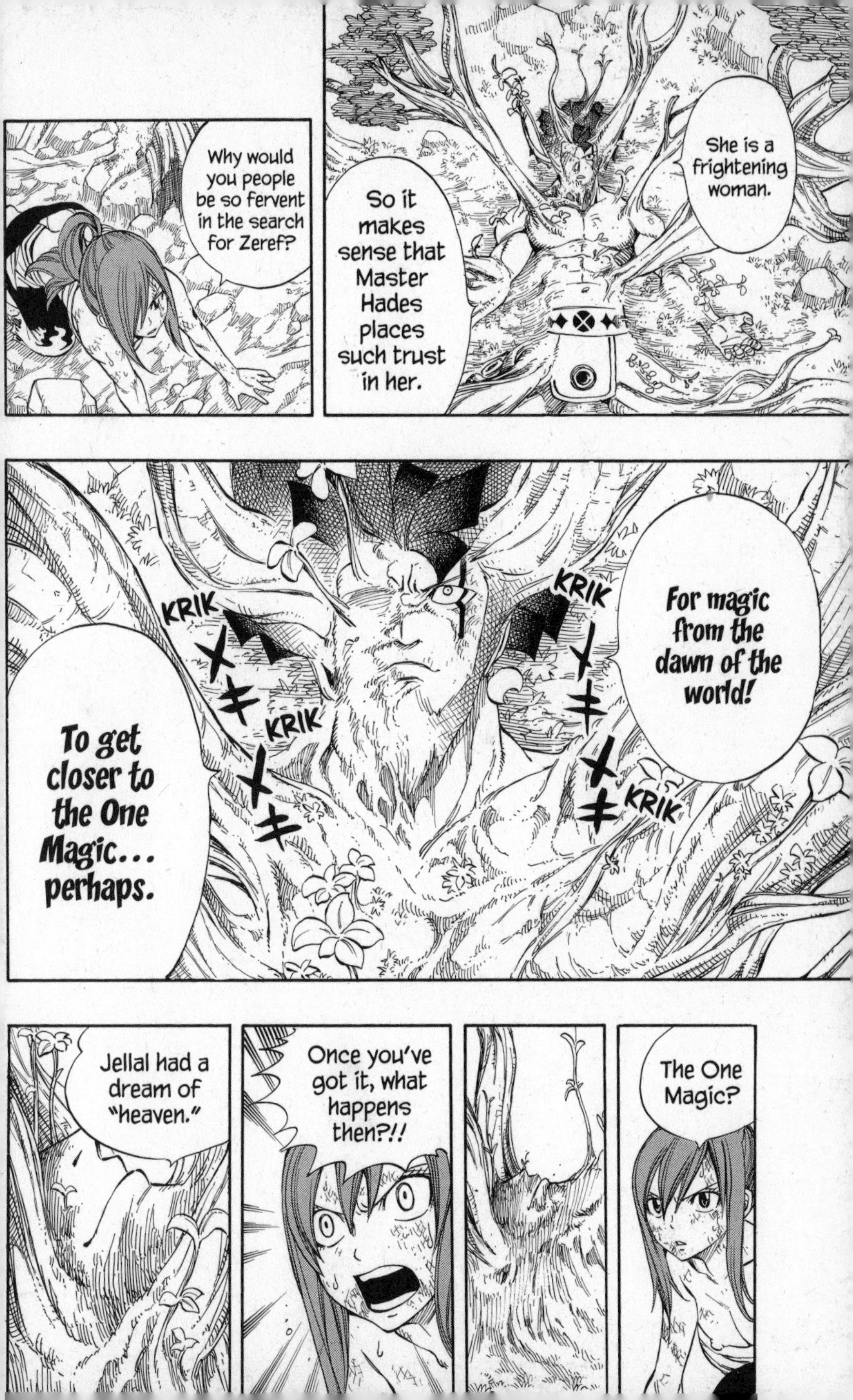

She is a frightening woman.
So it makes sense that Master Hades places such trust in her.
Why would you people be so fervent in the search for Zeref?
For magic from the dawn of the world!
KRIK
KRIK
KRIK
KRIK
To get closer to the One Magic... perhaps.
The One Magic?
Once you've got it, what happens then?!!
Jellal had a dream of "heaven."

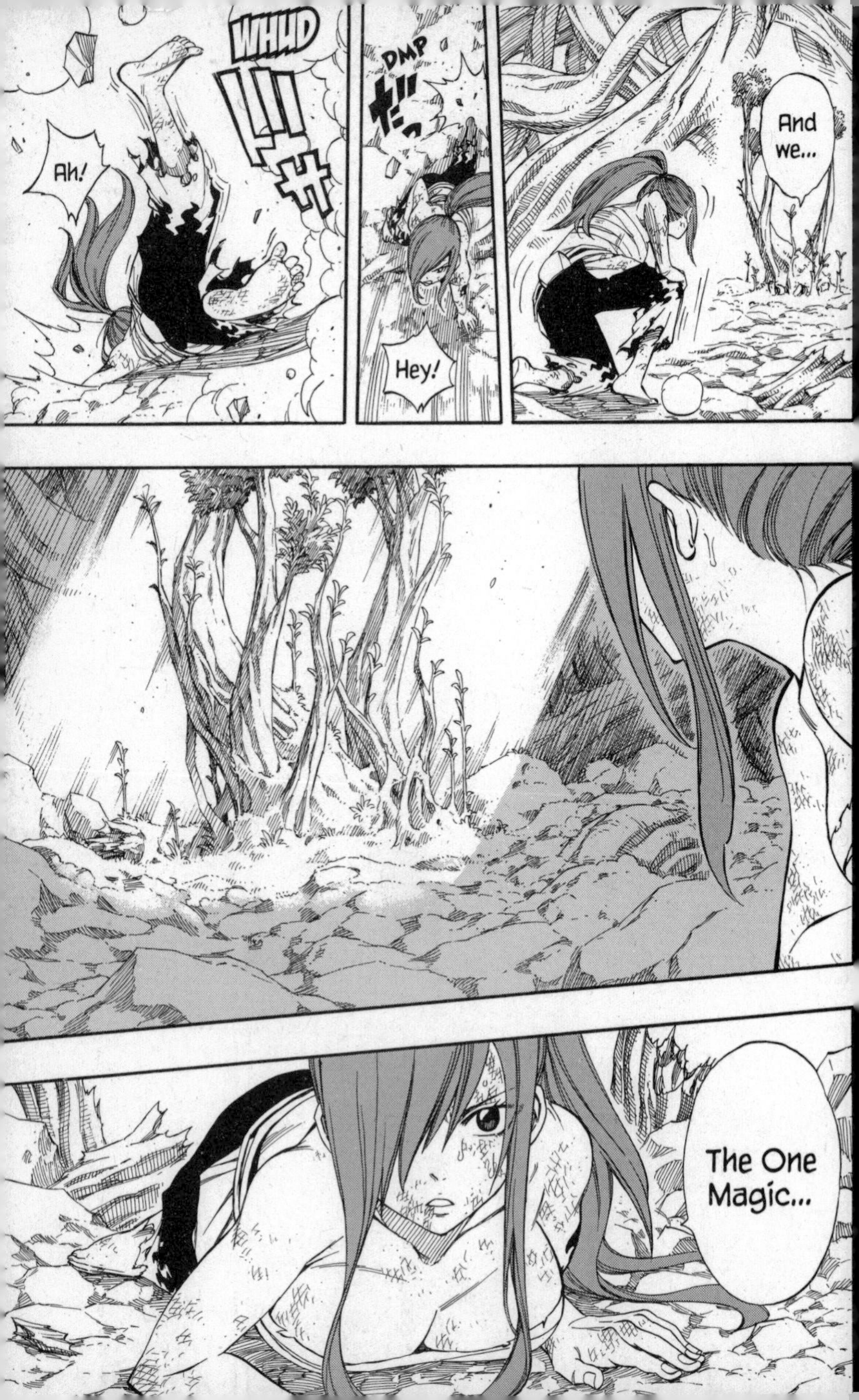
And we...
DMP
Hey!
WHUD
Ah!
The One Magic...

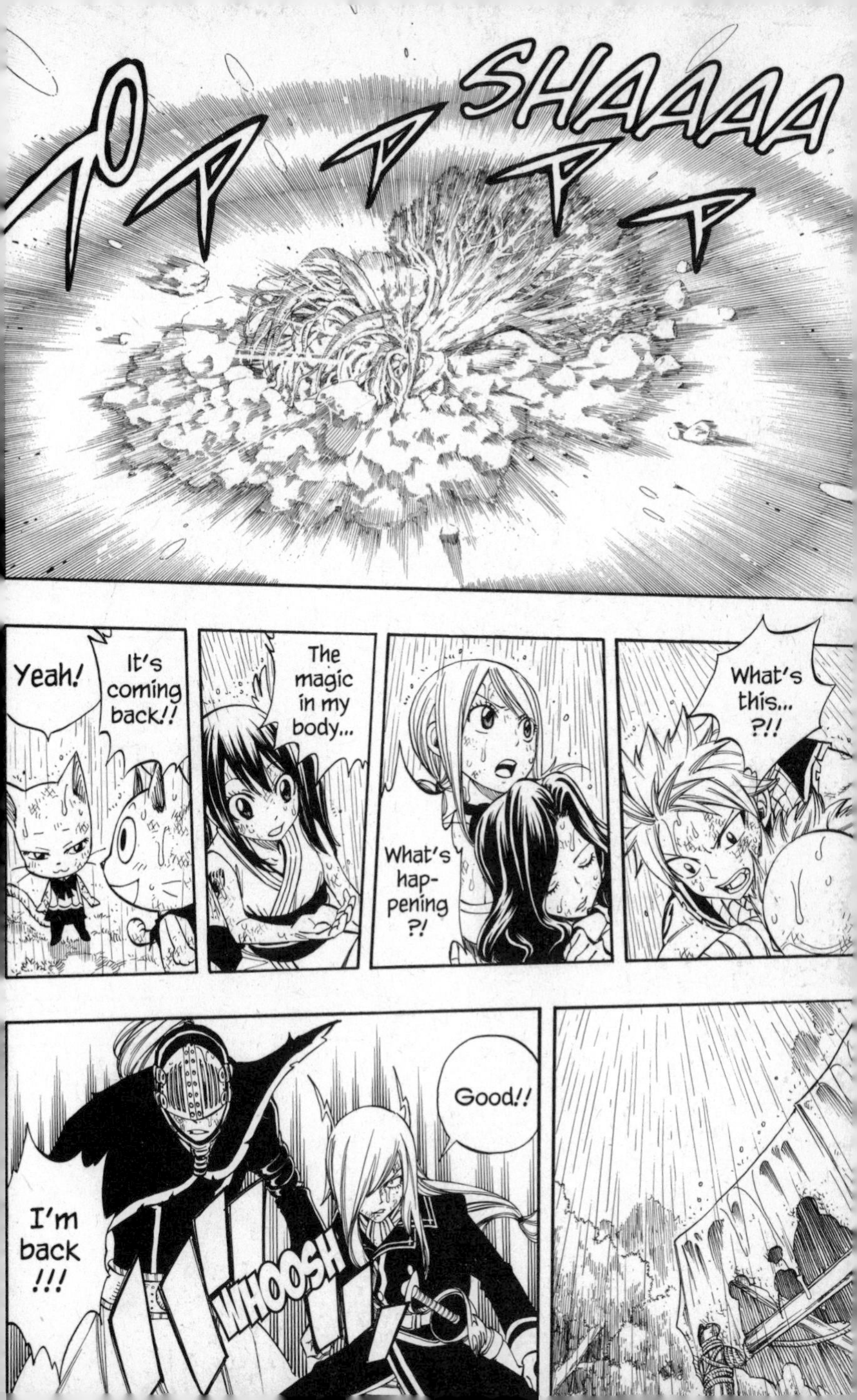
SHAAAAA
What's this...?!!
What's happening?!
The magic in my body...
It's coming back!!
Yeah!
Good!!
WHOOSH
I'm back!!!

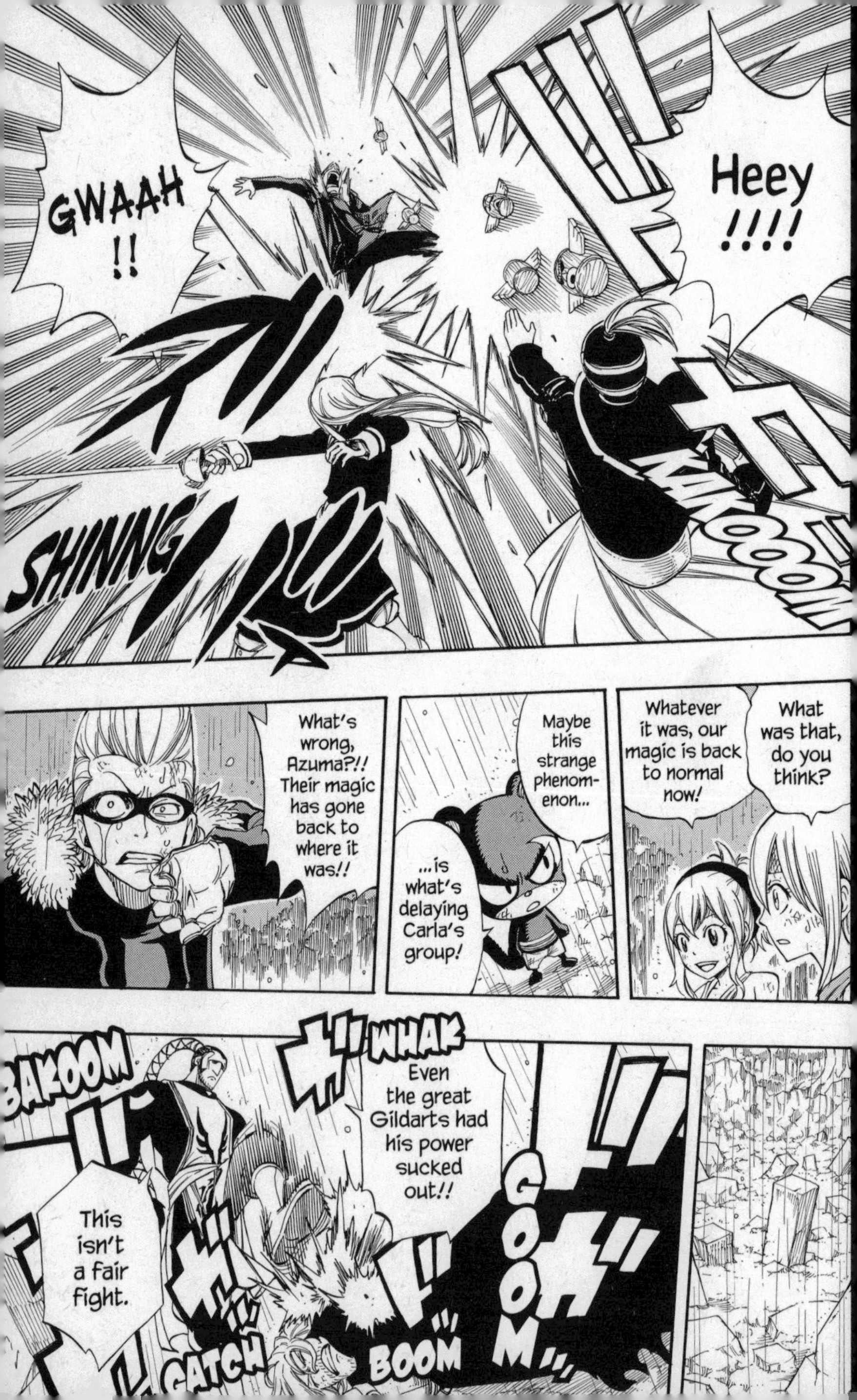
Heey !!!!
GWAAH !!
SHINING
What was that, do you think?
Whatever it was, our magic is back to normal now!
Maybe this strange phenom-enon...
...is what's delaying Carla's group!
What's wrong, Azuma?!! Their magic has gone back to where it was!!
GOOOM
WHAK
Even the great Gildarts had his power sucked out!!
BOOM
GATCH
BAKOOM
This isn't a fair fight.

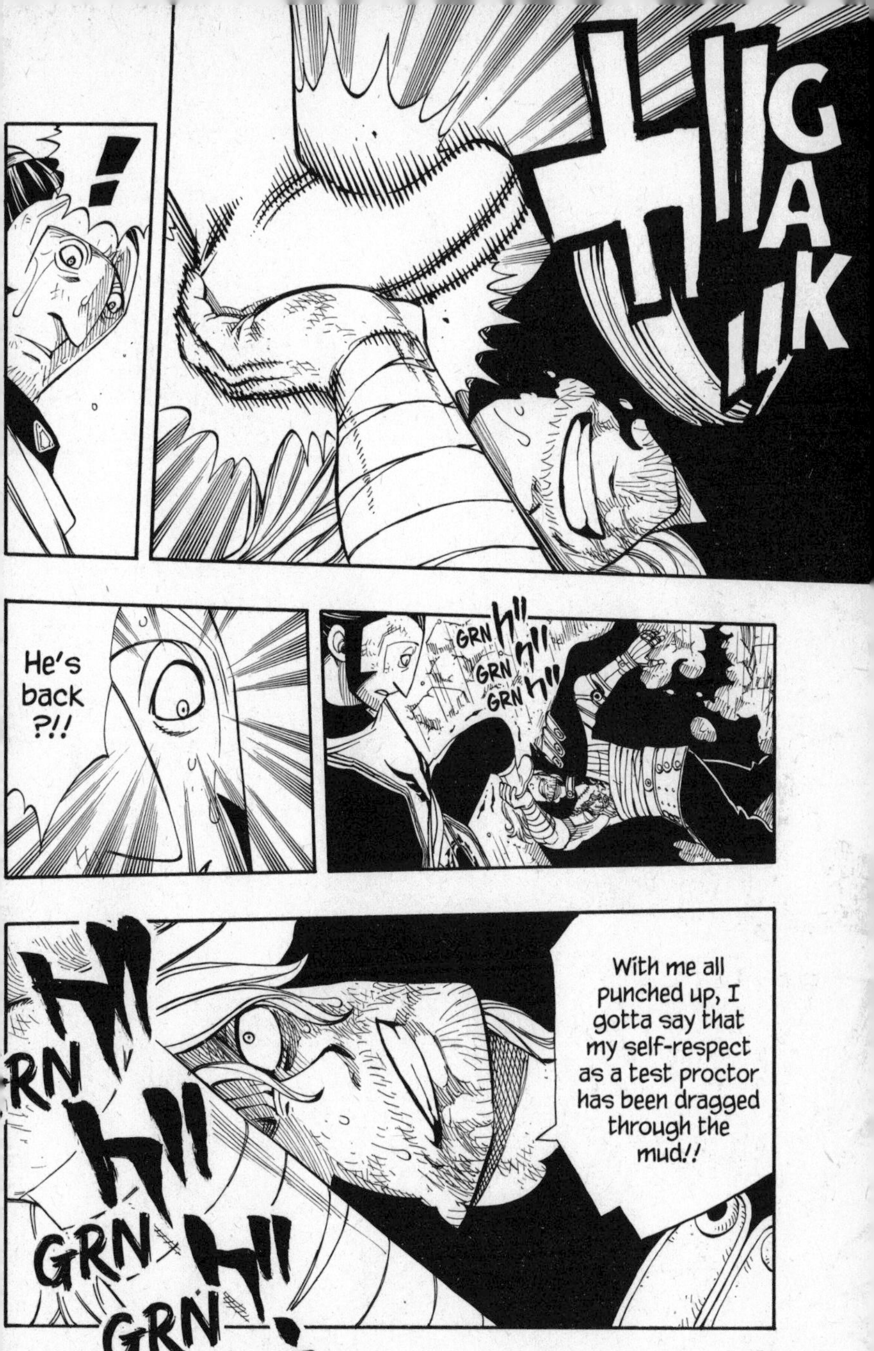
GAK
!
GRN h'' GRN n'' GRN h''
He's back ?!!
With me all punched up, I gotta say that my self-respect as a test proctor has been dragged through the mud!!
RN
GRN
GRN

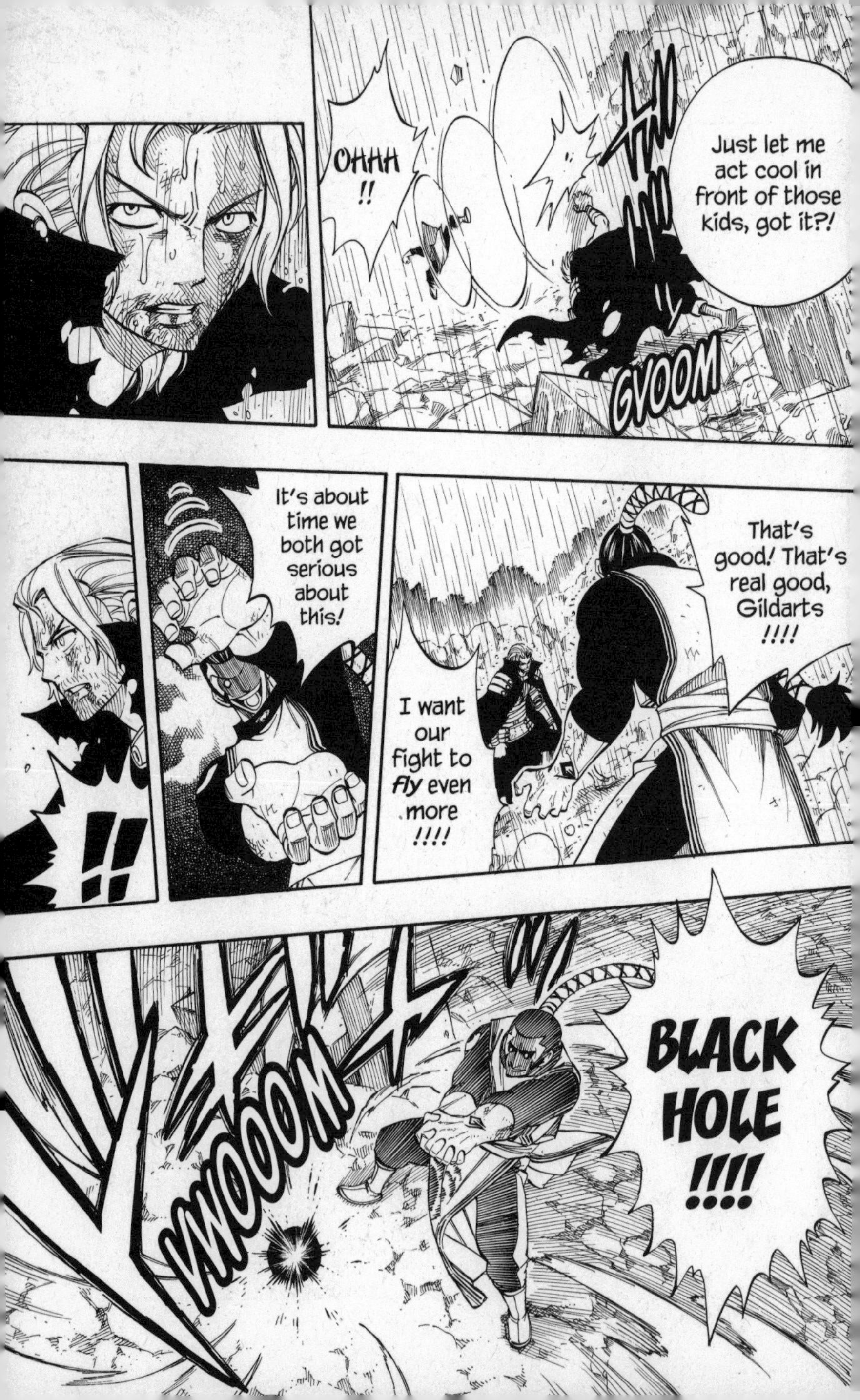
Just let me act cool in front of those kids, got it?!
OHHH !!
GVOOM
That's good! That's real good, Gildarts !!!!
I want our fight to *fly* even more !!!!
It's about time we both got serious about this!
!!
BLACK HOLE !!!!
WHOOOM

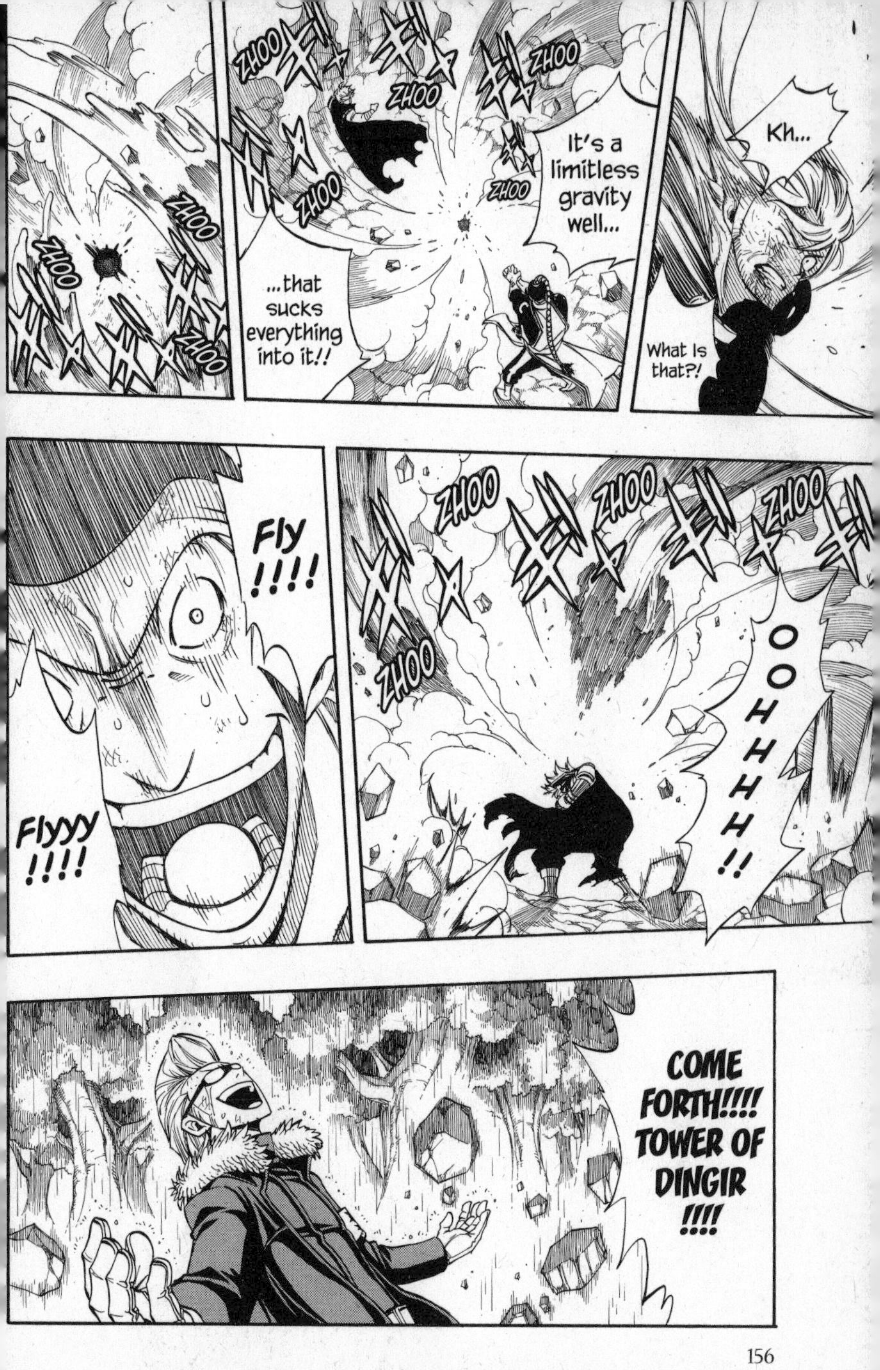
Kh...
What is that?!
ZHOO
ZHOO
ZHOO
ZHOO
It's a limitless gravity well...
...that sucks everything into it!!
ZHOO
ZHOO
ZHOO
ZHOO
ZHOO
ZHOO
ZHOO
OOHHHHH!!
Fly !!!!
Flyyy !!!!
COME FORTH!!!! TOWER OF DINGIR !!!!

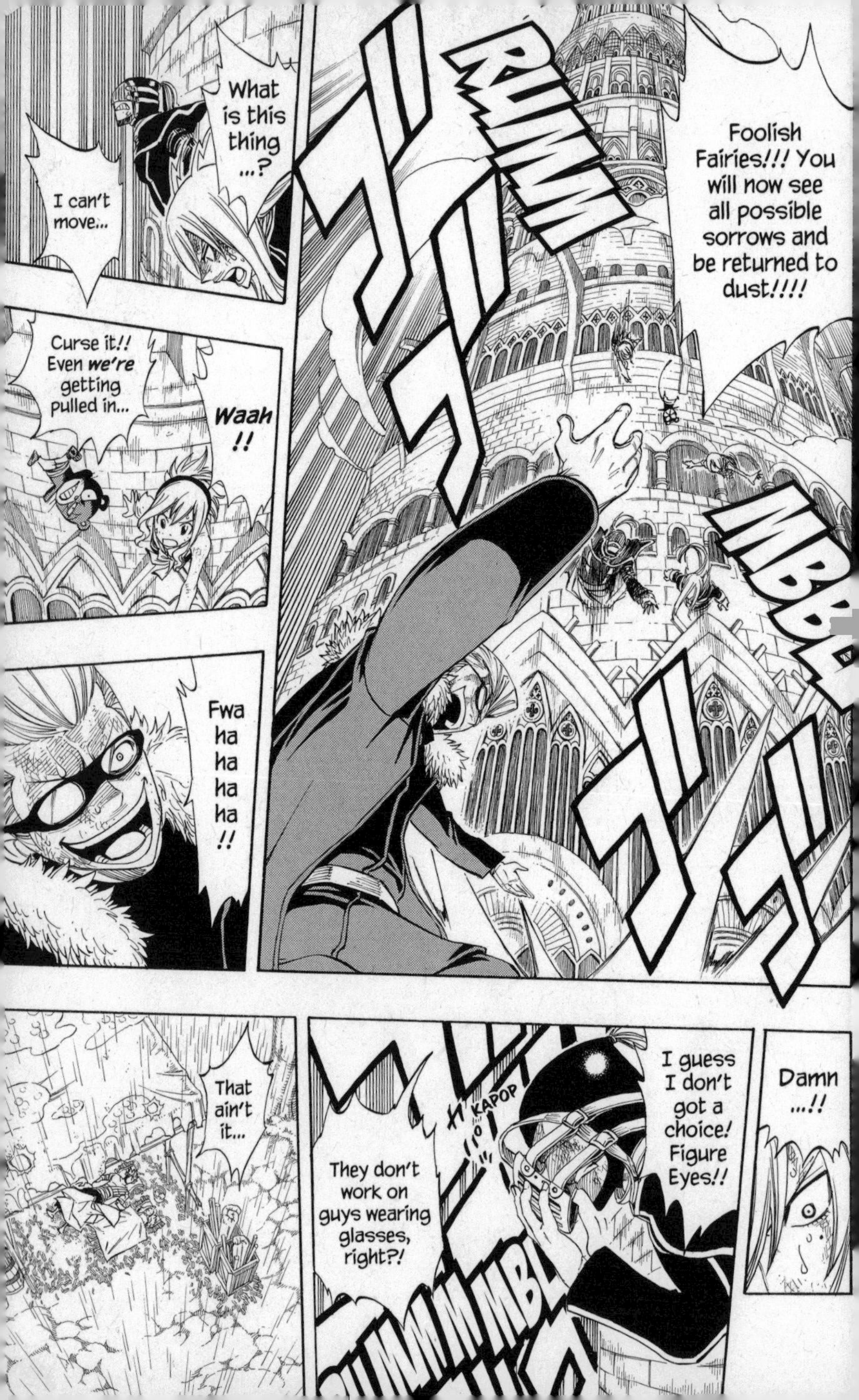
Foolish Fairies!!! You will now see all possible sorrows and be returned to dust!!!!
RUMM
NBBL
What is this thing ...?
I can't move...
Curse it!! Even we're getting pulled in...
Waah !!
Fwa ha ha ha ha !!
Damn ...!!
I guess I don't got a choice! Figure Eyes!!
KAPOP
They don't work on guys wearing glasses, right?!
RUMMMMMBL
That ain't it...

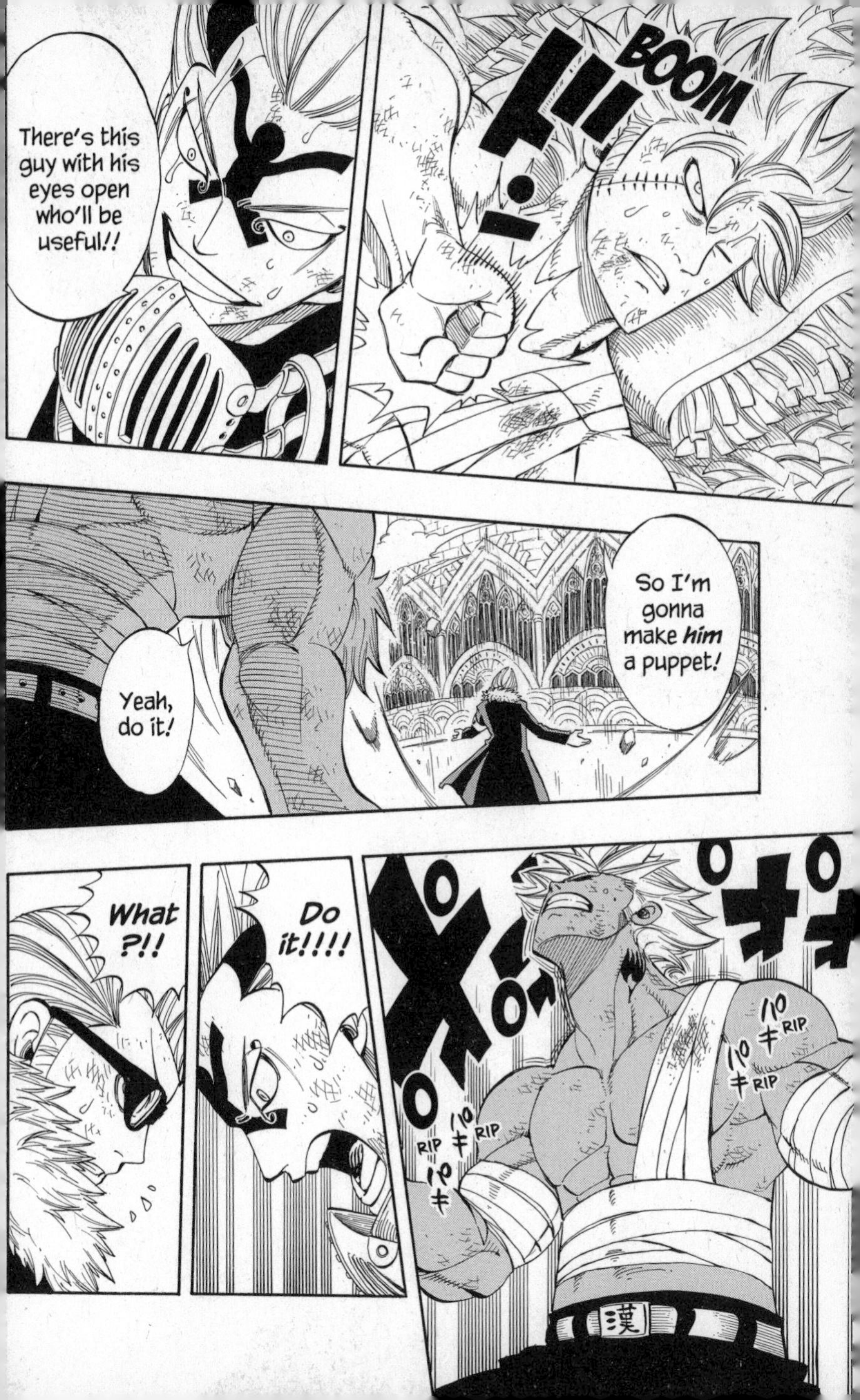
BOOM
There's this guy with his eyes open who'll be useful!!
So I'm gonna make *him* a puppet!
Yeah, do it!
パキ RIP
パキ RIP
パキ RIP
パキ RIP
Do it!!!!
What?!!

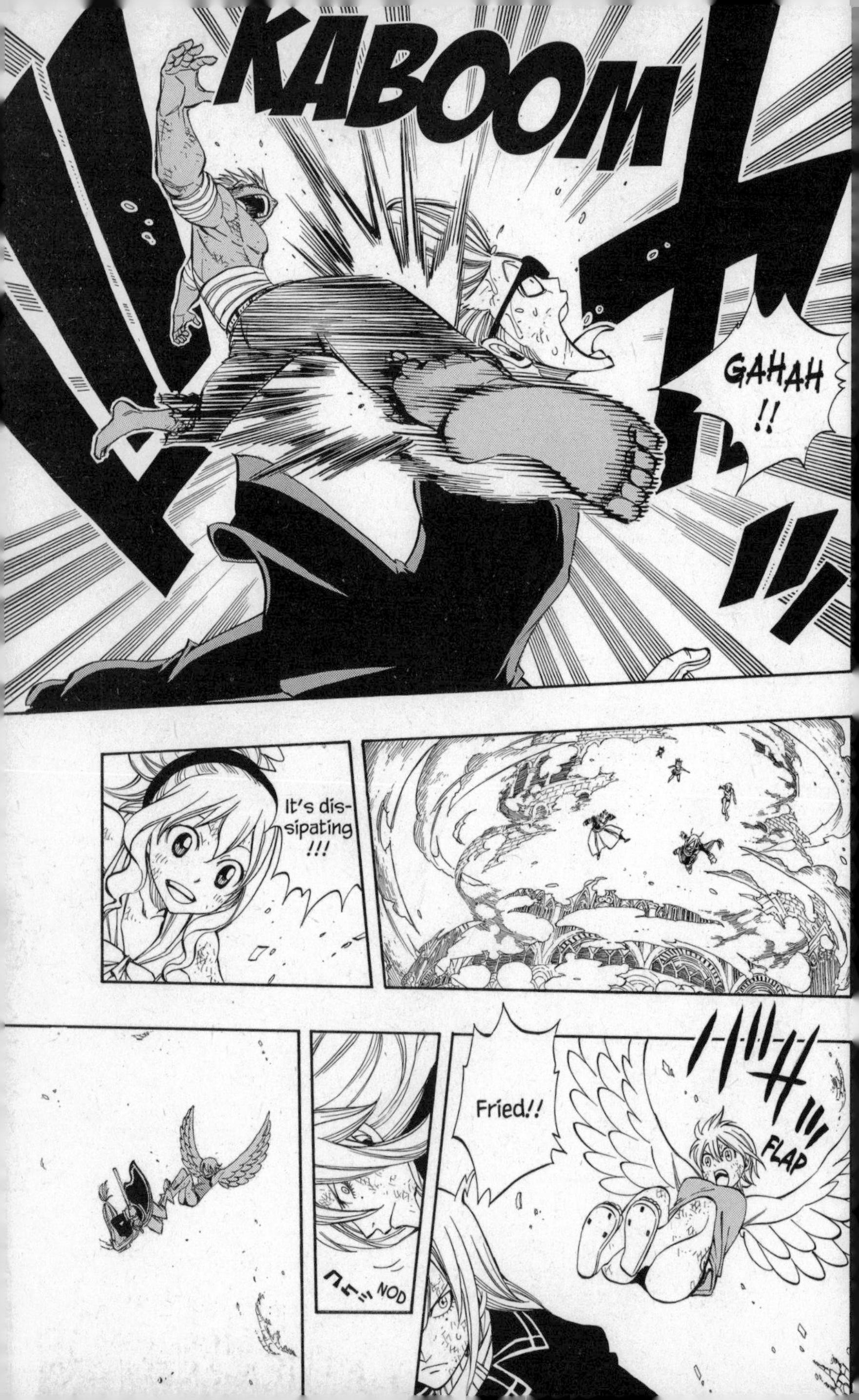
KABOOM
GAHAH !!
It's dis- sipating !!!
FLAP
Fried!!
NOD

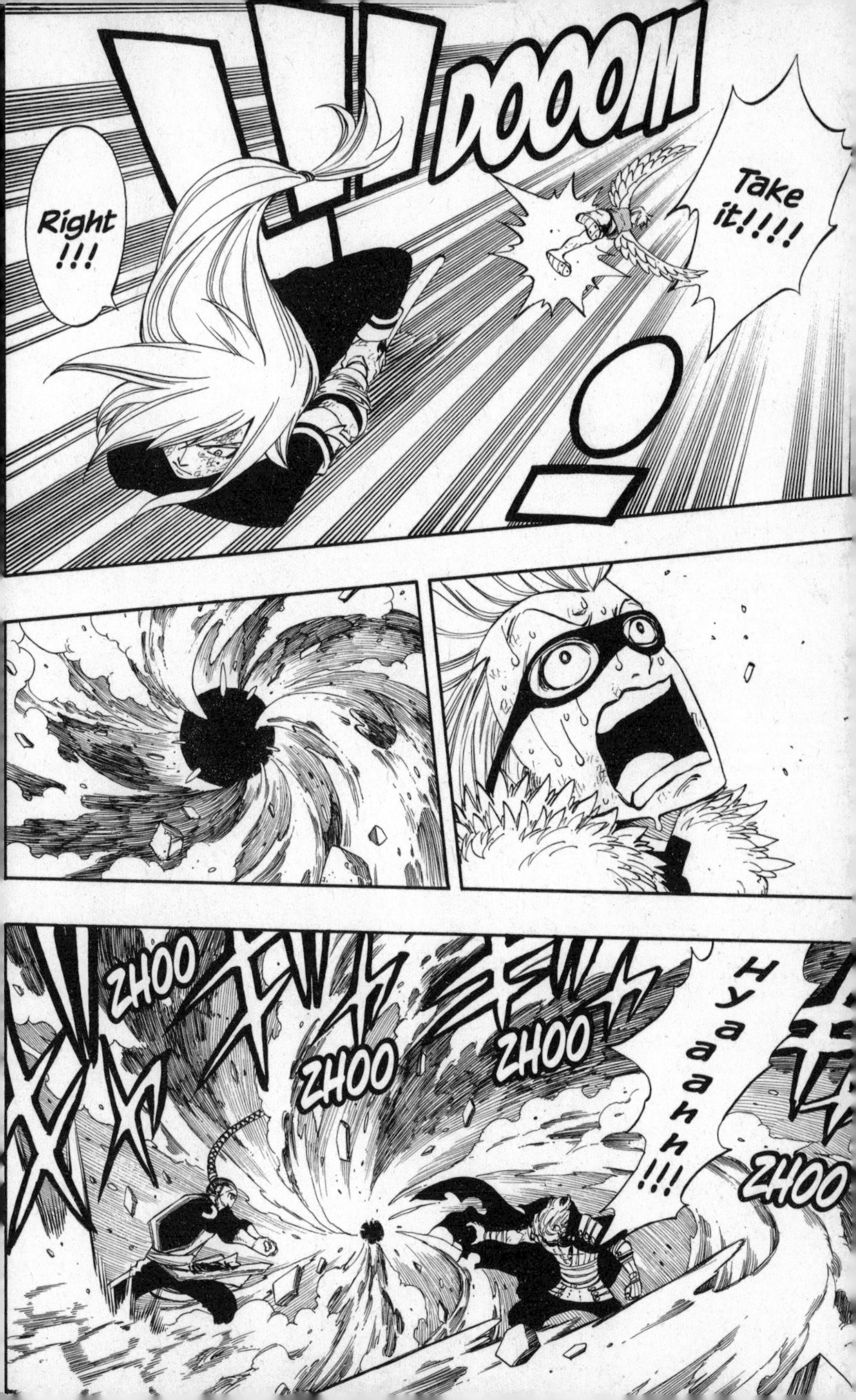
Take it!!!!
DOOOM
Right!!!
Hyaaaahh!!!
ZHOO
ZHOO
ZHOO
ZHOO

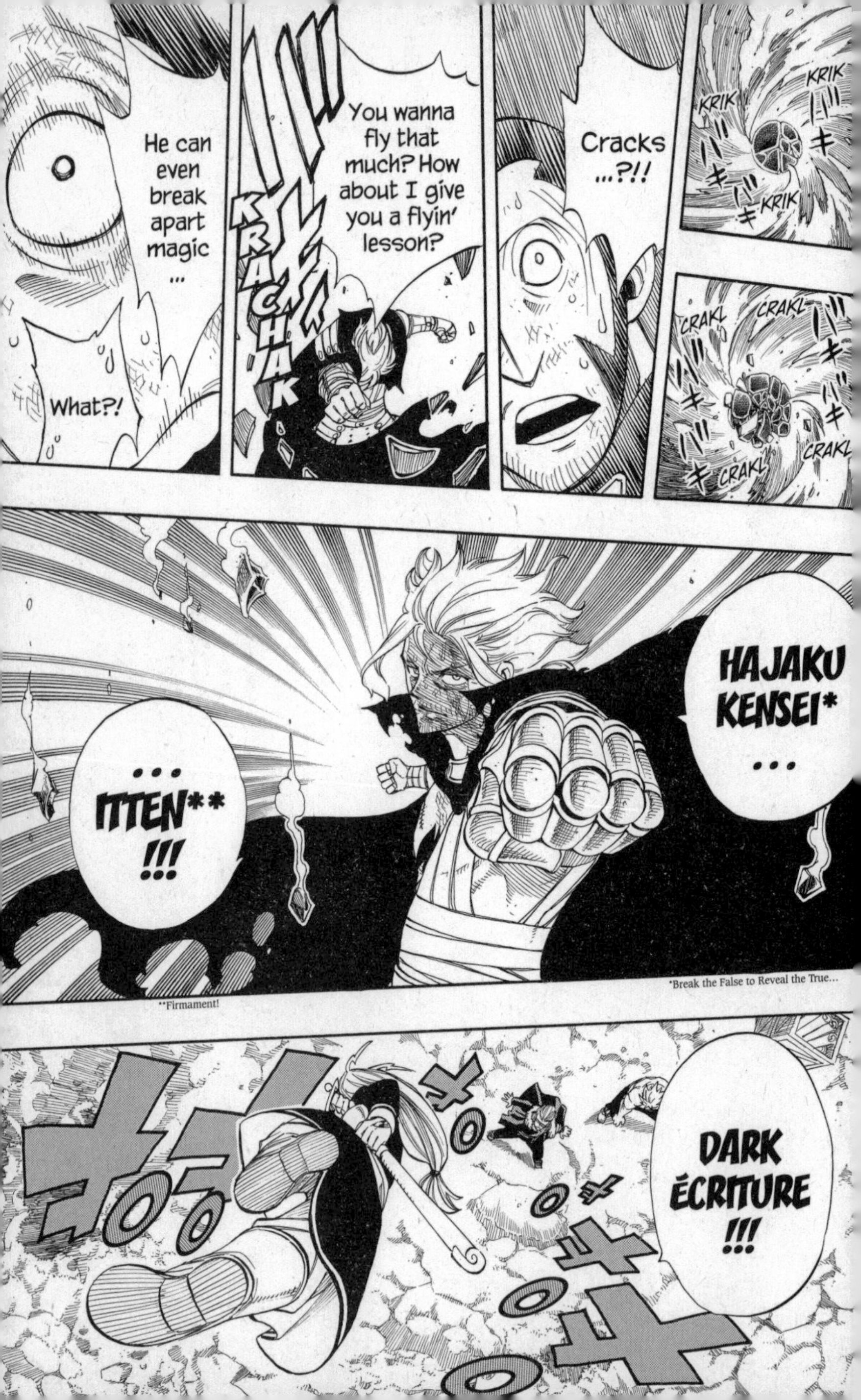
KRIK
KRIK
KRIK
CRAKL
CRAKL
CRAKL
CRAKL
Cracks ...?!!
You wanna fly that much? How about I give you a flyin' lesson?
KRACHAK
He can even break apart magic ...
What?!
HAJAKU KENSEI* ...
... ITTEN** !!!
DARK ÉCRITURE !!!

*Break the False to Reveal the True...

**Firmament!

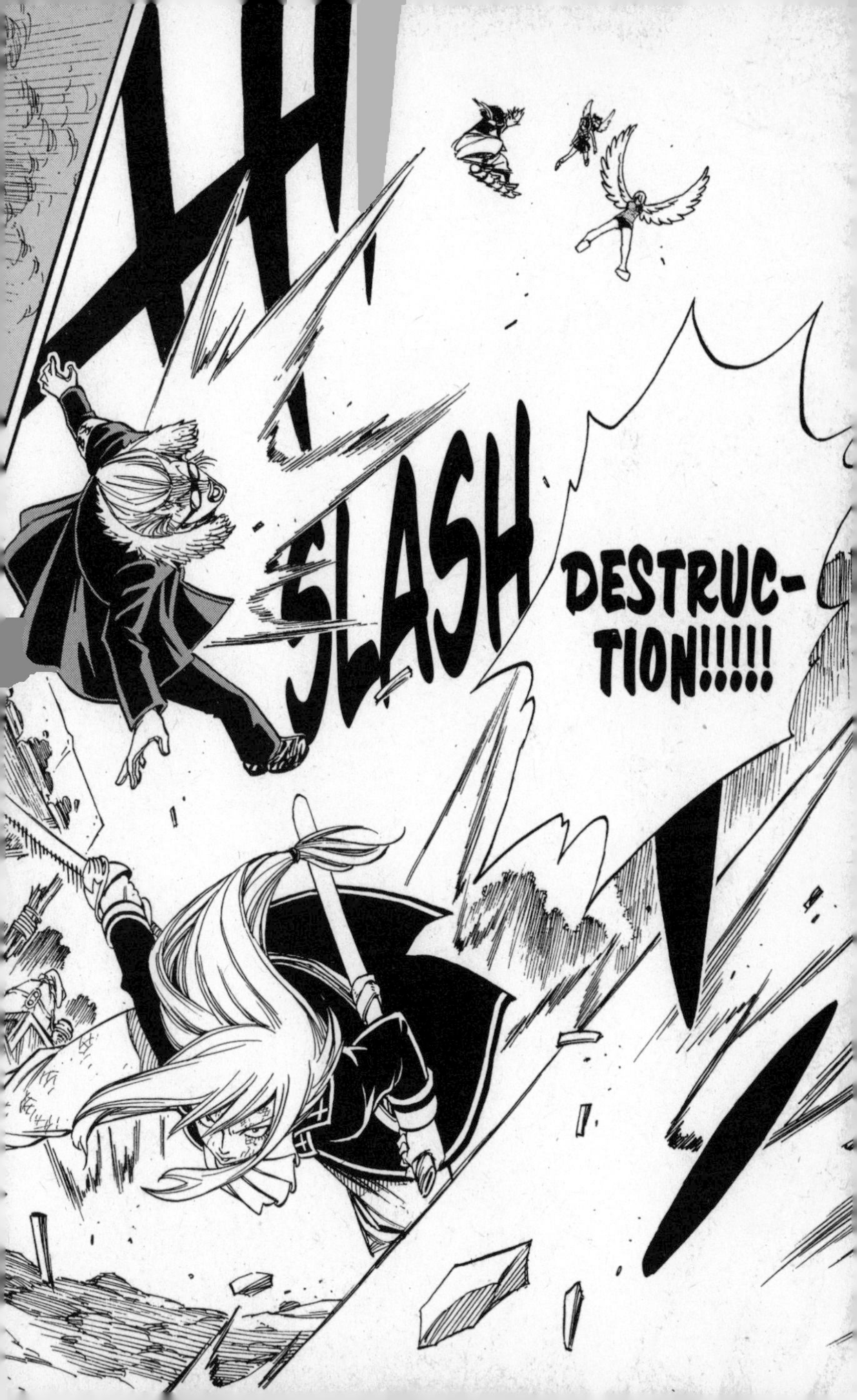
AH
SLASH
DESTRUC-
TION!!!!!!

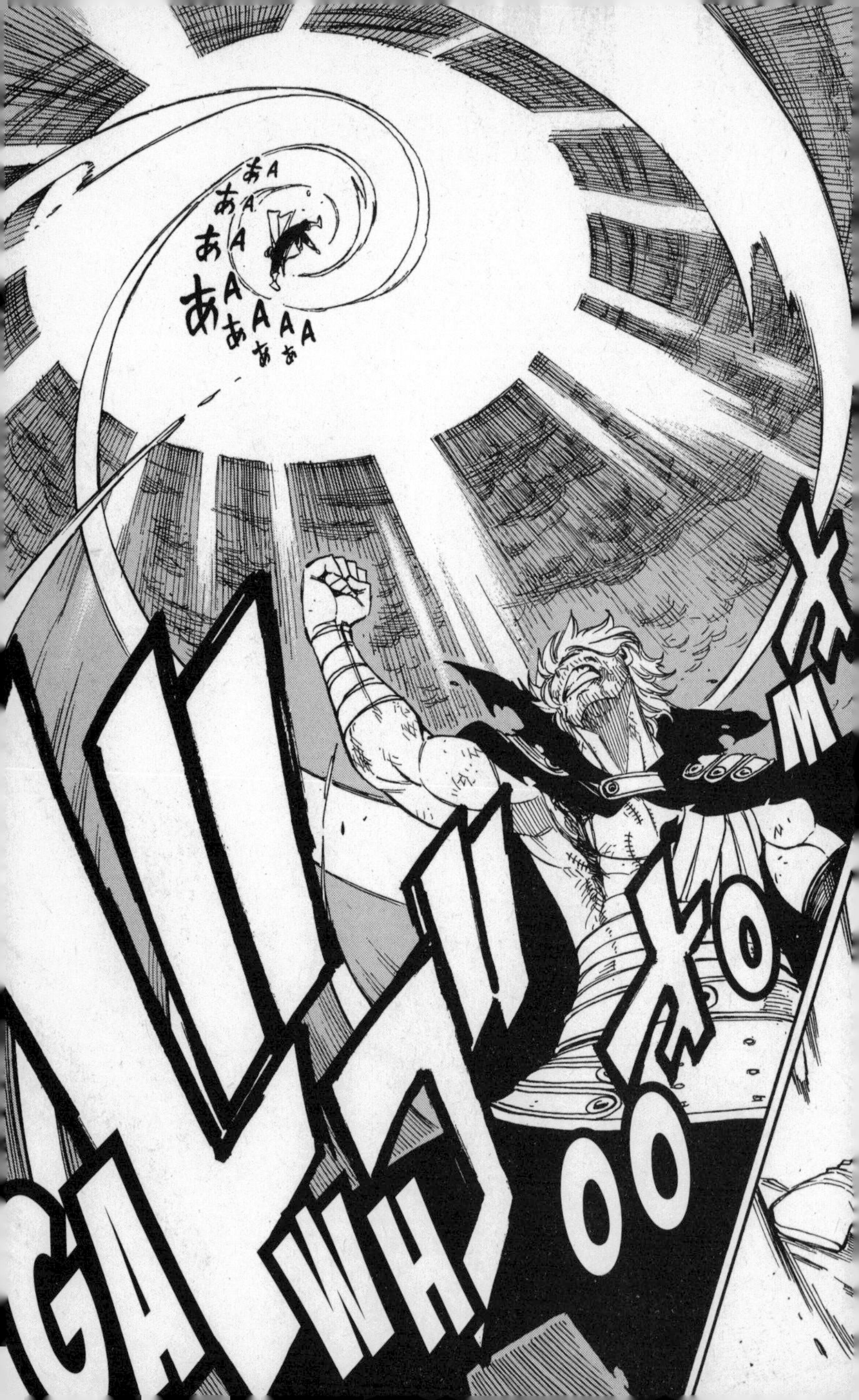
あAあAあAあAあAあAあA
GAWHOOOM

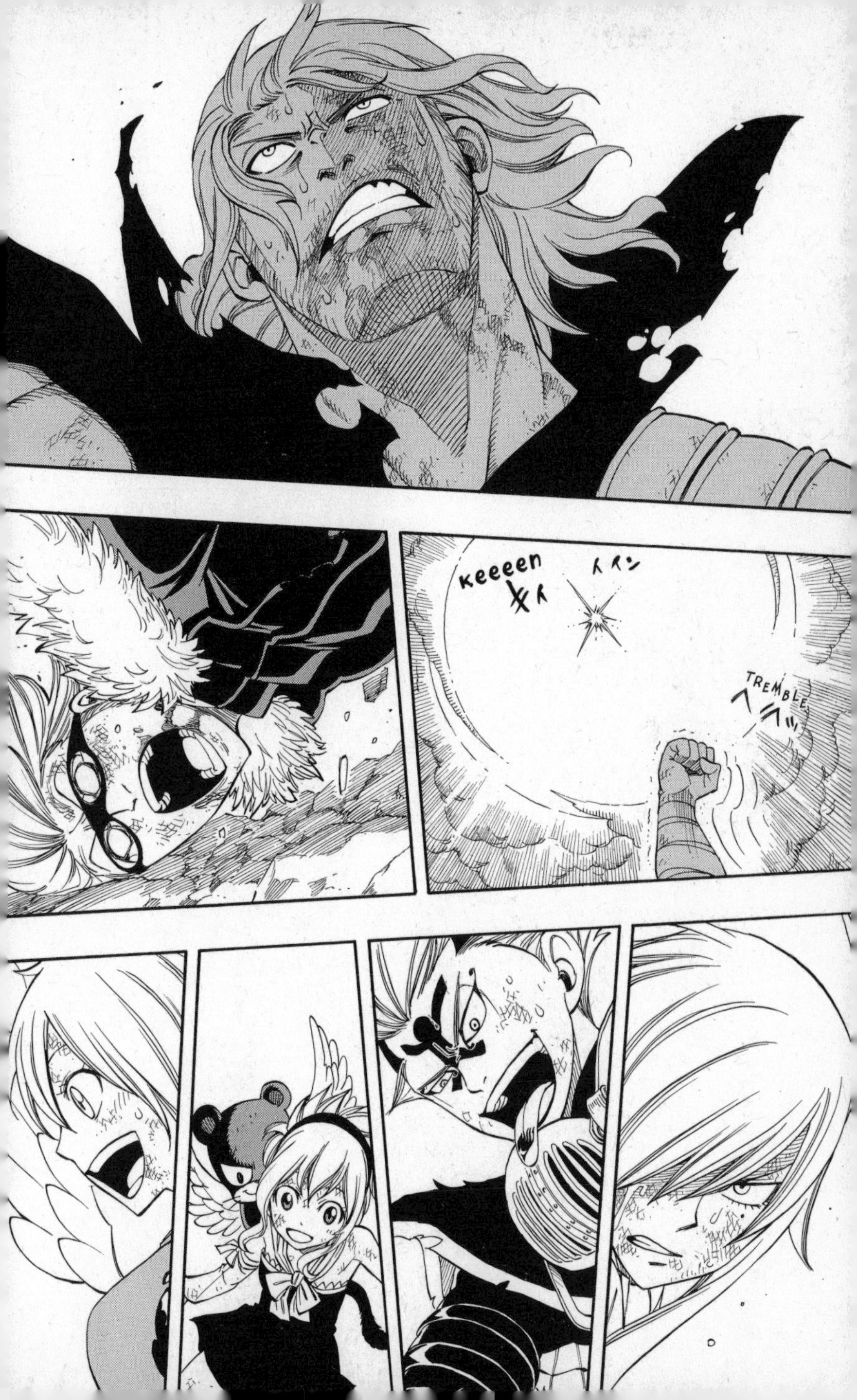
Keeeen
TREMBLE

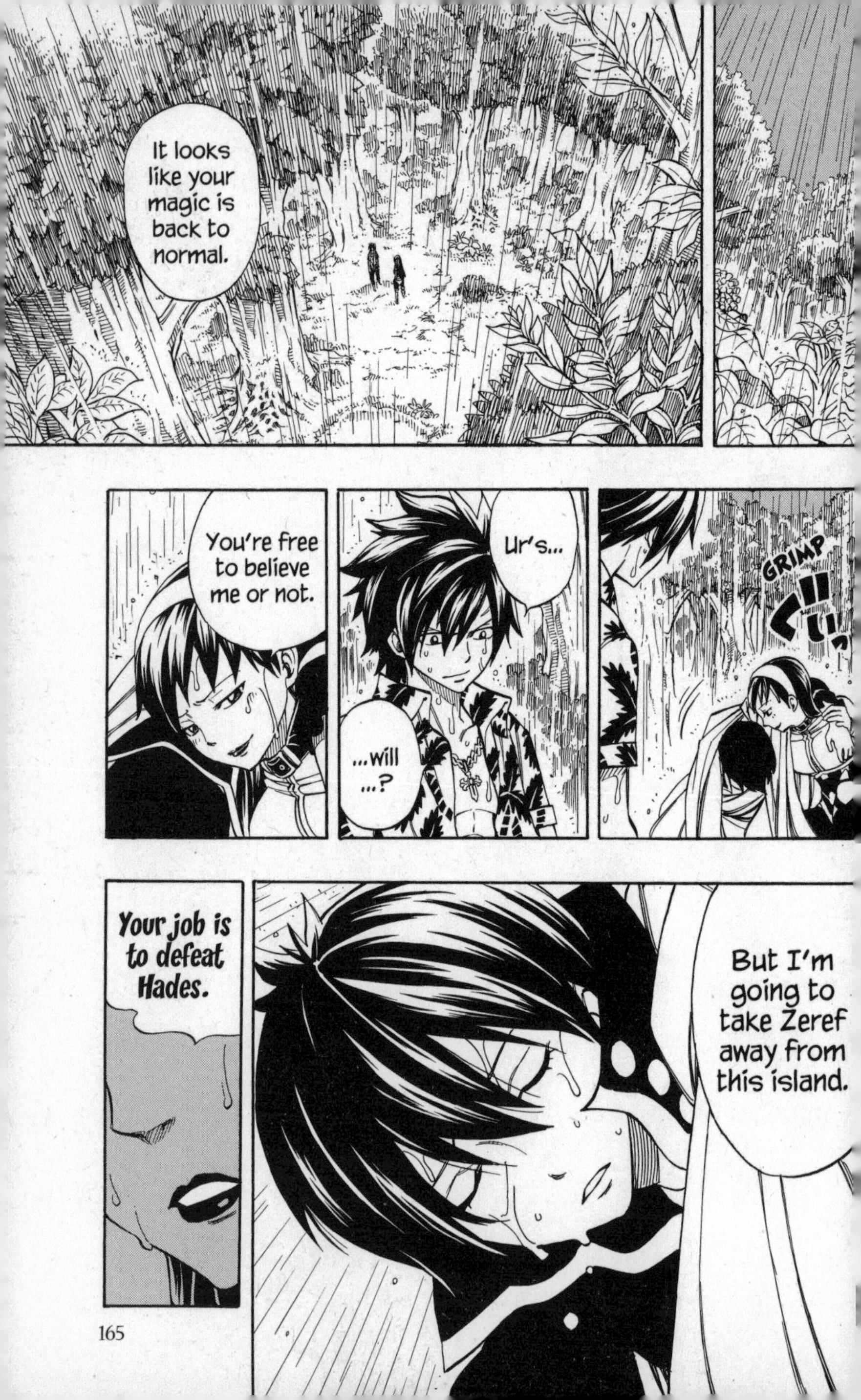
It looks like your magic is back to normal.
GRIMP
Ur's...
...will ...?
You're free to believe me or not.
But I'm going to take Zeref away from this island.
Your job is to defeat Hades.

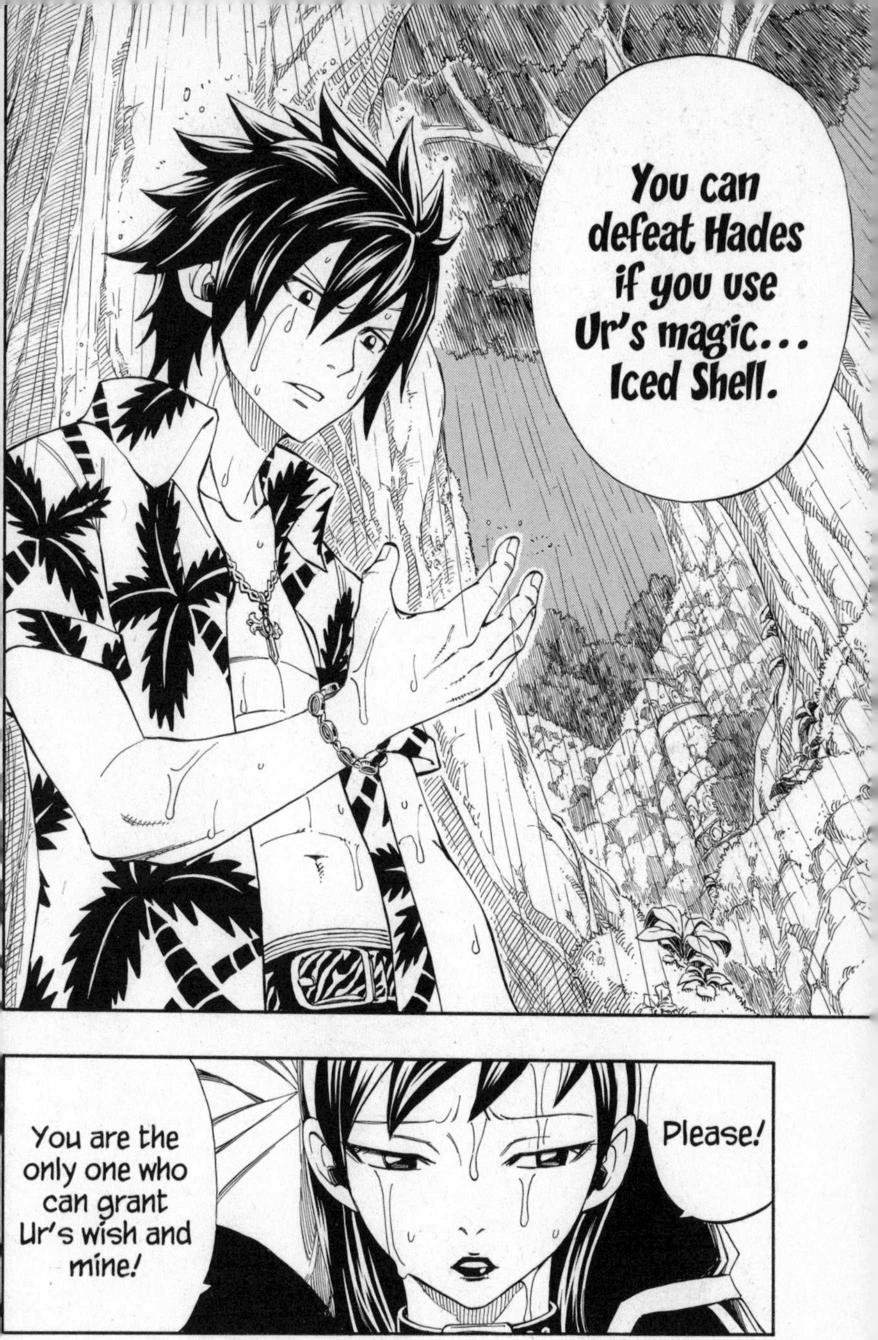
You can defeat Hades if you use Ur's magic... Iced Shell.
Please!
You are the only one who can grant Ur's wish and mine!

FAIRY TAIL

フェアリーテイル

Chapter 239: The Freezing Warrior

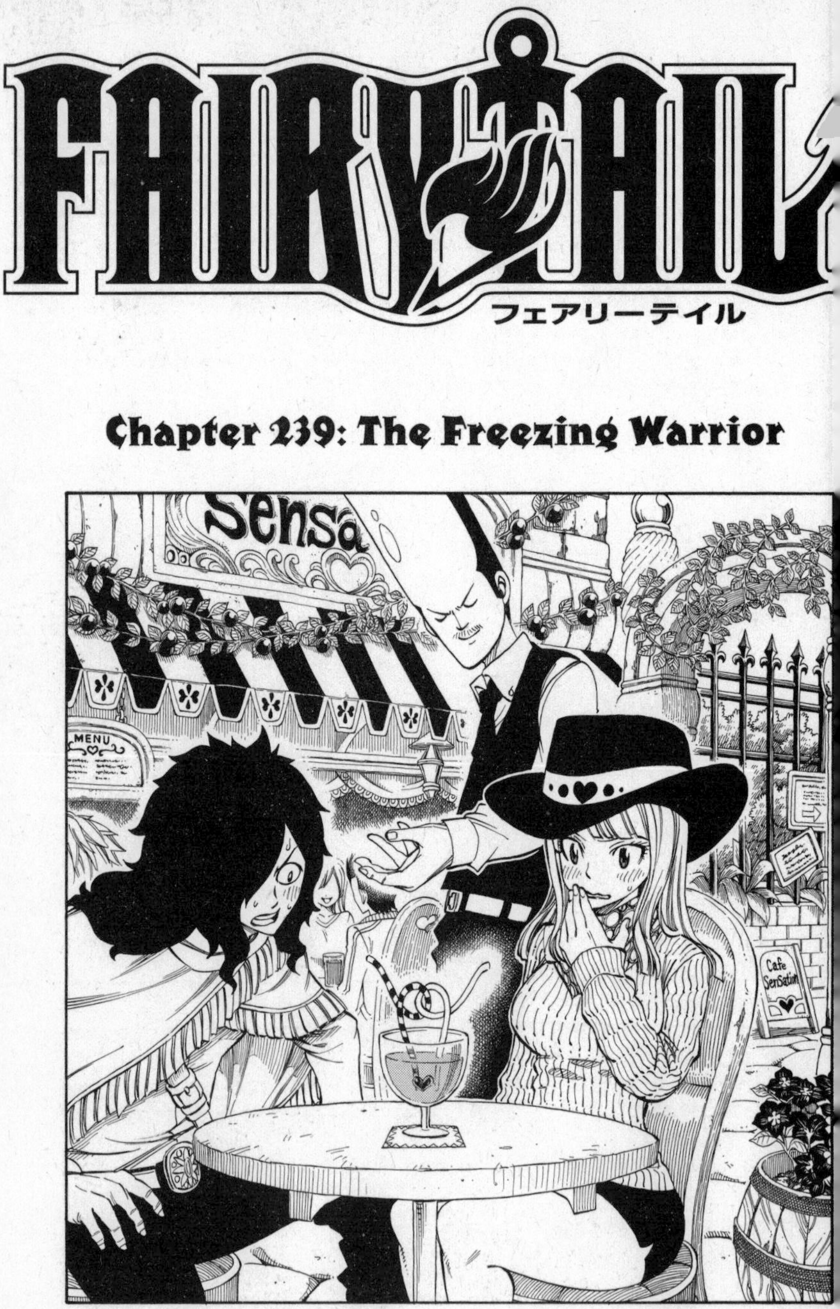
Sensa
MENU
Cafe SenSation

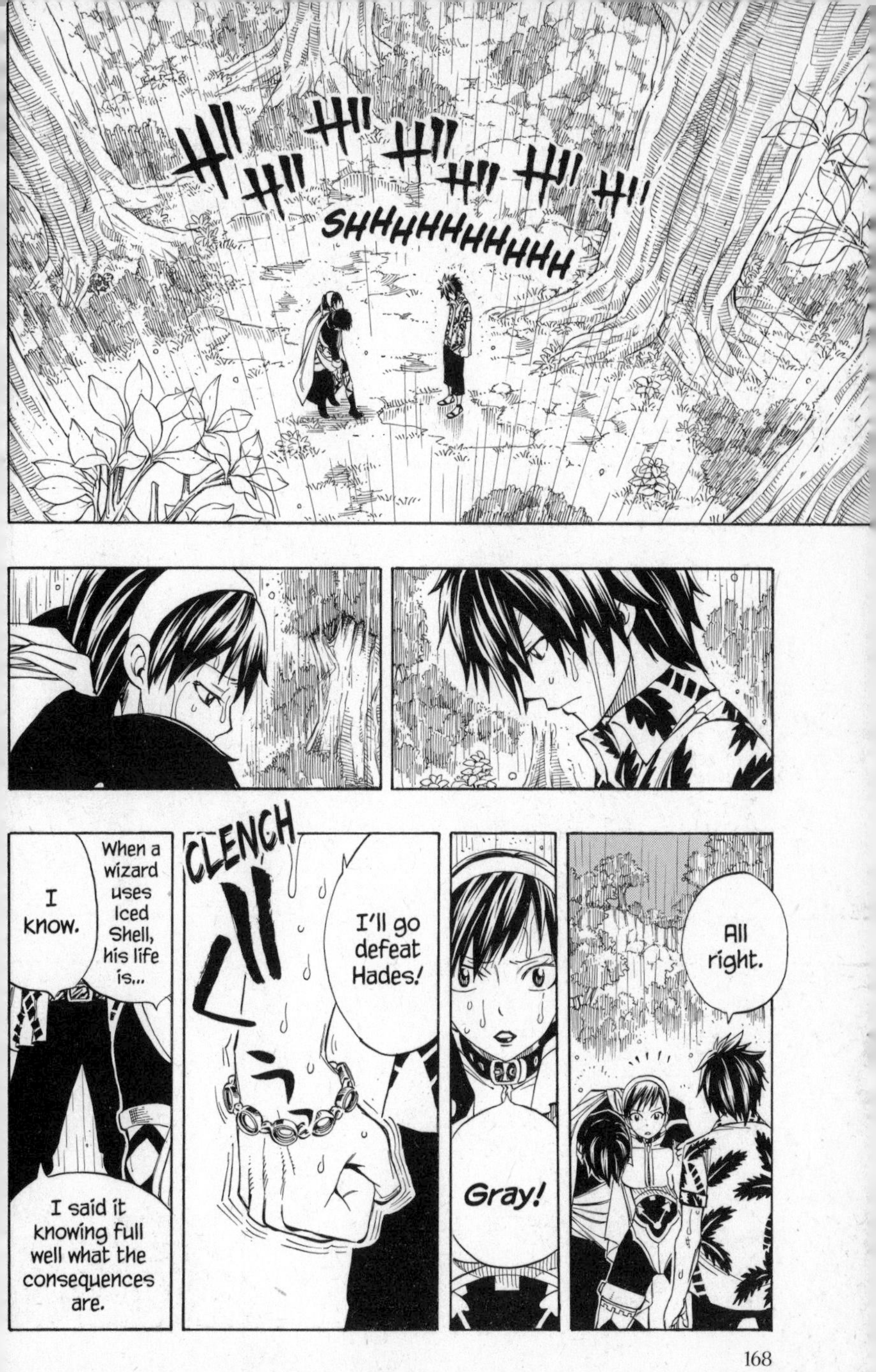
SHHHHHHHHHHH
All right.
Gray!
I'll go defeat Hades!
CLENCH
When a wizard uses Iced Shell, his life is...
I know.
I said it knowing full well what the consequences are.

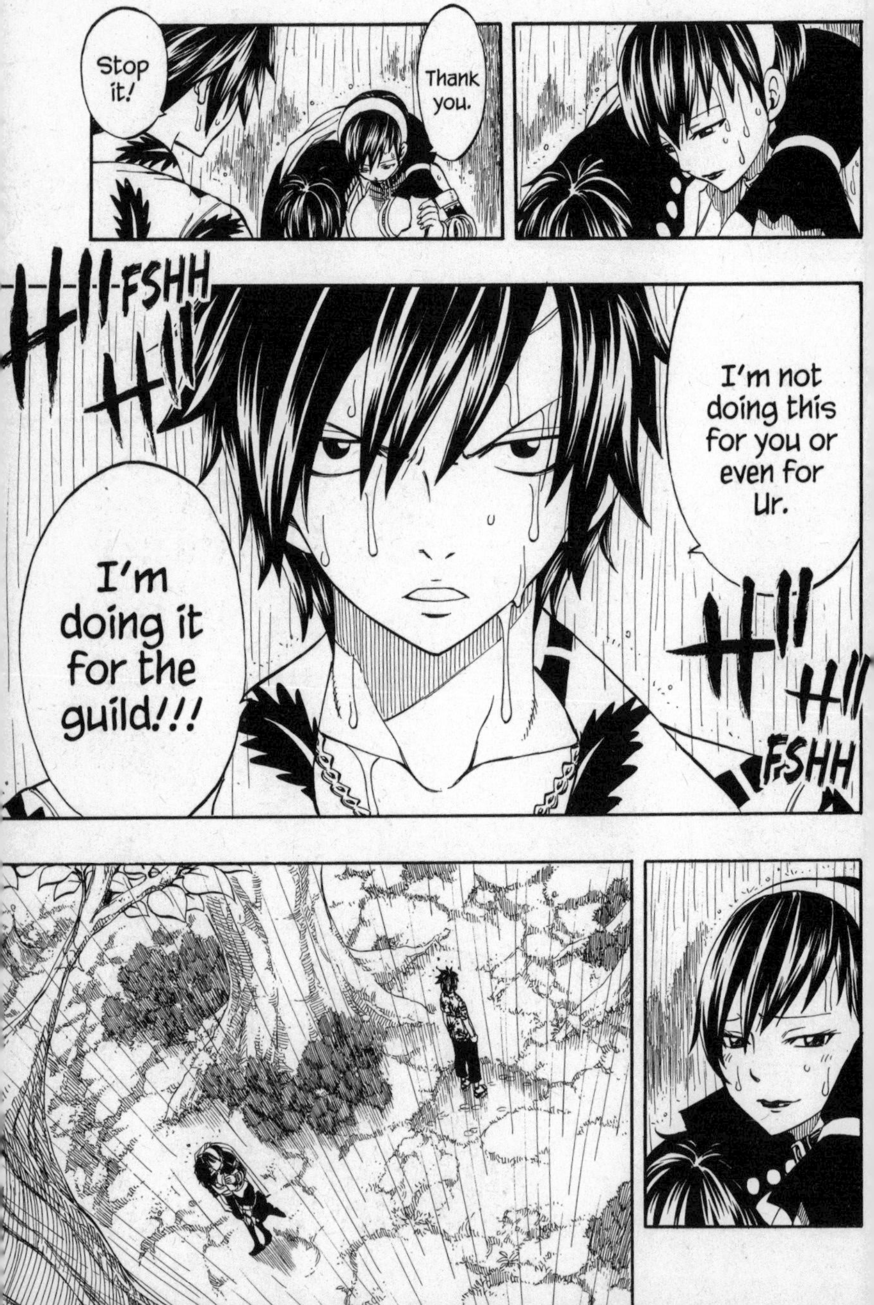
Thank you.
Stop it!
I'm not doing this for you or even for Ur.
FSHH
I'm doing it for the guild!!!
FSHH

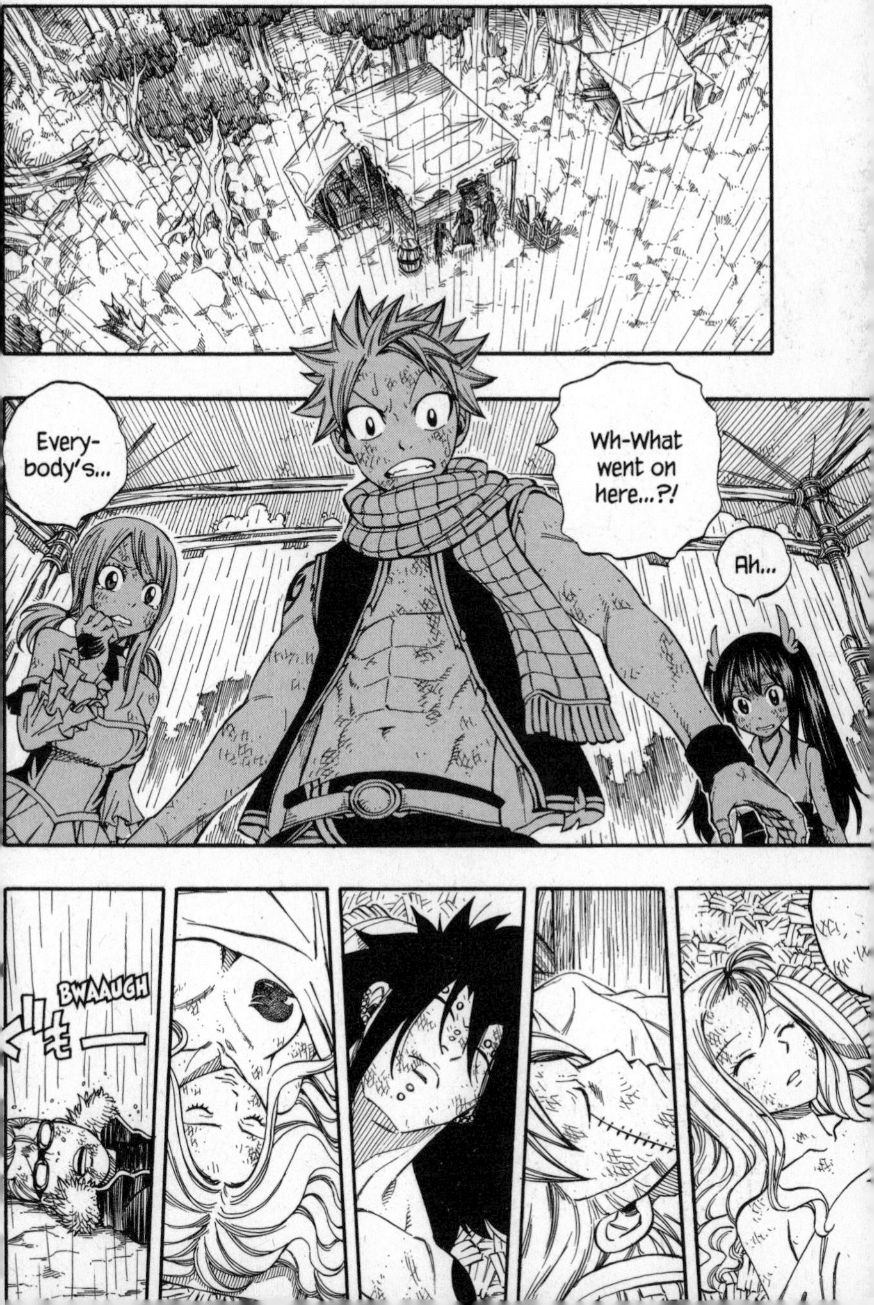
Wh-What went on here...?!
Ah...
Every-body's...
BWAAUGH

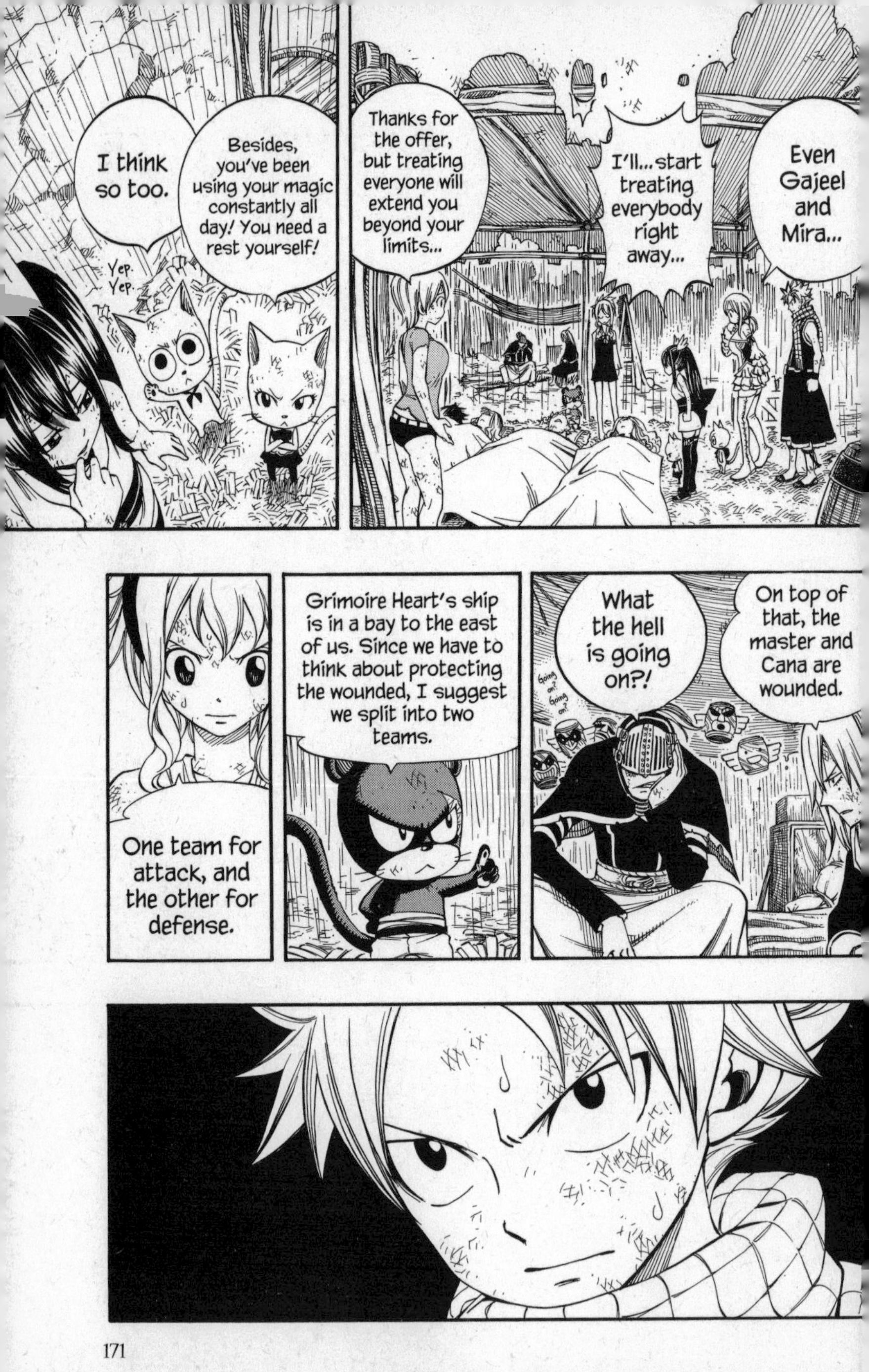
Even Gajeel and Mira...
I'll...start treating everybody right away...
Thanks for the offer, but treating everyone will extend you beyond your limits...
Besides, you've been using your magic constantly all day! You need a rest yourself!
I think so too.
Yep. Yep.
On top of that, the master and Cana are wounded.
What the hell is going on?!
Going on? Going on?
Grimoire Heart's ship is in a bay to the east of us. Since we have to think about protecting the wounded, I suggest we split into two teams.
One team for attack, and the other for defense.

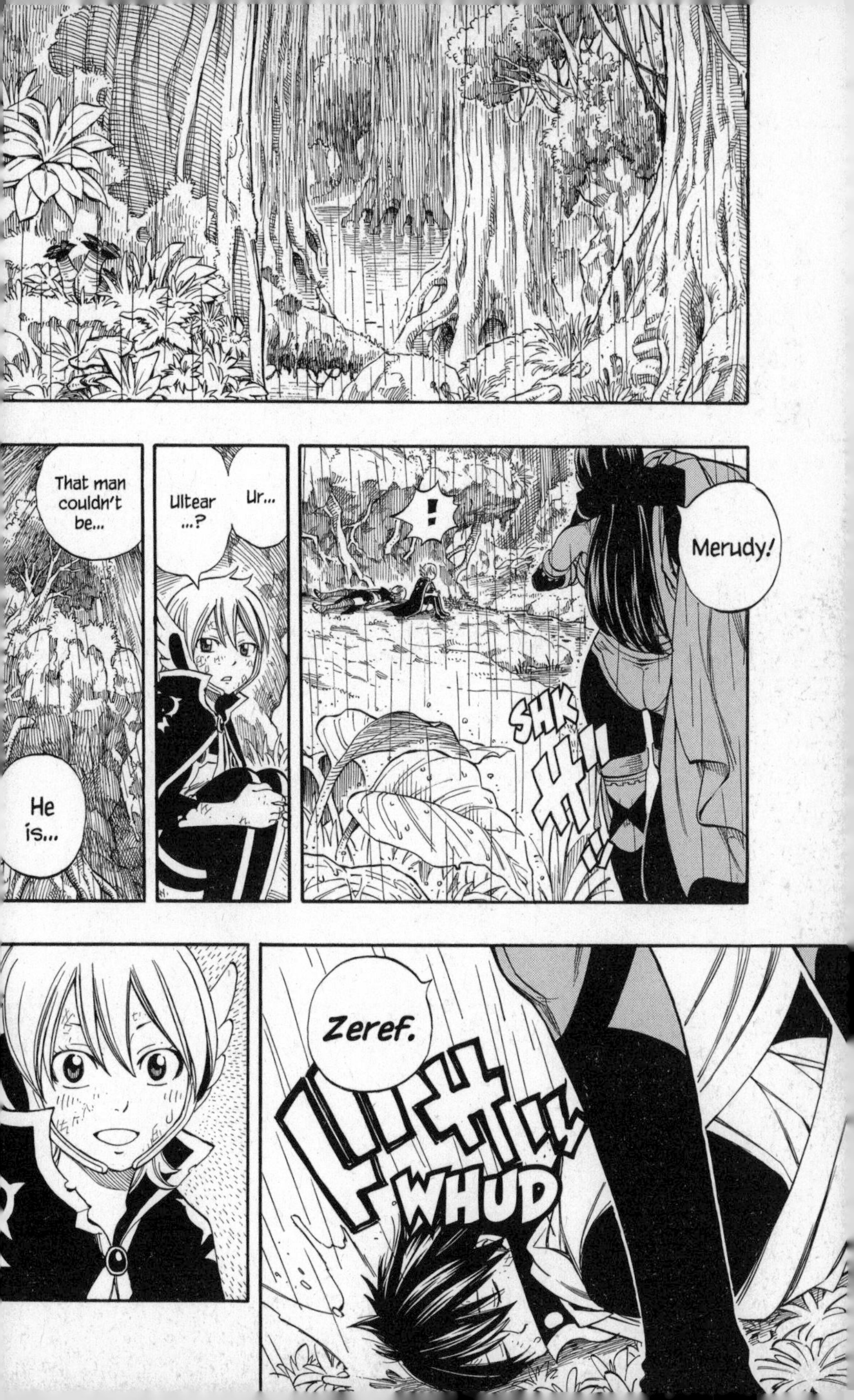
Merudy!
!
SHK
Ur...
Ultear ...?
That man couldn't be...
He is...
Zeref.
WHUD

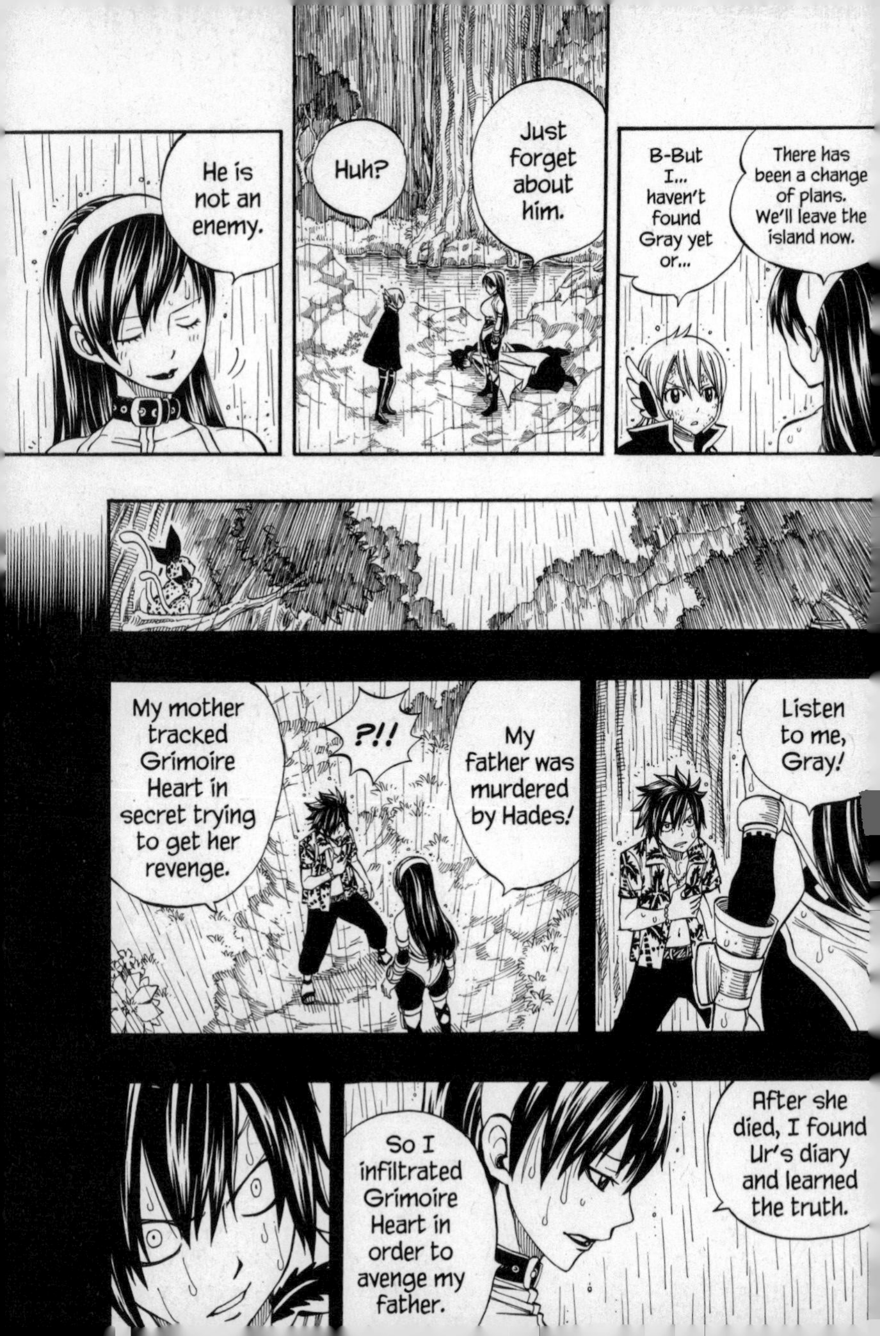
There has been a change of plans. We'll leave the island now.
B-But I... haven't found Gray yet or...
Just forget about him.
Huh?
He is not an enemy.
Listen to me, Gray!
My father was murdered by Hades!
?!!
My mother tracked Grimoire Heart in secret trying to get her revenge.
After she died, I found Ur's diary and learned the truth.
So I infiltrated Grimoire Heart in order to avenge my father.

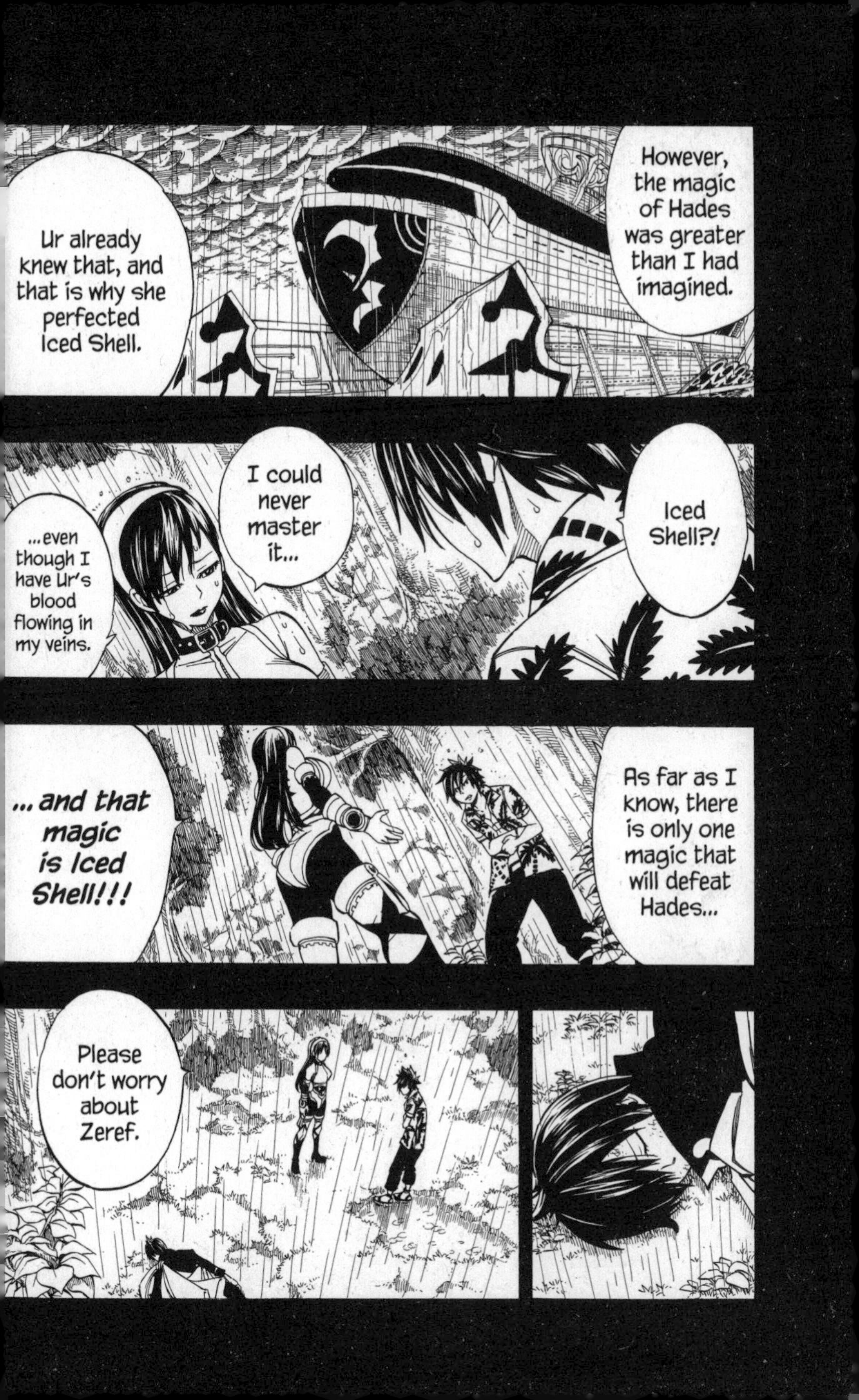
However, the magic of Hades was greater than I had imagined.
Ur already knew that, and that is why she perfected Iced Shell.
Iced Shell?!
I could never master it...
...even though I have Ur's blood flowing in my veins.
As far as I know, there is only one magic that will defeat Hades...
...and that magic is Iced Shell!!!
Please don't worry about Zeref.

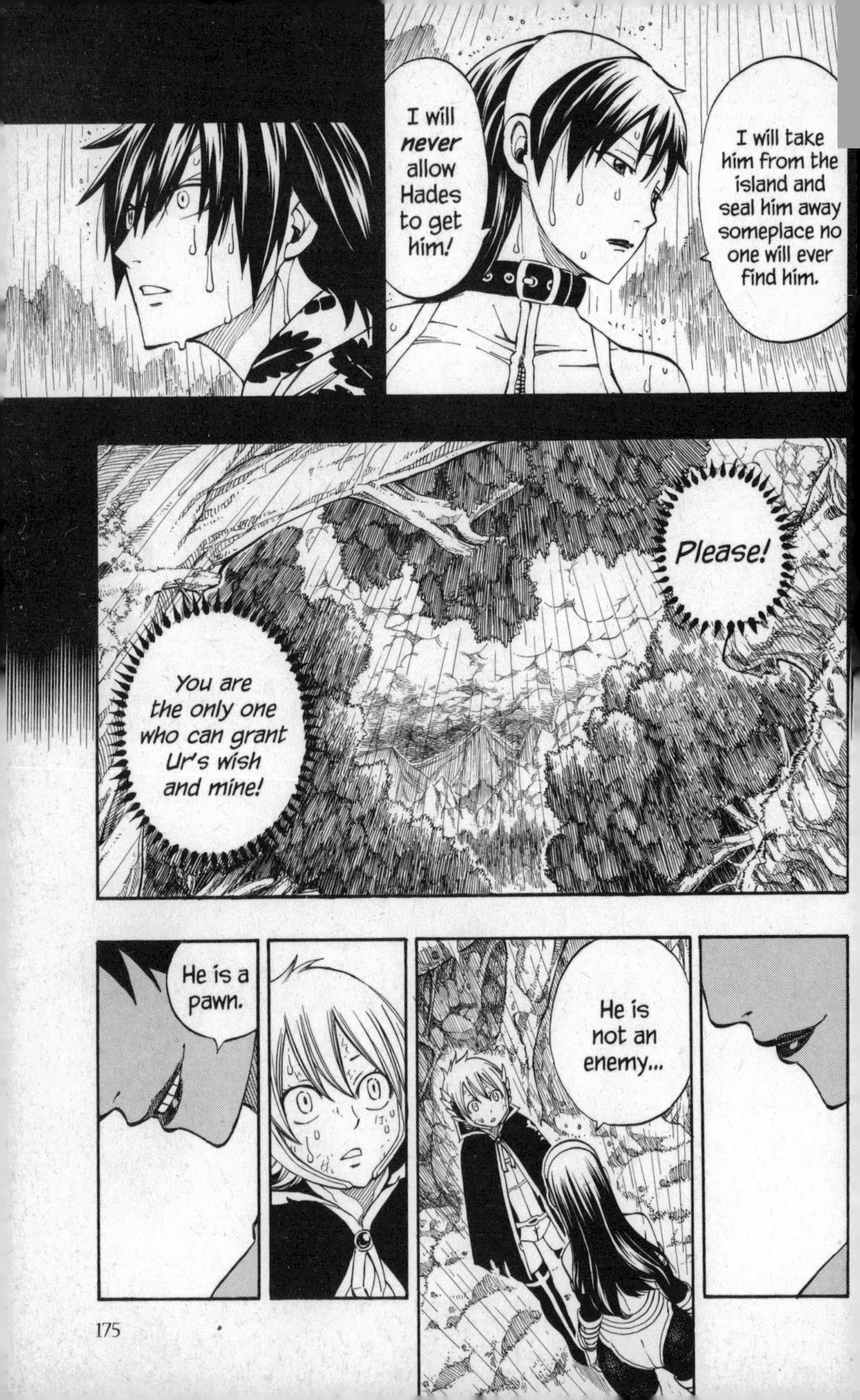
I will take him from the island and seal him away someplace no one will ever find him.
I will *never* allow Hades to get him!
Please!
You are the only one who can grant Ur's wish and mine!
He is not an enemy...
He is a pawn.

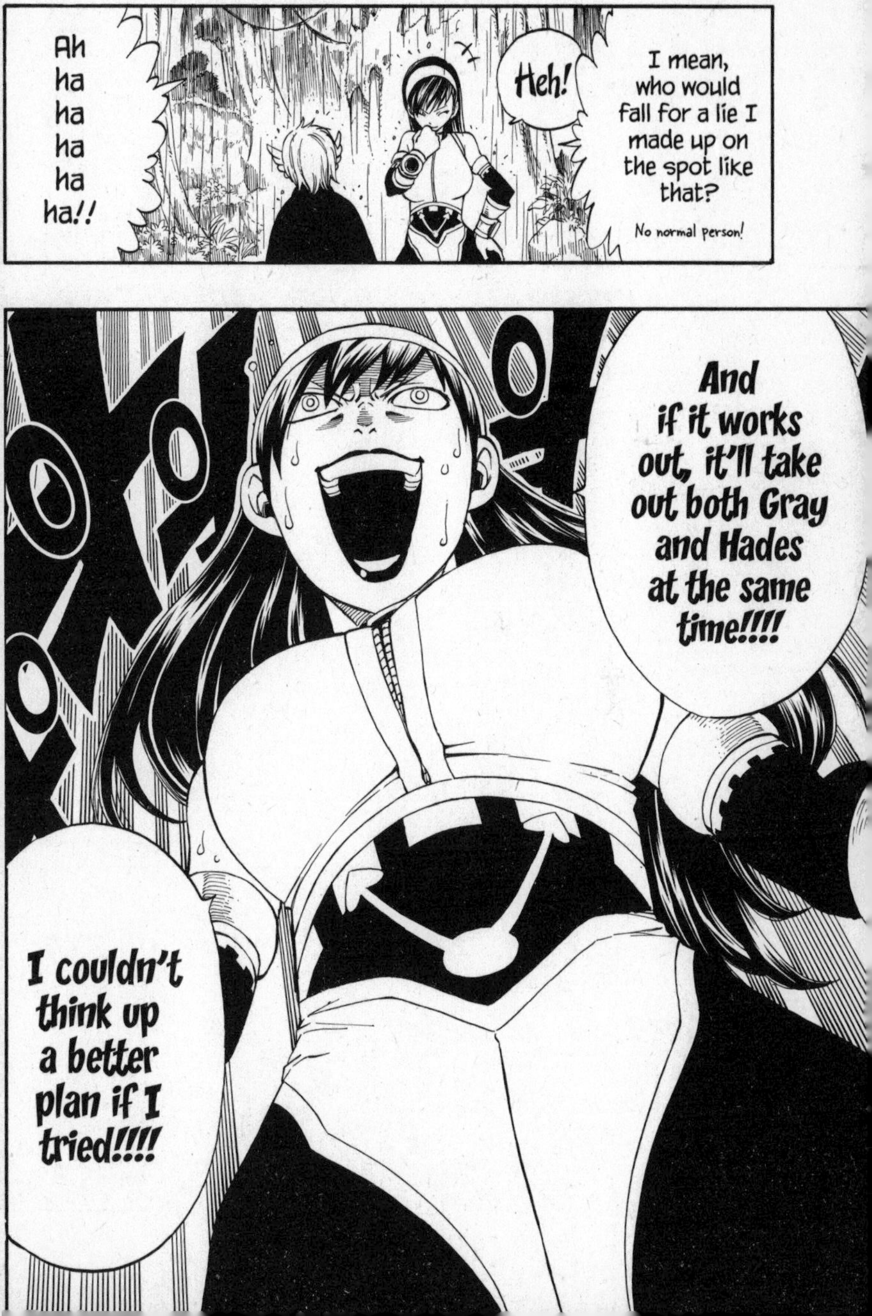
I mean, who would fall for a lie I made up on the spot like that?
No normal person!
Heh!
Ah ha ha ha ha ha!!
And if it works out, it'll take out both Gray and Hades at the same time!!!!
I couldn't think up a better plan if I tried!!!!

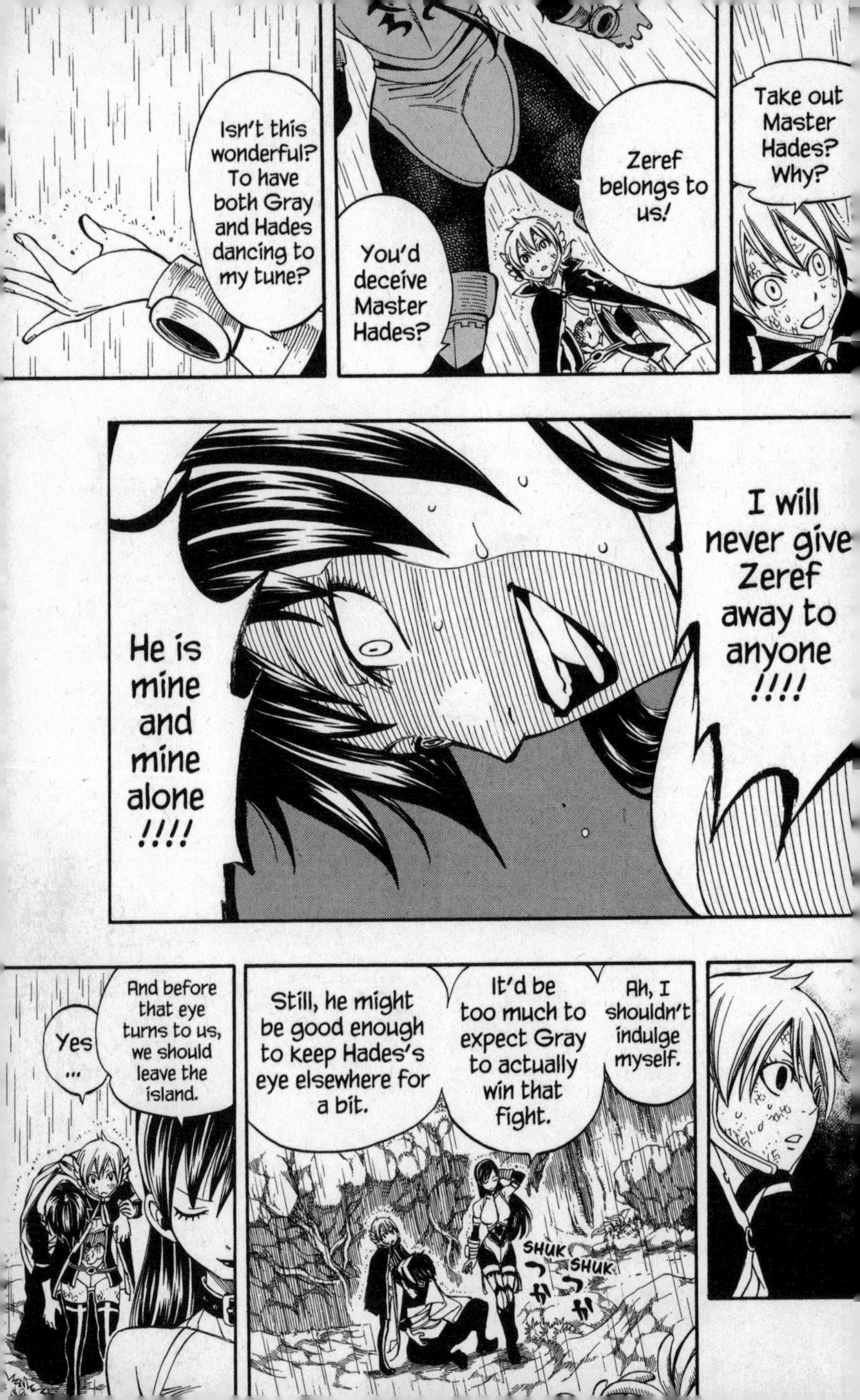
Take out Master Hades? Why?
Zeref belongs to us!
You'd deceive Master Hades?
Isn't this wonderful? To have both Gray and Hades dancing to my tune?
I will never give Zeref away to anyone!!!!
He is mine and mine alone!!!!
Ah, I shouldn't indulge myself.
It'd be too much to expect Gray to actually win that fight.
Still, he might be good enough to keep Hades's eye elsewhere for a bit.
SHUK
SHUK
And before that eye turns to us, we should leave the island.
Yes ...

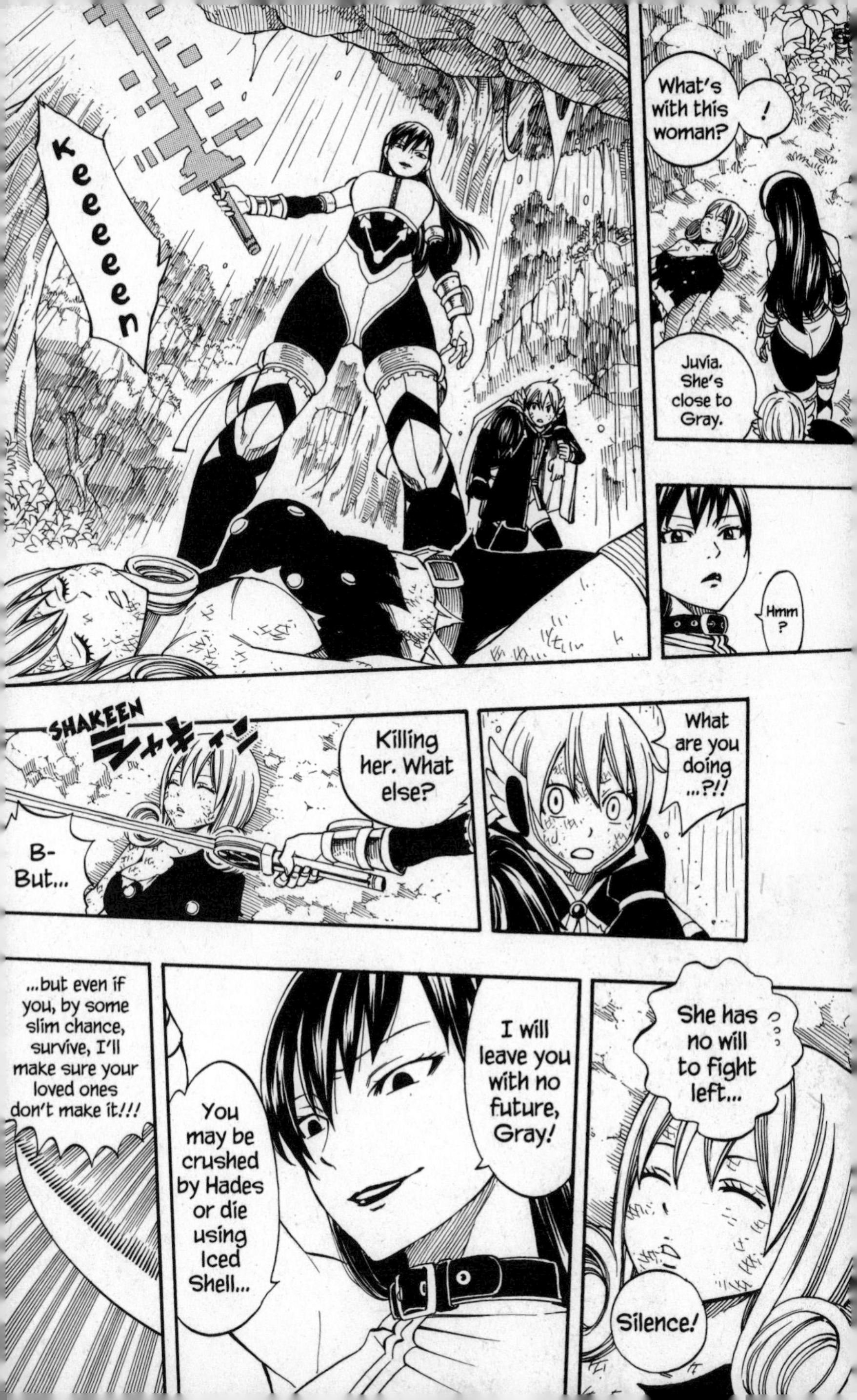
!
What's with this woman?
Juvia. She's close to Gray.
Hmm?
Keeeeeen
What are you doing ...?!!
Killing her. What else?
SHAKEEN
B- But...
She has no will to fight left...
Silence!
I will leave you with no future, Gray!
You may be crushed by Hades or die using Iced Shell...
...but even if you, by some slim chance, survive, I'll make sure your loved ones don't make it!!!

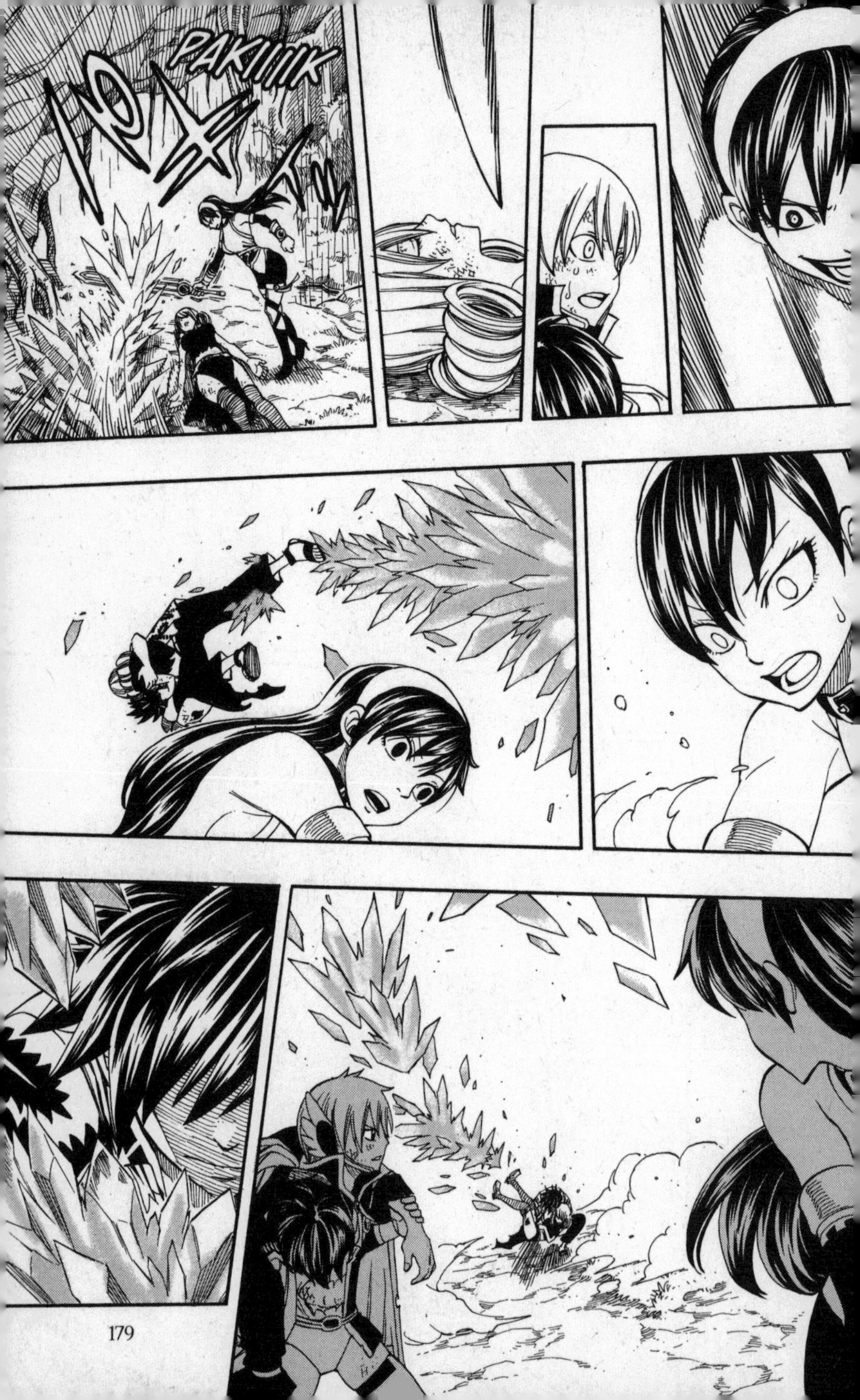
PAKIIIIK

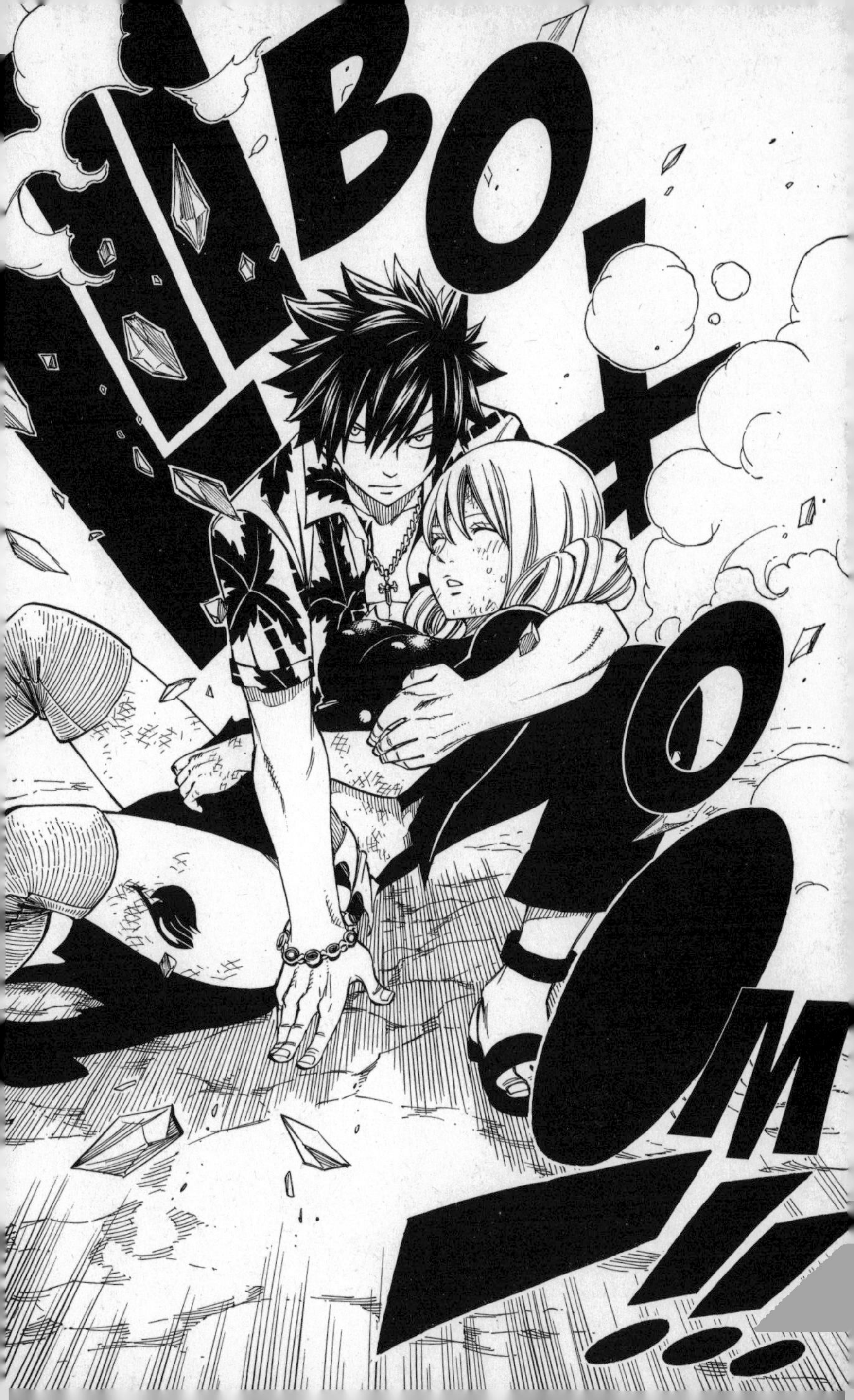
BOOOM!!

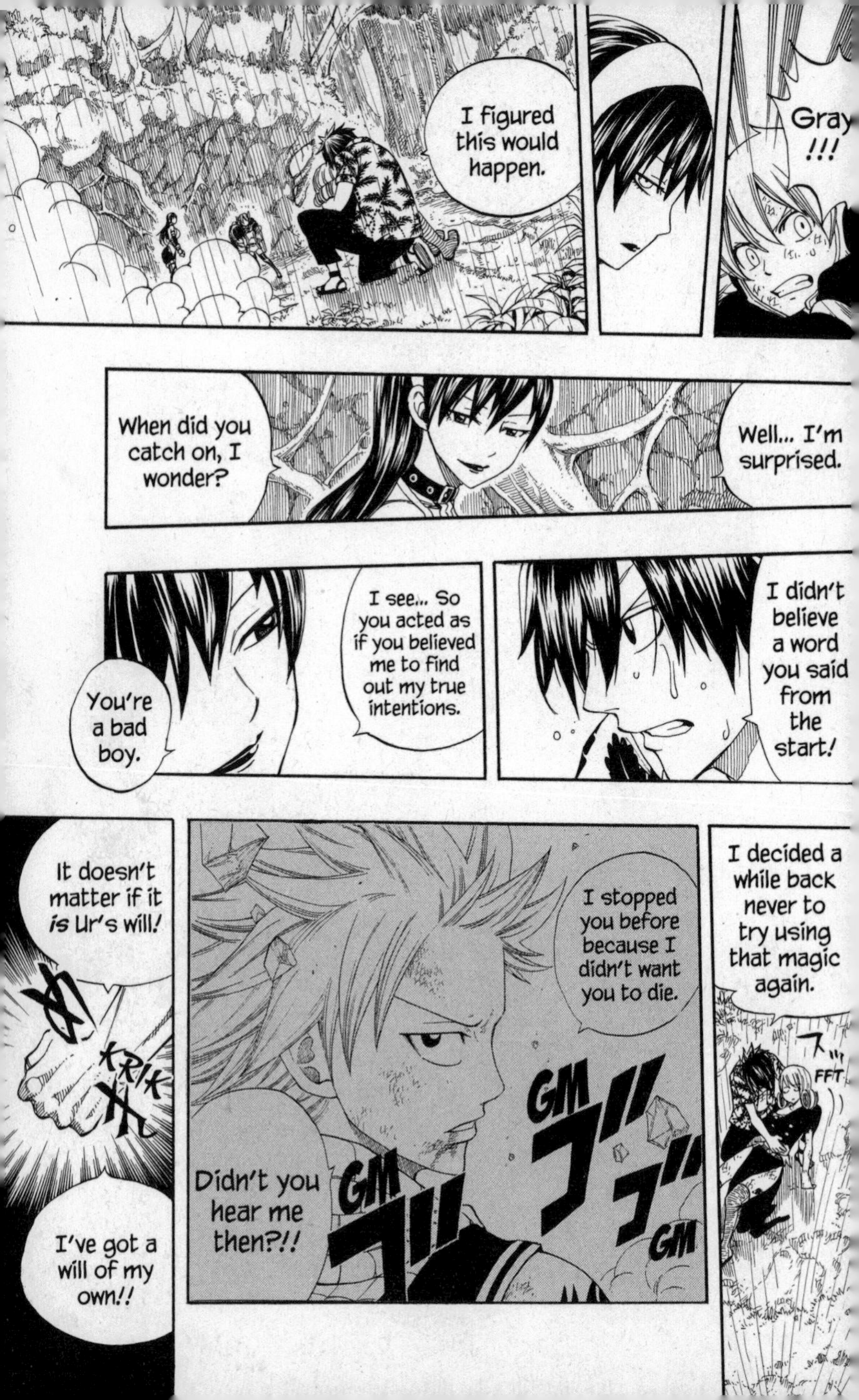
Gray!!!
I figured this would happen.
Well... I'm surprised.
When did you catch on, I wonder?
I didn't believe a word you said from the start!
I see... So you acted as if you believed me to find out my true intentions.
You're a bad boy.
I decided a while back never to try using that magic again.
FFT
I stopped you before because I didn't want you to die.
GM
GM
GM
Didn't you hear me then?!!
It doesn't matter if it *is* Ur's will!
KRIK
I've got a will of my own!!

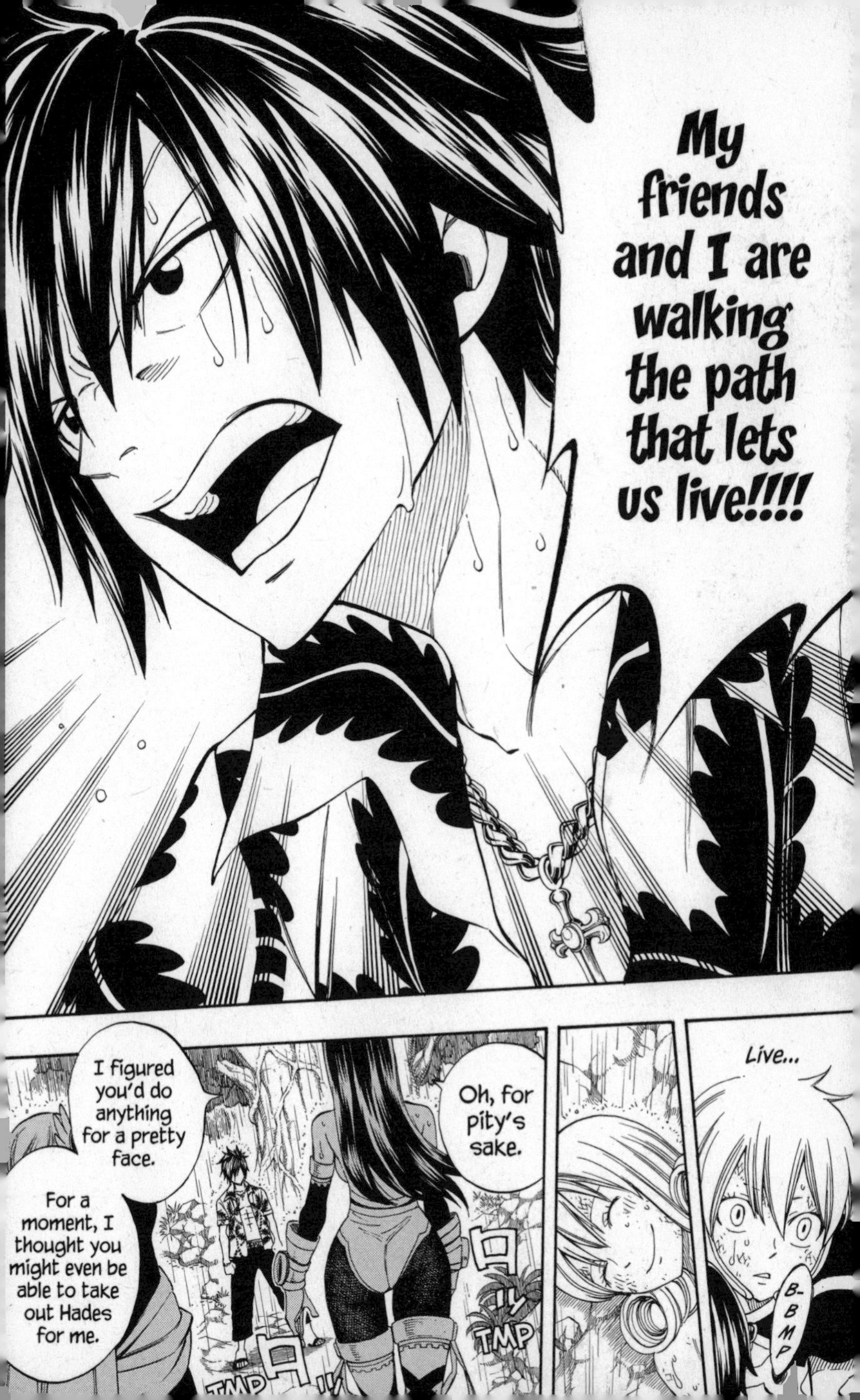
My friends and I are walking the path that lets us live!!!!
Live...
B-BBMP
Oh, for pity's sake.
TMP
I figured you'd do anything for a pretty face.
For a moment, I thought you might even be able to take out Hades for me.

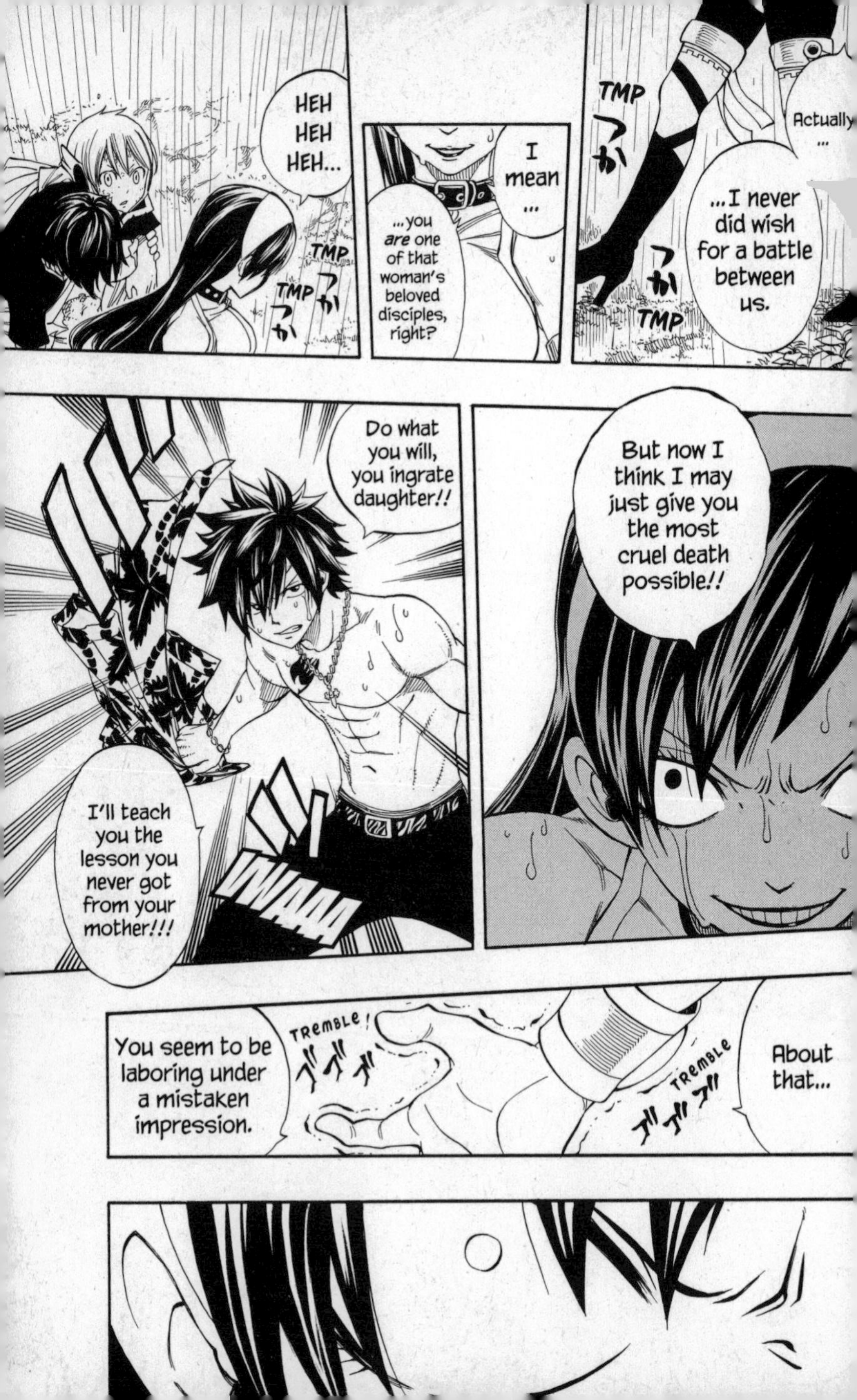
TMP
Actually...
...I never did wish for a battle between us.
TMP
I mean...
...you *are* one of that woman's beloved disciples, right?
HEH HEH HEH...
TMP
TMP
But now I think I may just give you the most cruel death possible!!
Do what you will, you ingrate daughter!!
I'll teach you the lesson you never got from your mother!!!
About that...
TREMBLE
TREMBLE!
You seem to be laboring under a mistaken impression.

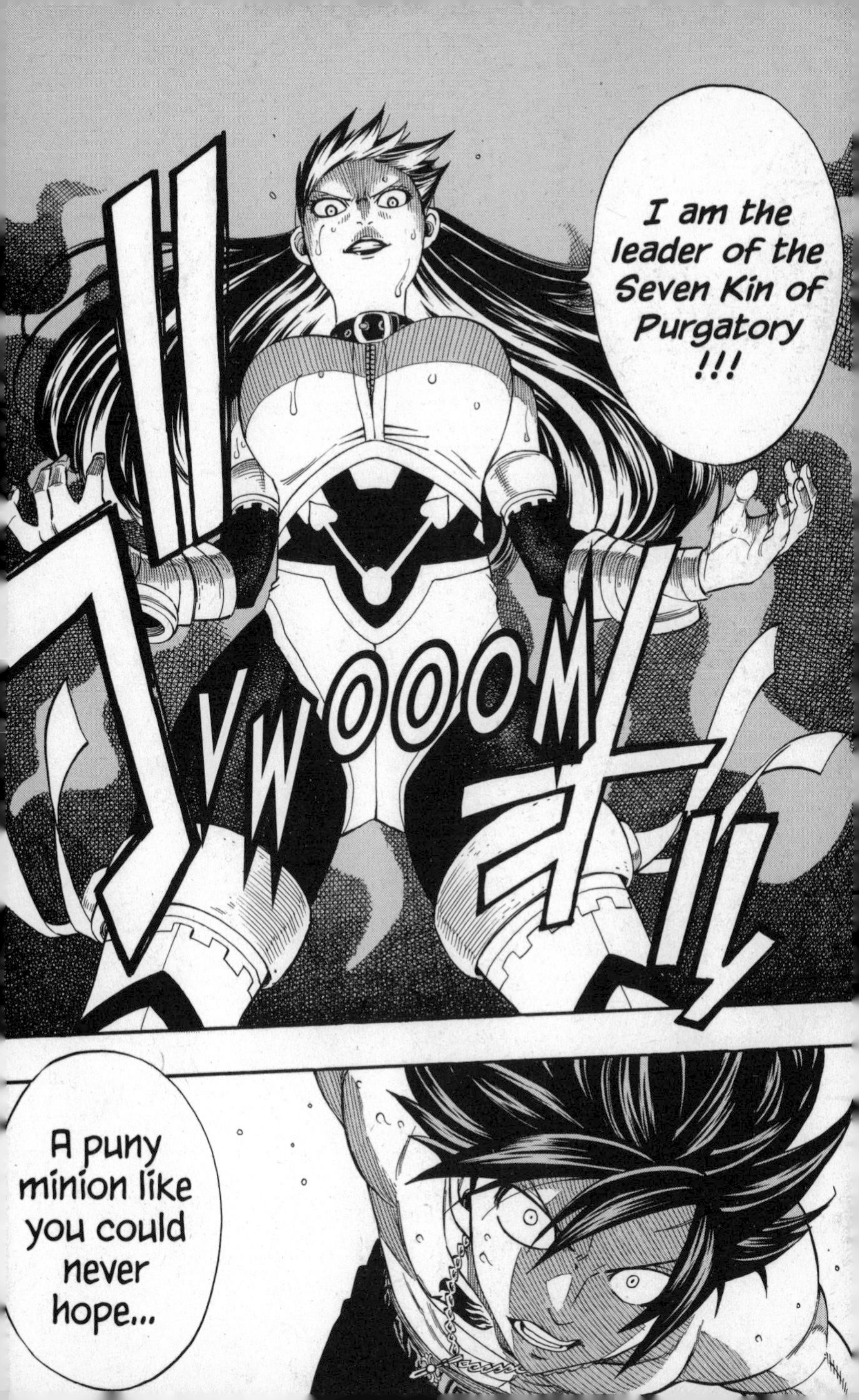
I am the leader of the Seven Kin of Purgatory !!!
VWOOOM
A puny minion like you could never hope...

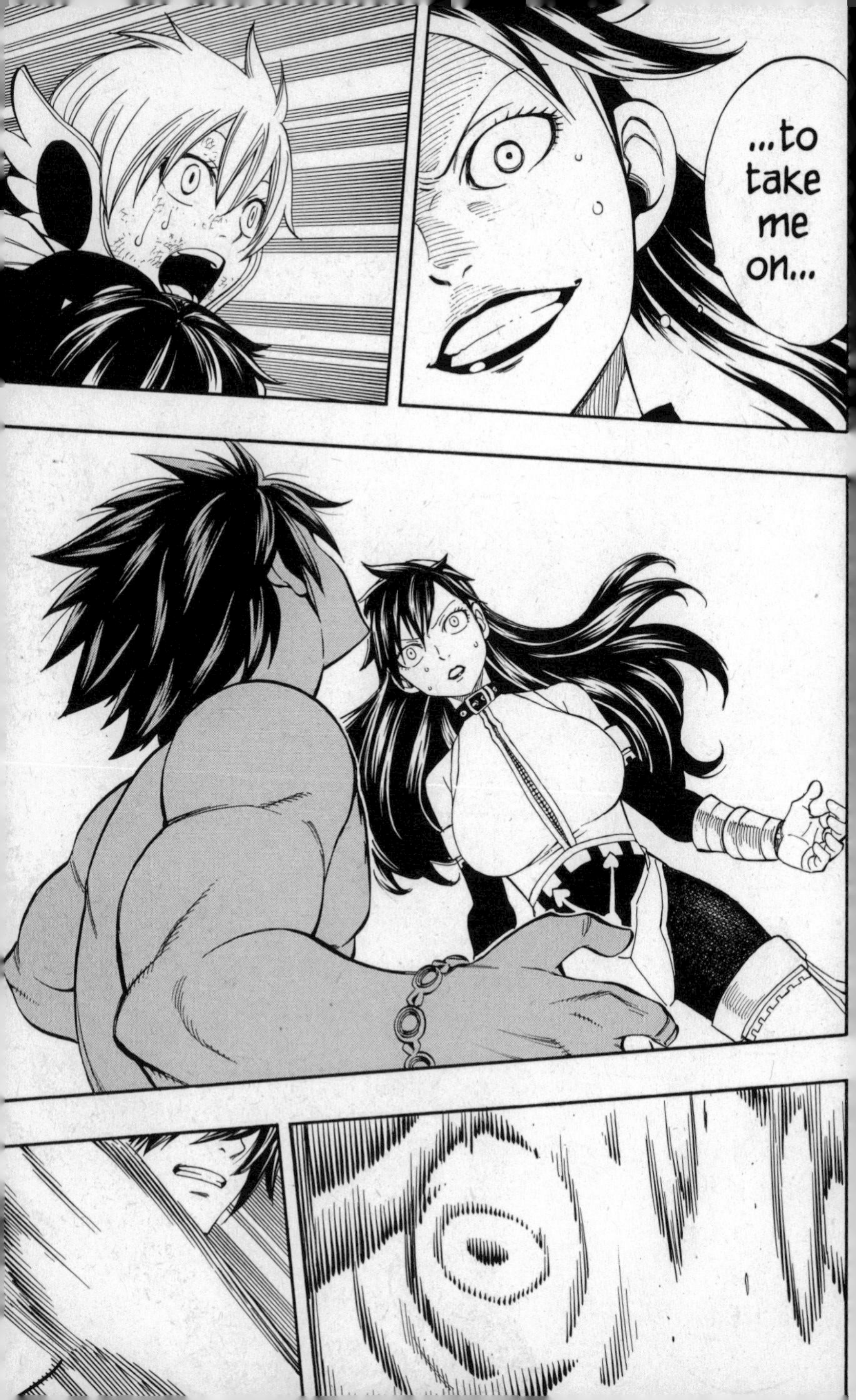
...to take me on...

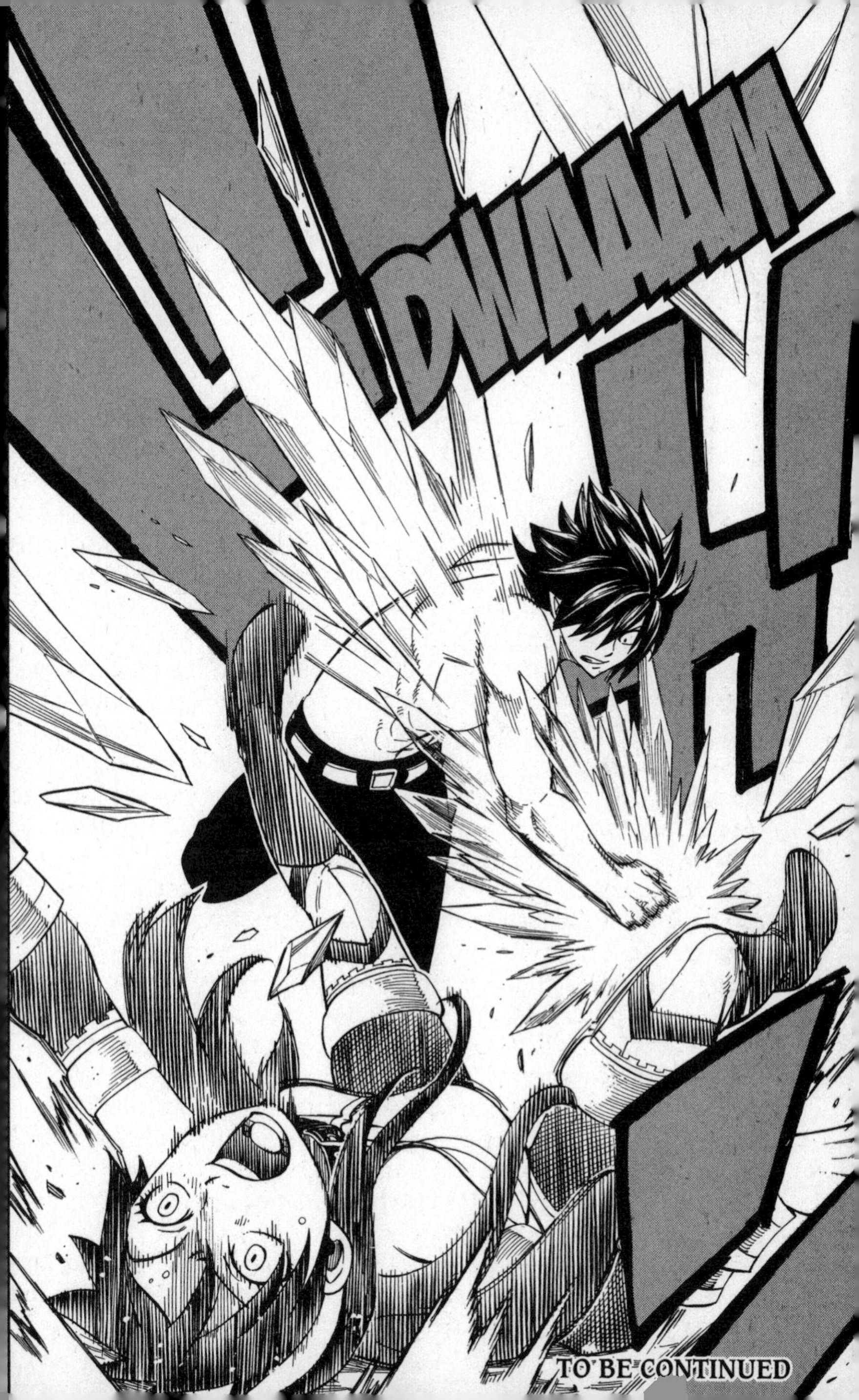
DWAAAM
TO BE CONTINUED

Afterword

There were a lot of drawing mistakes this time. Maybe I shouldn't limit it to "this time." But I had an especially hard time remembering to add in the pattern in Azuma's hair. (Hey!) I tried to fix all the ones that I managed to notice, but I may have missed a few... (cries). I get the feeling that I've told you how I've forgotten to add in characters' patterns or accessories before, but one reason I forget them is the person in charge of adding those patterns keeps changing. Sometimes I get caught up in it and add them myself then and there, and sometimes I save it for later, and sometimes I ask my staff to handle particularly tricky patterns. And sometimes I just forget. At the very worst times I find myself thinking, "Huh? What pattern went with this person anyway?" I do take time to check over my pages every time, but there are a lot of times when I've got other worries on my mind, and that ruins my concentration, so I manage to miss such things. Even though every time...every time I vow to be more careful on the next check!

They often compare manga creators to directors, and I have to admit that I agree with that assessment. Still, not every manga creator could make movies. But I'm talking about "total direction." He draws the *neemu* (which are like storyboards), writes the story and the dialog, maps out the pictures (camera angles), and when he draws, he includes the character layout (positioning), actions (blocking and expressions), backgrounds, props, lines of action, sound effects, lighting... It's all decided by one person. And even when the creator has staff working for him, it's the manga creator who gives the marching orders. In other words, the creator has a lot to do. And it's for that reason that creators sometimes put off applying the patterns until later or delegate it to their staff and then miss it in the checking stage.

I think the worst mistake I ever made was drawing a color picture of Lucy where she's showing the reader the Fairy Tail guild mark that she has on her hand, and I **forgot to draw the mark!** (Aw, man!)

Continued from the left-hand page.

When I've finished the PC-based line work, I make a copy and use that as the uppermost layer and paint it in the software's jôsan ("multiply") mode.

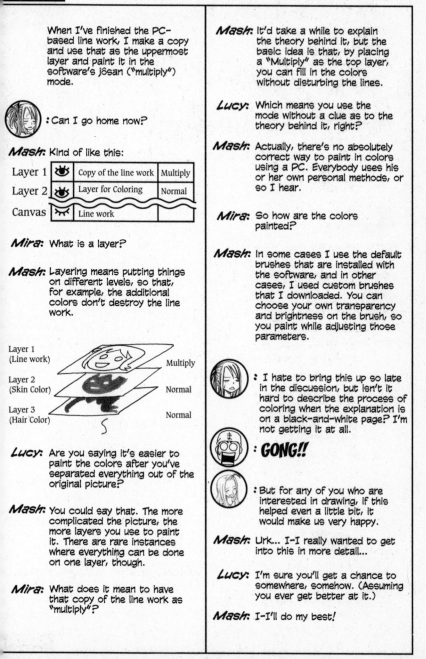

: Can I go home now?

Mash: Kind of like this:

Layer 1		Copy of the line work	Multiply
Layer 2		Layer for Coloring	Normal
Canvas		Line work	

Mira: What is a layer?

Mash: Layering means putting things on different levels, so that, for example, the additional colors don't destroy the line work.

Layer 1
(Line work)
Multiply
Layer 2
(Skin Color)
Normal
Layer 3
(Hair Color)
Normal

Lucy: Are you saying it's easier to paint the colors after you've separated everything out of the original picture?

Mash: You could say that. The more complicated the picture, the more layers you use to paint it. There are rare instances where everything can be done on one layer, though.

Mira: What does it mean to have that copy of the line work as "multiply"?

Mash: It'd take a while to explain the theory behind it, but the basic idea is that, by placing a "Multiply" as the top layer, you can fill in the colors without disturbing the lines.

Lucy: Which means you use the mode without a clue as to the theory behind it, right?

Mash: Actually, there's no absolutely correct way to paint in colors using a PC. Everybody uses his or her own personal methods, or so I hear.

Mira: So how are the colors painted?

Mash: In some cases I use the default brushes that are installed with the software, and in other cases, I used custom brushes that I downloaded. You can choose your own transparency and brightness on the brush, so you paint while adjusting those parameters.

: I hate to bring this up so late in the discussion, but isn't it hard to describe the process of coloring when the explanation is on a black-and-white page? I'm not getting it at all.

: **GONG!!**

: But for any of you who are interested in drawing, if this helped even a little bit, it would make us very happy.

Mash: Urk... I-I really wanted to get into this in more detail...

Lucy: I'm sure you'll get a chance to somewhere, somehow. (Assuming you ever get better at it.)

Mash: I-I'll do my best!

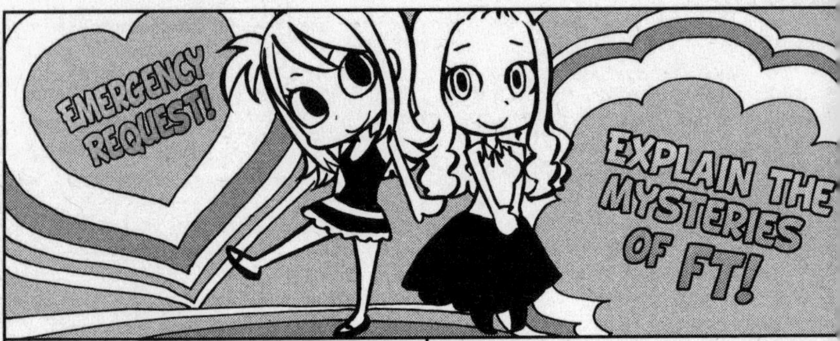
EMERGENCY REQUEST!
EXPLAIN THE MYSTERIES OF FT!

In the Magnolia Shopping District...

Lucy: Good morning, everybody!

Mira: Hello, people.

Lucy: Our corner today is for those fans who are real nerds.

Mira: Those who aren't can simply skip this column.

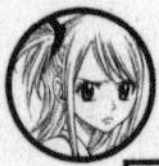
: This is the question!!

How are Fairy Tail's color pages painted?

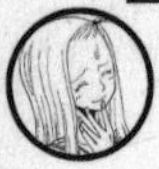
: I-I certainly do wonder about that, but for this we should have Mashima-sensei himself to drone on and on about the subject. Not that he's very good at it...

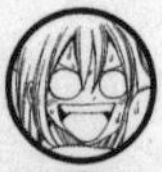
: You probably shouldn't be saying that...

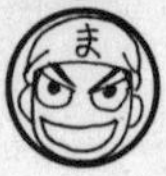
: And so, here I am to answer the question!

Mira: See? Here he is!!

Mash: I personally would divide my color illustrations into two big groups. One is drawing with a kind of marker called COPIC where I apply the colors directly to the drawing. The other is to use computer software to apply the colors digitally. Recently, I've been pretty much exclusively using the computer method, so that's the one I'll describe here.

Lucy: That was long!

Mash: First, I do a drawing on paper and trace it using pens or mechanical pencils to produce the line work. Then, I scan in the line work to my PC at a resolution of 300-400 dpi.

Lucy: You lost me after the word "first"...

Mira: Think of "resolution" like this: the higher the number, the more detail.

Mash: Once it's in a data file, I sharpen the image, cleaning up spots and such.

Lucy: Clean up? How do you do that?

Mash: Once it's on the PC, you can subtract whatever line you like at will. You erase it using a tool called "eraser."

Continued on the right-hand page.

TAIL d'ART

The Fairy Tail Guild is looking for illustrations! Please send in your art on a postcard or at postcard size, and do it in black pen, okay? Those chosen to be published will get a signed mini poster! ♪ Make sure you write your real name and address on the back of your illustration!

Fukuoka Prefecture, Shirayuki

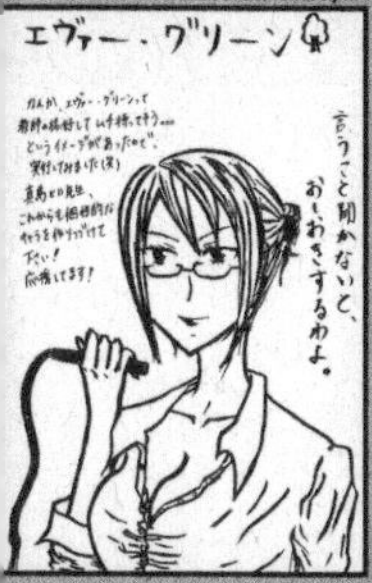
エヴァー・グリーン

▲ Pictures with Evergreen all by herself are unexpectedly rare. Thanks!

Kyoto, Kōsuke Kimura

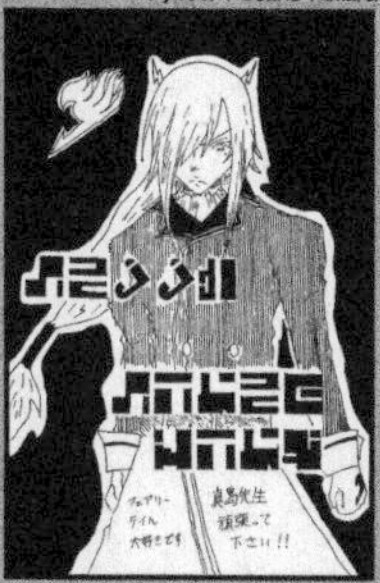
真島先生
頑張って
下さい!!

▲ First Fried in a long time! Pretty cool, huh?

Osaka, Sarukichi

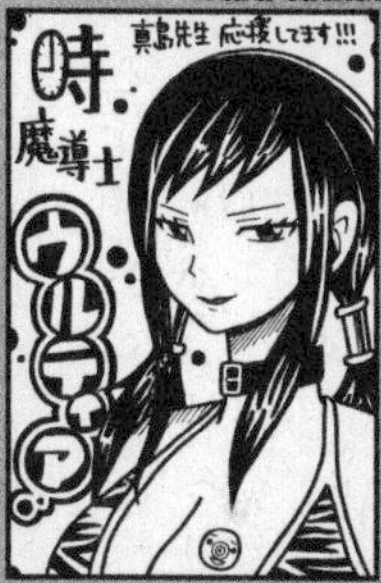
真島先生 応援してます!!!
時。魔導士
ウルティア

▲ I love the way this person drew the kanji for "time!"

Hyogo Prefecture, Nagamaru

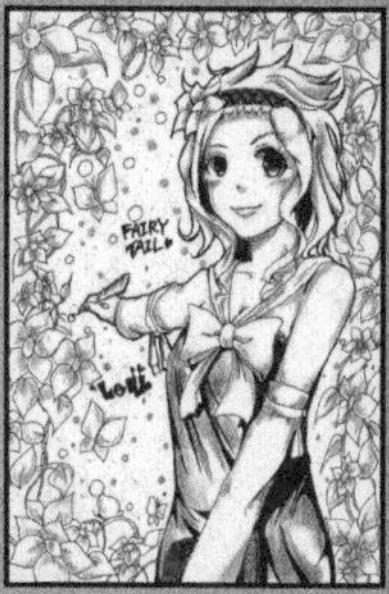
FAIRY TAIL

▲ Very good! Levy fans have really increased!

Kanagawa Prefecture, Risa Suzuki

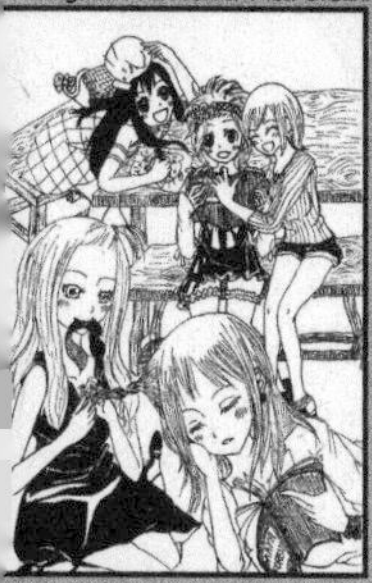

▲ The girls of Fairy Tail! Mira-chan is really cute here!!

Aichi Prefecture, Chizuru Kainuma

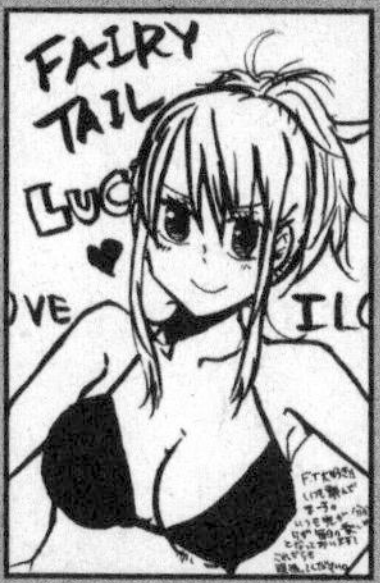
FAIRY TAIL

▲ A Lucy full of energy!!

Kanagawa Prefecture, Hiromi Funiyū

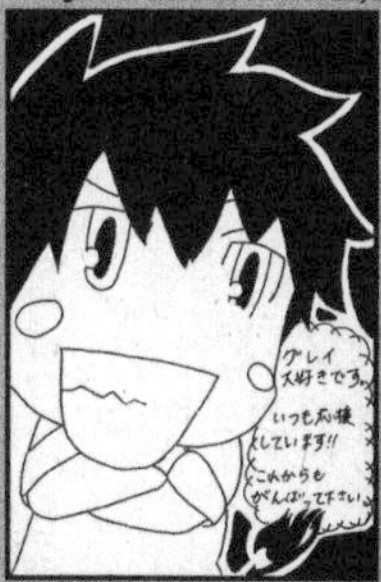
グレイ大好きです。
いつも応援しています!!
これからもがんばってください。

▲ Now this is one cute Gray! Especially the cheeks!

Nara Prefecture, Tsukasa

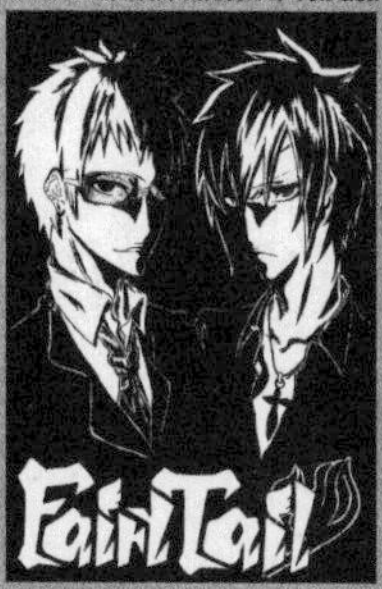
Fairy Tail

▲ This one's cool!

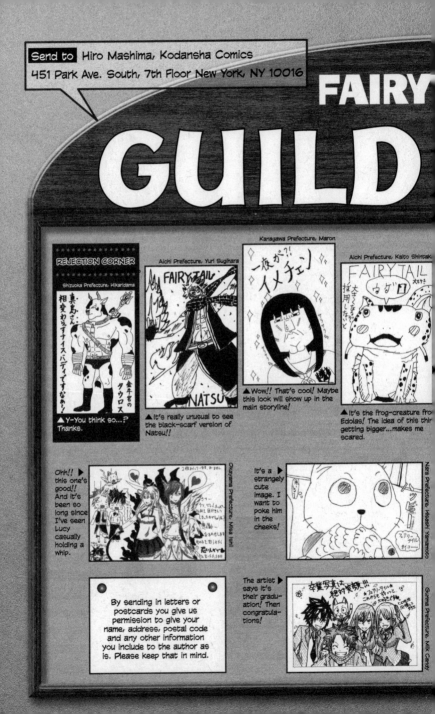

Send to Hiro Mashima, Kodansha Comics
451 Park Ave. South, 7th Floor New York, NY 10016

FAIRY GUILD

REJECTION CORNER

Shizuoka Prefecture, Hikaridama

真島さん相変わらずナイスバディですなあ!!
金牛宮のタウロス

▲Y-You think so...? Thanks.

Aichi Prefecture, Yuri Sugihara

FAIRY TAIL
NATSU

▲It's really unusual to see the black-scarf version of Natsu!!

Kanagawa Prefecture, Maron

一夜が?! イメチェン

▲Wow!! That's cool! Maybe this look will show up in the main storyline!

Aichi Prefecture, Kaito Shintak

FAIRY TAIL

▲It's the frog-creature fro Edolas! The idea of this thir getting bigger...makes me scared.

Okayama Prefecture, Misa Ishii

Ohh!! ▶ this one's good!! And it's been so long since I've seen Lucy casually holding a whip.

Nara Prefecture, Hisashi Yamamoto

It's a ▶ strangely cute image. I want to poke him in the cheeks!

フェアリーテイル サイコー

By sending in letters or postcards you give us permission to give your name, address, postal code and any other information you include to the author as is. Please keep that in mind.

Gunma Prefecture, Milk Candy

The artist ▶ says it's their graduation! Then congratulations!

卒業写真は絶対笑顔!!!

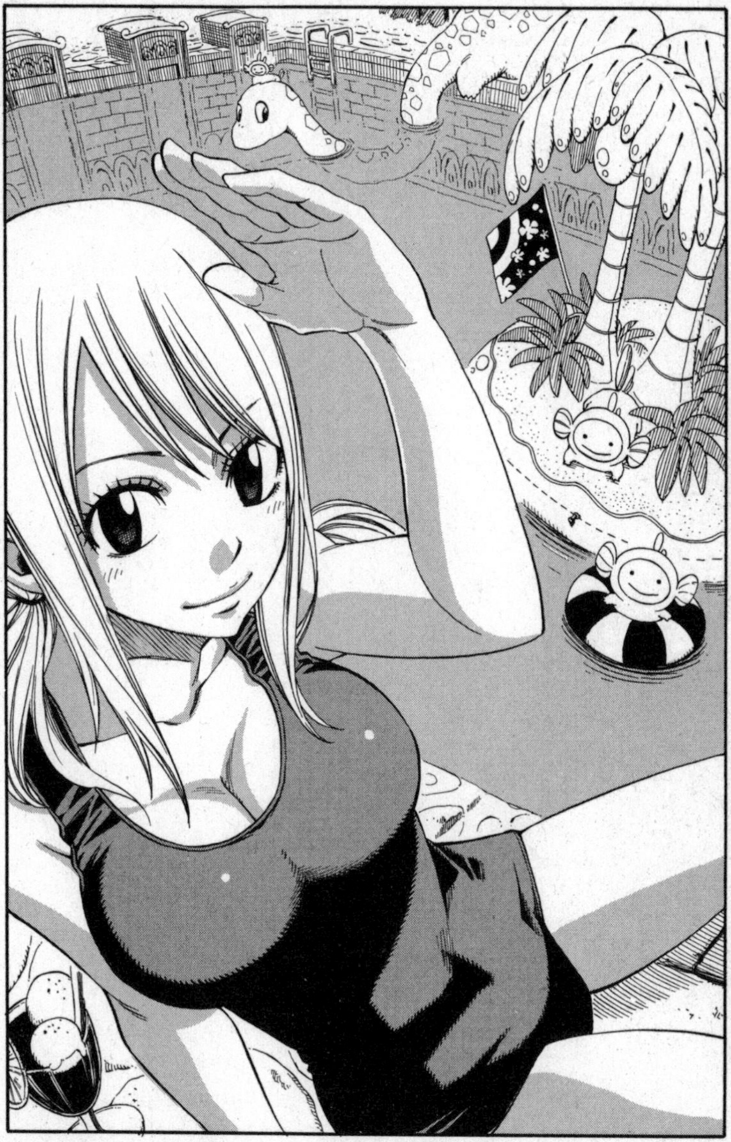

FAIRY TAIL 28

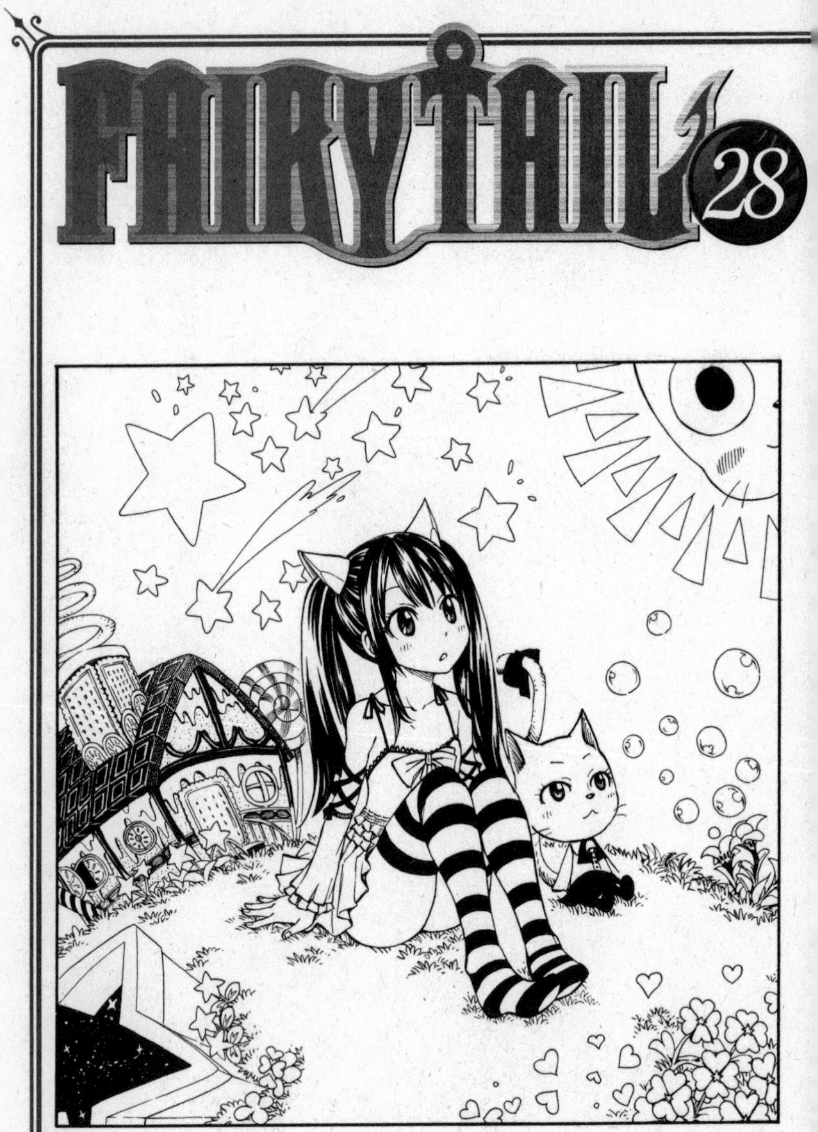

FROM HIRO MASHIMA

There have been ten opening and ending songs recorded for the first five seasons of the Fairy Tail anime, and a compilation album of them has just gone on sale in Japan! A huge number of them are really wonderful tunes! Some of the artists have also written original works especially for Fairy Tail, so I can't do much else but bow down in gratitude. I mean, I'd have just been happy if they had simply lent a song of theirs to the story, but for going the extra distance, I would like to take this opportunity to express my appreciation. Thank you so much!

Original Jacket Design: Hisao Ogawa

Translation Notes:

Japanese is a tricky language for most Westerners, and translation is often more art than science. For your edification and reading pleasure, here are notes on some of the places where we could have gone in a different direction with our translation of the work, or where a Japanese cultural reference is used.

Page 89, Brittia's Ghosts

The island of Brittia is described by the Byzantine historian Procopius in the sixth century A.D. He describes the island as a place where the souls of the northern European tribes go after they have died.

Page 114, Folium Sica

Azuma's attack names seem to be of Latin origin. *Folium* is Latin for leaf (and is the origin for the English word, "foliage") and *sica* is a kind of long knife used in Roman times for battle. The Japanese version agrees with that since the Japanese writing reads *ha no ken* ("Leaf Sword").

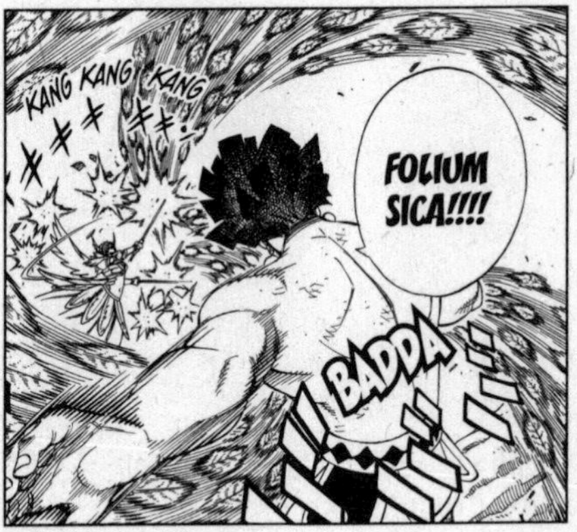
FOLIUM SICA!!!!
KANG KANG KANG
BADDA

Page 114, Ramus Sica

Like Folium Sica, this attack name comes from the Latin language. *Ramus* is Latin for branch, and *sica*, as mentioned above, is a knife weapon. This agrees with the Japanese writing in the Japanese version since *eda no ken* means "Branch Sword."

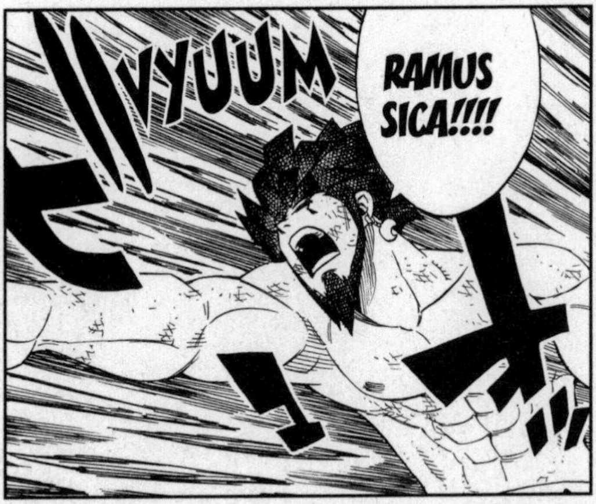
RAMUS SICA!!!!
VYUUM

Page 123, Terra Clamare

Like Azuma's other attacks, this name seems to be based in the Latin language. The Japanese version of the manga had this attack name in Japanese as *daichi no sakebi* (Cry of the Earth) with a *katakana* pronunciation guide of *tera kuramaare.* That would be how the Japanese would pronounce the Latin words *terra*, which means Earth, and *clamare*, which is Latin for invocation.

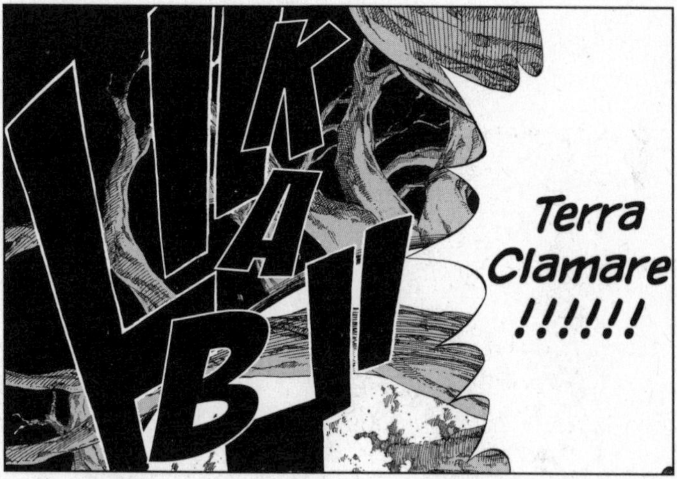
Terra Clamare !!!!!!
KLAK
BI

Page 156, Tower of Dingir

Although the Japanese version does not specifically designate what Dinger means, a cuneiform character from both ancient Sumerian and Assyrian has the same pronunciation and a meaning that seems to fit. In both ancient languages, Dinger means "deity," so a translation of the name of this attack would be "Tower of God" or "Tower of the Gods."

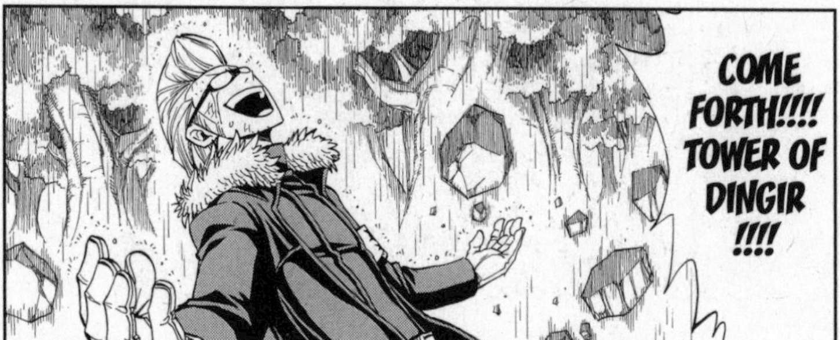
COME FORTH!!!! TOWER OF DINGIR !!!!

Preview of *Fairy Tail*, volume 29

We're pleased to present you with a preview from Fairy Tail, volume 29, being released digitally in May 2013 and in print in August. Please check our Web site (www.kodanshacomics.com) for more details!

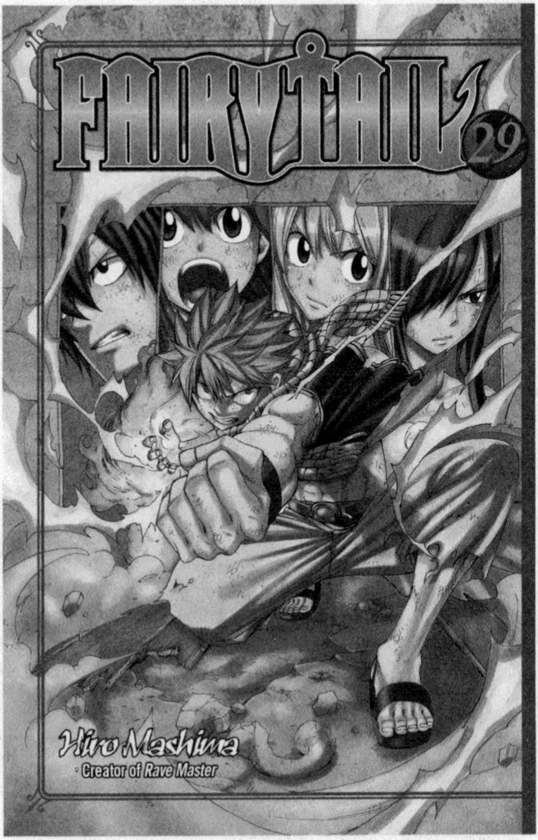
FAIRY TAIL
29
Hiro Mashima
Creator of Rave Master

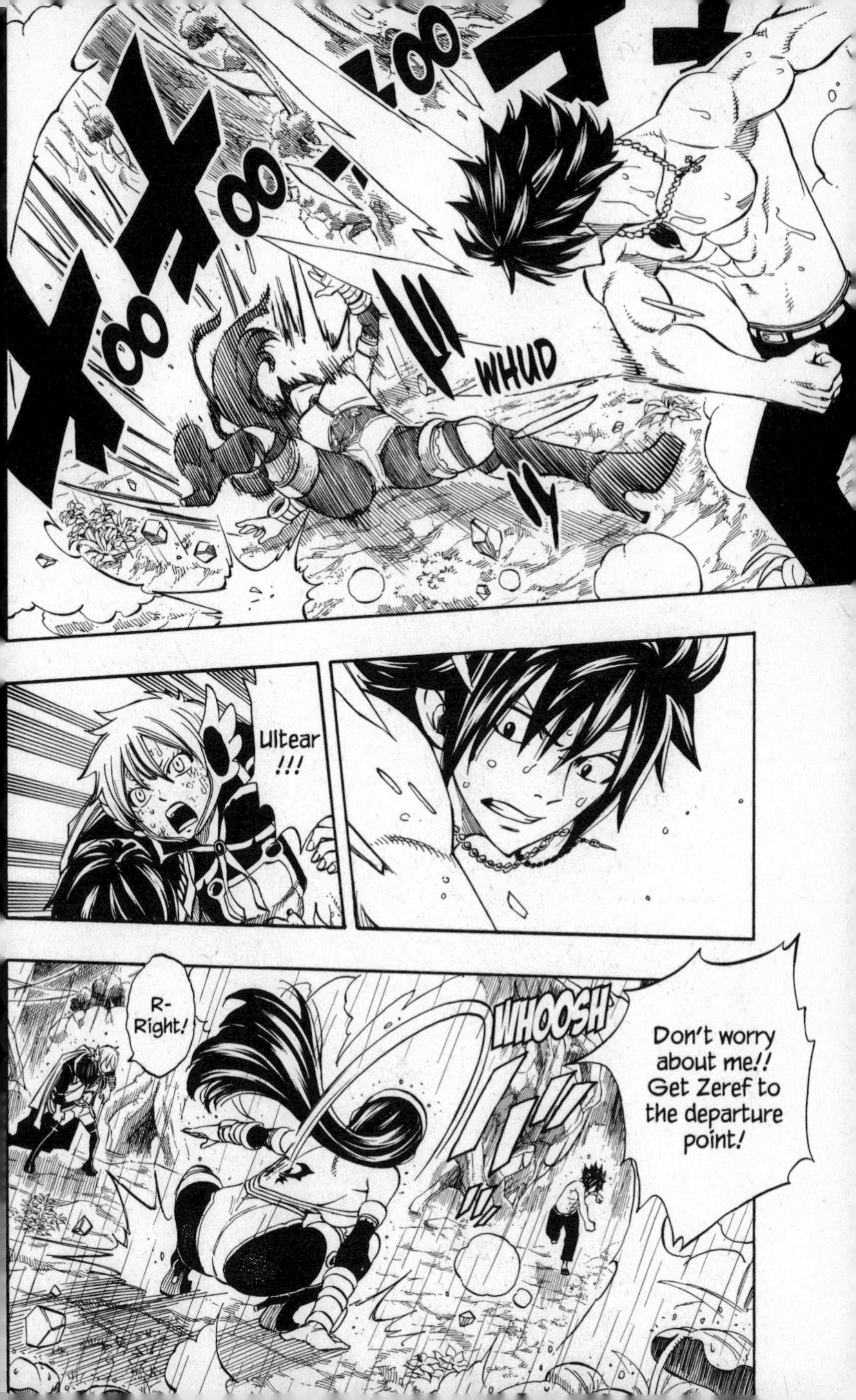
WHUD
Ultear !!!
Don't worry about me!! Get Zeref to the departure point!
WHOOSH
R- Right!

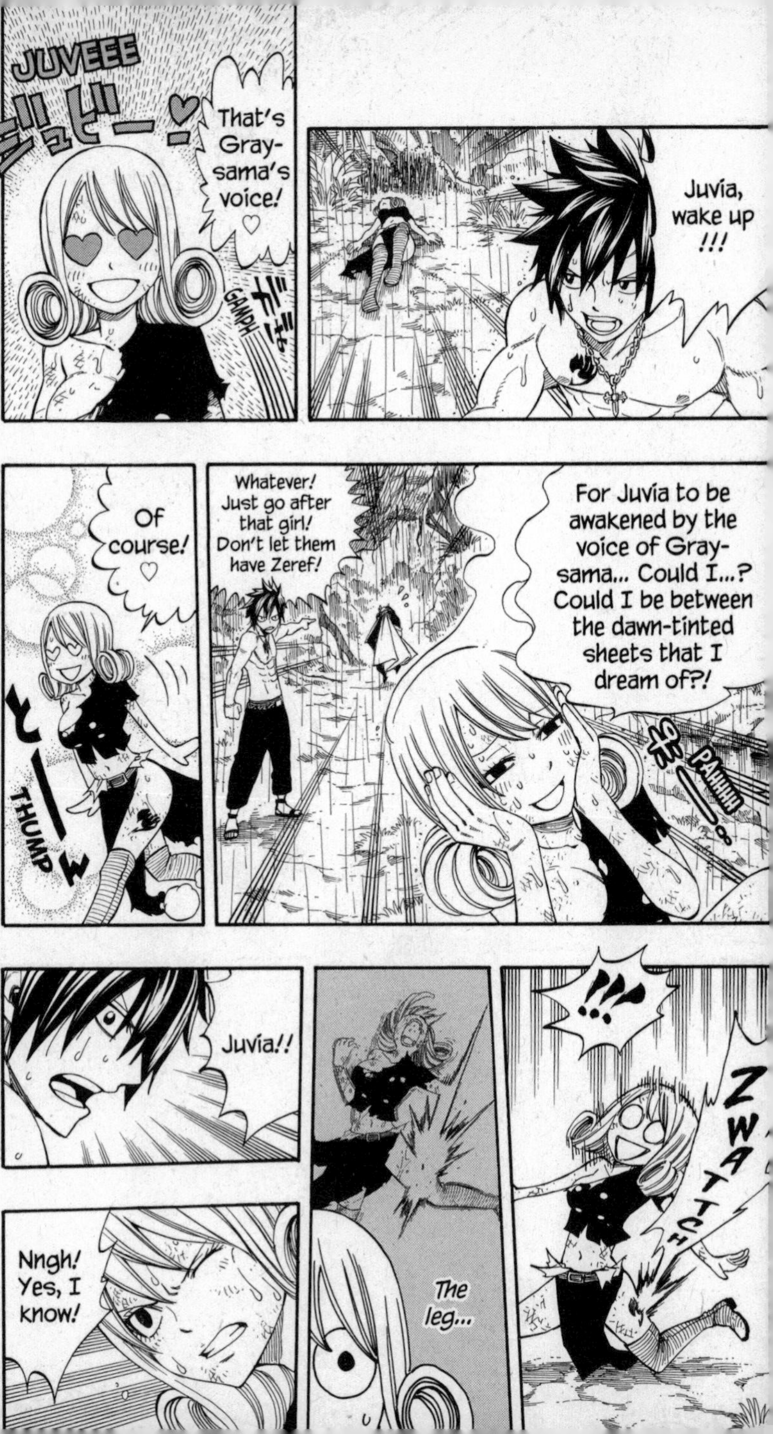
Juvia, wake up!!!
JUVEEE
ジュビー♡
That's Gray-sama's voice! ♡
GANPH
For Juvia to be awakened by the voice of Gray-sama... Could I...? Could I be between the dawn-tinted sheets that I dream of?!
PAHHHH
Whatever! Just go after that girl! Don't let them have Zeref!
Of course! ♡
THUMP
!!!
ZWATTCH
The leg...
Juvia!!
Nngh! Yes, I know!

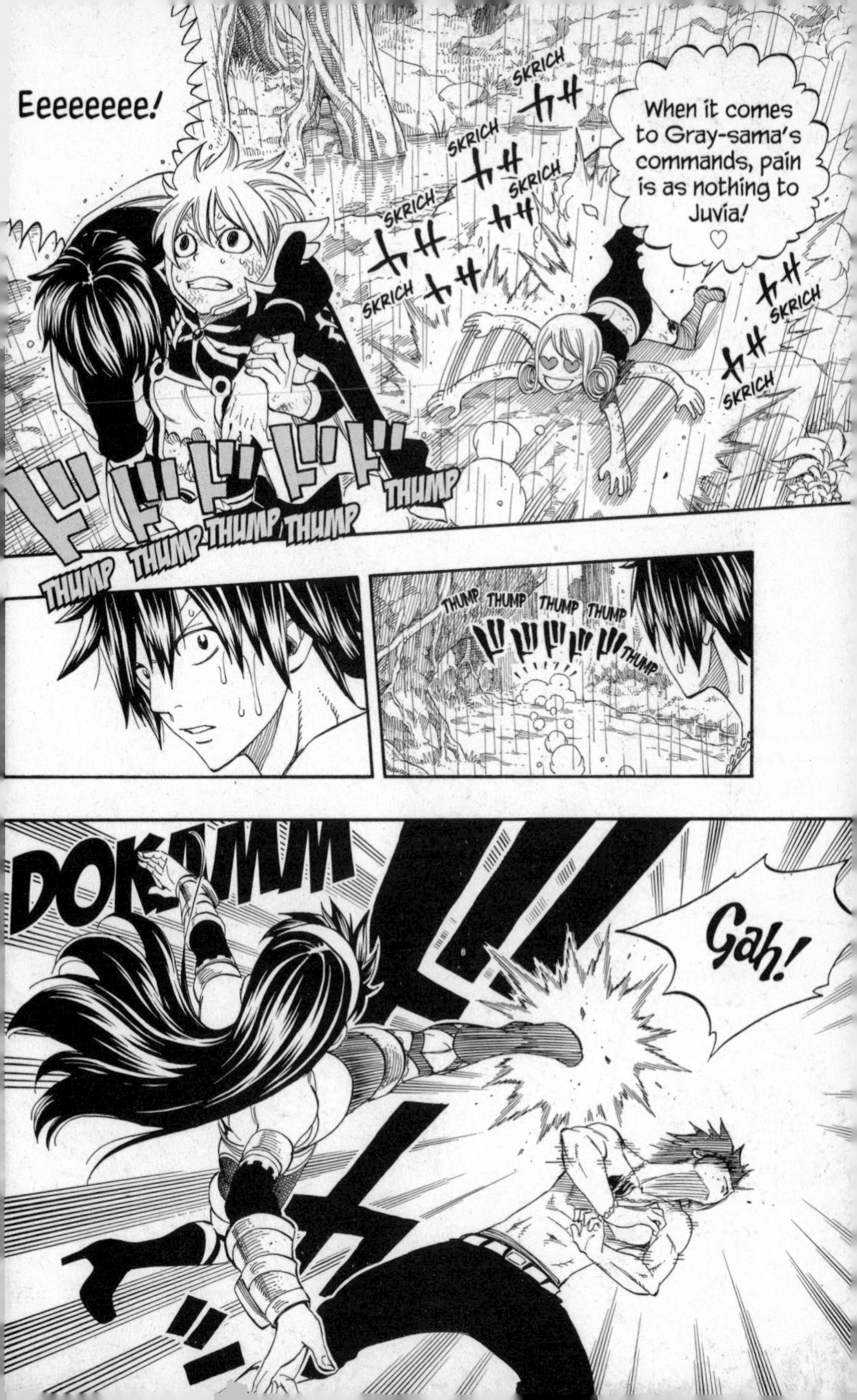

When it comes to Gray-sama's commands, pain is as nothing to Juvia! ♡
SKRICH
SKRICH
SKRICH
SKRICH
SKRICH
SKRICH
SKRICH
SKRICH
Eeeeeeee!
THUMP THUMP THUMP THUMP THUMP
THUMP THUMP THUMP THUMP THUMP
Gah!

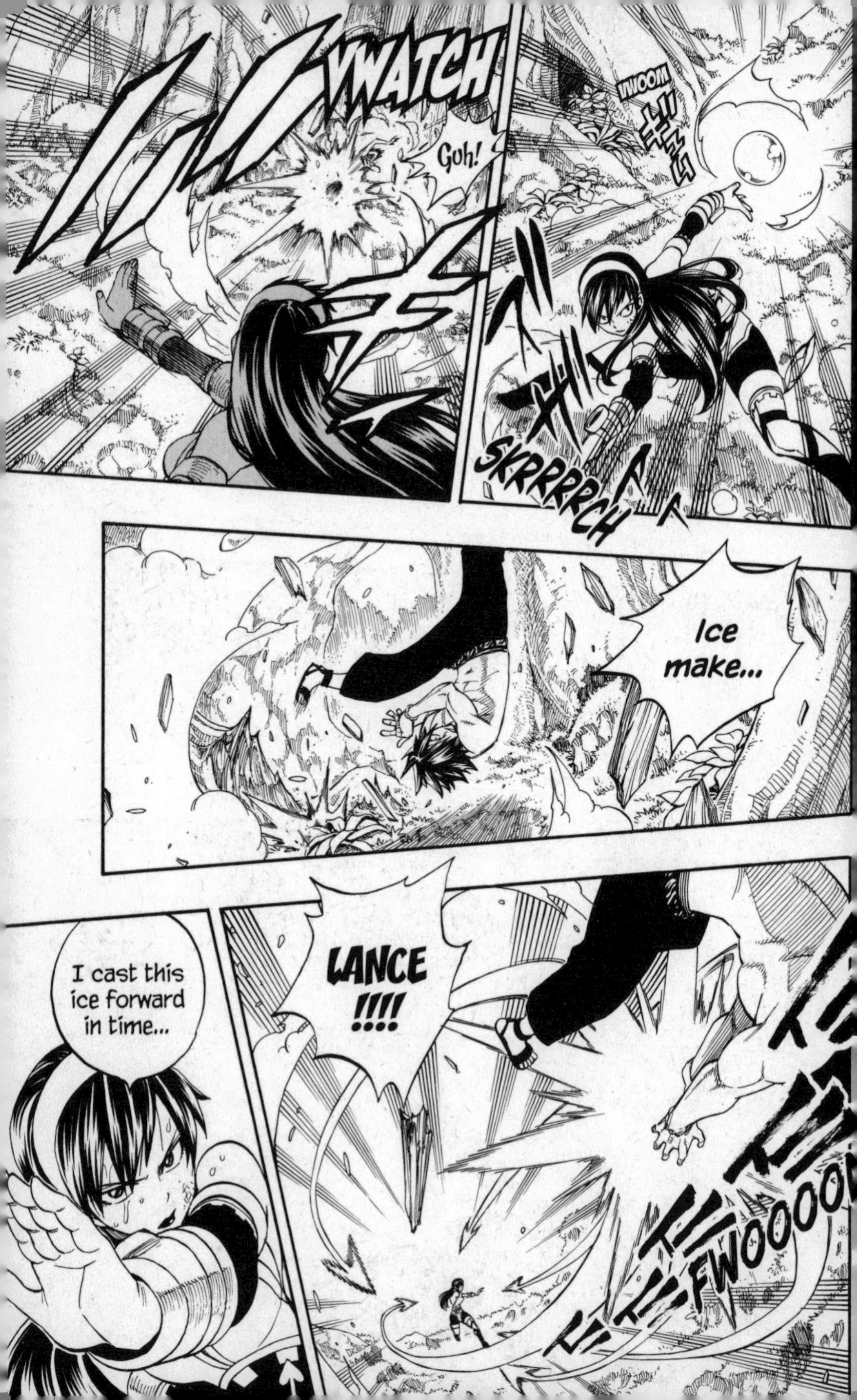
VWOOM
SKRRRRCH
VWATCH
Guh!
Ice make...
LANCE !!!!
FWOOOO
I cast this ice forward in time...

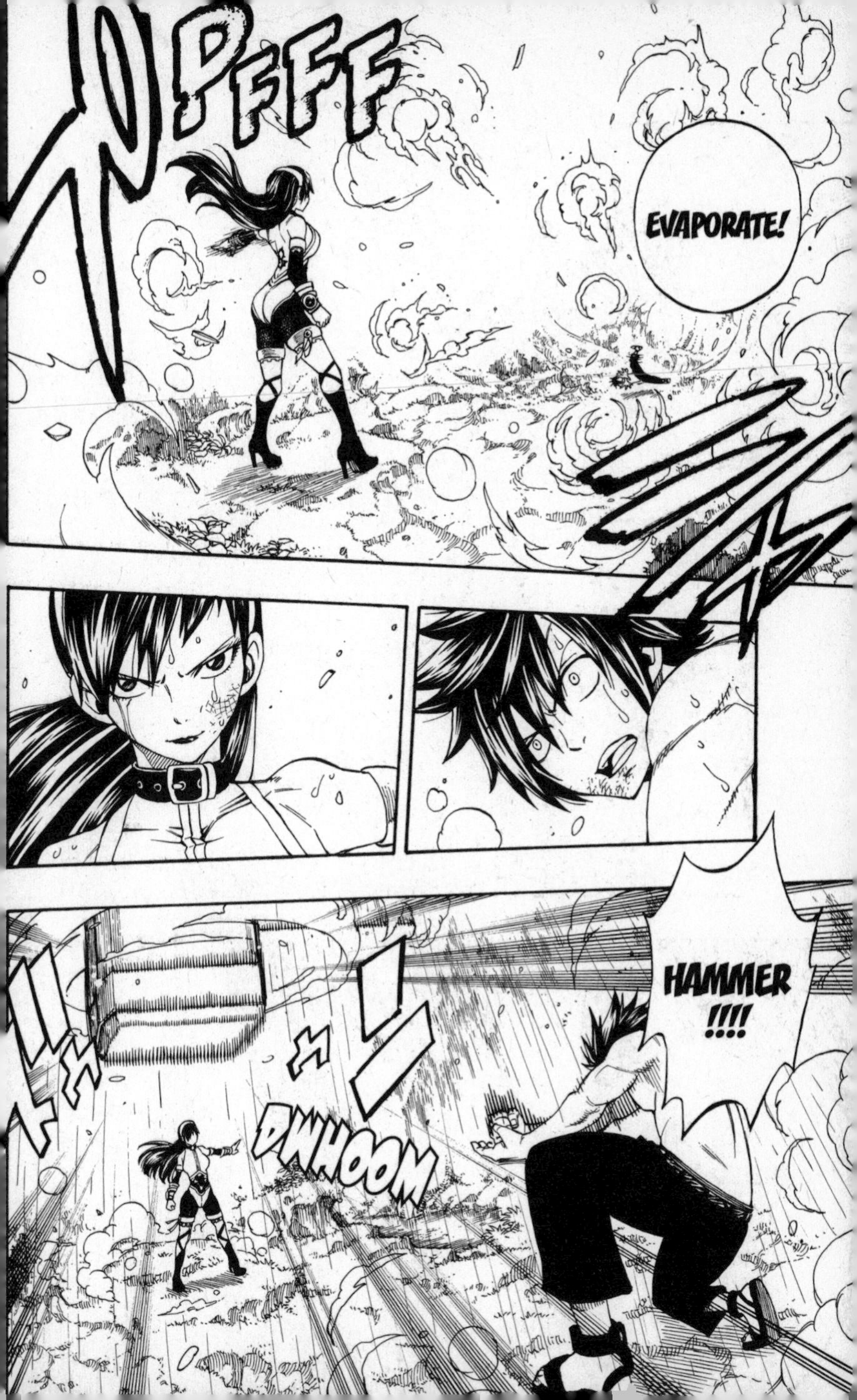
EVAPORATE!
PFFF
HAMMER!!!!
DWHOOM

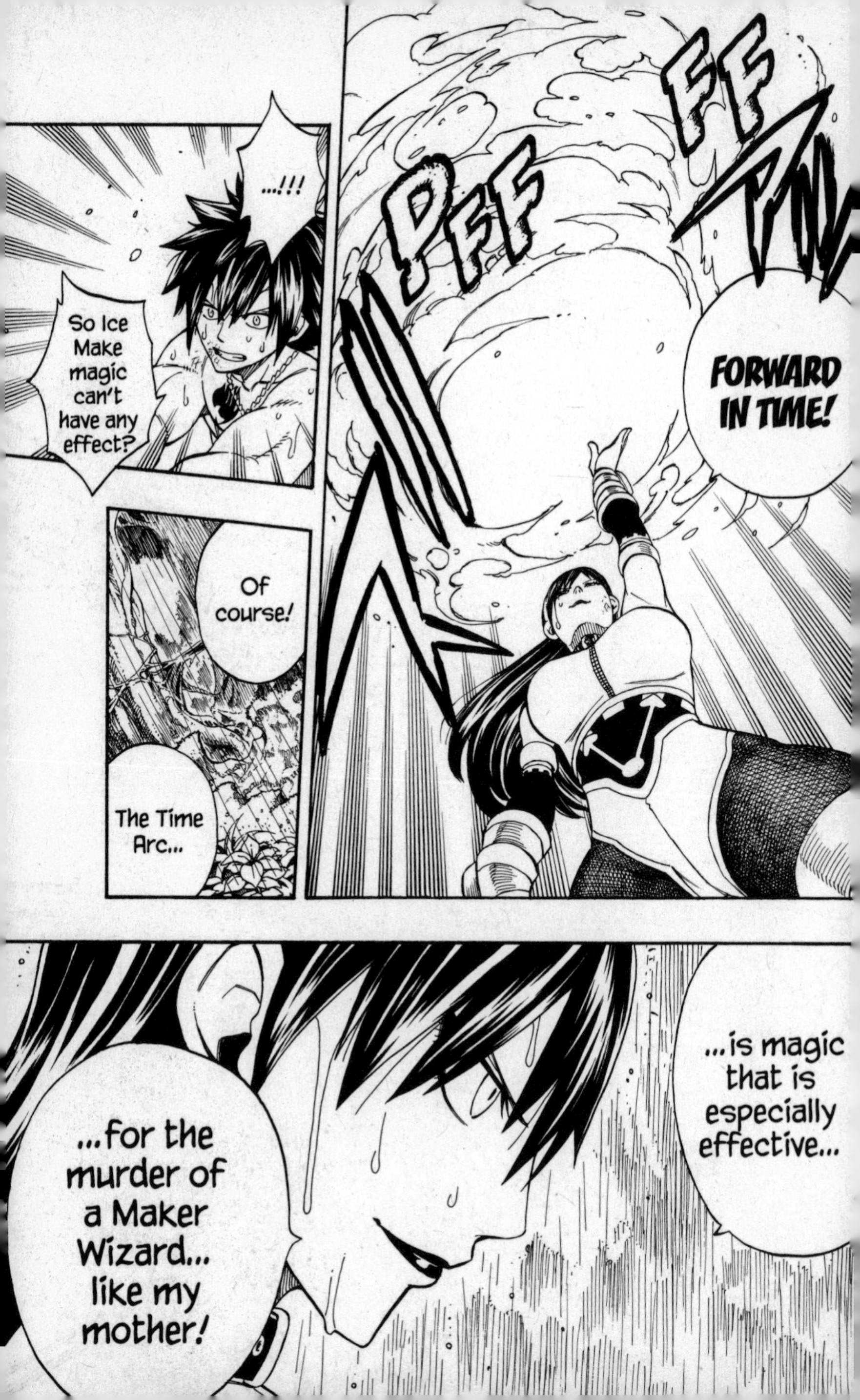
FF
PFF
FORWARD IN TIME!
...!!!
So Ice Make magic can't have any effect?
Of course!
The Time Arc...
...is magic that is especially effective...
...for the murder of a Maker Wizard... like my mother!

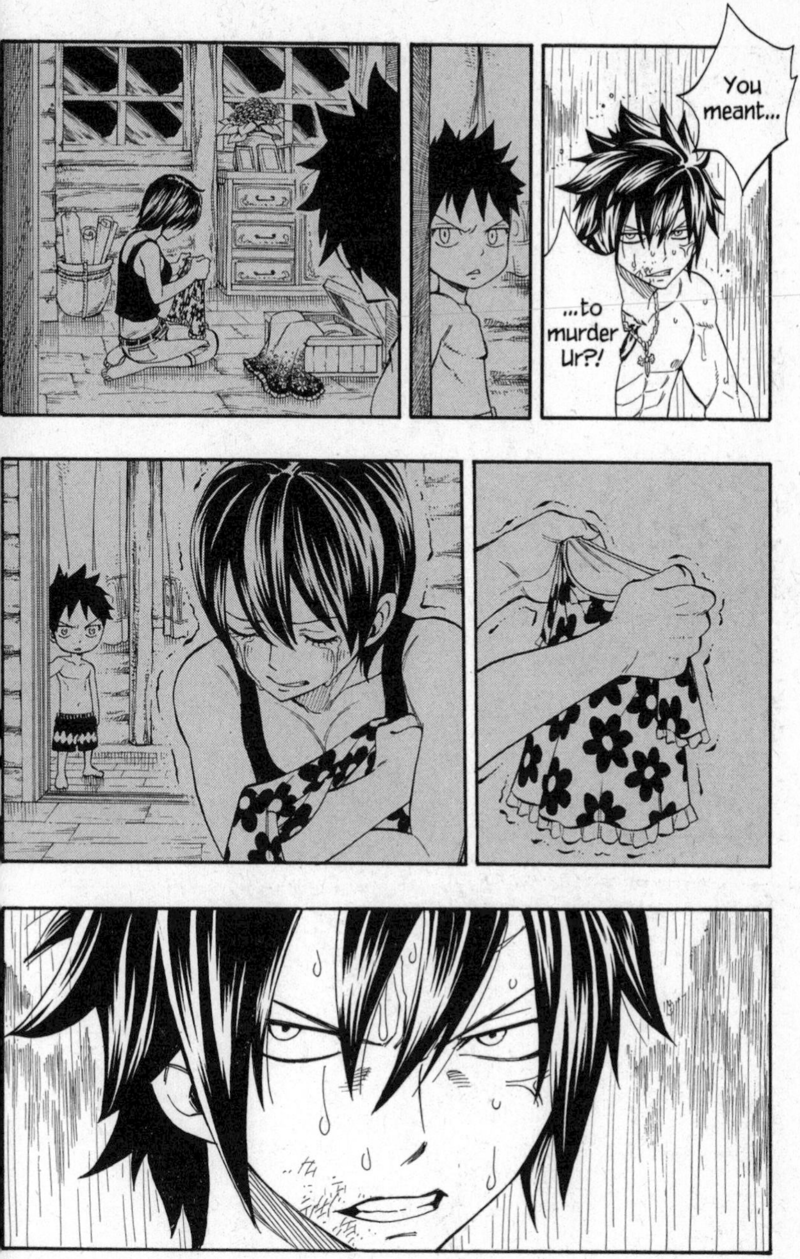
You meant...
...to murder Ur?!